P9-AOT-883

JOEL L. BURDIN, Ed.D., Michigan State University, is Associate Director, American Association of Colleges for Teacher Education and was formerly Associate Professor of Education, Indiana State University. Previously he was a public school coordinator of instruction, principal, and teacher. Dr. Burdin has had extensive experience in consulting for schools and colleges.

JOHN D. MCAULAY, Ed.D., Stanford University, is Chairman, Faculty of Social Science Education Pennsylvania State University. He was formerly Director of Education, Southern Oregon College, and an elementary and secondary school teacher and principal. Dr. McAulay has been a consultant to school districts and is the author and co-author of books and articles on various aspects of curriculum.

Elementary School Curriculum and Instruction

THE TEACHER'S ROLE

JOEL L. BURDIN
THE AMERICAN ASSOCIATION OF COLLEGES FOR TEACHER EDUCATION; FORMERLY INDIANA STATE UNIVERSITY

JOHN D. McAULAY
THE PENNSYLVANIA STATE UNIVERSITY

THE RONALD PRESS COMPANY • NEW YORK

1MP

Library of Congress Catalog Card Number: 78–155204
PRINTED IN THE UNITED STATES OF AMERICA

To our wives and children

Beverly Burdin and Linda, David,
Steven, Douglas, and Susan

Vera McAulay and Thomas Ewen

Preface

This textbook has been written to emphasize the role of the classroom teacher in promoting an effective curriculum. Curriculum is defined as the child's program of learning within the school environment and the organization of those instructional materials which will enhance the teaching process. The text should broaden the professional understanding of teaching and learning for both pre-service and in-service teachers in that it deals with concepts and issues which are fundamental to a sound curriculum. The teacher is shown how to examine basic educational principles and the varied dimensions of teaching. This book gives the teacher the necessary background to make classroom decisions in harmony with his personal philosophy of teaching. It helps him to analyze particular teaching and learning techniques and to arrive at his own conclusions. Too, the teacher is given a wide understanding of the needs of children and society's expectations from the school. This understanding should help the teacher formulate more precise and effective curriculum goals.

The authors have endeavored to present those skills, attitudes, and attributes which make teaching a profession and to give an inventory of potential decisions relating to classroom instruction so the teacher can plan for effective and efficient implementation of curriculum materials.

Because the majority of teachers are keenly interested in the improvement of particular areas of the curriculum, the book devotes almost half of its chapters to explaining new programs and how they may be incorporated into the classroom. The text is practical and realistic about the classroom situation and suggests solutions to problems for each elementary school subject within the curriculum. Numerous projects with each chapter provide for application of the basic principles.

This text, then, presents a varied learning program. It encourages the reader to regard teaching as a profession, to reevaluate the fundamentals of the school curriculum, and to develop his own techniques and methods of classroom behavior.

Joel L. Burdin
John D. McAulay

Washington, D. C.
University Park, Pennsylvania
July, 1971

Contents

I ANALYSES OF TEACHING AND LEARNING

II DYNAMICS OF CURRICULUM STUDY

III ISSUES AND TRENDS

PART I

Analyses of Teaching and Learning

Curriculum to a large degree is what the teacher and pupils *do* in the classroom. Part I provides an overview of the varied conditions that influence the kinds of learning which take place in the classroom. Part I should enable you to conceptualize the varied aspects of curriculum and place them in perspective. Having this kind of intellectual tool should enable you to examine objectives, processes, and content and to relate them to the big picture of curriculum. What is teaching? What is the structure of knowledge? What are learners like? How does the teacher design learning experiences and evaluate their effectiveness? These are some of the major curriculum questions that provide focus for Part I.

1

Introduction

KEYS TO CHILDREN'S "BECOMING"

In James Baldwin's book *Go Tell It on the Mountain* a first grade child is praised briefly by an elementary principal. She had said little while visiting his elementary classroom; she told him that he was a bright boy and encouraged him to keep up his good work. Baldwin describes the boy's resulting sense of "identity" in discovering "that with this power he might save himself; and that, perhaps, he might one day win that love which he so longed for . . . . It was his identity."[1]

Just think of the potentialities for helping pupils to open doors to living, to finding *who* they are and *what* they are to become! This book is written in the hope that it will aid you, whether a prospective or practicing teacher, in the process of "becoming"—that long process which involves your total being in relation to your total environment. The book hopefully will help you to analyze your personal reasons for selecting the teaching profession, organize your experiences and understandings, and improve certain skills needed in teaching.

Without a sense of awe of the potentialities of teaching and a clearcut understanding of the task, a teacher may become a mere taskmaster keeping children "occupied." Charles Dickens in his *Hard Times* gives us an example:

> "Bitzer," said Thomas Gradgrind, "your definition of a horse."
> "Quadruped. Bramnivorous. Forty teeth, namely twenty-four grinders, four eye teeth, and two incisive. Sheds coat in the spring; in marshy countries sheds hoofs too. Hoofs hard, but requiring to be shod with iron."
> "Now girl number 20," said Gradgrind, "you know what a horse is."[2]

[1] James Baldwin, *Go Tell It on the Mountain* (New York: The New American Library of World Literature, Inc., 1952), pp. 18–19.

[2] Charles Dickens, *Hard Times*, in John Ciardi, *How Does a Poem Mean?* (Boston: Houghton Mifflin Co., 1960), p. 665.

How pathetic that teaching ever degenerates into a monotonous repetition of facts, where words *represent* experiences *not yet experienced.* The task of a teacher's achieving more than this seems to be insurmountable. There are several resources, both within and without, to make the undertaking possible: (a) your own personal experiences in school and out of school, in which you developed some understandings of self, others, and environment; (b) the tremendous yearning for growth felt by children; (c) the collective wisdom of the teaching profession and experts in other fields which contribute to professional education. When a teacher utilizes these resources, he should be able to plan and execute a vital curriculum.

The Self as a Resource

The ability to reach into "the back of the mind" to produce new understandings from past experiences and knowledge is called insight. Everyone has experiences which may be helpful in understanding ideas presented in this book. These written verbal descriptions can help you to organize your present understandings and enrich them to the point where you become a growing *professional,* that is, you have personal and professional understandings, skills, and talents in unique combinations which the layman is not expected to have.

Rogers suggests that an individual can become "a more autonomous, more spontaneous, more confident person." You need to be "free" if you are to help children to attain their uniqueness and autonomy as individuals. Rogers, writing about counselors but later applying his generalization to teachers, traces the development of the free person:

> The client begins to realize, "I am not compelled to be simply the creation of others, molded by their expectancies, shaped by their demands. I am not compelled to be a victim of unknown forces in myself. I am less and less a creature of influences in my self which operate beyond my ken in the realms of the unconscious. I am increasingly the architect of self. I am free to will and choose. I can, through accepting my individuality, my 'isness,' become more of my uniqueness, more of my potentiality." [3]

Freedom for Modern Man. For citizens of a democratic society to be told that they are not free may be disturbing. Rogers uses *free* in a special sense and explains why people may lack personal freedom. Factors impinging on freedom include: (a) mass propaganda with preplanned beliefs and opinions; (b) social class, with values and ideas and understandings implanted during the preschool years; (c) hereditary fac-

[3] Carl Rogers, "Learning To Be Free," from a paper presented at a conference on "Conformity and Diversity," at the University of California School of Medicine, San Francisco, January 28, 1962, in Glen Hass and Kimball Wiles, *Readings in Curriculum* (Boston: Allyn & Bacon, Inc., 1965), p. 203.

tors which determine maximum limits of development; (d) conditioning by institutions such as family, school, church, and government.[4]

While admitting that modern man may be controlled to a large degree by environment, heredity, and circumstances, Rogers presents a way out of the dilemma in a quotation related to a former concentration camp experience of Frankl. Rogers notes that Frankl lost everything (possessions, outward identity, and choice) but that he claimed ". . . that everything can be taken from a man but one thing: the last of the human freedoms—to choose one's own attitude in a given set of circumstances, to choose one's own way."[5]

Personal Approach to Teaching. Combs, after a review of several approaches to determine what makes a good teacher, developed a "personal approach" to good teaching. His "self as instrument" concept encourages you to free yourself to become your best self.

> A good teacher is first and foremost a person. . . . Apparently, there can be no such thing as a "good" or "bad" method of teaching . . . . The good teacher is not one who behaves in a "given" way. He is an artist, skillful in producing a desirable result.[6]

Getzels and Jackson also have noted the importance of the teacher as a person. They call the teacher's personality ". . . the most significant variable," noting that the impact of the teacher can be traced not only to what he knows, "but in a very real sense to what he is."[7] Certainly there are limitations to this point of view. Teachers need more than an adequate personality, although this well may be the place to begin. *Uniqueness* is the point of departure for a developing professional.

Teachers, in common with other professionals, must transcend the feeling and fact of being laymen and must grow through professional education to utilize their uniqueness for guiding and providing learning experiences for children. This process includes: (a) learning about the profession, including its traditions, skills, sociopsychological factors, and methodology; (b) supervised practice under the direction of recognized professionals; (c) the all-pervasive but often subtle ways of learning to behave in a "correct" professional and personal manner. The transition is made subtly and gradually, yet radical changes occur during the process.

[4] *Ibid.*, p. 205.

[5] V. E. Frankl, *From Death-Camp to Existentialism,* translated by I. Lasch (Boston: Beacon Press, Inc., 1959); in Rogers, p. 207.

[6] Arthur W. Combs, "The Personal Approach to Good Teaching," *Educational Leadership,* XXI, No. 6 (March, 1964), p. 372.

[7] J. W. Getzels and P. W. Jackson, "The Teacher's Personality and Characteristics," in N. L. Gage, *Handbook of Research on Teaching* (Chicago: Rand McNally and Co., Inc., 1964), pp. 506–76.

Role Perception. The professional's life patterns develop according to his perceptions of his roles. Perceptual theory suggests that people behave according to what appears to be true and what appears to be self-enhancing. Professional education hopefully helps you to sharpen your perceptions of yourself and your role as a teacher or prospective teacher. Fusing an understanding of the teacher's role with an adequate self should produce an adequate teacher who knows what children need to experience and the most effective ways to bring about behavioral changes. The professional teacher plans experiences, called the curriculum, which are designed to bring out these changes.

The elementary teacher particularly needs to understand his role. The teacher of small children works primarily with them and thus has limited contacts with critical adult analysis and ideas. Teachers need to learn how to identify and promote desirable teacher roles.

We have claimed thus far that your experiences and understandings are fundamental resources in your professional education. It is important to emphasize that these, like natural resources, must be cultivated systematically and professionally. In their dormant state your experiences and understandings offer *potentialities* for converting an adequate personality into a lifetime of growth toward effective teaching. Cultivated through professional and liberal education, the potentialities can be channeled into societal service and self-satisfaction through teaching.

The Pupil's Yearning for Growth

Watching your children at work and play can easily lead you to a belief that children want to learn and grow. While observing children you will realize their *determination* (for example, the infinite and self-imposed practice when a child *wants* to learn endless variations of jumping rope, even on a hot day, or the number of times a child will endure falls on rough cement when he *wants* to master bicycle riding). You will note *perseverance* (a child often will surprise adults with the length of his concentration on a given task), and you will see *excitement* and *enthusiasm* when a task is completed. Watching a child experience the excitement of progress can easily lead you to believe that the teaching role is not *to force* him to carry on learning activities, but rather *to encourage and assist* the child to find and complete meaningful activities.

A fifth grade girl has captured her urge to learn. This illustrates the raw material you have to work with in teaching!

> I have the urge to grow,
> I guess I always will.
> I have the urge to know
> Why the world won't stand still,

Or why I keep on living,
Getting wiser by day,
Or why I like to be giving
In the things I do or say.[8]

Not all see children in a positive, dynamic context. There have been many who have a pessimistic view toward the young. Listen to this voice of more than twenty-five hundred years ago; similar voices are heard today:

> Children now love luxury. They have bad manners, contempt for authority. They show disrespect for elders, and love chatter in place of exercise. Children are now tyrants, not the servants of their households.[9]

A Positive Theory of Man. Maslow has drawn an essentially optimistic conclusion. After studying basic tendencies of people, he recognizes that children (and adults) indeed are physiological beings. This means that they first will seek means of maintaining their physical well-being. But he claims that man is more than a biological being, that after physical needs are satisfied people turn to "higher" goals. This implies a faith in persons to rise above the selfish, perplexing type of individual portrayed by Socrates and others with similar pessimistic views.

Maslow proposes that a person strives toward *a wholeness.* The child progressing toward a healthy wholeness seeks to develop a balance, a sense of well-being, in several ways. Maslow's concepts are summarized as follows.

1. The child seeks to meet his *physiological needs,* to maintain his normal state in relation to food, water, body temperature, and so forth.

2. He seeks to satisfy his *physiological appetites,* which are his unique ways and his cultural ways of meeting his physiological needs. For example, the child must eat, but the manner of eating, kinds of foods valued highly, and time when eating is desired are affected by the child's family patterns, social class, friends' ideas, and school instruction. Physiological needs assume psychological importance, as the individual finds security, satisfaction, and recognition in the manner of fulfilling appetites. Psychological needs may become more significant than physiological needs with the unhappy person who eats in excess of physical needs, or eats a disproportionate amount of certain kinds of food like candy.

3. After these needs and appetites are met, he can then turn to *"higher needs":* (a) safety; (b) belongingness and love; (c) esteem, including self-respect and self-esteem; (d) self-actualization, the effort to find a

[8] Karen Pearson, "The Urge to Grow," *American Jr. Red Cross News,* XLVII, No. 1 (October, 1965).

[9] Socrates, quoted in Earl C. Kelley, *In Defense of Youth* (Englewood Cliffs, N.J.: Prentice-Hall, Inc., 1962), p. 4.

unified personality, spontaneity, self-fulfillment, creativity, and the good life; (e) the desire to know and understand self and environment; (f) aesthetic needs, including poetry, art, music, and other forms of creative expression.[10]

It is important to remember that this is a *theory* of motivation. Maslow's theory was developed through a study of the healthiest one per cent of a college student group. He feels that theories in the past have been negatively oriented, that they have been blinded by what appears to have been true, rather than what might be under healthy environments. Maslow notes that the views of Hamilton were derived from a study of the poor, the views of Freud from the neurotic, and those of Hobbes from a study of persons in a poor socioeconomic climate.[11]

There are difficulties in proving Maslow's claim. Observing children's enthusiasm toward learning may create a willingness to capitalize on children's directions toward growth, whether inborn or developed. At least you will increasingly accept the child as a potential resource rather than as an enemy to be conquered and controlled.

Children's Nature. The school dedicated to serving the "whole child" recognizes that children's physical, emotional, social, and intellectual goals cannot be isolated into neat compartments, with rigid time allotments during the school day for each. The school tries to help the child attain all his goals concurrently, in the recognition that, when one phase of the child's goalseeking is restricted, the other phases cannot be completed satisfactorily. A child's goals are complementary, not conflicting. They all contribute to a need for a sense of well-being in an integrated human being.

You will want to examine regularly your *feelings* about the nature of children, since those feelings are a crucial factor in curriculum planning. There are some basic types of questions which can enlarge your understanding of your feelings. Your answers to these related questions can have a significant influence on how you plan your curriculum and your methodology, and this will tend to reflect your beliefs as well as your knowledge. Coleman gives the following suggestions for the need for self-examination of beliefs concerning the nature of man.[12]

Is a person basically good or evil? What are the theological, philosophical, and sociological bases for beliefs on this question? What are the educational implications of each position? For example, if you believe

[10] Abraham Maslow, "Theory of Human Motivation," *Motivation and Personality* (New York: Harper & Row, 1954), pp. 80–106.

[11] *Ibid.*, pp. 354–60.

[12] James C. Coleman, *Personality Dynamics and Effective Behavior* (Chicago: Scott, Foresman & Co., 1960), pp. 9–16.

that man is essentially good, you could consistently seek to help each child to assume more and more control and choice (in the assumption that there is potential for self-control and constructive choice which can be nourished), encourage him to find his own answers to his own significant questions, and aid him to grow into his best self (with the belief that each person has an aspiration toward "self-actualization"). Obviously there are many other implications for the "good" point of view.

Is a person rational or irrational? What are the bases for various views? What are the educational implications? For example, if you believe that a person is basically rational, you could seek to educate him in the processes of rational and critical thought, urge him to explore and initiate his own learning projects, and encourage him to acquire the ideals and skills of free men.

Is a person active or reactive? Is a person an active, self-directed organism; or does he essentially respond to stimuli from other persons and events? Is he a puppet and pliable clay, to be used and shaped by forces outside himself? Is he a purposive, seeking, selecting, and striving being? If you believe that he is essentially *active,* you probably could help him to pursue his own interests while you serve as guide, catalyst, and resource person; your school room could be organized around varied activities, interest centers, and places for individuals and small groups to investigate, experiment, explore, discuss, perform, and seek new experiences.

While there are different theories concerning the nature of people, there appears to be general agreement concerning the following conclusions, which may clarify the potentialities and limitations of children in relation to curriculum.

Heredity is "inherited capital" which sets the general potentialities and limitations. Children are not born with tendencies to be either troublesome or to meekly accept adult authority, with lazy streaks or flaming ambition, with interest or disinterest in school activities, or with desirable character or undesirable character. Heredity provides the potentialities; environment provides the stimulation and restrictions (in varying degrees and with varying influences) to determine the extent and direction of development. A simple example: A child may be born with good listening capacities, physical equipment for singing, and stamina; but he is unlikely to become a good musician if there are no important persons *in his life* who love music and practice it, and if there are no important persons to indicate that music is a "good" thing. An effective curriculum may help the child to develop his maximum inherited "capital."

The rate, direction, and intensity of development will depend upon diverse factors. These include the type of school curriculum and teaching, placement in family, attitude of parents, size of family, type of neighborhood, nutrition, climate, and personal illness. There are many conceivable combinations of influences, hence it is not possible to make ironclad predictions on what children will be like even if factors are known. The same factors may affect children differently at different times! Observations of a child's response to varied factors provide the observant teacher with *clues* to behavior and enable such a teacher to guide and stimulate children through a vital curriculum.

While there are general tendencies in the manner in which children develop physically, emotionally, socially, and intellectually, each child has his own unique pattern, his own "spurts" and regressions. A school program which rigidly forces all children through identical channels will push some too fast at the wrong times, encourage others at about the right rate, and retard still others. It is important to understand the general age group in your classroom; it is essential that you know the individual in all of his complexities. This factor will encourage you to seek ways to individualize the curriculum.

Sensitivity to Uniqueness. The spirit of positive acceptance of children as individuals with unique needs is captured by Kahlil Gibran, in an oft-quoted poem. He poetically notes that children are not our children in a possessive sense, that they do not belong to anyone, but that they are "Life's longing for itself." We can love children, but we cannot and should not attempt to fill them with our thoughts. What then is the adult role? Gibran tells us:

> You may house their bodies but not their souls,
> For their souls dwell in the house of tomorrow, which you cannot
> visit, not even in your dreams.
> You may strive to be like them, but seek not to make them like you,
> For life goes not backward nor tarries with yesterday.
>
> You are the bows from which your children as living arrows
> are sent forth.
> Let your bending in the archer's hand be for gladness.[13]

This poem implies a sensitivity to the subtlety of human relations, of seeing and of accepting each child entrusted to you. It is a matter of identifying with all conditions of childhood, or developing empathy to the point where as a fellow human being you can accept *each child* while exercising direction and restraint in maintaining society's expectations. And a child sensing your acceptance of *him* may accept your society and make it his.

Perhaps sensitivity can be increased through greater knowledge of and contacts with children of all kinds. You may experiment with some of

[13] Kahlil Gibran, *The Prophet* (New York: Alfred A. Knopf, Inc., 1959), p. 17.

the activities which follow to determine those which seem to further your understanding and acceptance of what people are while reserving your right to reject what they do, when their actions violate your understanding of what a "good" person does in this culture.

1. You may read biographical and fictional accounts of people in all walks of life and read or watch dramatic productions since these forms of communications are written by persons with unique sensitivity and perception of humanity. You may to a degree *experience* with the artist the dreams, problems, and accomplishments of many persons.

2. You may take a commercial bus trip and listen and look. You will note varied conversation patterns (perhaps discovering why some children have "atrocious" grammar). While waiting in a bus terminal and watching people you may note different behavior patterns: Some read "light" material while others are reading "educational" material; still others will doze or carry on time-killing conversation; some look healthy and energetic, while others convey expressions of defeat and hopelessness. The point is that when you look at individuals you find great variations; this sensitivity to individual differences among all ages should give some understanding of the familial origins of some individual differences found among children.

3. You may spend a summer vacation on a farm, in a slum social service center, or seaside resort; work in a recreation program; teach in a vacation church school; or work in a shoestore or factory. If you are seeking to broaden your understandings of people, you will select experiences which you have not had previously. If you are on campus, you may wish to ask for a roommate with a different background or at least from a different region of the United States.

4. You may develop a questionnaire to determine pupil preferences and dislikes on a variety of topics, particularly using sentences in which children complete the thought with their own words.

5. You may wish to live for a while in an area to be torn down for an urban renewal project to experience the sights, sounds, smells, and activities of such an area.

6. You may visit in children's homes, to help you develop a feeling that parents are doing the best they can with what they have (although sometimes they are limited in financial, educational, intelligence, and experiental resources).

7. You may participate in political activities, social groups, church groups, and service groups—places where you can extend your insights concerning yourself and others.

The previous point concerning increased sensitivity to varied human conditions may be belabored. However, there *is* a need for sensitivity and acceptance of varied human conditions. Children from certain backgrounds do feel that it is difficult to communicate (words, feelings, ideas) with teachers who *seem* to live in a world unrelated to the children's world. These children do not share the most important aspects of their lives with *strangers,* which teachers appear to be to some children.

Hopefully you will identify with individuals whenever you see them and especially when you come in contact with them. You can increase consciousness of eye expressions, voice and speaking patterns, physical reactions to situations—any clue which helps you to understand *why* and *under what circumstances* people behave as they do, perhaps why they react to you in various ways, perhaps why you react to different kinds of people in different circumstances. The goal is to see beyond the obvious in what people do and say; you want to look below the small fraction of an iceberg which shows above the water. The behavior of others can be viewed as an exhibition of symptoms of underlying causes. A casual observer, but not an effective teacher, misses the subtle yet significant factors which prompt people to respond the way they do.[14]

The Collective Wisdom of the Teaching Profession and Academic Disciplines

Certain persons seem to have a knack for helping boys and girls to learn. Mothers, church school teachers, and boy scout leaders with varying degrees of formal teacher education may teach children significant facts, skills, and attitudes. Likewise, school teachers in many cases seem to be "artists" in their ability to polish the rough edges into a better product. There is *to some extent* a collective wisdom of our society which contributes to your continuing preparation for teaching. More significant ideas are available in abundance in professional magazines, in many popular magazines, in newspapers, and in the broadcasting media. In addition, there is a growing fund of professional knowledge made available from various types of research into all aspects of education. Much of this book is a sampling of these sources of understanding the teaching and learning process which, combined with understandings of the self and the society, enable the teacher to plan a program of instruction, that is, *the school curriculum.* The professional is an expert in bringing about desired changes sought through the curriculum. Professional knowledge coupled with an adequate, mature personality increases the likelihood of stimulating significant changes in the lives of children.

[14] Some books which may extend your understanding of the process discussed here are: Edward T. Hall, *The Silent Language* (Garden City, N.Y.: Doubleday & Co., Inc., 1959) and Erving Goff, *The Presentation of Self in Everyday Life* (Garden City, N.Y.: Doubleday & Co., Inc., 1959). A recent, popularized treatment of the topic is Julius Fast's *Body Language* (New York: M. Evans and Co., 1970).

IMPORTANCE OF PEOPLE

The teacher himself must feel important if he is to feel secure enough to help children feel important. An analysis of a school environment will increase your awareness of ways in which teachers and children are perceived as important, with personal dignity and worth. The teacher both controls his teaching environment and is affected by it.

Involvement of Children

The basic generalization about a school's environment is that those affected by a decision should have a voice in making it. To permit decisions to be made otherwise is to create a disharmony between teaching and living. It is important to include children in democratic participation. Sometimes children are told to grow up in accepting responsibilities but to delay in securing their rights until they are 21. Children are becoming today what they will be tomorrow. It is important to coordinate the practice of responsibilities with the procurement of rights at all ages.

Children seem to know when they are playing games of *pretending* to have responsibilities and in securing rights. They are sometimes asked to pretend to be the President of the United States, a delegate to the United Nations, a banker or fireman, or a teacher. This kind of play *may* extend their imagination, as they "role play," and broaden their understandings of how others live. But to have them play at planning a lesson or learning activity when the teacher already has plans made and materials prepared is a hoax and shows contempt for the keen intelligence of children. To grant children "rights" as long as they blindly do exactly as the teacher wishes demonstrates disdain for children. Game playing (in which the teacher *pretends* to practice democracy or to show respect for children's ability and intelligence) fools no one, except perhaps the teacher who can convince himself that he really is "democratic."

It is indeed difficult to find a teacher or administrator who doesn't *believe* that he is promoting democracy. Some will at the same time limit children's democratic participation in the belief that: (a) They don't know what's good for them. (b) They have to grow up before they have rights. (c) Give them freedom, and they'll abuse it. There is an implied belief that when children receive their high school diploma or reach the age of 21 there is a magical transformation into maturity, responsibility, and personal worth. People are important; they have dignity and worth at all ages; they must be at all ages treated as free men capable of increasing responsibility *and* rights.

One student teacher in an effort to be democratic attempted to give the impression that her students were deciding how to study a unit in social studies. Her smiles, pleasantness, and invitation to pupils to help plan a unit were taken at face value. Several pupils immediately contributed alternate plans for proceeding in unit planning. While surprised, she fortunately was honest. She told them that she had made other plans but that since she had asked for suggestions, she would attempt to incorporate pupils' ideas with her own. She dropped her day's plans for social studies and then proceeded to another subject area. (She had neither made plans for pupil–teacher planning nor thought through how she might list their ideas on the board, organize them into categories, and help pupils to plan for follow-up with further suggestions on subsequent days.) She did sense, however, that classroom atmosphere as well as instruction helps children to learn, and delayed her own plans to enable her to respect and utilize pupils' ideas.

Teacher Involvement

Hopefully teachers also will be respected in school decision-making. Unless they have responsibilities and rights, they will be denied growth in group skills and dedication to democratic process. How can they teach something they have not experienced, except on an abstract, perhaps meaningless, level?

Some teachers even today resent being involved, for they conceive of their jobs in terms of working exclusively with children. They sometimes say, "Tell me what to do" or "Don't bother me with questions about the school curriculum; I don't have enough time as it is to teach."

While it does take time to involve many persons in curriculum decisions, there is potentiality for greater efficiency and effectiveness in decisions cooperatively reached. Here we are talking about teachers and administrators, parents and other citizens, *and children.* Everyone has something to contribute concerning what is to be taught, when it can best be taught, who should receive different types of instruction, and, to an extent, how it should be taught. However, the *how* questions of instruction are primarily for professionals. When everyone affected by decisions has some decision-making responsibilities, related to maturity, experience, and education, *he is likely to understand the who, when, what, why, and how of instruction.* Distrust is lessened; cooperation can become more effective; group pressures to complete decisions ("our" decisions) are effectively motivated to achieve group goals. Someone has suggested that we are inclined to distrust what we don't understand; involvement potentially contributes to understandings and support when objectives and methods are directed toward helping each individual to become his best self.

Group Dynamics

Involvement of affected persons in decisions is not automatically productive. Group dynamics is a specialized study which should be investigated at some time in your professional education. There are specific techniques and environments which are more productive than others. Some of the difficulties in cooperative decision-making include: (a) getting the total group adequately involved in the first place (some don't want to be involved); (b) channeling efforts into constructive lines (after sufficient airing of feelings, including hostilities, frustrations, and inadequacies; (c) establishing clear communication (to avoid the tendency toward participants hearing what supports their present personal viewpoints, tendencies, and experiences); (d) establishing an atmosphere in which all feel comfortable and secure in expressing true feelings and ideas; (e) establishing representation (getting varied views represented); (f) balancing efforts to get general agreement and pressures to reach decisions within a reasonable time (that is, avoiding extremes of railroading a decision or of endless talk while problems continue to interfere with education).[15]

Groups of people need assistance in defining issues, developing procedures, and carrying out decisions. Leaders are sometimes appointed (principals), elected (chairman of a teachers club), or accepted by general consent (informal influence exerted by a respected or feared member of a group). Leadership is affected by the situation under which decisions are made. Leadership of all kinds, including that exerted by the teacher in the classroom, is complex, with results that are unpredictable because of the number of human and other factors affecting decisions. There is no sure formula for success.

INFLUENCE OF LEARNING PRINCIPLES

It is important to expand your knowledge of learning principles which can serve as guidelines on what pupils can learn, when they can most efficiently learn, and the circumstances under which they learn, remember, and apply what they have learned. Understanding learners and their learning processes enables you to select curricular experiences which are most meaningful and to capitalize upon children's current characteristics and interests. Hopefully, you are interested in harnessing the power of the pupil tide rather than trying single handed to resist it with force. Collaboration with children in responding to their changing characteristics and needs provides a climate for growth.

[15] William VanTil, "Curriculum Improvement—Who Participates?" *Educational Leadership,* II, No. 6 (March, 1954), pp. 335–37.

An illustrative fable comes to mind. The sun and the wind were comparing their strengths one cold spring day. This led to some boasting, in which the wind challenged the sun to a demonstration of power. The wind said that he could make children playing below remove their coats fastest. The sun was agreeable to the test and suggested that the wind go first. The wind roared down in a mighty demonstration of power. The children grasped their coats to keep them from being ripped off. The harder the wind blew, the harder the children held on. Finally the wind gave up. The sun in quiet contrast gently increased the temperature. It grew warm and balmy, clearly inviting the children to shed their coats to make it easier to romp and play. Soon all had shed their coats in the soothing sunshine.

Children as "Allies" in Learning

Teachers seem to be adversaries to many children, as harsh as a March wind. It almost seems that the teachers are *against* everything the child is *for*. Of course, this is not the case as perceived as by the teacher. He is trying to "do what's good for them," or "to prepare them for the sobering responsibilities of adulthood." But when primarily past and future directed, the teacher may come into open conflict with childhood's love of living and excitement of learning related to the moment and the day. A two-pronged compromise may be in order: (a) Many of the activities of childhood are good for children's total growth now (and one might guess that the best preparation for the future is successful living today). (b) Many long-range societal goals can best be developed through a utilization of children's interests and abilities. Stated more simply, children enjoy meaningful activities and there are meaningful, enjoyable activities which can be utilized to broaden understandings which will be useful in adult life. Bruner[16] has suggested that children can learn concepts more easily when a teacher is able to organize learning activities harmonious with children's current level of development. This is to imply that even young children can begin to develop an understanding of difficult content. It is important of course to determine not only what children *can* learn but also what they *should* learn. The teacher can develop an atmosphere in which he is viewed as a person who can help a pupil to do *important* things. When doing personally important things, a child is quite willing to do difficult things.

In *The Elementary School We Need* there is an excellent discussion of learning principles.[17] The author gives reminders of ways in which

[16] Jerome Bruner, *The Process of Education* (Cambridge, Mass.: Harvard University Press, 1960).

[17] George Manolakes, *The Elementary School We Need* (Washington: Association for Supervision and Curriculum Development, 1965), pp. 26–33.

teachers violate some of these principles; examples include: (a) "failures" where children cannot meet arbitrary standards of what all children must do in order to pass into the next set of rigid grade-level expectations; (b) efforts to force all children to proceed toward adult goals at the same pattern, whether they are slow or fast learners (impossible tasks for slow learners, obvious and easy tasks for the fast learners); (c) rejection of children's interest when they invade learning content set aside for next year's curriculum.

In the same publication are some illustrations of how learning principles may be applied. You may want to read the following illustration and note ways in which learning principles are *applied* and how they are in harmony with individualized pupil growth patterns.

An Interage Group. Mrs. West's classroom is organized on an interage basis. There are six-, seven-, and eight-year-old children, and some who are nine. In most schools these pupils would be found in the first, second, and third grades. Since the children represent a wide range of maturity, interest, and ability, there are many centers of interest within this classroom. In one corner, there is a white rabbit in a cage. Nearby there is an easel with large sheets of white paper mounted in book form.

"What does a rabbit do in the winter?"

"How long do rabbits live?"

Often the rabbit is out of the cage. He is held by the children; he is fed by them; and his cage is cleaned by them. Sometimes a child who has been reading walks over to the cage and stands and merely watches.

Much of the learning in this room takes place on an individualized basis. Mrs. West and Tommy are reading together. When he comes to a word he does not know, he tries it because he knows he can get help when he needs it. At first Tommy was afraid to come to school, but he feels very comfortable with his teacher now. Tommy finds it difficult to sit still for very long, and he welcomes the change to move away from books and to help in building the garage in one corner. Sometimes he works at the easel with paints before he sits down again. There are times when he likes to play with some of the younger children in the room; and then at other times it makes him feel more grown up to be with the older children and to try out what they are doing.

Each child has many opportunities during the day to make choices. "What to do first?" "With whom to read today?" "What books to read?" There are also duties and responsibilities to be shared and things that the teacher asks him to do. Yet there is a freedom that each child senses. Freedom to go to the pencil sharpener, to the bathroom, to his coat pocket in the locker. There is also freedom to talk softly with the boy in the next seat, and the freedom to try out things, even if some of these projects turn out to be unsuccessful.[18]

The learner's tendency toward growth is a valuable asset in planning instruction. A study of principles of learning will enable you to capitalize on children's original tendency to learn about themselves and their en-

[18] *Ibid.*, pp. 28–29. Reprinted with permission of the Association for Supervision and Curriculum Development and George Manolakes. Copyright © 1965 by the Association for Supervision and Curriculum Development.

vironment. A curriculum which reflects children's needs is more likely to influence their learning and applications of that learning.

TIRED OLD WORLD OR BRAVE NEW WORLD?

January is named for a two-headed being who looks both backward and forward. The month of January is portrayed by artists in a variety of ways, quite often in terms of a tired old man glad to discard the struggles of the past and relinquish responsibilities to a brave young cherub who looks robust and happy. The artist may capture commendable sentiments in this portrayal in relation to New Year's resolution, but there is some question as to whether most of us do indeed shed the past and anticipate the future eagerly. It may be that the longer we carry a particular type of responsibilities the harder it is to change.

A teacher may become satisfied with present curriculum, methods, and results. He becomes secure in knowing almost exactly what will happen when certain plans are carried out. He establishes certain reputations, for being tough, creative, well-organized—whatever it is, he is recognized for what he does and for the results he obtains. He is *somebody.* Now if he selects *new* objectives, methods, and ideas, he may not get results he holds desirable; he may fail; he may be questioned by important persons around him; his lesson materials may not "fit"; his bulletin board displays may be inappropriate; he may not have glib advice to give to new teachers as he has in the past, for he himself is uncertain, *and in a real sense a beginner,* in relation to new situations.

Is it surprising, then, that change is often viewed with suspicion, sometimes with open hostility? A teacher may easily convince himself that what he is now doing is desirable, and he often can mention many students who apparently have benefited from the particular type of curriculum favored by the teacher. Under these circumstances, he may not admit that societal changes taking place, either slowly or explosively, are producing pressures for instructional revisions. The teacher's background and experiences *screen* and *interpret* his contacts with his environment. He may incorporate quite skillfully his present perceptions into past patterns of response. His curriculum may remain hopelessly obsolete, both in terms of the present and anticipated future.

The tendency to become entrenched with long-held views and practices is cleverly portrayed in *The Saber-tooth Curriculum.*[19] This is a satire in which the curriculum includes skills once functional but now dysfunctional as a result of changing circumstances. The curriculum

[19] Harold Benjamin (under the pseudonym of J. Abner Peddiwell), *The Saber-tooth Curriculum* (New York: McGraw-Hill Book Co., 1939).

depicted in the satire is for prehistoric times, and it logically includes catching fish with bare hands, defending self against saber-tooth tigers, and other such practical skills. Then conditions change: The rivers become muddied and catching fish with bare hands becomes almost impossible and a more efficient method, the use of the net, has been invented. Saber-tooth tigers become almost extinct. Still the curriculum includes catching fish with bare hands and techniques of defense against saber-tooth tigers. In the latter instance, an old saber-tooth tiger is found after much searching and brought down from the hills and chased through the village to enable the youth to practice what they are being taught. As the story ends a nearby village discovers that these people are going through meaningless motions. A formerly dynamic people with a functional curriculum which prepared its children for effective living is on the way to being conquered by the neighbor tribe.

Lifelong Professional Growth

You will want to avoid the trap of smugness and obsolescence. Professional growth *begins* in a vital teacher education program and extends *for a lifetime.* The alert professional takes courses, travels in a variety of situations, plans some vacations which are for both professional growth and pleasure, reads extensively in professional magazines and books and in a variety of fields, and participates in community civic and cultural activities—in short, he avoids the snare of the ivory tower that is carefully insulated from reality. He can understand the child better when he understands the world which molds the child (and he can regularly evaluate the changes in the present which may intellectually and emotionally separate the teacher—nurtured in a radically different world—from the child).

In addition to utilizing objective sources such as newspapers, magazines, and textbooks in varied fields to keep abreast of the times, you may find much stimulation in reading fictional and biographical books. Authors often have an ability to project now what will be possible in the future. An example from the past is Verne's *Twenty Thousand Leagues Under the Sea* [20] in which the author demonstrated an uncanny ability to foresee present capacities for scientific accomplishments. Of course it is important to accept a writer's hunches about the future with some reservations, to probe them for extensions of objective understandings of trends and possibilities, and to read such materials in conjunction with the writings of scientists, philosophers, and other academicians.

[20] Jules Verne, *Twenty Thousand Leagues Under the Sea* (New York: Charles Scribner's Sons, 1946, originally published in 1926).

The Inevitability of Change

Changes do occur regardless of our attitudes. Several predictions about the future should be considered by teachers: Starvation resulting from the population explosion, critical water shortages, imminent collapse of city governments, development of undersea colonies, experiments with human heredity, and political forms of government to permit rule by experts within the democratic ideal.

The elementary teacher needs to plan for his students in terms of specific dates, for example, 1980, 1985, 1990; to predict circumstances during those times; *and to plan present curricular experiences which are meaningful now and hopefully will be meaningful for the years ahead.* How else can elementary education today anticipate pupils starting families and beginning careers 15 years or more from now and assuming community leadership 30 years or more hence? A reading now, as well as later, of Chapters 11, 18, and 19 provides a picture of some of the issues facing you as you seek to understand curriculum.

The society painted by Grandma Moses has disappeared. She painted village life in its totality—homes, school, church, stores, farm life. A child who *lived* in this type of society could understand firsthand the simple economics, politics, religion, sociology, and other facts of its life, for he lived in a compact, understandable society *and participated in it.* The teacher who grew up in such a society may even today yearn for its simplicity and may be bewildered by the changes which occur at fantastic speed. He may grasp for facts to be memorized by children, giving both himself and the children a sense of accomplishment of sorts. With knowledge doubling at least every ten years, it is impossible to organize a curriculum around facts, since facts often become obsolete before elementary children graduate from high school.

Relation of Past to Present

It is possible to teach some pertinent and ageless values and aspirations based on children's experiences rather than in relation to the past (for example, 1776) or to distant places (for example, European events). After many *years* of concrete and vicarious experiences children may develop an ability to hurdle time, distance, and abstraction to understand and apply that which has not been experienced directly. To seek to force children to do this too soon may result in their using some words to describe other words. Another value of using the present as a launch for understanding the past's contributions and anticipating future directions is that children are more likely to be interested in their world as they have experienced it, in learnings which help them to experience that world more fully. It is possible then to relate school and total environment, to test the validity of school ways of thinking and learning in everyday life.

The teacher can and should be loyal to sturdy sources of strength from the past when they have relevance. The traditions can be brought up to date and made meaningful in terms of children's experiences. Examples of beacons from the past include the Magna Charta and the U. S. Constitution. It is well that children today identify with the heritage of free men, a heritage bought at such great price. Today's children should be reminded that each generation must find its own dedication to freedom.[21]

We reject a mechanical devotion to old creeds and deeds. The possibility that a meaningless study of our rich heritage will become a source of pupil desperation, rather than inspiration, must be overcome. How ironical it would be if today's children were to think of the past in terms of dreary lines to be memorized and recited monotonously day after day. Beymer gives an example of how our heritage can become distorted in this manner with the following effort of a child to verbalize a portion of our national heritage:

> I play the Legions/To the flag/And to the Public/Sandwich it's for/One action/Invisible/With Library and just is for all.

The child repeating this "Pledge of Allegiance" day after day is not being prepared for present or future social responsibility.[22]

Another example provided by Beymer is the following:

> Oh, saint can you see/By the donserly light/Was sew pronely we hailed/At the night's last grilling/The red rocks also burst in the air/Who's brought stripes and stars/Through the parilos fight/Will the twilight keep clammy/And round parts we watched/Were so caliently gleeming/Oh, say can you see/The Star Spangled Banner/And the home of the waves.

John Gardner, former president of the Carnegie Foundation and later Secretary of the Department of Health, Education, and Welfare, states the challenge this way:

> Instead of giving young people the impression that their task is to stand a dreary watch over the ancient values, we should be telling them the grim but bracing truth that it is their task to re-create those values continuously in their own behavior, facing the dilemmas and catastrophes of their own time. Instead of implying that the ideals we cherish are safely embalmed in the memory of old battles and ancestral deeds we should be telling them that each genera-

[21] Ernest W. Tiegs and Fay Adams, *Teaching the Social Studies* (Boston: Ginn & Co., 1959), pp. 1–14.

[22] Example provided by C. Lawrence Beymer, Indiana State University, Terre Haute, Indiana.

tion re-fights the crucial battles and either brings new vitality to the ideals or allows them to decay.[23]

The teacher who experiences with children the reality of the present can add as a result of educational background and experiences a dimension to children's understanding—the circumstances of the past which led to the present. The past need not be rejected; certain ideas, aspirations, and practices are not in themselves obsolete. Democracy, for example, has proven to be durable, although the nation itself has changed dramatically. Human dignity endures. Integrity binds people together. Talents are not color blind or class conscious. Our concepts of democracy have broadened; the problems of a democracy are changing and the methods for dealing with these problems also change. The teacher who is a part of rather than apart from the present can help children to link the best of the past and the emerging present. He can help children to develop critical thinking concerning past and present where they neither reject all of the past nor glibly assume that the new and modern are always the best.

KINDS OF CURRICULUM

Our present educational structures developed in the past, in response to a world different from the known present and the predicted future. Melby has noted this fact for administrators, and it seems to apply to all educators:

> But more important than *learning something*, education means *becoming something*. Becoming something results from the way the individual lives, and how he lives depends on who he lives with and how these persons act, how they behave.[24]

Instruction planned for individuals rather than a class group helps each child to *become important*. There is no organizational plan which can do away with differences. Goodlad notes that the mental range of first graders exceeds three years and that among fourth graders (defined as 4.0 and 4.9 in standardized tests) only 15 per cent are at "grade level." "This picture of gross variability persists even in classes contrived to be closely homogeneous in chronological age and is reduced only moderately through so-called 'ability grouping.'"[25]

The basic goal of curriculum organization, if one accepts this viewpoint, is to secure the greatest growth for the individual. Organizational

[23] From "Quotable," *Phi Delta Kappan*, XLVI, No. 8 (May, 1965), p. 479.

[24] Ernest O. Melby, "Needed: A New Concept of Educational Administration," *The Community School and Its Administration*, III, No. 11 (July, 1965), pp. 2–3.

[25] John I. Goodlad, *Some Propositions in Search of Schools* (Washington: Department of Elementary School Principals, 1962).

structures, content, and methods should serve the end goal of a more effective individual who ultimately will fashion the society at large.

A curriculum suitable for children is derived from several sources. It does not have to come exclusively from a study of children's interests and needs, although certainly this is a sound point of departure. Tyler in his *Basic Principles of Curriculum and Instruction* takes a position in favor of varied sources: ". . . no single source of information is adequate to provide a basis for wise and comprehensive decisions about the objectives of the school . . . . Each source should be given some consideration in planning any comprehensive curriculum program."[26] Tyler notes that in selecting curricular experiences, one should answer fundamental questions:

1. What educational purposes should the school seek to attain?
2. What educational experiences can be provided that are likely to attain these purposes?
3. How can these educational experiences be effectively organized?
4. How can we determine whether these purposes are being attained?[27]

He then delineates the basic sources of content for curriculum in the following manner.

1. *The child's interests, problems, and purposes.* A study of human growth and development can add much understanding of the child and contribute to the development of a curriculum which makes sense to the child.
2. *The cultural heritage, the accumulated knowledge of the century, the knowledge which has withstood the test of time.* A study of the humanities, for example, literature and the social sciences, may lead to a better understanding of the world which has such a significant effect in molding the individual child.
3. *The present society in which children are growing.* A study of subjects such as sociology, anthropology, social psychology, and other related disciplines can lead to a better understanding of pressing challenges of group and individual. A study of these problems and potentialities can help develop objectives which may lead to the "knowledge, skills, attitudes, and the like" needed to live creatively in the current world.
4. *Educational philosophers.* A study of educational philosophers may lead to an understanding of "basic values" selected for their enduring significance to a maintenance of the culture. These values are stable enough to enable the school to organize a long-range

[26] Ralph W. Tyler, *Basic Principles of Curriculum and Instruction* (Chicago: Syllabus Division, University of Chicago Press, 1950), p. 4.
[27] *Ibid.*, pp. 1–2.

study; they appear to be far enough removed from current controversies to enable pupils to study them objectively and calmly.[28]

Development of Objectives

While thinking through the many issues in organizing teaching and learning to bring about desirable pupil behavior, it is well to develop a skill in planning objectives which give direction to instruction. *The essential problem is to state an objective which clearly establishes what a pupil is to do or be like upon realization of the objective.* The objective should be stated in a specific fashion to enable the teacher and the pupil to determine when and if the pupil reaches the goal. If the teacher states that he wants the pupil to understand arithmetic computational skills, he does not know exactly what a pupil is to do. If, on the other hand, he states that a pupil should be able to secure a score of 70 or better on each section of the Smith and Jones' standardized test of computational skills, he can determine the extent to which each pupil attains the goals. Stating that a pupil should develop good sportsmanship is less specific than an objective of having all pupils be able to write the school's good sportsmanship code in their own words. It may be that some of the most significant objectives are the most difficult to state in specific terms. There is considerable doubt whether a teacher can teach for certain behaviors unless they can be stated in behavioral terms, that is, the manner in which pupils are supposed to be changed by a particular learning activity.

Having established varied yet specific objectives, the teacher is in a position to select materials, activities, and ways to appraise pupil progress and problems. The teacher can relate the current instruction to future teaching and can continue efforts to help pupils to attain objectives all during the year.

The alert teacher recognizes the changes in quantities of content available and the pressing need for helping the pupil to understand himself and the world through education. Curriculum planning consequently has taken the direction described by Goodlad:

> The selection of the most significant bits of content no longer is difficult; it is impossible. Consequently, teachers and pupils must seek out those fundamental concepts, principles, and methods that appear to be most useful for ordering and interpreting man's inquiries.[29]

[28] *Ibid.*, p. 4; see pp. 4–28 for Tyler's discussion in detail. Although published over two decades ago, it is still highly recommended as a recognized treatment of basic questions on curriculum.

[29] Goodlad, *op. cit., Some Propositions in Search of Schools*, p. 29.

PERSPECTIVE ON DIVERSITY OF TASKS

Personal Readiness

How can the prospective or relatively new teacher prepare for overwhelmingly varied tasks? Some of the ideas which follow may help to alert you to some problems faced by the teacher. In some cases the points are related directly to curriculum, while in other cases there are indirect connections to curriculum as it is usually defined.

You may benefit from an analysis of lists of teacher tasks to determine responsibilities for which you feel relatively competent and areas in which you feel need for study. You can develop a notebook, divided into major headings, in which you can place ideas for a year's instructional program. Another way is to organize the notebook chronologically, for example: before school, first week or two of school, September to Christmas, end of first semester, beginning of second semester, January to June, end of school year, and summer. The important goal is to be able to find what you need efficiently. (File folders can also be organized to serve this purpose.) As you teach, several of your ideas will be revised and certainly they will need to be up-dated regularly (hence always date everything). Aim for efficiency in finding materials to enable you to concentrate upon their use in teaching–learning processes. Perpetuate no procedures and retain no ideas unless they are productive; evaluate what you are doing or plan to do and revise it on a regular basis. Develop a philosophy of education, educational objectives, and instructional perspectives which will enable you to make decisions about routines which are harmonious with *major goals.* Each teaching decision should not be an isolated act; it should fit into the year's pattern. Decision-making then is part of an interlocking pattern of teacher behavior which promotes pupil growth. Do not feel that you can know everything at once; professional and personal growth covers a lifetime. Select areas of needed and attainable improvement for reasonable periods of time. During the early years of teaching, turn to many persons with good ideas and helpful assistance: the principal, other teachers, pupils, and their parents. Rejecting these sources, you are indeed a lonely person with an overwhelming task. If you cooperate with others, your tasks can become increasingly manageable challenges and opportunities.

An ability to honestly evaluate yourself, even if the results are discouraging, may be a start toward sharpening your perceptions of your potential strengths and weaknesses as a teacher. Following your private assessment, you may wish to have a trusted person react to your self-rating. You may find it helpful to write out your present understanding of yourself in relation to your feelings and reactions to others. This is difficult to do, for one tends to resist an indication from any source that he does not do things "right"; it is not easy to see one's deficiencies. The experience of self-analysis may be needed on several occasions to improve perceptions of self, but it should not be carried on to the point that it decreases self-confidence.

A difficulty in using checklists and summaries of characteristics needed by teachers is that no one can live up to such high standards. Awareness of effective teacher characteristics may help the teacher utilize his competencies more effectively as a professional. No one reading the characteristics of good teachers should attempt to become a carbon copy or to cultivate blindly "good" qualities. The teacher may grow through enriched perceptions of self and others. "A deeply deprived self cannot afford to give itself away."[30]

Growth Activities. You may find that your perceptions of self and others can be expanded to enrich your life as you expose yourself to varied experiences and persons. Experiencing music, literature, art, and other artistic expression endowed with rich perceptions may further stimulate personal perceptions. Reading varied types of printed materials for educators and interacting with educators on all levels in varied situations should enrich your perceptions. Experiences with children and adults outside of education should also be helpful. The perceptually rich teacher is alert to his total environment and is constantly expanding his perceptions of self, of others, and of total environment.

Hurley suggests the need for the teacher to examine his own mental hygiene, an emphasis which reinforces Combs' general emphasis upon knowing self. The teacher then, according to Hurley, is more conscious in efforts to develop sound conditions for children. Creating a good climate for growth implies friendliness, informality, psychological freedom, human autonomy, opportunities to find useful work, and constructive associations with friends."[31] The teacher hopefully is among the child's unique friends and helpers, one who opens the doors to many constructive activities. The teacher has education and experiences which provide a mature understanding of what can be done safely and constructively and of which activities must be firmly but fairly blocked. The child of course needs a different kind of friendship with his age group, with its diverse personalities and unique contributions.

[30] Arthur W. Combs, *The Professional Education of Teachers* (Boston: Allyn & Bacon, Inc., 1965), p. 68. For a basic presentation on this viewpoint, see A. W. Combs (ed.), *Perceiving, Behaving, Becoming,* 1962 Yearbook (Washington: Association for Supervision and Curriculum Development, 1962). This is one of the best general references for teachers.

[31] Beatrice Davis Hurley, *Curriculum for Elementary School Children* (New York: The Ronald Press Co., 1957), p. 70.

Presumably the teacher who is personally secure and challenged by teaching and the learning process seeks ways to help each child attain his maximum growth. In a permissive yet challenging and productive climate, children will find the personal satisfaction and security which come through progress toward personal and in-group goals.

School Calendar

A copy of the school calendar should be helpful in determining when blocks of uninterrupted teaching time are available; hence, only a short unit would be planned for the period between Thanksgiving and Christmas recesses. You should avoid beginning a unit three days before Christmas only to have two weeks intervening! Your school calendar may include special seasons and emphases; but in some cases it may be possible to capitalize upon these or to lighten instructional demands before an exciting season, for example, just prior to the school's Halloween parade. An example of a school calendar planning follows: school dismissed for state teachers association meeting, October 22–23; Veterans Day recess, November 11; Thanksgiving recess, November 26–27; Christmas recess, December 18–January 4; Easter recess, April 12–16. Blocking out the days when students are not at school you can plot the number of consecutive days available for instruction. Major units should not be started in some communities where it is a custom for pupils to leave early or return late from vacation recesses.

Your calendar probably will include observances such as Columbus Day, UN Day, United Fund Week, Be Kind to Animals Week, and others for which there may be considerable local and national publicity in the news media and for which free and inexpensive materials often are available. Magazines for elementary teachers have special suggestions for such occasions. It is well to start and maintain a file of observance ideas.

Sources of Planning Dates. Browsing through back issues of teachers magazines can be helpful in beginning a planning calendar; and many memorandum books for teachers have information on special dates, events, and personalities. Bulletin boards, special programs, and other practices can be used in special observances. A reminder: There are literally hundreds of days and weeks proclaimed by different special interest groups. The wise teacher plans carefully to select the most meaningful ones for his own class. Some school staffs may wish to select a few basic observances for all grades, and then select others for specific grades to provide variety for pupils and also avoid needless repetition. You may develop an instructional planning calendar for each month by dividing regular typing paper into daily squares, or you may purchase a teacher's plan book which already is divided into blocks equaling the number of school days in a year.

An investigation of school procedures related to securing instructional materials will help to plan for obtaining them on time, both those purchased by the school and those which are free. Some districts provide all materials needed for instruction, others provide only basic textbooks, and still others charge fees for all materials. You need to know not only what the school provides but also what you may ask students to bring, for example, paints or only scrap materials such as oatmeal cans. Adequate time is needed even when salvage materials are requested. Parents are sometimes pressured to make purchases or become scavengers at the last minute, as the father who received a frantic request to buy an apple one night at 10:30 P.M. His daughter had forgotten about the apple, to be used in an applesauce project, until she happened to awake at 10:30 P.M.! Some parent–teacher groups regularly provide instructional materials, while others insist that the regular school budget should supply needed materials.

Instructional Objectives and Unit Planning

You may use several criteria for examining units of study, either your own or those prepared by other teachers in your building, available in teachers magazines, or printed in books. Unit plans are guides and not binds. Early examination of sample unit plans may make many broad curriculum questions meaningful.

Questions related to instructional planning are so numerous that only a few will be touched at this point. Succeeding chapters will bring out many more points. The *content* of the curriculum continues to be a major concern, as efforts are made to discover the *structure* of the different content areas (for example, to determine how mathematics differs from grammar) to ascertain how the pupils can master the skills needed to study these areas. A significant curriculum concept is that *process* is as significant as *product*. Understanding and using mathematics (process) rather than possessing just an ability to get answers through memorized formulas (product) is an example. Learning to understand interrelationships between man and his environment (process) rather than merely memorizing the main manufactured and agricultural products of a region (product) is another.

While much emphasis is now being placed upon the uniqueness of the subject areas (structure), there are continuing questions concerning the ways in which these areas can be correlated, integrated, and fused in such a way that the pupil sees relationships and uses concepts and skills learned in one subject area to clarify and reinforce learnings from others.

Another basic question ought to be: To what extent should a school be subject centered, pupil centered, and society centered? Can the school's instructional program combine its varied obligations and in a sense be all things to all people? How does the teacher combine the many who, why, when, and where questions into meaningful instructional plans, the *how*?

Procedures and Problems in Securing Instructional Supplies and Materials. Procedures for securing supplies and equipment vary from school to school. However, it may be helpful for you to examine a faculty handbook from a teaching materials center on a college campus or to examine one in current use in some school. Your planning for instruction during student teaching or early teaching experiences will be more realistic, and hence more functional, if your curriculum planning takes varied factors into account.

It is helpful to become conversant with mandatory and prohibited instruction for the type of class or general grade level on which you hope to teach or are teaching. There are related policies in the use of free and inexpensive materials. Variety, or lack of it, of instructional materials, should be reflected in curriculum planning. Sometimes a school system has its own instructional materials center, where varied materials are available; and as a result of state and federal assistance, there are an increasing number of area curriculum centers. These centers in addition to prepared materials may have equipment to enable you to prepare materials uniquely suited to your particular instructional goals, and they may have specialized personnel who can either instruct or assist you.

Finally, there are parents and other laymen who often have valuable materials, equipment, and/or experiences which they are pleased to share with students. There are at least two major potential problems in using community resources: (a) They may not be of high quality as a result of age, manner of presentation, or other factors. (b) They may be offensive to community values or so controversial that their use would undermine community trust and support.

Effects of Classroom Routines. It may be of some value when studying curriculum to peruse a textbook on classroom management, for unless classroom routines are well planned and executed, much valuable instruction time can easily be wasted. In some classrooms this time may become substantial.

Attendance. Routines are needed to provide a means of checking on children whose absence cannot be explained. In relation to curriculum, attendance irregularity may suggest illness or home factors which may interfere with learning; it may also imply that certain children feel so uncomfortable about school that they find real or imaginary reasons for staying home whenever possible.

Clerical Functions. A simple yet effective filing system is needed if you are to find materials which are best for a particular unit of instruction. An orderly system is needed for collecting pupil work, grading it, recording grades and progress, and returning pupils' papers. Teachers may become preoccupied with clerical duties and neglect curriculum planning.

Effects of Building Routines. Building routines should be studied even in an elementary school with "self-contained" classrooms. You will need to know if building bells determine your schedule, and if passage to the playground, into the neighborhood, or within the school is rigidly structured. Building procedures may control the use of special facilities and equipment. The amount of supplies and times when they are available to you may be affected by decisions of either the principal or the faculty. Certain reports such as those on needed supplies, attendance, and discipline problems will have some effect on the amount of time available for curriculum planning. Your failure to be reasonably efficient in these matters may affect the quality of your relationships with the principal and with other teachers.

Student Activities. Distinctions between curricular and extra curricular activities fade in the light of definitions such as those used in this book—that curriculum includes the planned activities of the school. Outside activities may be considered a part of curriculum, but they are considered separately here for purposes of analysis. They tend to differ from the more commonly accepted curricular activities by their lack of structure, traditional goals, and marks, and by their relative absence of instructional materials. In some schools they may include elements of all or some of these distinguishing characteristics. The teacher in cooperation with children, parents, and associates should plan school activities which are meaningful to varied types of children, and feasible in terms of necessary costs, available pupil and teacher time, and required materials, equipment, and facilities. Some illustrative activities include school assemblies, class parties, safety patrols, student councils, school stores, and intramural sports. These activities should be regularly appraised and revised to maintain good human relationships, support good home–school relations, and most importantly contribute to pupils' mental, physical, social, and emotional health and growth.

Teacher and School Relations. Some beginning teachers say, "If only *they* would leave me alone in *my* room, I could do a better job with *my* pupils!" There are times when the principal, other teachers, custodians, secretaries, speech correctionists, psychologists, and a variety of other persons seem to be conspiring to keep the classroom teacher from teaching. Indeed there are times when even the teacher of the self-contained classroom has difficulty in finding time for a period of uninterrupted instruction when all children are in their room and when no other member of the school staff is present.

The teacher who in exasperation complains about interruptions probably would not want to lose the assistance of the varied persons who interrupt his classes; he is expressing a sense of frustration at the fact that the elementary school today is expected to do all that was done in previous years *plus* seemingly unending additional tasks. As the school has been given increased responsibilities in the areas of physical and mental health, recreation, community service, and other functions, the number and kinds of special personnel have increased. Likewise as the curriculum has expanded, varied personnel other than classroom teachers have been needed, including art, music, and physical education teachers. In planning the curriculum you need to account for your own unique curriculum responsibilities in relation to those of others, and you must correlate your activities with those of others. This will avoid needless duplication and capitalize on the competencies and programs of others.

Curriculum planning should include an inventory of possible aids, human and material, which can be related to your own resources. It should also include an inventory of what general types of experiences children have had in the past and will presumably have in the future. There will be questions about school-wide emphases and observances, the extent to which you are expected to consult with or receive permission from the principal or system consultants prior to planning learning experiences, and the types of instructional content which are either required or prohibited (by state law or local board of education policy or administrative dictate). Increasingly a team of adults works together, using varied resources, to promote total pupil growth.

Pupil Records. The ultimate way to evaluate your curriculum is to determine its effectiveness in changing pupil behavior. You will need to have much information concerning each child to capitalize upon his interests and strengths as well as to help him solve his problems. Of course it is possible to become so concerned with a child's past that you ignore the possibility that he has changed his behavior or is passing into a new stage of development. The past records of a child should be used as *a rough index* of what you may expect of him. They should not be considered indelible branding irons which restrict teacher's perceptions. Certain questions concerning children's records should be asked: (a) Can you telephone the previous school for records? (b) Who sends for pupil records? (c) What informal and formal tests and other analyses can you secure? (d) What can parents tell you? (e) What can the child tell you about himself? (f) When the sending school is unfamiliar to you, how can you evaluate the meaning of the records? (g) What kinds of information may be helpful in diagnosing factors which contribute to pupil growth or retard it? Records may include summaries of parent–teacher conferences, telephone calls, and notes; report cards; reading records; reports of special consultants and personnel; anecdotal records; health information, including results of hearing and vision testing, and special treatments; summaries of intelligence and achievement tests; family data, including child's placement among children in the family, parents' occupations, and parents' educational attainments; attendance checks; and physical problems which may restrict kinds of activities safe for individual children. Records are valuable in helping you to diagnose the needs of the total child.

Class Grouping. Class size and composition should be considered in planning instruction, and since they vary from system to system and even in the same building from year to year it is necessary to develop instructional plans which can be adapted to different class groups. An example of a serious instructional problem is a class of 40 in a small room, where plans for several groups working on projects may be very difficult but not impossible to carry out.

Varied grouping procedures should be anticipated when developing resource units, lesson plans, and materials files in view of the diversity of grouping plans used. Some schools divide the number of pupils per grade by the number of teachers available for each grade, randomly assigning pupils to teachers regardless of the abilities or characteristics of either. Other schools place students into classes on the basis of sex (separate rooms for boys and girls), academic abilities (good grades and bad grades), types of problems (good readers and poor readers), age (old pupils and young pupils), pupil preference for particular teachers, means of getting to school (bus riders and neighborhood children), level in an ungraded unit (for example, reading level five in a nine-level primary unit), recommendations of previous teachers (to note one example, to avoid placement of children who create problems when together), and almost endless other variations beyond those just noted as illustrations. These plans affect instruction tremendously, and the teacher once assigned to a group often must adapt to the situation.

If you are willing to experiment and change grouping plans, this will enable you to utilize your unique competencies with a unique group of children. Many grouping plans are adopted in an assumption that they will decrease problems related to individual differences. Grouping plans may decrease the range of differences by eliminating extremes (bright and dull), or they may decrease differences in a specific skill, for example, phonetics. Individual dissimilarities still remain. Dedicated to democracy, schools should actually *increase* individual differences by providing a rich learning environment.

End-of-Year Planning. Planning for the end of the year should start at the beginning. Representative samples of pupil work can be collected, slides and pictures can be taken of learning activities, and sample projects can be saved for summarizing activities of the class, for sharing with other classes, or with parents and other interested persons. A careful diagnosis of each pupil, showing basic learnings accomplished and suggesting goals for summer learning, can be established. A growth chart, showing basic learnings anticipated for a year, can be used to guide individual and class learnings all year and help in end-of-year evaluation. In addition to listing elements of the pre-planned curriculum, the growth chart can have space for learning activities which arise during the year for the group, and also individualized activities and goals established by the pupil and/or the teacher. With adequate information, the teacher finds that grading is largely routine; there are few surprises since pupils and parents have been involved and informed during the year.

End-of-year planning also includes planning for completing an inventory of equipment, instructional materials, and supplies. A check on the instructional file is also in order to eliminate bulletin board items, unit plans, and other means which did not live up to expectations or which are obsolete. Pupils can aid in evaluating the materials which should be retained for future use.

Some Additional Issues. Many other points should be investigated by the prospective and beginning teacher, and they include the following considerations.

1. *Drill and practice.* How much is needed? How can drill and practice be varied for individuals, both in type and amount of activity? How can drill be used judiciously to increase retention of meaningful learnings?
2. *Critical thinking and problem solving.* How can all types of pupils be challenged to a level of thinking needed for an uncertain and changing world?
3. *Diagnostic and remedial teaching.* How can individual strengths and weaknesses be diagnosed and instruction provided where and when needed?
4. *Motivation.* What are some of the ways to increase and broaden pupil desire to learn (intrinsic motivation)? What are the *pros* and *cons* of grades, stars for good work, threats (extrinsic motivation) administered by the teacher?
5. *Transfer of training.* What are the ways in which pupil learning in one situation can be applied to others, both in school and outside?
6. *Concept formation and generalizations.* How can a series of related learning activities be planned to promote broad understandings of general applicability? How can concept formation be

promoted to provide children with a way of learning about both present and future?

7. *Transportation safety/fire safety/disaster planning.* How can pupils develop safety consciousness? How can varied aspects of instruction and classroom routines be used to develop safety as a way of life?
8. *Cafeteria's educational potentialities.* In what ways can the school cafeteria services supplement classroom instruction?
9. *Religious education.* In what ways can religion be studied for its relationship to American values? How can this be done without promoting sectarian bias and without infringing upon any individual's religious views?
10. *Creativity.* How can children's unique tendencies toward exploration and mastery of self and environment be accepted and accentuated? In what ways can individual growth be encouraged concurrently with instruction in societal values?
11. *Site, facilities, and equipment utilization in instruction.* What facilities, equipment, land areas, and living things around the school can be used for learning?
12. *Faculty in public affairs.* To what extent and in what ways can a teacher participate as a democratic citizen and still avoid narrow partisanship while teaching? How can participation increase teacher effectiveness?

The Right Teacher for the Right Job. We have tried to emphasize the personal and professional nature of teaching, since the teacher is the key determinant of the type of learning that occurs. To function at his best the teacher should attempt to find a job where his particular competencies and interests can be applied. There are many questions that teachers should ask when applying for a position. It is indeed important to secure information concerning salary, payroll deductions, vacation periods, and other personal data but it is also crucial that questions be asked concerning the instructional setting which either helps or hinders the ways in which you can teach. Questions should derive information on: (a) the school's philosophy of education; (b) regular instructional materials available and expectations for instructional methods; (c) special resources and personnel available; (d) special grouping plans used and other provisions for individual differences; (e) testing and other processes for evaluating pupil growth plus the ways of reporting to pupils and parents; (f) in-service growth opportunities, both within the system and also in the area; (g) system attitudes toward professional activities, both local and beyond; (h) extent of extra-class responsibilities, to determine the amount of time available for direct instructional activities; (i) the philosophy of teacher evaluation and how it is conducted; (j) community expectations and involvement and the extent and manner in which community factors help or hinder education. Many of these questions will arise in a formal interview. If you know what information you wish to obtain, you can mentally keep track of what comes out in the interview and what questions you need to raise after your interviewer has completed his questioning. It is helpful to hold part of your conversation in a typical classroom, if possible, to stimulate instruction-centered discussions; also to meet the principal where you may be teaching and observe and talk with teachers there. A professional interview viewed constructively is not an interrogation period for either prospective teacher or interviewing official; it is a time to determine whether a teacher can make a unique contribution in a particular school.

This chapter has provided an overview of the many factors in curriculum planning, teaching, and learning. Many of the points discussed will be elaborated further in subsequent chapters and it is important to view discussions in these chapters as a beginning. Curriculum is the totality of planned school learning activities; therefore, it is apparent that its scope and subtleties cannot be learned and applied in less than years of study and practice.

A Suggestion. This chapter and each of the following seventeen chapters conclude with a section entitled Projects and Readings. It should be carefully read, studied, and, where possible, applied as an integral part of the total chapter. We have made an effort to suggest ways to extend your understanding of how people are involved in curriculum and the processes which are used to attain objectives, to ultimately develop a product—new knowledge, changed behavior, modified attitudes and ideas, and so forth. Curriculum viewed in the perspectives suggested in Projects and Readings is dynamic. This is true whether related to teachers or pupils. The basic goal of this section, from our standpoint, is to encourage you to *do* something—reading, discussing, visiting—which should in turn provide *new leads* to active growth in understanding elementary curriculum. This broad objective should be kept in mind whether you are asked a question, told how to apply a concept, or given information.

PROJECTS AND READINGS

1. One of the most potentially productive means of enlarging your understanding of this textbook is to browse in the library. For each chapter there is at least one library section where related materials are stacked. It is not necessary to read whole books each time you find a good one. Tables of contents and indexes can lead you to a few sections which are most valuable for your reading.

If your library uses the Dewey Decimal System, you will find that the 370, 371, 375, and 379 sections—with their breakdown into sub-categories—are most closely related to materials in this textbook. The 370 section includes professional education, student teaching, and the use of equipment. The 371 section includes grouping, tests and evaluation, promotion and retardation, methods of teaching, discipline, student government, school facilities, hygiene and health, and special education and exceptional children. The 372 section includes elementary school levels of teaching and the elementary subject areas. The 375 section contains several aspects of curriculum, including theory. The 379 section comprises governmental relationships to education.

If your library uses the Library of Congress system you will find that the "LB" and "LC" classifications are most closely related to this textbook. There are sub-categories comparable to those found in the Dewey system.

2. It is particularly desirable to keep abreast of current ideas and information, which a textbook can only partially report. You will find that certain headings in *Guide to Periodical Literature* and *Education Index* are most productive in relation to curriculum topics. It is helpful to develop a list of these headings and examine the reading guides regularly to find clues to desirable reading.

3. A fictional, biographical, or autobiographical account of the life of a teacher could supplement your reading of this chapter. You can then contrast another writer's perceptions of teaching. You can look critically at the viewpoints presented in this chapter to see in what ways others' opinions seem to be supportive or contradictory, either for teaching situations in general or for specific kinds. Reading comparable chapters in other curriculum textbooks also would be informative.

4. A very brief statement of your views on curriculum, written after you have read this chapter, could be contrasted with your viewpoints after you have completed reading the book. You could, among other things, determine how much change occurs as a result of exposure to facts and ideas, and you could try to decide what is most likely to alter your behavior and analyze how human behavior in general may be changed.

5. An examination of a faculty handbook will reveal many factors related to curriculum. How many, in your estimation, apply to non-curriculum matters? Which factors look as if they might interfere with the development of the kind of school you now think is desirable?

6. One of the world's most comprehensive idea and information systems is the Educational Resources Information Center (ERIC) of the U.S. Office of Education (USOE). It is valuable as a means of keeping abreast of what is going on in education as well as of identifying the contents and availability of reports and articles (and of objectives and activities of federally funded educational projects). The ERIC system is an indispensable companion resource to libraries and textbooks. *Research in Education* (RIE) is a journal of abstracts with an indexing system enabling you to identify documents under many different terms and further permits you to learn the nature of a document to a much greater degree than do typical library tools; it also indexes many projects which are in process and provides information on them. *Current Index to Journals in Education* (CIJE) uses the same indexing system and includes annotated citations of journals and other periodic literature. A *Thesaurus* of terms used by the ERIC system is an aid to finding index terms (used in RIE and CIJE), which are specifically related to the topics about which you are seeking ideas and information. The system is designed to prevent ineffective and inappropriate searches for ideas and information. You

are provided information on each document's availability, and in many cases you may secure it through the ERIC Document Reproduction Service (EDRS), in Bethesda, Maryland. In the latter case the documents often are available in microfiche form (which for a few dimes per sheet makes up to 60 pages of materials available on a 4 x 6" film card which requires a machine reader) and sometimes in hard copy form (which for a few cents per page provides paper copies readable to the naked eye). The average reader will use his library's copies of the monthly, semi-annual, and annual publications noted above and also the microfiche collection rather than buying them.

Many school districts also have these resources. While the ERIC system can be used with the aid of computers, the means noted above provide a major source of ideas and information needed by pre- and in-service school personnel.

2

An Analytical Study of Teaching

To a great extent curriculum can be defined in terms of what the teacher does in the classroom. This statement is an oversimplification, but it does focus attention upon the role of the teacher. It is important to develop a clear understanding of the teacher's role; such insight can help to organize learning activities to bring about changes in pupil behavior—how the pupil thinks, acts, and believes—and what he becomes. This chapter summarizes some efforts to analyze teaching and learning acts, as an aid to understanding curriculum itself.

It is appropriate to acknowledge the contribution of LaGrone and others in the development of the outline used in this chapter and to a great extent Chapters 3 to 5. The sources of information and ideas suggested in a study by LaGrone and others furnished much of the content of Chapters 2 to 5. Footnotes are provided to enable you to read original sources or other materials by the authors cited.[1]

Some persons entering teaching or professional education courses may be seeking a "bag of tricks," a series of gimmicks, a set of clearcut responses for situations faced by teachers—that is, simple answers to complex questions related to teaching and learning. Indeed it would be possible to develop an encyclopedia of answers for a variety of situations, but these "answers" would apply to no specific teacher and no specific group of

[1] See Herbert LaGrone, *A Proposal for the Revision of the Pre-service Professional Component of a Program of Teacher Education* (Washington: American Association of Colleges for Teacher Education [AACTE], 1964). A final report on the same study is entitled *Professional Teacher Education: A Programed Design Developed by the AACTE Teacher Education and Media Project* (Washington: AACTE, 1968).

children. Answers which seek to respond to everyone's questions indeed may answer few pertinent questions!

It is better for *you* to develop a unified, harmonious way of looking at teaching and learning and to acquire a set of generalized responses based upon sound concepts of teaching. Through observing, teaching, experimenting, and discussing, you can internalize the teacher role, enabling you to act like a teacher because you have learned *to think and behave* like a teacher. As experienced teachers will admit, this is a lifelong process, never completed, since new insights arise whenever a teacher seeks to combine theory and practice, which are being revised constantly.

The basic goal of this chapter is to enable you to understand certain analytical tools which have been developed through scientific studies of classroom behavior. The observational and analytical procedures also provide means for an individual or an elementary, secondary, or collegiate class (or other group) to study teaching in a manner which leads to a broad understanding of teaching and learning. These procedures may help you to analyze your own teaching or that of others.

This process of developing understanding has been summarized by Taba into three steps.

1. Individuals inevitably build mental schemes with which to organize the information they encounter.
2. The individual fits the information he receives at any moment into the conceptual scheme he already possesses.
3. When the requirements of the situation do not fit his current scheme, the individual is forced to alter or extend it to accommodate new information.[2]

You have at this moment, as a result of attending school, studying, or teaching, certain ideas about teaching and learning. These ideas are organized to some degree. Hopefully, experiences such as reading, observing, and analyzing teaching acts will revise some of your ideas concerning teaching which are not valid in relation to research findings and expert opinion. This suggests that each person should open himself to the experience of analyzing his views of teaching and revising them when it appears that greater effectiveness could be attained.

This chapter is based on an assumption that you cannot study every teaching act all day long, but that with practice you can select and study some teaching acts, both your own and those of others. After analysis and study of these selected acts, you should be able to determine broad reaction patterns which fit generalized situations. In a given day you have thousands of perceptions picked up by the senses. To analyze these

[2] Hilda Taba *et al.*, *Thinking in Elementary School Children*, Cooperative Research Project No. 1574 (San Francisco: San Francisco State College, 1964), in LaGrone, *op. cit.*, p. 9.

individually while teaching would become physically exhausting and would lead to a series of halting, unrelated—perhaps conflicting—reactions. Children would sense indecision and resent inconsistency. They could be counted on to create action to fill vacuums caused by teacher hesitation resulting from doubts about what to do next.

Teaching cannot, and should not, become automatic sets of responses to children's actions. However, it should be possible to anticipate generalized responses to teaching acts. Ryans, who has completed a major study of teaching, provides a degree of optimism concerning consistency and predictability in teaching: (a) There is "some degree of consistency." (b) There is "a limited number of responses." (c) Teaching behaviors may be classified as various "core components" which yield "generalized descriptions." (d) Teaching–learning acts are classifiable qualitatively and quantitatively." [3]

The teacher who has an overall confidence that he can plan for *general pupil behaviors* with a consistent reaction can concentrate upon promoting constructive *individual behaviors.* This kind of confidence should be promoted by a knowledge of what is significant and what is not, what needs considerable attention and what can be passed over lightly. While pupil behavior is unique, it also can be related to generalized teaching and learning patterns. The individual pupil responds much like others in his classroom; but the manner, timing, intensity, and duration of his individual actions depend upon his immediate perceptions as to what will advance whatever goal may predominate at a given moment.

Presumably, training, including the use of procedures summarized in this chapter, can increase your perception of the diversity and unity of pupil behaviors. Gibb notes:

> It is likely that the more experience the teacher has, the more meaningful will his observations be. However, any person will tend to select aspects of his social environment when observing it. Perception is a selective process. Training will improve one's observational abilities. A frame of reference will serve as a guide to systematic observation.[4]

An accurate measure of teaching and learning acts can add to the practice of teaching as a science. An effort to become a scientific practitioner should not eliminate concern for teaching as an art.

The complexity of teaching, both as an art and as a science, is illustrated by Maccia:

[3] David G. Ryans, *Characteristics of Teachers* (Washington, D.C.: American Council on Education, 1960), pp. 13–26.

[4] Jack R. Gibb, "Sociopsychological Processes of Group Instruction," in Nelson B. Henry (ed.), *The Dynamics of Instructional Groups,* Fifty-ninth Yearbook, National Society for the Study of Education (Chicago: University of Chicago Press, 1960), p. 116.

Unlike apples, students with identical measures add up to more than students with identical measures. There is interaction between one student and another, between each student and another, between each student and the teacher, between all the students and the teacher, and between all of the group taken as a whole. Also there is interaction with oneself and other aspects of the classroom environment other than persons. Furthermore, this interaction which takes place in the classroom takes place with increasing complexity in the school and in the school district.[5]

CLASSROOM INTERACTION

An attempt to analyze teaching is based on certain assumptions: (a) There are generalized patterns of teaching and learning which can be observed, analyzed, and studied. (b) The task is complex and demands considerable effort. The potential result is an understanding of what can and does occur when teaching and learning take place *or* are restricted. Let us now examine some of the observational tools available to the pre-service and in-service teacher.

Classroom Interaction Analysis Categories

Flanders and Amidon recommend that a group of teachers may develop skills needed to analyze teaching:

> (a) ability to accept, clarify, and use ideas, (b) ability to accept and clarify emotional expression, (c) ability to relate emotional expression to ideas, (d) ability to state objectively a point, (e) ability to reflect accurately the ideas of others, (f) ability to summarize ideas presented in group discussion, (g) ability to communicate encouragement, (h) ability to question others without causing defensive behavior, and (i) ability to use criticism with least possible harm to the status of the recipient.[6]

Flanders and Amidon in the same discussion encourage teachers to role play, that is, *imaginatively* act out roles of teachers and students to provide a variety of vicarious experiences and reactions. A group of teachers can "live" more experiences than one individual teacher can. The elementary teacher perhaps more than any other needs to develop an ability to analyze his teaching behavior; he will be working largely apart from other adults, and thus will be cut off from critical analyses of other adults.

Initially you may feel embarrassed at "playing" teacher, parent, or pupil or varying your present teaching role. As you become actively in-

[5] Elizabeth Steiner Maccia, George S. Maccia, and Robert E. Jewett, *Construction of Educational Theory Models,* Cooperative Research Project No. 1632 (Columbus: Ohio State University, 1963), p. 139.

[6] Edmund J. Amidon and Ned A. Flanders, *The Role of the Teacher in the Classroom* (Minneapolis, Minn.: Paul S. Amidon and Associates, Inc., 1967), p. 3.

volved in helping yourself and others, role playing can become creative, somewhat in the manner of dramatics, musical stage productions, and many games. It is important to build up semi-automatic general responses to varieties of situations. Exact responses, of course, cannot be determined since they will vary with situations. Faced with the classroom need to react, the teacher finds a long listing of "dos and don'ts" cumbersome in contrast, for the memorized list of possible responses must be translated from a mental abstraction into action alternatives.

Amidon and Flanders also suggest that tape recordings can be used for later analysis. It appears that two uses could be planned: (a) a pre-service or in-service group analysis of tape recordings of a teacher's interaction with students or of a group's role playing, (b) self-analysis of a recording.

The Flanders analysis system focuses upon *verbal* teacher–student relationships. The system of analyzing teacher behavior has been refined to the point that different trained observers can get similar scores for the same teaching situation. Each observer in the Flanders system is essentially rating teaching acts on a system of categories related to the amount of freedom of expression permitted and encouraged.

Put another way, the scale enables the observer to determine the extent of teacher domination of verbal interaction, typically a major classroom teaching activity. The verbal factor is not the only important one, but it is indicative of many aspects of the teacher's personality, philosophy, and procedures. Flanders and others have sought to develop a scale which is both adequate and simple, that is, it has enough dimensions but not so many that it becomes cumbersome to mark and analyze.

The teacher who attempts to use this chart must commit it to memory, in order to make rapid and sufficient analysis of classroom verbal interaction. When a group uses it, someone should study Amidon and Flanders' book for full interpretation and in turn train the group interested in using the process. An individual can profit from reading and using the scale to increase his sensitivity to classroom verbal interaction. It appears, however, that a group setting is more appropriate to capitalize on the potentialities. It will take considerable group practice both to record numbers reflecting the type of verbal behavior going on and to develop objectivity and accuracy in recording. A mark is made every few seconds, to indicate either that the previous type of behavior is continuing or that new behavior has been started by teacher or pupils.

Amidon and Flanders suggest that an analysis of classroom interaction may point to certain conclusions:

> When a teacher uses extensive lecture, is he taking time to find out whether or not he is communicating? A question–answer period, or a pattern of question and clarification by the teacher of student ideas, may indicate that the

Categories for Interaction Analysis[7]

TEACHER TALK	*INDIRECT INFLUENCE*	1. **Accepts Feeling:** accepts and clarifies the feeling tone of the students in a nonthreatening manner. Feelings may be positive or negative. Predicting and recalling feelings are included.
		2. **Praises or Encourages:** praises or encourages student action or behavior. Jokes that release tension, not at the expense of another individual, nodding head, or saying "uh hm?" or "go on" are included.
		3. **Accepts or Uses Ideas of Student:** clarifying, building, or developing ideas or suggestions by a student. As teacher brings more of his own ideas into play, shift to category five.
		4. **Asks Questions:** asking a question about content or procedure with the intent that a student answer.
	DIRECT INFLUENCE	5. **Lecturing:** giving facts or opinion about content or procedure; expressing his own idea; asking rhetorical questions.
		6. **Gives Directions:** directions, commands, or orders with which a student is expected to comply.
		7. **Criticizing or Justifying Authority:** statements intended to change student behavior from nonacceptable to acceptable pattern; bawling someone out; stating why the teacher is doing what he is doing, extreme self-reference.
STUDENT TALK		8. **Student Talk-Response:** talk by students in response to teacher. Teacher initiates the contact or solicits student statement.
		9. **Student Talk-Initiation:** talk by students which they initiate. If "calling on" student is only to indicate who may talk next, observer must decide whether student wanted to talk. If he did, use this category.
		10. **Silence or Confusion:** pauses, short periods of silence and periods of confusion in which communication cannot be understood by the observer.

[7] Ned A. Flanders, *Teacher Influence: Pupil Attitudes and Achievement,* U.S. Office of Education Cooperative Research Project No. 397 (Minneapolis: University of Minnesota, November 30, 1960), Interaction Analysis Manual, p. 5.

teacher is taking time to relate the responses of children to the material or to determine how effectively he is communicating his ideas. Conversely, a pattern of extended lectures with few questions, or one of only direct questions with specific answers required, may indicate limited attempts on the part of the teacher to find out how well he is communicating or to find out whether or not there is a clear relationship between student ideas and the content being discussed.[8]

Certainly there is need to examine objectively what goes on in the classroom quantitatively (amount) and qualitatively (value in terms of goals). The teacher interested in quality cannot blindly take content and teaching suggestions from a textbook or course of study guide. He must be able to evaluate what happens when the teacher and pupils teach and learn a particular unit. Analysis of taped recordings of one's teaching or of someone's observed teaching could contribute to the ability to select content and teach it with an analytical ability to discover "what the score is" in terms of what is happening in the classroom. The use of Flanders scale is one way to develop this ability.

Among the questions which Amidon and Flanders suggest for each teacher are: (a) Do I do too much talking in the classroom? (b) Am I typically a direct or indirect teacher? (c) How do I react to student verbal behavior? (d) How much time do I spend lecturing? (e) Do I spend enough time in the extension of student ideas? (f) Do students tend to resist my influence? (g) Do I accept, clarify, and use student emotion? (h) How effectively do I use praise? (i) How effective am I in communicating subject matter to my pupils? (j) How effectively do I use criticism in my teaching? (k) Is there adequate pupil participation in my classroom?[9]

These authors point out that there is no absolute answer to these questions. However, becoming aware of many factors opens keys of understanding to one's teaching or potential teaching. Research has proceeded to the point where knowing your scores on the Flanders' scale provides useful information about your teaching strengths and weaknesses.

Amidon and Flanders caution against assuming that one type of interaction is better than another. Interaction analysis can provide clues on the main characteristics of teacher behavior which will tend to become the predominant pattern in the classroom. Thus a teacher who seeks to promote democratic behavior presumably would practice interaction patterns which would emphasize acceptance of diverse views, encourage active participation of those affected by a decision, and instill strong respect for the dignity of the individual.

[8] Amidon and Flanders, *op. cit.*, pp. 49–50.
[9] Amidon and Flanders, *op. cit.*, pp. 43–49.

Classroom Observation Report

Another kind of analysis has been developed by Ryans as part of the most extensive study of teacher characteristics ever conducted. The Ryans scale for evaluating classroom climate—the general type of relationships which prevail—includes criteria for determining both pupil and teacher behaviors but stresses teacher behaviors. The analysis form was revised in a 1960 study at the University of Florida and is used in this book (see Appendix, pp. 457–64). A study and use of this guide hopefully will increase your understanding of the *range of behaviors* which may occur in a classroom. In observing another's teaching or analyzing your own teaching from a tape recording or from memory, you should become very familiar with the criteria for determining whether teaching behavior is apathetic or alert, to name but one category. No teacher exemplifies or elicits all "good" or "bad" characteristics. All criteria for a given characteristic may not be evident during a particular class period. This extensive form is included in the Appendix to provide an additional tool for determining what happens in a classroom—in effect, an analysis of the curriculum in action—as well as the potentiality for constructive teacher–pupil interaction. A careful study of the form can contribute to a conceptualization of teaching and learning which is the heart of curriculum study. It should *not* be used as a means to evaluate teacher effectiveness or to develop conclusions on classroom environment.

Management Moves

Continuing in the assumption that what the teacher *does* largely determines the curriculum, we turn now to an analysis by Bellack and others. They have divided teaching or pedagogic moves into four types. In instructional planning you will need to anticipate specific ways to manage these moves. The processes used ("moves") in large measure determine learnings ("products").

1. "Structuring moves" are those which direct student thinking upon topics which are to be studied during a particular lesson. They establish procedures and the kinds of teacher–student relationships which are to prevail.
2. "Soliciting moves" are teacher efforts—in the form of questions, commands, or requests—to get students to respond mentally or physically.
3. "Responding moves" are those taken in response to soliciting moves. The student reacts in direct response to teacher moves.

4. "Reacting moves" are made in response to one or more of the previous kinds of moves but not in direct response. There may be acceptance, rejection, or modification. Teaching moves may not be along lines anticipated.[10]

Bellack and others explain that they have sought to analyze teaching through an analysis of language behavior of teachers and pupils. Language seems to them to be the main source of communication between teachers and pupils. These researchers note that their effort is to find who "speaks, about what, how much, when, under what conditions, and with what effect."[11] Conclusions from the research of Bellack and others include:

1. The pedagogical roles of the classroom are clearly delineated for teachers and pupils. Teachers are responsible for structuring the lesson, soliciting responses from pupils, reacting to pupils' responses, and, to some extent, summarizing aspects of the discourse. The pupil's primary task is to respond to teacher's solicitations. Occasionally, pupils react to preceding statements, but these reactions are rarely evaluative. Pupils do not overtly react evaluatively to teachers' statements, and they evaluate other pupils' responses only when the teacher asks them to do so. There are deviations from this pattern, but they are infrequent.

2. By far the largest proportion of the discourses involved empirical meanings. This includes fact stating and explaining, which accounted for between 50 and 60 per cent of the total discourse in most of the classrooms studied. . . .

3. The core of the teaching sequence is a teacher's question, a pupil's response, and a teacher's reaction to that response. . . . In fact, the significance of this sequence of pedagogical moves was probably recognized 40 or 50 years ago in teacher training, when a substantial part of the technical education of teachers was concerned with the skill and art of asking questions. . . .[12]

Another Verbal Analysis System

Smith and others also emphasize verbal interchanges between teachers and pupils in their categories for analyzing classroom verbal behavior. Their system of categories includes thirteen major ways of analyzing verbal interactions.

[10] Summary based on Arno Bellack, "The Language of the Classroom: Meanings Communicated in High School Teaching," in James B. MacDonald and Robert R. Leeper (eds.), *Theories of Instruction* (Washington: Association for Supervision and Curriculum Development, 1967), p. 104.

[11] Arno A. Bellack *et al.*, "The Language of the Classroom," in Michael D. Usdan and Frederick Bertolaet, *Development of School–University Programs for the Pre-service Education of Teachers for the Disadvantaged Through Teacher Education Centers,* Cooperative Research Project No. F–068 (Evanston, Ill.: Northwestern University, 1965), p. 199.

[12] Bellack *et al., op. cit.,* pp. 203–5.

1. *Defining*	To provide the meaning of terms
2. *Describing*	To represent something by word or drawing, to tell about something
3. *Designating*	To identify something by name—word or other symbol . . .
4. *Stating*	To state formulas, issues, rules, ideas, etc.
5. *Reporting*	To report on what a book or document says
6. *Substituting*	To perform a symbolic operation, usually of a mathematical nature
7. *Evaluating*	To estimate the worth, justice, dependability, etc., of something
8. *Opining*	To express a conclusion based on *inference* from several sources of evidence rather than to report a single fact
9. *Classifying*	To make explicit reference to an instance or class of things or both (Words like type, class, group)
10. *Comparing and Contrasting*	To compare two or more things—actions, factors, objects, processes (Words like difference, compare, correspond, same)
11. *Conditional Inferring*	To give an *antecedent*, that is, the conditional part of a statement. *Example: When it rains,* the streets are wet. ("If" statements)
12. *Explaining*	To give a reason to account for a fact, judgment, action (How? and Why? questions)
12.1 *Mechanical*	To describe the way the parts of a structure fit or work together
12.2 *Causal*	To give events to be accounted for and ask that information be cited to explain them
12.3 *Sequential*	To cite a sequence of events to account for a happening
12.4 *Procedural*	To describe the steps of operations by which a given result or end is attained
12.5 *Teleological*	To *justify* or account for an action, decision, or state
12.6 *Normative*	To mention or assume something that must be justified or citing a definition or characteristic of both
13. *Directing and Managing Classroom*	Activity with little or no logical significance to keep classroom activities moving (assignments, examinations) [13]

Taba's analysis of verbal behavior stresses the questions teachers ask. She states that "the role of questions becomes crucial; the way of asking questions is by far the most influential teaching act. A focus set by the teacher's questions circumscribes the mental operations which students can perform, determines the points which they can explore, and which

[13] B. Othanel Smith and Milton O. Meux *et al.*, "A Study of the Logic of Teaching," in Usdan and Bertolaet, *op. cit.*, pp. 196–97.

modes of thought they learn." [14] An analysis of verbal and other classroom interactions is a helpful means of understanding what learnings are taking place.

NON-VERBAL COMMUNICATIONS PATTERNS

A non-spoken communications system as well as a verbal system exists in a school. The non-spoken communication may support what is said verbally, or it may negate a verbal statement. The teacher who is totally dependent upon words eliminates much meaningful communication, and the teacher who is not conscious of the *varied ways* in which he communicates may be surprised at what he is communicating, both during times of verbal and non-verbal communication.

Much of what children learn is through non-verbal communications. A silence, a shrug of the shoulder, a scornful look, an open hands expression—these and other means—encourage, discourage, insult, and communicate a variety of other feelings and reactions to children. Children from different sub-cultural groups may learn and communicate their understandings differently from others. A teacher may, for example, expect children from a particular cultural group to volunteer their understandings of an assignment, whereas they may consider it undesirable to "show off" knowledge, or to "show up" those who do not know an answer to a teacher's question. Curriculum planning in this type of setting might include relatively non-verbal pupil responses and communications patterns.

People communicate with their whole bodies. The teacher who insists upon a child's use of complete sentences or "good" English at all times may limit communications; many children may not have mastered detailed, verbalized abstractions for experiences. If the teacher insists on a formal communications pattern, he may make it difficult for children to communicate. A teacher therefore may wisely attempt to teach acceptable standards of communication, including the "correct" words, sentence structure, spelling, pronunciation, and distance appropriate for persons to stand or sit from one another when conversing. However, he may also help children to accept the fact that there are different communications patterns, for formal situations (for example, a rare formal speech), informal patterns (for use among friends and in a relaxed situation), and slang at times. *The context determines the message and the real meaning,* through the tone used, the person speaking, the person spoken to, and so forth, almost indefinitely. Most words have many meanings, determined by both the person communicating and the person receiving the communication.

[14] Hilda Taba *et al.*, in LaGrone, *op. cit.*, p. 23.

ASSESSMENT OF CLASSROOM CLIMATE

That the teacher is the single most important person (and factor) in determining the type of climate prevailing in a classroom is the finding of Withall's research. Further, he holds that a sampling of the teacher's verbal behavior is a representative sample of total behavior. Withall's system includes an index of climate based upon a ratio of learner-centered to teacher-centered statements. The following listing of statements is in a descending order from the most supporting to the least supportive:

1. *Learner-supportive statements* express agreement with ideas, actions or opinions of the learner, or commend and reassure him. The dominant intent of these statements or questions is to praise, encourage, or bolster the learner. Statements of this kind frequently take the form of a single word response such as, "Right," "Yes," or "Good."
2. *Acceptance or clarifying statements* show considerable understanding by the teacher or restate clearly and succinctly in the teacher's words the ideational or emotional content of the learner's statements. The dominant intent of these statements is to help the learner gain insight. Statements of this kind are rather infrequent; but the following is an example, "In other words you think that if we decide to go back again we should plan to spend the entire day."
3. *Problem-structuring statements* offer facts, ideas, or opinions to the learner about phenomena or procedures in a non-threatening, objective manner. The dominant intent of these statements is to sustain the learner by facilitating his problem-solving activities. A good example of this kind of statement is the following, "What is special about twins? Two brothers are born on the same day one year apart, are they twins?"
4. *Neutral statements* evidence no supportive intent, being neither teacher-centered, learner-centered, nor problem-centered. The dominant intent of these statements is to facilitate the administrative and procedural detail of class management. Examples of neutral statements are the following, "Children, there will be no movie today, since our school projector is broken." "Who is going to march in the St. Patrick's Day parade tomorrow?"
5. *Directive statements* advise the learner regarding a course of action and offer him no choice or severely limit his choices. The dominant intent of these responses is to have the learner take up the teacher's viewpoint and pursue a particular course of action. An example of a directive statement is the following, "If there are any words which you do not know, put them down in your notebooks; and we will go over them tomorrow."
6. *Reproving, disapproving, or disparaging statements* express complete or partial disapproval of the ideas, behavior, or personal characteristics of the learner. The dominant intent of these statements is to admonish the learner for unacceptable behavior; to instruct the learner in societal values as interpreted by the teacher; or to impress upon the learner that he has failed to reach certain standards of excellence. A good example of mild reproof is the following, "Children, you think you are whispering; but you are not." Stronger reproof is found in the statement, "You knew that yesterday, but now you've forgotten it completely."

7. *Teacher-supportive statements* are those in which the teacher refers to herself, expressing a defensive attitude, or refers to her present or past interests, activities, or possessions in order to reassure herself and confirm her position. The dominant intent of these teacher responses is to assert, defend, or justify the teacher. An example of this type of statement is the following, "You must say 'Excuse me' when you interrupt me; I say 'Excuse me' when I interrupt you. Now we will go on without any interruptions." [15]

The classroom climate is a major determinant of how pupils feel about themselves and their work. It is worthy of study as the setting for curriculum.

LEADERSHIP IN SOCIAL SYSTEMS

Thus far we have stressed the central importance of the teacher to learning. The way he acts, speaks, and questions is the main factor in determing the emotional, social, and intellectual climate of the classroom. It is now time to discuss briefly the role of the teacher as part of an overall classroom social system and the manner in which teacher and pupils exercise leadership.

A Democratic Setting for Curriculum

Several studies suggest that when leaders are accepted and trusted more change in behavior can be developed than if hostility and mistrust prevail. Thus it would appear that while the teacher legally has *power over* pupils he is more effective if he exercises his *influence with* pupils. Rogers claims that "acceptant-democratic" leaders are most "growth facilitating" in several ways: (a) "accelerated intellectual development," (b) "more originality," (c) "more emotional security and control," (d) "less excitability." The person who influences leadership in a democratic fashion appears to be warmly emotional, respectful of others' individuality, and characterized by non-possessive caring. Their attitudes and feelings rather than their theoretical viewpoints and precise techniques seem to be significant in determining the degree of acceptance of the influence (leadership) exerted with another person. Some of these conclusions are based on studies outside of teaching, but there appears to be some consistency in conclusions about human relations and leadership regardless of the setting.[16]

Democratic leadership does, or helps others do, some of the following:

[15] John G. Withall, "The Development of a Technique for the Measurement of Social-Emotional Climate in Classrooms," *Journal of Experimental Education,* XVII, No. 3 (March, 1949), p. 347.

[16] Carl R. Rogers, "The Characteristics of a Helping Relationship," *Personnel and Guidance Journal,* XXXVII, No. 1 (September, 1958), pp. 6–16.

> . . . identifies, clarifies, strengthens, supports, suggests new alternatives and arrangements, provides new structure or means of operation, creates new understandings, motivates, provides new perspective and conceptualization.

Certain conditions contribute to democratic leadership:

> . . . goal centered, value oriented, communicative, catalytic, energizing, initiatory, and/or creative.

Leadership may be defined as:

> . . . that action or behavior among individuals and groups, which causes both the individual and the groups to move toward educational goals which are increasingly mutually acceptable to them.[17]

The teacher interested in attaining certain results with children is not interested so much in his *rights* as he is in exercising leadership which is productive. He is also interested in helping pupils to develop concepts and skills needed for leadership and group membership not only through intellectual (classroom) studies about democratic practices but also through living in a democratic classroom society.

A Sociological Analysis of the Classroom

The teacher who exercises, and helps pupils to exercise, democratic leadership needs to understand the nature of the group as well as the nature of leadership. Elkin has stated this imperative in the following way, from the perspective of the child; presumably the statement applies to the teacher as well:

> He must know what to expect from people of given statuses, how he himself fits in with the various groupings, what is considered proper and improper in given situations, and the range of acceptable behavior in those segments of social life which are rapidly changing. This is the world which the socializers, knowingly or unknowingly, pass on to the newcomer.[18]

You are not expected to be a sociologist in examining your classroom and the school in which it functions. However, you may wish to examine the sociological questions which follow, to determine their influence upon your relationships with pupils, parents, and other professionals; upon the content you teach; and upon the methods and materials which are available and acceptable in the social system in which you function. As a representative of a state and local educational system you are the *societal representative* in relation to education for a specific group of children. From your understanding of the school in relation to society you can more intel-

[17] Association for Supervision and Curriculum Development, *Leadership for Improving Instruction* (Washington: The Association, 1960), p. 27.

[18] Frederick Elkin, *The Child and Society* (New York: Random House, Inc., 1960), p. 10.

ligently develop an educational program which fits into the total social experiences of children.

Dahlke suggests a number of questions which could be helpful in analyzing the social structure of a school. A summary of his questions appears in the following:

1. To what extent do school norms (or acceptable standards of behavior) match or differ from the general cultural norms? Do the norms change as children grow older?
2. What rewards and punishments are established to enforce norms? Do children have a role in evaluating and revising the norms?
3. Do school activities seem to be interrelated with school norms?
4. What are the bases for teacher and pupil prestige within the school? To what extent does the prestige system support school norms?
5. How are school relations and behavior rated? Who does the rating?
6. How are school relations affected by community groups which influence the school?
7. How significant is sex and age status, as well as class status, in school social relationships?
8. What factors contribute flexibility or rigidity in school procedures?
9. What general American values are upheld by major national groups, and what influences do they have in the school?

The norms of a school may vary greatly from norms of schools with which you are familiar. There are standards which are generally accepted by Americans as a nation, while there are many variations in interpretations and applications of the norms within different segments of a community, and within the school. Knowing the norms and their relationships to the curriculum, you can make adjustments where possible to capitalize upon the norms or at least to anticipate probable pupil and community reactions.[19]

The school social system functions within a larger social system, composed of many special interest groups, national and religious groups, and socioeconomic classes. The American school tends to reflect middle class, western European, Caucasian, and Protestant values. If the school is to communicate with and serve all children effectively, it will probably have to become classless and more cosmopolitan. Teachers, either from the middle class or motivated by middle class aspirations, may be largely unconscious of the effects of their orientations. In fact, they will sometimes express shock that anyone could suggest that their values are not *the*

[19] H. Otto Dahlke, *Values in Culture and Classroom* (New York: Harper & Row, 1958). See pp. 11–12 for a more precise and extended discussion of the above points. See also pp. 313–14 for Dahlke's excellent contrasts of lower and middle class values.

values of all Americans. While the school may select the middle class value systems as the standard, you will want to accept the child—regardless of his background—as an individual to the point that you may attempt to change his values without minimizing his sense of his value.

You should take into account varied pupil experiences with different kinds of social systems when making instructional plans. Their background will in large measure determine the kinds of classroom experiences and materials which will be meaningful, the types of motivations which will produce results, and the manner in which parents can be included as resources. "Lower" and "middle" class is a description rather than a value judgment and such labels of class-related behaviors are sometimes overly generalized. It is important to see that these are extremes and that individual families may be placed somewhere on a continuum of socioeconomic class differences. Understanding these generalizations can help you understand *why* children may be behaving the way they do. You may also increase your willingness to accept behavioral variations within individual children while attempting to change their behavioral patterns accepted by school personnel.

As previously noted, the teacher's instructional program is affected vitally by the social system which establishes and maintains schools. The raw materials of instruction are to a large extent molded by the society and they include the teacher as an individual and as a professional, pupils as individuals with expectations and motivations, parents as a prodding and restrictive influence, and the community as a system which determines what, to whom, when, and where instruction shall take place and under what conditions.

The teacher in addition works in two sub-societies: (a) the school building and school system, (b) the profession at large. You will lead and be led within these systems. They will affect the *what* and *how* you will teach. Where they are effective in exercising community leadership, these social systems may be crucial in determining curriculum materials. Professional groups have been increasingly significant in state and national educational programs.

Local vs. Cosmopolitan Orientations

Of the many other ways of characterizing persons interacting with others, there is one model which attempts to delineate them according to their orientation to the community. The "cosmopolitan" is interested mainly in the world outside the local community, and the "local" is interested primarily in the community. An individual in small or large, urban or rural communities may be either local or cosmopolitan. The terms used

Structure of Social Relationships

The Building-oriented Teacher	*The Profession-oriented Teacher*
Is loyal to the building staff and the local school district.	Is loyal to the education profession and perhaps to a particular sub-professional group, e.g., National Council of Teachers of English.
Is interested in teaching in the local school district or at least in home state.	Is ready to move elsewhere if professional advancement appears possible; at least he considers the possibility that a move *could* be desirable.
Is influenced more readily by those around him, including those in the community.	Is influenced by those with comparable professional education and experience.
Is tradition-oriented, especially to the dominant tradition of local building and district.	Is future-oriented, especially toward goals of professional groups, for example, The Department of Classroom Teachers.
Has spent most of his life in his present area.	Is a relative newcomer to the school district.
Is of any age group.	Is of any age group.
Is concerned with maintaining contacts with his own building and district associates.	Is concerned with selective associations, primarily with those interested in his particular professional interests.
Is relatively unconcerned with heavy teaching assignments and low salaries.	Is critical of heavy loads and low salaries.
Seeks recognition within his own local groups.	Seeks recognition in regional, state, and national groups.
Believes in adhering closely to rules.	Views rules in a flexible manner, believing that they can be compromised when they interfere with professional goals.
Resents criticisms of local efforts by national groups.	Accepts criticisms of local efforts by national professional groups.
Is unlikely to become a profession-oriented teacher.	Is more likely to become a building-oriented teacher than becoming a profession-oriented person.

Avenues of Interpersonal Influence

Depends upon a network of personal interactions to make the building effective.	Depends upon his professional skills and knowledge to improve the effectiveness of the school program.
Has difficulty in establishing a professional image over his image as a local citizen.	Arrives on the scene with his professional image established elsewhere.
Is less vulnerable to criticism within the school.	Is more vulnerable to criticism within the school.

Social Status in Action: Interpersonal Influence

Is sought out by others for his sympathetic understanding and personal interest.	Is sought out by others for his specialized knowledge and skills.
Is more interested in giving personal advice.	Is more interested in giving advice related to academic progress.

The Building-oriented Teacher	*The Profession-oriented Teacher*
Extends his influence through both personal and professional channels.	Extends his influence primarily through his professional activities.
Tends to be conservative in the sense that he upholds the dominant views of the local schools.	Tends to be more liberal in the sense that his values are derived from the profession on the national scene.
Tends to dominate the school which is "second rate."	Tends to have great influence in the school which is "first rate" (in relation to standards of accrediting agencies and professional groups).
Is more secure in facing criticism from the local school.	Is less secure in facing criticism from the local school.

in the following discussion are related to states of mind rather than place of residence.[20]

The local is concerned with how he is regarded locally, while the cosmopolitan is interested in making his mark within his professional group. Jewett translated his original interpretations, which applied to citizens in general, to the university community. In the following discussion, Jewett's model of local versus cosmopolitan will be freely adapted to an elementary school staff. Jewett's category of local-influential, institution-oriented professor will be translated into an elementary-school-centered or building-oriented teacher, and his cosmopolitan-influential, discipline-oriented professor will become—for our purposes—the professional elementary teacher who sees his role interpretation as one derived from the total profession rather than from the teachers assigned to one building.

The distinction is an important one, for the teacher particularly is under pressure to demonstrate loyalty to the teachers around him by making their goals his goals, by absorbing their dislikes, and sometimes by parroting their clichés. These statements apply to the teacher whose main aspiration is to be accepted by those whose professional world largely ends at the school doors (often at their own room doors). The cosmopolitan teacher, in contrast, may be more likely to avoid any sign of *disloyalty* to the building faculty in personal and social relations but at the same time will identify with the total profession. The cosmopolitan teacher *may* be more inclined than is the local toward deriving instructional goals from many sources, including local persons (professional staff, parents, and other citizens), state and local professional organizations, and researchers. *The cosmopolitan, concerned with the larger society, may be better equipped intellectually to adapt curriculum to present and anticipated changes.* These are conjectures. In analyzing yourself in relation to these

[20] Robert E. Jewett, "An Educational Theory Model: Theory of Local and Cosmopolitan Influentials," in Maccia, *et al., op. cit.*, pp. 282–97. Originally his theory was published as Occasional Paper 63–140, Bureau of Educational Research, Ohio State University, 1963.

two alternatives, seek possible implications for instruction. It appears that the profession-oriented teacher would be more likely to adopt a relevant curriculum based on his wider perspective.

The School Structure's Demands

A school is a social structure with rather specific demands upon persons who work and study there. George S. Maccia uses certain basic words which clarify the various dimensions of school operations.[21] The structure demands what curriculum can be implemented, and with what means. Demands upon schools vary, but for the elementary school the main pressure is to develop children's personalities.

1. *Regulations* are transmitted to the local buildings of a school system through faculty meetings, bulletins, reports, newsletters, courses of study, and other forms of written communication. The building staff in turn makes demands and exerts pressures upon the central administrative staff. The central staff may be arbitrary in curriculum matters; curriculum guides may specifically *demand* that certain content be taught in certain grades at a given time of the year. Curriculum experts are inclined to believe that persons affected by decisions should help to make them. Even in large school systems representatives may be involved with central office subject-area consultants in determining content, selecting instructional materials, and developing teaching methods.

2. *Adaptations* are adjustments to the local setting by the school faculty. The neighborhood in part determines the attitudes of pupils toward school and learning. Local conditions may determine the extent of energy levels available for school tasks; for example, malnutrition, poor sleep, and poor health conditions may severely limit energy applied to learning. Cramped home conditions may limit the amount of homework which a teacher may expect. The backgrounds of students will affect the manner in which they study. Each school develops a "personality" as staff, parents, students, and other neighborhood personalities interact. Instruction is adapted, and the type of learning which occurs is different for different schools within a school system. There should be a recognition of the uniqueness with which each teacher teaches and each learner learns.

3. *Stability* refers to the degree of turnover in staff in a school. If too many teachers enter a school year after year, it is difficult to establish harmonious teaching relationships, educational goals, and relationships with parents and children, and otherwise operate as a functioning organization. Instability of school staffs often reflects the condition of the neighborhood, for teachers in unstable neighborhoods seek transfers more often

[21] George S. Maccia, in Maccia *et al., op. cit.*, pp. 139–86.

than do teachers in stable ones. Teaching in the traditional sense is more difficult in unstable areas, and it may break down to the point where the teacher spends as much time maintaining order as in teaching. Currently efforts are being made to educate teachers to work in such communities. Some school districts are providing financial incentives and promotional advantages for those who will dedicate themselves to teaching in unstable areas and also are saturating these areas with special personnel, limiting class sizes, and making other adjustments. Recent guides to educational literature point to the tremendous growth of thinking concerning unstable neighborhoods. These communities are usually slum areas, although instability may occur in other settings, as for example, near large military establishments.

4. *Compatibility* means that the school's products are harmonious with the community's expectations. Compatibility also relates to a school building's output in relation to the expectations of the school system. The school which adapts to local conditions but still functions within the guidelines of the system is attempting to be compatible with both.

The Elementary School's Products

Both industrial and agricultural explanations ("models") of organizational endeavors have been modified to analyze educational functions. A model based upon agriculture has been modified by Jewett to describe a school setting. A school society organized into "self-contained classrooms" is described by Jewett. This type of organizational pattern is common in the United States, although it is under attack by critics. They advocate differentiated staffing to permit utilization of varied competencies of teachers and claim that no one teacher can meet all of the needs of a group of children. Jewett's model of a self-contained classroom when applied to other organizational patterns (see Chapter 5) can help you to understand the teacher as "producer" and teaching outcomes as his "product."

1. The teacher is a generalist. He does not center his efforts in producing within his pupils understanding and skills, within a particular discipline to the exclusion of attention to other disciplines. His background, his competencies, and his commitment is such as to direct him to a consideration of the whole child. He is attempting to produce a general education for the pupil, not a specialized or vocational education.

2. The purposes of education are determined by the teacher. Since the teacher is promoting general education rather than specialized education, the demands of the job market do not determine educational purpose. The teacher determines the goals of general education, of course, within the limits set by the norms of the society.

a. The quantity of learning desired is determined by the teacher.

b. The type and quality of learning to be achieved is determined by the teacher.

3. The elementary school does not produce within the pupil specialized knowledge and skills which can be utilized on the labor market

4. The nature of the nurture given the pupils is determined by the teacher.

5. The selection of types of content and the quantities of content afforded the pupils is determined by the teacher.

6. The knowledge and skills acquired by the pupils justifies the existence of the elementary school. The personal-social development of the pupil through general education, not the acquisition of marketable skills through specialized education, places the elementary school in a unique and essential role in society.

7. The productivity of the pupil is dependent on the teacher's skill and the nature of the individual pupil.

8. Combining (6) and (7) above we arrive at a type of symbiotic relationship between the pupil and the elementary school. The self-development of the pupil justifies the existence of the elementary school. The pupils are dependent on the school for this development.

9. The teacher knows and evaluates each pupil on the basis of a wide range of the pupil's characteristics. The teacher knows the habits, the behavior, and the intellectual capacity of each pupil. He evaluates each pupil on the basis of the total behavior of the pupil, not solely in terms of intellectual capacity.

10. The teacher has little incentive to gain command of content in excess of the needs of his pupils.

11. The teacher has little incentive to teach skills and knowledge appropriate for vocation. He is not preparing pupils directly for the job market. He is not in the business of developing salable skills. All of the understandings which he develops in his pupils are used by the pupils in becoming a person.

12. The teacher has neither the incentive nor the facilities to carry on the scholarly research necessary to produce new content for his pupils. He must rely on the university and other centers of scholarly research whose purposes and facilities are geared for such activities.

13. The teacher provides his pupils with the type of content designed to further their general education. He does not select content for his pupils of the type that will promote vocational training. He does not "press" content upon them to promote intellectual development at the expense of emotional and physical development.

14. The teacher accepts and attempts to bring about the maximum general development of all pupils. He does not reject the slow learner. He is oriented to citizenship education and self-development for his pupils, not specialized education for vocational ends. Therefore, he is interested in the general education of all pupils.

15. The type of content which the teacher acquires is that which has meaning for his pupils within the context of general education.

16. The teacher values his teaching career as a way of life. He views teaching as a profession.

17. The teacher tends to have a few common interests with the university professor who is engaged in educating students for a vocation or a profession. He tends to believe that the professor is not sufficiently sensitive to the overall development of students, and that the professor is too concerned with specialized education.

18. Other teachers in the elementary school, in judging the worth of the teacher, place emphasis on the quality of the teacher's care of his pupils.

19. The teacher has a community of interests with other elementary teachers. He finds it easy to communicate with them.[22]

ANALYSES IN CURRICULUM STUDY

We have suggested that instruction does not function within a vacuum, that instructional goals cannot be selected arbitrarily by the teacher. What you do is a result of: (a) what you are, personally, socially, and professionally; (b) what the school expects to occur in the classroom, in reaction to what the larger culture expects; (c) what each child brings to the classroom in the way of personal expectations, and communication, behavioral, and socioeconomic patterns. An ability to analyze the complex processes occurring in the classroom can help you to select, organize, and carry out meaningful instruction, and an understanding of them may increase your confidence, competence, and productivity.

A careful analysis of teaching, particularly when you and your peers discipline yourself to use numerical analyses scales, may increase your awareness of the behaviors needed to promote the type of learning you seek. Until the dynamics of classroom behaviors are understood, it appears unlikely that you can plan instructional activities effectively. When you have increased your awareness of what happens when teachers and children work together in a classroom, *in a large measure you understand curriculum.* The actual mastery of content—which is the goal of much teaching—and the techniques used to teach specific content are means to an end, that of contributing to effective teacher and pupil behaviors. Indeed, educational objectives should be stated in terms of what you expect to happen as a result of classroom activities and interaction, in so far as this is possible.

It is important to avoid attaching undue significance to analyses derived from models and lists such as you find in this chapter. They are, after all, experimental indices of teaching and learning. Only sophisticated researchers and specialists should use the tools for in-depth analysis. Teaching and learning are a series of complex and interacting phenomena. Analytical tools are inadequate to *prove* what goes on in a school, but they can broaden perspectives and extend understandings of curriculum.

[22] Jewett, in Maccia *et al., op. cit.,* p. 171, pp. 179–81.

PROJECTS AND READINGS

1. It is profitable to increase your awareness of the many kinds of interactions between teachers and pupils. Using the materials in this chapter, you may develop a rough estimation of the kinds of interactions which *predominate* in a classroom which you are able to observe. You can keep count of the number of times the teacher or pupil acts in a certain way described in one of the sub-categories of any of the analytical systems included in this chapter. (Some of you may desire to secure a manual which describes *in detail* how to record observations in a systematic manner.) All of the systems of analysis reported in this chapter have been extensively described in many publications.

2. You may discover that non-verbal communications patterns are more prevalent than most persons realize and might find it informative to observe and tabulate the kinds of non-verbal communications that might occur in different situations. You may find it stimulating to attempt to carry on a "conversation" without words—somewhat in the manner of "charades." As a further exploration you could attempt to use a variety of non-verbal communications patterns to depict the kinds of reactions which pupils and teachers exhibit during a lesson.

3. In a textbook on educational sociology you can find comparisons of socioeconomic classes. It is informative to rate acceptability or non-acceptability of the traits for a socioeconomic class other than your own and to contrast your ratings with those of others in a college class or teacher's group. You may further refine the approach by breaking down the system to include ratings such as "highly objectionable," "objectionable," "acceptable," "highly acceptable." How do you think that teachers should react to pupil behavior that is highly objectionable to teachers but acceptable to parents and friends of the children?

4. The number of books emerging from publishing houses and professional associations is almost limitless. It is good to regularly develop a habit of seeking out publications by a number of associations, including the Association for Supervision and Curriculum Development, Association for Childhood Education International, National Society for the Study of Education, American Educational Research Association, and subject-matter associations such as the National Council of Teachers of English.

5. A number of educational journals are good sources of continuous renewal of educational understandings. These include *Educational Leadership* (Association for Supervision and Curriculum Development), *Childhood Education* (Association for Childhood Education International), *Elementary Principal* (National Association of Elementary School Principals), *American Education* (U. S. Office of Education), *Today's Education* (National Education Association), journals of the various subject-matter professional groups (*Elementary English, Reading Teacher,* etc.).

6. Novels, biographies, and autobiographies are good sources of insights on children, even if they do not have school settings. There are a number of books of this nature which do have teacher and pupil as main characters. They tend to have secondary or private school settings, but are nevertheless good reading that will prove beneficial in adding meaning to your study of learning and teaching.

7. Other artistic expressions often offer insights on human behavior. The artist, musician, sculptor, and architect have perspectives which can increase your sensitivity to the human factors in teaching.

8. Descriptions of 54 outstanding teachers selected by *Look* Magazine and the Council of Chief State School Officers are given in warm and appealing terms in William Jeremiah Burke's *Not for Glory: Who Are Today's Great Teachers?* (New York: Cowles Education Corp., 1967). Written by the man who travelled to the teachers' hometowns, this book is desirable reading to keep perspective on the basic humanness of teachers—their philosophies of education, teaching methods, community influences, and personal and family activities. (For several years, a spring issue of *Look* has included a pictorial feature on the "Teacher of the Year.")

3

The Structure of Knowledge

FROM MEMORIZATION TO MEANING

The school has assumed many roles over the years and has parted with few. To impart knowledge has survived as a basic concern and it has been the almost exclusive domain of the school, since many other school roles have been shared with other institutions and agencies. Expertness in selecting and teaching appropriate knowledge to the young is a crucial distinction between the professional teacher and the layman.

In the past, knowledge was equated with memorization of unrelated facts presented by the teacher and reported back to him in an uncritical, partially digested manner. Teaching was telling. Elementary arithmetic, for instance, was taught as a series of discrete computational skills and no effort was made to relate addition and multiplication. Other aspects of arithmetic were taught in a similar manner through memorization of formulas and endless drill. The structure of mathematics was left as a mystery. The task in arithmetic—each and every day—tended to be rote drill without meaning.

Traditional teaching stressed assignment, recitation and drill, and taking tests on materials selected and presented by the teacher. The pupil was supposed to recite passively, do drill assignments, and take tests; regurgitation of teacher-selected knowledge—however meaningless and unstructured—was the test of a "successful" pupil. The teacher presumably knew the structure; the child was to do as he was told to do. If he questioned *why* something was so, he often was considered impertinent.

Today, discussions of knowledge, especially its structure, are stated in terms of the interaction between the learner and the *organized ways* of searching for truth and understanding as presented in the several subject matter disciplines. The emphasis is upon the learner's assuming the *role* —the way of thinking and seeking—of mathematician, scientist, historian, or artist within the bounds of his own experience, insights, and knowledge. The teacher is seen as a person skilled in helping the learner find structure and applying it. Later chapters suggest ways of combining content, materials, and method to encourage mastery of structure of the subject areas.

Structure of Knowledge

In current proposals for elementary and secondary school curriculum reform, there is much emphasis upon structure of knowledge, not only in subjects such as mathematics and science but in the social sciences and arts as well. In order to put these curriculum proposals to use, you will need to experience self-discovery of the structure of knowledge—to find relationships, to discover implications and applications. You then can apply your understandings of the structure intellectually and in other ways. You continually can revise your understanding of structure, for meaningful knowledge opens the door to new knowledge. Knowledge is always tentative, always stimulating additional growth.

Throughout this book, there is encouragement for you to seek out additional ideas and information which can help you to organize in your own mind the structure of curriculum and those related experiences and subject areas which are useful in a vital curriculum. When you the teacher have an understanding of the structure of curriculum and its component subjects and activities, you should be able to help children find their own understandings of the relatedness of knowledge.

While the academic disciplines over the years will be modified by new knowledge, the learner who has mastered the unifying *regularities of knowledge* and the methods of learning through various intellectual disciplines can replenish and revise his knowledge during his total lifetime. Having learned the structure of the various disciplinary contributors to man's knowledge, the learner should not allow himself to become obsolete. The *process* of mastering the structure of knowledge is self-renewing and continuously self-validating. The *product,* factual knowledge included, is significant only as long as it is valid and as it contributes to learner conceptualization.

You should have a conceptual framework for understanding the structures of knowledge—integrated, related, and drawn from various disciplines—from which the objectives, content, and methodology of the school in large measure are derived. This will enable you to select from the present curriculum as well as from among the many proposals for curriculum reform those which are consistent with your own educational objectives, those of the school system, and those of pupils and of the community.

You should learn a great deal about the content areas in which you plan to teach and should also be a professional teacher knowledgeable in the teaching and learning process. In this sense you should be able to mediate between the needs and expectations of children and community and the academic disciplines. The difficulty of becoming competent in both subject matter and teaching–learning processes is compounded by the fact that elementary teachers commonly teach many subject areas. This problem has been one of the factors in the demands that the elementary school staff be organized along some type of subject matter plan, for example, team teaching. This matter is discussed in more detail in Chapter 5.

While there are advantages and disadvantages (based on the concept of the structure of knowledge) of curriculum proposals of recent years, it does seem feasible to carefully consider these proposals, which are based on studies of the structures of knowledge and organized into various disciplines. You will find many conflicting opinions concerning this common emphasis on structure of knowledge. You may find yourself in a teaching situation where the local school has adopted an entire curriculum "package"—coordinated content, materials, equipment, methods—developed by national organizations, subject matter specialists, or private industry. Some of the issues related to new subject matter curriculum patterns are discussed further in Chapter 9. This chapter primarily is a study of the emphases upon the structures of knowledge rather than their direct applications in the elementary curriculum, and is an introductory rather than an inclusive chapter. It can become more meaningful when supplemented by your study of articles, books, and proposals for curriculum reform as well as samples of curriculum materials.

STRENGTHS AND WEAKNESSES OF EMPHASES

Bruner is a pioneer among those who stress curriculum implications of the structure of knowledge. His basic claim is that "Grasping the structure of a subject is understanding it in a way that permits many other things to be related to it meaningfully. To learn structure, in short, is to learn how things are related." The learner, it is assumed, having learned the essential relationships of a given content area can discover much more about a given type of knowledge. He does not learn isolated bits of knowledge and later attempt to put them together into meaningful relationships. Learning the structure of knowledge enables him to place it into a larger picture, as well as enlarge his understanding. Learners retain more for longer periods of time when relationships, significance, and meaning have become evident to them. Seeing connections and applying them to subsequent learnings is not accidental. Transfer from one situation to another is neither accidental nor incidental—it must be actively and consciously sought. The teacher should be a specialist in bringing about transfer, both in the immediate classroom situation and in subsequent comparable or related occurrences wherever and whenever the occasions arise.

Bruner makes several claims for his position on the structure of knowledge. In contrast to unstructured knowledge, restructured knowledge provides several benefits:

1. The structure of knowledge, containing fundamental ideas, is more comprehensible.
2. Details in a pattern—the structure—are most easily remembered than those not in a structure.
3. Details in a pattern are more easily transferred into comparable situations.
4. Articulation—the unfolding of learning from one situation to another—is improved through continued analyses of knowledge.[1]

The emphases on the structure of knowledge have not received universal acceptance. Some criticisms have grown from a concern that subject matter specialists who know the structure of their specializations often are not adequately well grounded in understanding children and the teaching process. Goodlad notes: (a) the *isolation* of in-depth studies conducted in a particular discipline, for example, geography, from studies of other disciplines; (b) *lack of consideration of educational psychology* in such studies resulting from domination of subject matter specialists; (c) excessive concern of specialists for what *should* be taught children in *preparation for further development* in a particular content area while minimizing here-and-now learning problems such as motivation, retention of knowledge, and other factors of immediate or general applicability. In terms of the structure of the subjects, what specialists determine should be learned, ought to be related to the needs and objectives of a child as well as to those of the society.[2]

In *The Process of Education,* Bruner develops several questions or

[1] Jerome S. Bruner, *The Process of Education* (Cambridge, Mass.: Harvard University Press, 1960), pp. 23–26.

[2] John R. Goodlad, in William A. Jenkins (ed.), *Nature of Knowledge* (Milwaukee: Uhrig Foundation, 1962), pp. 86–87.

themes which summarize his major positions on the nature of knowledge.[3]

1. *How can pupils with limited experiences with knowledge experience a lifelong impact?* Give them an understanding of structure of the content being studied. The opposite approach is memorization of facts, as selected, organized, and presented *by the teacher.*

2. *When are children ready to learn certain knowledge?* The foundations of any subject can be taught in some manner to children regardless of age. As children experience knowledge of the basic kind, they develop capacities for more abstract or verbalized learnings. Bruner gives an example of fourth graders developing an understanding of the plight of mankind through a study of myths.

3. *What is the nature of intuition?* It is the technique of developing tentative yet reasonable hunches without taking organized steps to prove them. Intuition—growing out of concrete, early learning experiences—becomes a basic tool for relating new learnings by providing insights into how new things are related to previous learnings.

4. *What is the difference between learnings at different levels?* Bruner states the answer well: "The difference is in degree, not in kind. The school boy learning physics *is* a physicist, and it is easier for him to learn physics behaving like a physicist than doing something else." (This suggests a kind of learning environment in which children are learning ways to learning by utilizing the processes of the specialists to seek out relatedness—the structure of knowledge.[4]) Bruner claims that the emphasis on learning the structure of knowledge is as desirable for low achievers as for others.[5] Learning the structure of knowledge can be particularly helpful to slow learners who often experience knowledge in unrelated, discrete forms—experiences which are bewildering.

DETERMINANTS AND USES

To the extent that you understand the nature of knowledge and its structure, you will be more competent to select and arrange for teaching knowledge and learning experiences appropriate for children at a particular age. Distinct content and methodology are required for the different uses of knowledge—ways of knowing—selected for a school's curriculum. Four school uses of knowledge have been identified by Broudy, Smith, and Burnett.[6] These uses suggest how varied learnings become meaningfully related. The following summary is based largely on the dis-

[3] Bruner, *op. cit.,* pp. 11–13.
[4] Bruner, *op. cit.,* p. 13.
[5] Bruner, *op. cit.,* p. 9.
[6] Harry S. Broudy, B. Othanel Smith, and Joe R. Burnett, *Democracy and Excellence in American Secondary Education* (Chicago: Rand McNally & Co., Inc., 1964), pp. 45–55.

cussion by Broudy, Smith, and Burnett, but some additional points have been added.

1. *Associative* uses of schooling. Much learning is somewhat accidental according to Broudy and his colleagues. A new situation reminds a person of a previous one and sets off a chain reaction of related ideas, whether or not they are appropriate to the situation. It would be possible to attach unconsciously incorrect significance of new knowledge, however related. Responses on tests and in discussions may be associative in nature. On the other hand, association may be an aid to memory. Much of the feeling and mood evident in the fine arts is a consequence of associative learning. This kind of learning is enhanced by "resemblance, contiguity, and satisfaction." The problem in analyzing associative thinking is its "highly idiosyncratic and uncontrollable" nature. Content recommended for a particular teaching objective may suggest quite different meanings and relationships to individual pupils. It is not a substitute for logic.

2. *Replicative* uses of schooling. This use is quite different from the associative use. Practice makes perfect is a related cliché for overlearning which is based on previously learned skills and knowledge. Repetitions and meaningful drill are a major school strategy for teaching map reading, spelling, arithmetic, and comparable skills. Since there are few life situations in which elements are repeated identically, there is limited value in replicative learnings. Those learnings which are repeated regularly and functionally may be learned replicatively. There can be transfer from one situation to another under specific circumstances. In a dynamic, changing world, excessive use of replicative learnings could be a serious handicap to learners and society.

3. *Applicative* uses of schooling. This use involves the application of past and present cues to develop new learnings through "principle, generalization, or statement of fact." Broudy and his colleagues claim that applicative thinking is used primarily by scholars and scientists in creating new knowledge. It is important to lay an early foundation in understanding the applicative use of knowledge. It is also important to help those children likely to become specialists to develop thinking processes needed to develop new knowledge. Some citizens will become specialists; all as citizens need to understand the applicative processes and to provide intelligent support of specialists.

4. *Interpretive* uses of schooling. This kind of thinking is based on efforts to attach meaning to experience "as we categorize it, conceptualize it, or classify it." People do this through language, science, and works of art. They learn to perceive, feel, and understand life in meaningful relationships. Interpretive uses of schooling provide perspective on living,

yet they are not particularly useful in problem-solving and action situations. This kind of thinking provides form to the diverse perceptions and experiences of individuals. It is an organizer of thinking out of which other kinds of thought processes may develop. Understanding, the consequence of effective interpretive thinking, is the necessary antecedent to the other kinds of thinking. Interpretive thinking is realistic for children when they study their environment over which they have little control. The development of understanding—the interpretive use of knowledge—is called *general education.* It is presumed that all citizens need this kind of education, while relatively few attain the applicative knowledge used in the creative arts and sciences, from which new knowledge is generated.

LOGICAL STRUCTURE

Pupils as well as scholars use both inductive and deductive methods in studying and in deriving meaning from various facets of knowledge. Hickey and Newton make major efforts to differentiate between inductive and deductive thinking. It is important to know which kind of thinking is significant in learning of various kinds in order to guide content selection and strategies for teaching and to ascertain which kind of thinking can be most productive in terms of relating various learnings. Hickey and Newton carefully specify aspects of inductive thinking; the opposite of the following would characterize deductive thinking.[7] Inductive thinking has several characteristics:

1. It begins with the simplest concepts and incorporates increasingly complex ones which ultimately can be combined into principles.
2. It begins with the concrete and proceeds to the abstract. The authors illustrate with economics: (a) At the concrete level, it is possible to observe economics in operation in a store. (b) Ultimately economics can be generalized to high mathematical levels.
3. It begins with examples, from which concepts are derived by learners.

Depending upon the nature of content being taught, it is appropriate to proceed from the inductive to the deductive, or *vice versa.* Whichever the direction, there is need to carefully designate sequential steps which are in *logical* order. One of the findings of research into programmed learning materials is the importance of planning relatively small

[7] Albert E. Hickey and John M. Newton, *The Logical Basis for Teaching: The Effect of Sub-concept Sequence on Learning,* Final Report to U. S. Office of Naval Research, Personnel and Training Branch, Contract Nonr–4215(00) (Newburyport, Mass.: Entelek, Inc., January, 1964), pp. 3–4.

conceptual steps. If the steps from one sub-concept to another and to the next are sufficiently small, the learner is more likely to combine them into meaningful generalizations.

Still another process for studying relationships is that of analysis and synthesis. When simpler elements of understanding are combined to lead to broader concepts, this is called synthesis. A less complex process is called analysis, wherein a broad concept is broken into small components for study. In either process, pupils can be aided in mastering the structures of knowledge. A basic objective should be the encouragement of pupil discovery of relationships.

Another aid to self-discovery of structure involves study steps moving from the concrete to the abstract or the opposite. The sequence of study in either direction should lead to an understanding of relationships.

Learning relationships can be derived from deductive–inductive, analysis–synthesis, and concrete–abstract steps, or their reverse. It is important to have an orderly, logical progression of manageable learning from beginning to end. A related series of steps (for example, analysis to synthesis) should be pursued actively by the pupil until he comprehends the structure of the knowledge under study. It is then time to proceed to another series of related experiences with knowledge (concrete to abstract or inductive to deductive).

You should understand the structure of content in order to help pupils attain a similar comprehension on their level of maturity and ability. A sound understanding will enable you to aid each pupil in selecting significant concepts which help him to master structure, and the sequenced and orderly steps as well.

STRUCTURE AND FORM

The manner in which knowledge can be characterized provides still another aid in your efforts to conceptualize its nature. These ways may be selected on the basis of their appropriateness for specific content and learners. Provision for these varied ways of building understanding of relationships should be a continuing part of curriculum planning.

Bruner shows that any knowledge can be characterized three ways:

1. *Mode of representation.*
   a. *Enactive* representation—actions designed to achieve specifications and results. This refers to something which can be done or built; it is concrete experiencing. The appropriateness of this mode is related to age of learners, their style of learning, and kind of subject matter. It is learning through experiencing.

b. *Ikonic* representation—images which stand for a thing or a concept but which do not explain fully; it is the use of verbal or graphic symbols. It is imagery derived from experiencing. An example given by Bruner is the representation of English common law by the Magna Carta.
c. *Symbolic* representation—symbolic and logical propositions governed by well-defined laws which can be used to form and transform propositions. This is formal and abstract representation, for example, mathematical formulas and linguistics.

2. *Economy*—information which is processed to create comprehension. The number of steps prior to comprehension—economy—is a consequence of a number of items that must be dealt with. Some concepts are simple and easily comprehended; others are complex and must be developed through a series of sequential steps. Economy suggests movement from the simple to the complex wherein concepts become building blocks for generalizations.
3. *Effective power*—the capacity to generate new knowledge through the connection of apparently disconnected knowledge. Knowledge that has effective power is likely to be economical as well.

The manner in which knowledge can be presented is dependent upon the differences in learners (age and learning styles) and subject matter being studied. Bruner notes that while the three ways of representing knowledge are parallel they may be pursued independently. He claims that the sequence of learning followed by children provides "optimal orchestration" for learners of all ages: enactive representation to ikonic and finally to symbolic. After children have an adequate experience with symbolic representation derived from experiences with enactive and ikonic representation, they may be able to think primarily in the symbolic level.[8] The first two modes should not be neglected too quickly and never should be completely ignored.

As Parker and Rubin point out, it is sometimes difficult to delineate the various kinds of structures found in the subject areas and their appropriateness for varied ages.[9] A good teacher knows enough about content *and* children to provide both the proper sequence for, and the depth of, learnings which are appropriate for each child. Translating Bruner's ideas into a discussion of curriculum practice is a difficulty of considerable magnitude. His ideas seem to be a practical means to enhance your conceptualization of knowledge and they should increase your com-

[8] Jerome S. Bruner (ed.), *Learning About Learning: A Conference Report,* Cooperative Research Monograph No. 15, OE–12019 (Washington: Office of Education, 1966), pp. 201–3.

[9] J. Cecil Parker and Louis J. Rubin, *Process as Content: Curriculum Design and the Application of Knowledge* (Chicago: Rand McNally & Co., Inc., 1966), p. 16.

petence in selecting content to be taught and the manner in which it can be presented most effectively.

LOGICAL ASPECTS OF TEACHING

Pupils of all ages need to develop a vigor in their thinking as they explore the world of knowledge. Children at an early age can be helped to go far beyond their "because" explanations to a knowledge of structure and beyond verbal discussions without substance to clarity of expression. Logic is a key factor in establishing structure for various intellectual disciplines.

Learning precision in using sentences is valuable in the logical use of language. LaGrone notes the desirability of learning how to use several kinds of sentences as learning tools. A balanced curriculum should provide experiences with them as a means of increasing pupil precision in expressing ideas and integrating partial knowledge into structured knowledge.

1. "Value sentences"—sentences which include opinion and worth.
2. "Definition sentences"—sentences which define the meaning of a word, concept, or fact.
3. "Analytic sentences"—sentences which delineate the nature and relationships of parts of knowledge.
4. "Empirical sentences"—sentences which provide verifiable proof of statements of fact.
5. Other kinds of sentences—"In addition, there are sentences which state particulars, sentences which express generalizations, prescriptive sentences giving directions as to how something is to be done, and counterfactual sentences which state what might have been the effect had something occurred but which in fact did not occur."

LaGrone claims that "Intellectual rigor consists in the ability of the student to handle logical operations with marked precision and to think clearly and consistently." [10]

The capacity to analyze classroom verbal patterns is a valuable tool in developing thinking abilities. The use of logical discourse should enable children to establish purposeful relationships between their past and present learnings and to share their knowledge with others. Language that is precisely used can be an indispensable aid to a study of knowledge.

[10] Herbert LaGrone, *A Proposal for the Revision of the Pre-service Professional Component of a Program of Teacher Education* (Washington: AACTE, 1964), pp. 36–37. See also 1968 AACTE revision of the report entitled *Professional Teacher Education: A Programed Design Developed by the AACTE Teacher Education and Media Project.*

SUBJECT MATTER ILLUSTRATIONS

Thus far we have tried to show that knowledge organized into meaningful relations (structured) is more easily learned, retained, and applied. While there are strengths and weaknesses of current curriculum emphases upon the structure of knowledge, the advantages seem to outweigh the disadvantages. Further, we have noted different intellectual tools which contribute to an understanding of knowledge—for example, studying uses of knowledge, using logical structures, and understanding the ways in which knowledge can be represented.

This chapter should be studied concurrently with articles or books on the structure of knowledge as well as with curriculum materials. There is a rich potentiality for conceptualizing curriculum in a meaningful manner. Indeed curriculum itself is a study of relationships—how people, processes, and products become related and help to promote pupil learning. Your mastery of the concept of the structure of knowledge—and the development of an ability to help pupils to attain and apply it—is a most difficult task.

In a further effort to make the concept purposeful, let us now turn to a discussion of subject matter and of the structure of knowledge. Subject matter derived from the academic disciplines is a basic component of curriculum. Whether traditional or progressive, or at some point between, educators tend to recognize the necessity for helping children to learn appropriate portions of the organized wisdom and knowledge of the culture. Disagreements, when they exist, tend to be concerned with *degree* and *kind* of subject matter content.

Balance Between Subject Matter and Child-Societal Needs

A seminar of outstanding curriculum and subject matter specialists proposed a solution to a related two-pronged problem: (a) how to avoid a power struggle between influential academicians seeking to promote their fields at the expense of a balanced curriculum, (b) how to avoid the blandness which can occur when non-specialists seek to synthesize the various disciplines and simplify them for elementary pupils. Their solution was to suggest two kinds of curriculum, labeled *nuclear curriculum* and *cortical curriculum.*[11]

Recognizing the needs of children and of society at large, the specialists called for some nuclear aspects, that is, materials selected *primarily* to meet the needs of children and societal expectations. Of course,

[11] National Education Association Project on Instruction, *The Scholars Look at the Schools* (Washington: The Association, 1962), pp. 50–52.

these materials should be sound in terms of subject matter itself, but this is not the primary intention.

Cortical components, say the specialists, should be selected for their conceptual framework as well as processes of discovery and verification. If such content can also make a contribution to children's and society's needs, that is desirable; it is not the prime criterion for selection. There is an implication that knowing the structure of knowledge is important for the welfare of both child and society.

How much nuclear and how much cortical content is appropriate for elementary grades where traditions have been strong in favor of a child-centered curriculum? The specialists admit that there is no clear evidence to support them, but they advocate the following guidelines:

1. In the earlier grades, cortical content should be as low as 10 per cent of the total (reaching as high as 90 per cent for seniors in high school).
2. Teacher preparation for different grades should correspond in emphasis, that is, subject matter specialization should increase proportionately as teachers prepare to teach older pupils.
3. Perhaps the time pupils spend in school may need to be increased as pupils are expected to learn and apply both nuclear and cortical components of the curriculum.

Some Curriculum Examples

It now seems appropriate to note some examples of what structure means in some subject areas. A study in depth of proposals for curriculum reform is recommended again, especially in subject matter areas which you are most likely to teach. This recommendation is particularly pertinent to pre-service and in-service upper elementary teachers.

English. Children may enter school with a considerable knowledge of the English language. They have learned much of the *structure* through listening and talking and hence formal study of what they have unconsciously acquired can be a valuable learning aid. Wilson notes that children know: (a) how to sort out sounds of different letters in combination and separately, (b) sentence patterns which they can manipulate, (c) linguistic devices such as analogy (for example, making comparisons by adding *er* and *est* to words they know), (d) the influence of inflection of meaning. He claims that formal grammar is not based on the structure of the language a child learns prior to attending school; rather it is a Latinized version of "correctness."[12]

[12] Graham C. Wilson, in G. W. Ford and Lawrence Pugno (eds.), *The Structure of Knowledge and the Curriculum* (Chicago: Rand McNally & Co., Inc., 1964), pp. 73–77.

Hanna reports a study which indicates that 80 per cent of 3,000 words commonly found in spelling lists follow regular rules of orthography (representation of sounds). Noting that English is primarily a language of predictable structure, Hanna advocates teaching the words that fit structural rules first, irregular words last. This would build on what children know from experiencing language structure.[13]

Social Studies. Illustrations of structure can be cited for social studies. There, the effort is to develop understandings of how space, time, resources, and people are interconnected. Different examples of structure have been developed to show interrelationships. Scriven attempts to show the relationships of various social sciences through the following illustration. A platform rests on a tripod which in turn rests on a base. The *base* includes the arts, biology, chemistry, physics, engineering, and other disciplines. The base disciplines provide an understanding of the conditions under which learning takes place. The *tripod* itself represents history, geography, and psychology; history and geography are traditional school subjects while psychology is a needed supplement in understanding internalized behavior. These three subject areas provide a basis for understanding other relationships, notes Scriven, and they have the added advantage of being simpler to teach. Psychology (for example, in the form of group dynamics) can be taught in applied form to elementary age children. In the Scriven scheme, methodology, logic, and mathematics provide horizontal support for the tripod in the same manner in which chair rounds could be represented as holding chair legs together.

The elevated *platform* in Scriven's illustration includes sociology, anthropology, economics, and government—with a central core of ethics. While often not included separately in the elementary social studies, this content is important in understanding human behavior singularly or collectively. Ethics or value judgments affect the manner and extent of response to economic, geographic, and other factors. Scriven has thus provided a *structure* for the social sciences.[14]

Hanna provides a more applicable structure for understanding the content of elementary social studies. He establishes categories for understanding relationships in terms of several "basic human activities": "organizing and governing," "educating," "transporting," "creating new tools and techniques," plus five other basics. These topics provide an *organizing framework* for understanding human endeavors everywhere. They can be used for analyzing conditions among peoples, and for studying human activities in relation to environment. By using such a framework during several elementary grades, a child can apply concepts learned in

[13] Paul H. Hanna, in William A. Jenkins (ed.), *The Nature of Knowledge* (Milwaukee: Edward A. Uhrig Foundation, 1962), p. 72.

[14] Michael Scriven, in Ford and Pugno (eds.), *op. cit.*, pp. 88–93.

a study of his home community (the here and now) to faraway places, where he finds it necessary to transcend space, time, and culture to develop sound ideas of human differences and similarities. Hanna's announced goal is to encourage children to learn how to live in several communities of mankind from the local to the world.[15]

The organizing topics of Hanna could be used in conjunction with a utilization of the various social sciences. Each social science has its unique way of studying human and natural phenomena. Pupils pursuing discovery as social scientists would do are on the way to securing an enduring conceptualization of man and his world—a foundation on which to lay later related facts and understandings. This is a desirable contrast to the kind of emphasis on factual knowledge which becomes the basis for assignment, memorization, recitation, and examination—knowledge which often is not meaningfully related for the pupil.

If indeed the elementary pupil is to experience learning as a social scientist in the bud, method should match motive. For example, the historian pursues his studies through varied sources. To have as a curriculum *objective* imparting the structure of history and as the *method* studying from one textbook—pre-digested history—is self-defeating. Curriculum objectives are feasible through a use of rich and diverse learning resources now available. As an example, we note that it is possible to secure reprints of historic documents, actual letters written during a given period, and old newspapers and magazines. The single textbook approach not only defeats the curriculum goal of teaching the structure of knowledge, but also interests relatively few. After all, a single summary or a digest of history is a poor substitute for history derived from several sources. The textbook writer's thoughts are a poor substitute for pupils' self-discovery of the processes of the social scientist.

PROJECTS AND READINGS

1. As noted previously, children may enter school with considerable knowledge of the structure of the English language. What do you feel the school should do for those children whose deprived environment has not enabled them to gain such an understanding? What can be done to help them learn the structure while the more fortunate—those with sound early childhood experiences—are helped to build on those early understanding of structures? It is interesting also to consider the special problems of children from homes where English is not the basic language, hence the English structure is relatively unknown.

2. If children learn mathematics rather than *about* mathematics, difficulty may be a relative matter, according to Page. He claims that with understandable, interesting materials children can learn mathematics. "It may be that

[15] Paul R. Hanna, in Jenkins (ed.), *op. cit.*, pp. 76–78.

nothing is intrinsically difficult" (David Page, in Bruner, *The Process of Education,* p. 40). What are the differences between learning mathematics and learning about it? To what extent can an elementary teacher be expected to know enough about the structure of mathematics to be able to teach the "new math," which stresses structure and self-discovery by pupils?

3. The "AAAS Science Curriculum for K–6–A Process Approach" is still another example in which there is an emphasis upon structure. There are three "basic tenets" in this science curriculum: (a) "Logical thought and action" must be repeated with increasing sophistication as children proceed through the school program. (b) The basic test of the process of learning science is the effectiveness of pupil thinking and acting. (c) The discovery of relationships (structure) by pupils and the resulting self-discovery is the basic plan for an effective science curriculum. [Mary M. Blatt, in *Nature and Science Teachers Edition,* II, No. 8 (January 18, 1965). The American Association for the Advancement of Science, Washington, D.C., has extensive descriptions of its curriculum.] Are there kinds of science instruction that do not lend themselves to the self-discovery method? Are they sufficiently valuable to be included in the elementary school program?

4. Mathematics is a study of relationships of abstract forms and structures, according to Lange (L. H. Lange, in Ford and Pugno, *op. cit.*, p. 52). Mathematics is different from other subject areas in that it is not evident to the senses, notes Schwab (Joseph J. Schwab, page 7 of the same publication). What kinds of concrete experiences can be provided to enable children to find the structure, abstract though it is, of mathematics? What are the particular problems that disadvantaged children have as a result of limited experiences with applied mathematics?

5. Bruner claims that teachers should know the structure of knowledge for two reasons: (a) in order to know how to present it, (b) in order to know how to break it into units for instructional purposes without destroying the structure in the process (Bruner, *Learning About Learning: A Conference Report,* p. 253). The elementary teacher, often responsible for teaching several subjects, would have a difficult time in learning enough about all the academic disciplines to understand their structure in depth. In your opinion, what are the advantages to plans which enable an elementary teacher to specialize—for example, team teaching and departmental organizational plans—and what are the disadvantages in terms of presumed advantages of self-contained classrooms wherein one teacher is responsible for most instruction for a year?

6. "If students discover how one body of knowledge succeeds another, if they are aware of the substantive structures that underlie our current knowledge, if they are given a little freedom to speculate on the possible changes in structure which the future may bring, they will not only be prepared to meet future revisions with intelligence but will better understand the knowledge they are currently being taught" (Joseph J. Schwab, in *The Structure of Knowledge and the Curriculum,* p. 30). Earlier (p. 13), Schwab notes that knowledge imparted in teaching structures is of limited duration since particular concepts disclose "new complexities" which in turn bring forth new concepts. What limitations, if any, do you see in teaching knowledge as being tentative, as being the means of discovery of new knowledge? What practical difficulties do you see in terms of keeping up-to-date instructional materials and curriculum guides? What difficulties are you experiencing in your college-level studies which would be most likely to bother elementary children as well?

7. What alternatives to stressing the structure of knowledge, especially for elementary children, do you find most defensible? What are the primary weaknesses of such alternatives?

8. Foshay notes that subjects taught in schools have not been what they are claimed to be. Examples include: (a) facts and dates as history, (b) computation as mathematics, (c) grammar as composition. He claims that school subjects are sterile to the extent that they close inquiry as a method of pupil learning (Arthur W. Foshay, in Jenkins, ed., *The Nature of Knowledge*, p. 33). Is Foshay too critical? Is he making a valid point? How could facts and dates, computation, and grammar contribute to an inquiry approach?

9. In order to grasp the structure of curriculum and its component knowledge, you will need to read what subject matter specialists have to say, books on subject matter itself, ideas on organizational patterns, and proposals on how teachers and pupils can seek *cooperatively* to learn the structure of knowledge. Understanding the structure of curriculum, you can then help children to learn by helping them to seek out and organize time, materials, and knowledge.

10. Several sources are good for additional reading in depth:

a. Jerome S. Bruner, *Process of Education* (Cambridge, Mass.: Harvard University Press, 1962), especially pp. 41–48 for examples of the use of structure in several subject areas.

b. Jerome S. Bruner, "Some Theorems on Instruction Illustrated with Reference to Mathematics," *Theories of Learning and Instruction*, Sixty-third Yearbook, National Society for the Study of Education (Chicago: University of Chicago Press, 1954), chapter XIII. A good basic reference on theories of learning and instruction.

c. William A. Jenkins (ed.), *The Nature of Knowledge* (Milwaukee: The Uhrig Foundation, 1962).

d. G. W. Ford and Lawrence Pugno (eds.), *The Structure of Knowledge and the Curriculum* (Chicago: Rand McNally & Co., Inc., 1964).

e. J. Cecil Parker and Louis J. Rubin, *Process as Content: Curriculum Design and the Application of Knowledge* (Chicago: Rand McNally & Co., Inc., 1966).

f. John Dewey, *How We Think* (Boston: D. C. Heath & Co., 1933).

g. *The Scholars Look at the Schools* (Washington, D.C.: Project on Instruction, National Education Association, February, 1962).

11. Behaviors on which to spend much instructional time and those on which less time should be spent have been identified in a publication of one of the relatively new "learning corporations" which have been active in recent years. The publication urges that much time be spent on conducting diagnostic and didactic inquiry, facilitating decisions, leading small group discussion, tutoring, and giving positive verbal and non-verbal messages. Less time should be spent on giving solutions, providing content, giving negative verbal and non-verbal messages, managing records and computer materials, and managing materials and equipment. See Margaret T. Steen and Dewey Lipe, *The Use of the Teacher Observation Scale in the Development of the PLAN Teacher Training Program* (New York: Westinghouse Learning Corporation, 1970). What do these points suggest relative to curriculum? What generalizations can you make concerning activities which are recommended for much attention and less attention?

12. There are many descriptions of individual classroom observation systems but few which relate many systems to each other. J. T. Sandefur *et al.*, in *Classroom Observation Systems* (Washington, D.C.: ERIC Clearinghouse on Teacher Education, 1970) classify several affective, cognitive, and multidimensional systems and claim that most of the efforts are to study verbal behavior. To what extent can observational systems, developed originally for research purposes, be used productively by pre- and in-service teachers (after some training) to analyze teaching–learning situations and to determine the extent that the curriculum is producing desired behavioral patterns? How can those teachers create an atmosphere in which they seek the assistance of peers to analyze classroom behaviors through varied observational systems? On the basis of reading about research results derived from the systems what changes appear to be needed in the elementary curriculum?

4

Human Development and Learning

Children are the obvious reason for schools. Children, seen as blobs or as a "class," may be viewed as seething sources of despair and frustration. Known as *individuals,* children are challenges and sources of inspiration in curriculum building. Children are the dynamic "raw material" in curriculum. Their drives toward living and experiencing learning are a basic resource in planning school curriculum. Consider for a moment a true series of events involving children during 30 minutes prior to bedtime.

At snack time:

The unexplainable value placed upon a small plastic toy in the cereal box.

Why the younger children rather than older children enjoy clearing the table after the snack is over.

While getting upstairs to bed:

A five-year-old carefully backing *down* stairs rather than continuing on to his bedroom.

A five-year-old and a six-year-old carefully counting the stairs while going up to bed, and coming out within ONE of getting the same count.

After getting in bed:

A two-year-old carefully turning back his covers, putting them back, repeating the process several times, then attempting to climb into the top bunk, then continuing a monolog which has been going on for some time.

Before going to sleep:

The extraordinary interests of children:

5-year-old: Can a lion fight an elephant?
6-year-old: How does a snake's skeleton help him move along? Do you know how to kill a snake?
8-year-old: Did you hear Davy say that a bull could push over our house? (This in turn leading to a discussion of terms such as a "bull in a china shop").

The emerging sense of responsibility:
An older child offering to rock a younger child to sleep.

The characteristics and needs of children provide some general guidelines for curriculum planning, as do some curriculum objectives. These objectives also are based on society's needs. Each type of objective is assigned to grade levels, essentially age levels. Activities then are planned to reflect children's capacities and interests. Unit plans not only provide for *groups* of children but also for *individual* variations. Daily lesson plans likewise reflect general objectives for an age group and each individual. Chapter 5 provides further discussion of instructional planning to develop individual intellectual, social, and physical potentials. Chapter 11 and subsequent chapters reflect efforts to stress a meaningful curriculum for each child. The teacher is the society's representative in converting human plastic potentiality into personal worth and valuable citizenship.

Since the mid-1800's, efforts have been made to simplify the teaching of individual children. Attempts have included various grouping plans, types of curriculum programs, materials and equipment, plans for "accelerating" or "retaining" pupils, and organizational patterns of teachers. Yet the differences not only persist but *increase*, particularly under the stimulus of good teaching. A knowledge is needed of the many factors which help to mold a relatively plastic baby into a distinct human being.

The precise way in which multiple factors combine to affect a human being varies with each individual. The manner in which he responds is unique. Identical twins, with a similar heredity, raised apart may have both comparable traits and distinctive traits. Knowing about the many factors which affect children is *one* curriculum tool. It cannot simplify your teaching task, but it can sensitize you to its complexity and can aid in your diagnosis of the instructional needs of children.

A major emphasis of this chapter is intellectual development; but other aspects of development, and the environmental factors which affect them, will be analyzed and discussed. Of course the total child is of concern to the school. However, the school has a unique role—the development of intellectual competencies—and this should be a primary interest. Care for the total child is shared with other agencies, while the school has primacy in its concerns for the intellect. Intellectual competency should spill over into all factors which affect the total child. It is always important to relate intellectual development—broadly conceived—to environmental, physical, emotional, and social factors.

COGNITIVE DEVELOPMENT AND NURTURE

Development of intelligence continues its traditional primacy in American school objectives. Pressures from abroad and increased complexity at home combine to create drives for achieving effective intellectual development. The launching of Russia's Sputnik unleashed a continuing interest in brain power, and the results can be seen in curriculum content, grading practices, and grouping practices. Several topics related to cognitive development and nurture are discussed below. Until intelligence is developed, children must depend for many years upon others for nurture and protection. Helping children to unlock and utilize their great *potentialities* through learning is the major task in teaching. A good curriculum provides those learnings which enable each child to develop his intelligence to its greatest potentiality.

Intelligence

Intelligence is a basic human characteristic. It is the capacity to learn —within the limitations of heredity and environment. Intelligence is applied potentiality. It is the raw material for learning. Unlike animals, humans don't come into being genetically programmed. The relative plasticity of learning potentialities is a basic factor in individual differences.

Intelligence is the capacity to analyze and respond in a manner which will contribute to goal attainment, varied applications of learnings, and adaptations to changing circumstances and needs. Intelligence enables an individual to modify behavior from the specific to the general, concrete to the abstract, present to future, the immediate to the distant, and the actual to the potential. Intelligence permits an individual to experience beyond only the "here-and-now" which can be perceived through varied senses.

Structure of the Intellect

There has been some tendency to think that the intellect is a generalized entity which functions on a generalized level in all situations. A single I.Q. score is a partial reflection of this incorrect assumption. In contrast Guilford has identified *three basic processes,* broken into *120 intellectual factors,* which can be applied to analyses of intellectual functioning sought in curriculum.[1] Verduin summarizes the three intellectual

[1] J. P. Guilford, P. R. Merrifield, and Anna B. Cox, *Creative Thinking in Children at the Junior High Level,* U. S. Office of Education Cooperative Research Project No. 737 (Los Angeles: University of Southern California, September, 1961). Also described in other publications by Guilford.

processes and defines some of them.[2] They require, in some instances, more than one reading to develop clarity and determine significance.

> The first classifying unit is that of the level of operation or processes performed. Within this system are the five major groups of intellectual abilities such as cognition, memory, convergent thinking, divergent thinking, and evaluation.
>
> Cognition, in this case, is the discovery or rediscovery of information and includes comprehension and understanding. Memory is the retention or storage of information. From this known and remembered information come the two productive kinds of thinking: divergent thinking and convergent thinking. Divergent thinking is the generation of new information from known information with the emphasis on variety and quantity of information. In this case thinking goes in a variety of directions, with no real "right" answer being sought. Convergent thinking is the generation of new information which leads to the right or conventionally accepted answer. In this case, the given or known information usually determines the correct response. Evaluative thinking is the intellectual process by which judgments and decisions are made regarding the goodness, correctness, adequacy, or suitability of information, based on some criterion of consistency or goal satisfaction that resulted from productive thinking.
>
> A second classification system offered in the intellectual process is based on the kind of material or content involved. These broad classes of information are identified as figural, symbolic, semantic, and behavioral content. Figural content is that which is concrete material and is represented by itself. This content is taken in through the senses and has some degree of organization. Symbolic content is that which is composed of letters, signs, numbers, etc., usually with some organization such as the alphabet or number system. Semantic content is information in the form of meanings to which words are attached, and is used primarily in verbal communication. Behavioral content is that information, mostly non-verbal, which deals with human interactions in which attitudes, needs, desires, and perceptions of others and oneself are important.
>
> At this point, then, when a certain operation is applied to a selected kind of content, the intellectual process involves a kind of outcome or product. The variety of products involved here are identified as units, classes, relations, systems, transformations, and implications. Units are relatively segregated items of information that have a single character. Classes are sets of items of information that are grouped by common properties. Relations are connections between the units of information based upon certain points of contact that are applicable to them. Systems are organized complexes of interrelated or interacting items of information. Transformations are the changes in existing, known information or in the actual use of the information. Implications are the extrapolations of information, which can take the form of expectancies, predictions, concomitants, or consequences.

Verduin further provides an illustration of how questions can be phrased to bring out different kinds of thinking.[3] It is important to note that each kind of thinking illustrated by Verduin has a place in the curriculum.

[2] John R. Verduin, Jr., *Conceptual Models in Teacher Education* (Washington: American Association of Colleges for Teacher Education, 1967), pp. 85–87.

[3] *Ibid.*, p. 93.

Examples of Productive Thinking Operations

Subject Area	*Divergent Thinking*	*Convergent Thinking*	*Evaluative Thinking*
Science	How might life be different on Mars?	Explain why there could be no life on Mercury.	Do you think there is life on Mars?
	Name as many possible detrimental effects of the use of insecticides as you can.	How are humans modifying their environment through the use of insecticides?	Are insecticides more harmful or more beneficial?
Social Studies	What would happen if there had not been a Bering Strait?	How did the Bering Strait influence the settlement of North America?	What is the most important contemporary use of the Bering Strait?
	What would have happened if Lewis and Clark had arrived at the mouth of the Frazier River instead of the Columbia?	Explain the impact of the Lewis and Clark expedition on the development of the Oregon Territory.	What were the two most influential contributions of the Lewis and Clark expedition to the development of the Oregon Territory?
Language	Here is the beginning of a short story. How many different endings could be developed from it?	Tell why you think the short story developed in American literature rather than European.	What is more important in the development of the short story—character or plot?
	In what ways has American English changed as a result of advertising?	Explain the impact of advertising on the level of acceptable spoken English.	What kind of advertising made the most valuable contribution in changing American English?

Questions, and other instructional activity, should be planned as means of attaining varied curriculum objectives.

A knowledge of the categories of Guilford and others is potentially useful in analyzing the kinds of intellectual activities to be practiced or planned. In observing classroom activities, you can determine whether or not balanced intellectual development is being encouraged. In analyzing curriculum guides and textbooks, you can discover whether balanced intellectual development is an objective and if it is planned adequately. Certainly this does not imply that 120 intellectual categories should be sought in every lesson or teaching unit, or even that it would be feasible. Awareness of the factors should enable you, formally or informally, to analyze curriculum planning and practices. Gallagher and Jenne report that 50 per cent of the questions asked in five observed class sessions were of the cognitive-memory variety, followed next by those appropriate for convergent thinking.[4] Excessive attention was given to "right" answers in the classroom observed. It seems probable that this was more typical than atypical. Only if you consciously seek varied kinds of thinking will the classroom intellectual atmosphere advance beyond the read-recite-and-repeat level.

Cognitive Growth

This ability has often been considered a generalized or global one, and once learned in any form utilizable in others. It was presumed that the mind grew in a manner comparable to muscles. Therefore, any type of use could, it was thought, cause general cognitive growth. This concept of cognitive growth has been generally rejected, yet there are still people who stress the general value of "tough" subjects in developing the mind.

Cognitive growth occurs as a child perceives, experiments physically or mentally, evaluates his experience, and plans and carries out other experiences. The child learns to make sense of his world. He organizes, systematizes, evaluates his experiences and perceptions, and changes his behavior in ways which contribute to personal objectives.

Taba claims that formal thinking begins in second grade and continuously increases thereafter, but in a rather irregular pattern. To Taba formal thought includes "abstract symbolic relationships," "if–then" principles, projection of hypotheses, and "high level categorizations." [5] In her study of thinking, Taba identifies three cognitive tasks: (a) "grouping and classification of information," (b) "interpretation of data and the making of inferences," and (c) "the application of known principles and facts to explain phenomena." [6]

A different analysis of thinking, that of Piaget, is found in Chapter 10. His conception of cognitive development is being widely studied today.

The experiences which stimulate and modify cognitive growth are screened by individual perceptions. Differences are a consequence of individual physical perceptual equipment and experiences. An individual is not a robot responding to stimuli and growing in a steady progression. A child learns selectively, that is, he learns that which seems to contribute

[4] James J. Gallagher and William Jenne, *Productive Thinking of Gifted Children*, U. S. Office of Education Cooperative Research Project No. 965 (Urbana: University of Illinois, 1965), reported in Verduin, *op. cit.*, p. 89.

[5] Hilda Taba, *Thinking in Elementary School Children*, U. S. Office of Education Cooperative Research Project No. 1574 (San Francisco: San Francisco State College, 1964), pp. 173–74.

[6] *Ibid.*, p. 30.

to himself. A child is educated; an animal is trained by a series of stimuli which develop rather predictable responses.

The psychologically secure person is more likely to have perceptions which correspond to reality. He is more likely to trust himself and his world, to open himself to new experiences. Cognitive growth is more likely to occur when perceptions are freed from distortions which occur when an individual is fearful, mistrusts himself and others, uses psychologically unsound reactions, and so forth.

Perceptions, and ultimately cognitive growth, are affected by a number of feelings. Cognitive growth often is thought of in abstract and rational terms. In *Learning More About Learning,* a number of non-rational factors and illustrations are discussed: [7]

1. *Beliefs.* What people believe affects what they learn and how they behave—for example, the old belief that the world is flat.
2. *Values.* What people feel is important and affects what they see and experience.
3. *Needs.* Whether physical, psychological, or emotional, needs influence perceptions, for example, reminders of food when hungry. (Breakfasts are being served in some schools in the assumption that little learning is likely to occur on empty stomachs.)
4. *Attitudes.* An emotionalized belief about worth of someone or something has a bearing on perception and learning.
5. *Self-experience.* How one feels about himself (self-concept), what he would like to be, and how he sees his role are vital forces in perceptions. These factors in turn contribute to attitudes toward what is being taught.
6. *Threat.* Fear leads to defensive, distorted perceptions and limited cognitive growth. Faced with a fearful situation, individuals tend to retreat to the tried and true, to the relatively safe idea or action, and to conformity.

For emphasis, let us say again that cognitive development is not carried on in splendid isolation in the cerebrum. The total body feeds in perceptions which provide and extend learnings or restrict them. Empty stomachs, fear, threat, mistrust, low esteem—these are poor ingredients for valid, constructive perceptions. They are inadequate bases on which to build for continuing cognitive development. While aiming at cognitive development, you will of necessity deal with other factors which influence perceptions and thereby intellectual activity. The total child cannot be fragmented to permit an isolated brain to develop and grow. Some highly disciplined and mature adults may function on a high intellectual level

[7] Association for Supervision and Curriculum Development, *Learning More About Learning* (Washington: The Association, 1959), pp. 57–62.

without being affected by varied perceptions. Such individuals should not be used as illustrations to support claims that the school should deal only with the mind.

Maturation and Readiness

With the development of large schools the administrative device of graded schools arose, with rigid expectations for each grade level. Sometimes curriculum demands placed on children were realistic in terms of maturation, in other situations expectations were arbitrary and unrealistic. Children in large schools had to be grouped some way, and to an extent grouping by age groups was a satisfactory way—as long as flexibility prevailed within the classroom.

Maturation is the sequential unlocking of the inherited potential of a child. A fairly consistent growth pattern is built into *each child's genetic inheritance.* In general, developmental patterns for children of a comparable age are similar. Unlike maturation of lower animals, human maturation is affected by personal and cultural factors. Since each child has a unique hereditary, home, and societal foundation, the precise manner and time when one child reaches a level of development will be unlike the pattern for any other child. Fortunately, from the standpoint of grouping, there are children on the same *general* levels of development, and therefore comparable learning tasks can be planned for them.

There is readiness for a particular task when society expects it, maturity permits it, and the child's personal inclination facilitates it. To force children toward learning tasks prematurely is not productive. To wait too long is equally objectionable. To assume that a child matures as a total being along a smooth line and is equally ready for growth tasks—whether physical, mental, or social—is not realistic for some children, although true for many. Hence, a physically very mature child *may* be intellectually immature but socially average.

Havighurst has identified "developmental tasks" for each broad age group. These are defined as tasks that are normal for "healthy and satisfactory growth in our society." Havighurst notes:

> A developmental task is a task which arises at or about a certain period in the life of the individual, successful achievement of which leads to his happiness and to success with later tasks, while failure leads to unhappiness in the individual, disapproval by the society, and difficulty with later tasks.[8]

Havighurst's developmental tasks are arbitrary, by his own admission, yet they furnish a basis for analyzing what children of a general age *can*

[8] Robert J. Havighurst, *Developmental Tasks and Education,* Second Edition (New York: David McKay Co., Inc., 1948, 1950, 1952), p. 2. Used by permission of David McKay Co., Inc.

do and are expected to do. They provide a compromise in viewpoints on selection of content and are not exclusively individual-centered, child-centered, or society-centered.

Let us examine one of Havighurst's developmental tasks to illustrate their dimensions. Readiness based on maturation and in harmony with societal expectations is a factor in the middle childhood task of learning to read, write, and calculate, and it is a task peculiar to this period, according to Havighurst. *Biologically,* children of this age have overcome their earlier farsightedness and can manipulate pencils. *Psychologically,* they are capable of learning the basic mental processes of the tasks. *Culturally,* they usually are by this age ready to meet the minimal expectations of the society. *Educationally,* expectations have been adjusted to harmonize demands with what is desired and what is reasonable. When there is maturational and social readiness, learning proceeds most efficiently. Readiness is a vital consideration in curriculum planning, and is only one factor in the many developmental tasks identified for several age groups. They should be considered in more depth in relationship to other factors described in this chapter. Curriculum planning carefully related to developmental tasks is apt to be more realistic than is possible on a hit-and-miss basis. Such planning for a particular age also should be adjusted to the reality of *individualized* patterns of maturation and readiness.

Concept Formation

In a facts-centered curriculum the emphasis is upon memorization. The assumption is that facts thus stored in the mind *can* and *will* be applied in future situations. Facts in themselves are inadequate intellectual tools, for they: (a) become obsolete quickly, (b) tend to be forgotten rapidly, (c) are likely to be transferred to new and varied situations only under certain conditions, (d) are so numerous that teacher selection and pupil retention become very difficult. In view of these and other difficulties, concepts increasingly are emphasized in the modern curriculum. They have few of the disadvantages just noted and several distinct advantages.

Woodruff provides an extensive general definition of a concept:

> A concept is a relatively complete and meaningful idea in the mind of a person. It is an understanding of something. It is his own subjective product of his way of making meaning of things he has seen or otherwise perceived in his experiences. At its most concrete level it is likely to be a mental image of some actual object or event the person has seen. At its most abstract and complex level it is a synthesis of a number of conclusions he has drawn about his experience with particular things.[9]

[9] Asahel Woodruff, in Verduin, *op. cit.,* p. 102.

A concept is an intellectual or verbalized representation of experience. Without sufficient experiences, channeled into the brain through the senses, children may resort to the use of words to discuss words. Words, of course, are abstract in themselves. Through experiences with reality, a child can develop and verbalize concepts which will help him to interpret new perceptions and attach organized meaning to them. In a sense concepts are skeletons which serve to hold together diverse elements. The organization of instruction to facilitate the development of concepts, and other curriculum objectives, is discussed in Chapter 5.

Meaningful concepts have been developed by scholars and practitioners for the various subject areas. There are relatively few concepts to be taught in contrast to the number of available *facts*. There are still fewer *generalizations*, which are descriptions *of relationships of concepts* in a field of knowledge. While facts tend to change, concepts are relatively stable and provide children with some capacity for organizing and predicting their environment. You can help children to secure those experiences in school and capitalize on others which contribute to the development of significant concepts and generalizations. Lacking such organizing frameworks for new and old bits of sensory inputs, a child lacks an important tool in interpreting his world and relationships to it. His behavior may become random, confused, and unproductive. Specialists in learning are still studying the best time for learning specific concepts and the best methods to be used in developing them.

Since a rich background of experiences is important in concept development, there is presently much interest in studying the consequences of limited experiences available to the disadvantaged. Much of the school's curriculum traditionally has been organized in the assumption that all children have had certain experiences. It is now clear that many children have had inadequate or inappropriate experiences for developing meaningful concepts and generalizations. It is a small wonder that such children may find school a place of an endless array of unrelated words and facts. If the curriculum is built on and seeks to enrich the experiences of disadvantaged children, concepts and generalizations can be developed. The close-to-home and the here-and-now experiences are the most easily translated. Fortunately they are of greatest interest to children as well as of use to teachers. This provides a clue to the concept development of children with deprived experiences.

Cognitive Learning Styles

It is important that children learn appropriate intellectual processes for the various kinds of learning needed in a complex society. Some would have us believe that intellectual development is semi-automatic, that with exercise (read–recite–repeat) the mind can be developed. Bruner and Clinchy suggest that there is balance in learning styles when children learn to use both analytical and intuitive processes. Neither process is simple or semi-automatic.[10]

Analytical and Intuitive Approaches. The analytical approach places primacy on the collection, analysis, and interpretation of data, and Bruner and Clinchy note that computers will increasingly perform this type of task.[11] The school should prepare children to think intuitively—to anticipate the applications of results derived from computerized analytical processes. Computers can do what they are "told" to do. Once programmed, they can complete certain kinds of processes with remarkable speed, to a great extent making humans obsolete in analytical processes.

The computer is amoral and acultural—it responds in a comparable manner anywhere in the world. The school is responsible for establishing educational goals compatible with the *American* heritage, which emphasizes individuality, rationality, and democracy. That heritage cannot be transmitted through indoctrination or exclusive utilization of analytical thinking. The intuitive approach should be taught in conjunction with the analytical. Each child needs to experience and grow in the ability to process both approaches to *knowing*.

Bruner's ideas on teacher-related factors which encourage *intuitive* thinking include: (a) teacher willingness to *guess* on questions and then proceed with critical analyses, (b) provision for varied experiences, (c) emphasis on content structure, which in turn gives freedom to experiment with thinking, (d) heuristic teaching—the encouragement of guessing by students before proceeding to learn facts through analytical processes.[12]

Intellectual Freedom. Several writers emphasize the importance of intellectual freedom as a means of encouraging intellectual development. Taba discusses the importance of exploratory activities, properly paced to permit pupils to assimilate the *significance* of the activities. Higher degrees of participation seem to encourage the development of high levels of thinking.[13]

Crutchfield has experimented with student booklets designed to encourage thinking by making provisions for: (a) the identification and definition of the problem, (b) avoidance of hasty answers and conclusions, (c) discovery of discrepancies in details, (d) generation of ideas, (e) ac-

[10] Jerome S. Bruner and Blythe Clinchy, "Towards a Disciplined Intuition," in Bruner (ed.), *Learning About Learning: A Conference Report* (Washington: U. S. Office of Education, 1966), pp. 71–72.

[11] *Ibid.*, p. 82.

[12] Jerome S. Bruner, *The Process of Education* (Cambridge, Mass.: Harvard University Press, 1960), p. 66.

[13] Taba, *op. cit.*, pp. 163–68.

ceptability of "silly" ideas.[14] Crutchfield seems to caution against a teacher's rushing in with the answers before pupils experiment with thinking.

Writing in the same volume, Kessen advocates tolerance for plural approaches, ambiguity, and variability while children learn.[15] Johnson calls for the nourishment of the "intuitive and imaginative powers" of students. He believes that these powers may result in "new forms of thought and conduct, new vistas, and even new social institutions and systems."[16]

Curricular Constraints. Crutchfield suggests that cognitive skills are limited in the typical school curriculum:

1. Tasks are too easy.
2. They are meaningless, repetitive, and of "low order."
3. There is excessive recognition for "successes" in mastering simple demands.
4. Immediate feedback on the adequacy of pupil's responses is limited, partly as a result of large classes.

Several steps should be taken to plan a curriculum which stimulates cognitive developments. According to Crutchfield these steps are:

1. Curriculum materials should be developed to stress complex problem solving.
2. The materials should aid pupils in developing creative and critical thinking.
3. Pupils should be helped to transfer specific learnings to complex situations.
4. Pupils should be aided in their organization of personal resources, for example, skill in analyzing problems at hand and planning appropriate strategies for solving them.[17]

Pupils' Roles in Thinking. Reference to this point has been made to *teacher responsibility* for encouraging thinking. It is time now to look at thinking in terms related to pupils.

Intuitive thinking occurs when pupils use what Bruner and Clinchy call "short-cut approximations"—a beginning step that determines what analytical tools are needed to guarantee against error.[18] Children at the *intuitive level of thinking* will exhibit certain kinds of behavior: (a) absence of carefully designed steps in thinking, (b) involvement in processes not easily explained to others, (c) use of processes dependent upon knowl-

[14] Richard Crutchfield, in Bruner, *op. cit., Learning About Learning: A Conference Report,* p. 258.

[15] William Kessen, in Bruner, *ibid.*, pp. 100–2.

[16] Earl S. Johnson, in William A. Jenkins (ed.), *The Nature of Knowledge* (Milwaukee: Edward A. Uhrig Foundation, 1961), p. 25.

[17] Richard Crutchfield, *op. cit.*, pp. 66–67.

[18] Jerome S. Bruner and Blythe Clinchy, in Bruner, *op. cit.*, pp. 71–74.

edge of structure of the content, which permit freedom to experiment and search for personal understanding. While intuitive thinking in its formative stage lacks the precision of the more commonly accepted analytical thinking, Bruner claims it is better than "articulate idiocy." In contrast, when a child seeks to verify his intuitive thinking through *analytical processes,* his behavior is characterized by: (a) development of explicit steps which can be explained to others, (b) use of careful reasoning, logical operations, *and step-by-step experiments.*[19]

At the intuitive level, children should have some freedom to experiment with thinking, with the opportunity to make some mistakes and enter some blind alleys. After all, productive thinking does not develop instantaneously at any age. Children at this point need a teacher who can help with the intuitive stage and then aid them in proceeding to analytical processes to check out the validity of conclusions. The two thinking processes are complementary.

In a world where the unknown is as significant as the known, the old "scientific method"—the lockstep process of proving facts already known to the teacher—is obsolete. The changing world challenges us to use intuitive thinking as a springboard to analytical thinking. Intuitive thinking provides imaginative exploration of the hypothetical while analytical processes help to avoid error and to systematize thought conclusions.

Creative Thinking. A closely related process is *creative thinking*—the ultimate application of individuality in intellectual development. Creative thinking is an individual's unique and intuitive application of sound thinking and problem solving. It is not chaotic on the one hand nor rigid on the other. It has its personalized timing, its own processes, and its own productivity.

Calling attention to the autonomous nature of creativity, Hallman suggests that it cannot be *planned or forced* on a group. "Rather it flourishes on the unforeseen," he claims. He advocates self-initiative and self-responsibility as replacements for facts dispensing and authoritarian teacher behavior.[20]

Hallman has also developed some criteria for creativity, a term which tends to be used rather loosely. He specifies characteristics of creativity and conditions under which it is likely to flourish: (a) *connectedness:* the act of producing novelty through the combination of old materials, past learnings, and present experiences; (b) *originality:* surprise characteristics of the product; (c) *non-rationality:* operations below the rational level, on the spontaneous level and manifested through images and ideas; (d)

[19] Bruner, *Process of Education, op. cit.,* pp. 55–60.

[20] Ralph J. Hallman, "Creativity and Educational Philosophy," *Educational Theory,* XVII, No. 4 (January, 1967), p. 7.

creative traits: psychological health, non-defensiveness, valuing of independence, sensitivity to problems, capacity for ambiguity, and aesthetic interests; (e) *creative environments:* non-authoritarian and open.[21]

Creativity is a way of living which permits an individual to open himself to new experiences, ideas, and processes. The results ultimately can be tested and proven through conventional means. In a society in which it is difficult to know what the questions are, creative thinking is needed to cope with change and complexity. Fresh thinking is needed to produce new insights on old data and to bring about the discovery or invention of new data.

It seems inconceivable that there should be a shortage of fresh, imaginative thinking among children when they begin school in that way. To observe a young child is to watch seemingly inexhaustible energy. To talk with him is to subject yourself to constant *who, when, why, where,* and *how* questions. What happens to such children when they enter school and grow progressively *less* eager and enthusiastic in interest and activity?

Inquiry Methods. Suchman has studied methods of inquiry in elementary classrooms [22] and wondered whether teachers actually train children *out of* tendencies to ask questions. Teachers were found to ask eight to ten times as many questions as did children? Suchman then sought to stimulate children to ask questions. He used movies as stimulants to discussions. Interviewers responded to children's questions with "yes" or "no" responses, thus putting discussion responsibility on the *children.* The temptation appears to be for an adult to enter into a monolog when a child gives a brief response or question. In the Suchman study this approach was rejected in favor of patience: to provide *time* for children to ask questions leading to inquiry skills.

Formal steps for pupils in the Suchman study included: (a) "episode analysis"—the verification of facts shown in the movie, (b) "determination of relevance"—delineating the necessary conditions to what happened, (c) "induction of relational constructs"—the attempt to predict what else might have happened and might happen under different situations.

In helping children to develop inquiry skills, you will need to develop the ability to encourage children to go beyond superficial or premature conclusions. It will also take self-discipline to avoid telling children when and why they are wrong or partly wrong. Telling children the "right" answers appears to be a temptation for teachers. It *is* faster, but your role is promoter of learning rather than conserver of time. Some formal exercises in inquiry training may be useful in elementary schools. Encourage-

[21] *Ibid.*, pp. 3–4.

[22] J. Richard Suchman, *The Elementary School Training Program in Scientific Inquiry,* Title VII 1958 (Urbana: University of Illinois, June, 1962).

ment of questioning minds should be a continuing practice where child learning has priority over teacher talk.

It appears that a curriculum based on much freedom to explore and experiment with ideas and things is implied in Suchman's findings. Each pupil brings to the classroom his own thought "organizers." He has had unique experiences and his own system of analysis. The curriculum should provide experiences which will broaden each pupil and furnish systems for objective classification of the child's thoughts.

Critical Thinking. Another analysis of thinking focuses upon *critical* thinking. "By critical thinking, we mean the scrutiny of discourse for truth and validity," state Broudy, Smith, and Burnett. They suggest several criteria for analyzing critical thinking: (a) truth of the statement, (b) extent to which it follows from available evidence, (c) probability of the evidence available in comparison to alternatives.[23]

Children cannot be expected to attain this level of sophistication easily, particularly in their early years. Over the years they can develop cognitive skills necessary for critical thinking. It is a long, hard path from "because" explanations of behavior and statements to critical thinking.

Problem Solving

Varied cognitive skills should lead ultimately to the ability to solve several kinds of problems. Problem solving in a scientific manner, according to Sears, includes: (a) the ability to perceive problems and sift through solutions rather than be defeated by frustrations, (b) the ability to select from alternatives the ones to be tested "actively and economically," (c) the development of persistence with increasing age to the point where it is possible to master *difficult* problems.[24]

Henle has delineated some aids to problem solving capabilities. Classroom living should be seen as part of a total laboratory experience where thinking is *practiced rather than talked about until adulthood.* Steps suggested by Henle include:

1. Learning to ask right, relevant questions
2. Learning to look at details and seek inconsistencies
3. Learning to be interested in ideas
4. Holding critical ideas in abeyance to keep idea channels open
5. Learning to plan properly, to ask questions, and to delimit problem areas

[23] Harry S. Broudy, B. Othanel Smith, and Joe R. Burnett, *Democracy and Excellence in American Secondary Education* (Chicago: Rand McNally & Co., Inc., 1964), p. 55.

[24] Robert Sears, in Bruner, *Learning About Learning: A Conference Report, op. cit.,* pp. 4–5.

6. Learning to contemplate before reaching conclusions
7. Learning to test ideas and conclusions [25]

Learning to solve problems rationally should be an objective of the elementary curriculum, and pupils should be taught the principles of such thinking. These principles should then be practiced during each day. Problem solving should not be limited to "science" classes. Furthermore it should not be confined to formal learning situations. There are occasions in cafeterias, on playgrounds, and in other informal situations where children should be aided to rationally think through problems and solve them. While much school content will be obsolete very shortly, the ability to solve problems is a tool useful for a lifetime.

The preceding discussions concerning thinking processes and problem solving should not be seen as separate and distinct. You have read brief summaries of several experts on how they view different aspects of thinking and approaching problems. They share several emphases, including the need to provide children the freedom and time to explore the realms of thinking, and encouragement to attach personal meanings and ultimately verify their findings and conclusions. A curriculum based on these and similar viewpoints will provide many opportunities to learn the *processes* of thinking and problem solving. Facts will be incorporated when needed (as will drill and other learning activities) to develop the creative thinker for the present and future.

Motivation

Differences in motivation partially explain why children with apparent similarities often are very dissimilar in school achievement. A basic curriculum task is planning to stimulate, create, or extend each child's desire to do his best.

There is both short-term and long-range motivation. Short-term motivation is likely to be most functional for elementary children. It is based on current interests and needs. Limited interest spans and time concepts, particularly for the disadvantaged, limit the effectiveness of encouraging that type of learning which is based on what is good for children in the future. The present, with its personal and peer significance, is much more meaningful than is the future. Curriculum content which helps the child in the here-and-now is likely to create interest in and inclination to learning in the present and lead to long-term learning.

Both intrinsic and extrinsic motivations are used widely in schools. *Intrinsic motivation* is that which arises from within. It causes learning actions without threats, punishment, or rewards, and it can drive a child

[25] Mary Henle, in Bruner, *Learning About Learning: A Conference Report, op. cit.*, pp. 58–59.

to endless effort to attain a desired goal. The resulting interest is a learning stimulant. *Extrinsic motivation* occurs from without. There are various "softsell" and "hardsell" techniques. They range from subtle things such as grades and stars on a chart to harsh punishments.

Children engaged in meaningful activities seem to be highly motivated to learn. Learning can be pleasant and challenging. Good curriculum is basically good motivation since it is relevant to children.

Factors of Repetition, Drill, and Retention

"Pounding sense" into someone's head is a common reflection of faith in repetition and drill. Stressing the desirability of tough subjects reflects the belief that the mind can be strengthened like muscles. While these assumptions may have some validity if properly interpreted, they have severe limitations in relation to cognitive development. Let us briefly consider four related topics.

Repetition. Practice is a common process in learning. When repeated in a meaningful manner, learnings can be made permanent and transferable to other situations. Some subject areas provide many opportunities for repetition of related skills. Language is an example, for it is used continuously. Many forms of mathematics, on the other hand, are not used in normal pupil experiences. Repetition, if meaningful and interesting, can stimulate intellectual development. If dreary and worthless, it may cause daydreaming and rejection of other experiences valuable in cognitive development. Repetition which is identical is rarely stimulating; that which is supplementary, interpretive, and broadening can be provoking. The art and science involved here is to know how much repetition —and in what form—will contribute to intellectual development.

Drill. There are occasions when repetition of identical learning components may be of value. Drill is common in situations where memorization is the goal. Spelling is a case in point. Multiplication tables are another. These are low-level cognitive functions which may have some value if meaningful to pupils. When pupils reach an understanding of processes, they may desire to attain semi-automatic responses when they are faced with a need such as knowing how to spell a word or do an arithmetic problem. "Practice makes perfect" is a cliché which is used too casually. Drill probably has its place when a pupil sees that continuing errors are slowing him down or limiting his effectiveness.

Retention. If teaching could be equated to telling, it would be both easy and boring. Retention is far more than memorizing what the teacher talks about, and it more likely will occur if pupils are interested in the content and if there is personal meaning.

Structure. A further aid to retention is an understanding of the structure of the subject. Materials arranged in a fashion which shows relationships are more easily retained. An example which violates all of these factors is the requirement that pupils memorize the alphabetically arranged names of the more than ninety counties in their home state!

PHYSICAL AND PSYCHO-SOCIAL GROWTH

To observe children when they are alert and interested is to see how they respond with their whole beings. The "whole child" is an important factor in curriculum planning. The physical and psycho-social development of children will be considered only briefly in this textbook, but the aspects of development most significant for curriculum will be the main focus.

Physical Development

Curriculum planning and programs for healthy development are an accepted elementary school responsibility. (This is discussed at some length in Chapter 16.) Physical education is justifiable for its contribution to physical, social, character, and intellectual development.

General curriculum planning should reflect an awareness of the many physical factors which affect the potentialities and limitations for learning. The brain varies in its inherent efficiency, and it may even be damaged as a result of birth. While learning determines the extent and manner of development, inherited intellectual capacity places a *ceiling* on development. The nervous system provides the basic means for the individual to perceive his environment. The functioning of the senses of sight, hearing, touch, smell, and taste are determined in large measure by heredity. Sometimes the senses may be damaged, or they may be poorly stimulated by a defective or deficient environment. Learning is severely limited by such handicaps. A mulfunctioning digestive system may leave a child sick much of the time. Glands may improperly regulate bodily functions or fail to trigger a developmental stage. The combined consequences of physical factors are significant in terms of what a child can do and how he functions.

Maturation Factors. Physical maturation patterns in part determine the kinds of grade placement, scope, and sequence of content and learning activities appropriate for a particular age group. Formal reading is delayed until eye muscles have matured, and initial reading materials are printed in large type with much white space. Writing paper has wide spaces, and writing pencils used are large until the end of the primary grades when there is finer muscle control. The scope or depth of learning experiences planned is limited by physical endurance and agility, for example, primary grade field trips which must be brief and relatively free of difficult climbing. Sequence in the curriculum is planned to harmonize with physical factors such as extent of control and coordination of muscles, speed and endurance, length of time children can remain relatively passive, and extent of bone development.

Maturation refers primarily to inborn behavioral tendencies. Human beings seem to have few in comparison to animals. The longer they live, the fewer characteristics or actions which can be attributed *primarily* to genetic factors, although there are generalized growth patterns for humans. The length of time it takes for a human being to reach maturity increases the probabilities of other influences counterbalancing hereditary factors. Non-hereditary factors include nutrition, medical care, and environment, and the importance of such factors can be seen through a study of other cultures. Man has a common biological inheritance, yet the manner and timing of growth into that inheritance varies from culture to culture.

Man is *educable* as a consequence of his flexible growth patterns; animals are *trainable* within the limited responses built into their heredity. Yet man may also have some limitations built into his heredity. Retarded or limited physical potentialities should be recognized in curriculum planning. Physical handicaps, impaired vision or hearing, heart murmurs, and a number of other conditions affect not only physical education but also other types of activities which can be planned for some children.

Physical factors may vitally affect how a child feels about himself. They may determine to a degree what chances he is willing to take when faced with new situations. If he feels awkward, he may hesitate to give a report, point out a city on a large map in front of his peers, or experiment with painting. If he feels uncomfortable about being or seeming to be ugly or gangly or fat or thin or tall or short, he may withdraw from open participation in class activities. On the other hand, if a child is attractive, healthy, energetic, and agile, he may develop a confidence and drive which extend into his learning attitudes and activities. How others see physical conditions is less significant than how a child *perceives* his physical self and how he *feels* about it. Inherited characteristics and those influenced by environment are important largely to the extent determined by an individual and those around him. Achievements of those with great physical handicaps point out the potentialities when an individual believes in himself as he is and in what he can become.

Home Influences. Home conditions reflected in a child's development are significant in curriculum planning. In part they determine the extent and direction of the development of native intelligence and physical potentialities. Intellectual capacities largely unreached as a result of a barren environment may remain dormant. Uncomfortable, crowded beds may lead to tired bodies and minds. Uncorrected vision, hearing, or other physical defects sorely limit learning potentialities. Chaotic, unhappy home conditions may produce tenseness, nervousness, and irritability. Children may arrive at school hungry. They may be tired from long bus rides or walks to school. They may be frightened from experiences on the way to school. As a child responds physically to these conditions, his readiness and capacity for curricular experiences are affected positively or negatively. Curriculum planning should reflect awareness of physical factors affected by home conditions.

It is important to know the general curriculum implications of normal and defective physical development patterns for different ages. Even if you know the physical factors for a particular grade, you will find that there is a wide range of behaviors in that grade resulting from individual factors, and they should be considered in relation to average growth patterns when planning curriculum for a class.

Psycho-Social Development

Children's psycho-social development, according to Erikson, progresses through a series of steps.[26] Success in one contributes to success in future steps; failure in one blocks success in future ones. This suggests that curriculum planning should be compatible with children's developmental stages, including both physical and psycho-social. Likewise a sound curriculum includes provision for compensating for earlier inadequacies of children. The extent to which this can be done successfully is debatable. At a minimum, you can attempt to be understanding and supportive when children continue to suffer from previous failures in their developmental stages.

Erikson's early stages are labeled "infancy," "early childhood," and "play age." Successful completion of these ages, according to Erikson, contributes to a basic trust of self and world, good will for others, and a sense of dignity and independence. The "successful" child has experimented with himself and his social and physical environment. He has found that it is "good" and safe to master himself and his world and that he is not alone in meeting his challenge. On the other hand, he has not been smothered. He is an *individual* with dignity and worth, and independence.

The child who has not experienced success in his preschool years may feel somewhat a part of the world and yet apart from it. He may feel

[26] Erik Erikson, *Childhood and Society* (New York: W. W. Norton & Co., Inc., 1963).

negatively about himself and others. He may rebel against those perceived as blocking his needs and wishes.

The child who has been successful is prepared to enter school. He is likely to trust school personnel and to open himself to their assistance. Having richly experienced his world, he is interested in learning even more. Confident of his capacities, he enters school with minimal hostilities and frustrations. He is reasonably free of distorted perceptions of himself and his world and willing to enter into productive relations with school peers and adult personnel. The successful child is likely to have the kinds of experiences, motivations, and intellectual functioning which contribute to school success.

The child who "failed" in the preschool years may lack the positive attributes noted previously or may even develop pathological tendencies. In the latter case, the classroom teacher can do limited teaching unless supplementary professional help is available. The "curriculum" for a sick child is therapy and counseling. The regular curriculum assumes a minor role until the effects of preschool years can be offset to a degree.

During the elementary school years, the successful child experiences strengths Erikson calls "method" and "competence." The child learns to use his energies to produce things and thereby earn recognition. Structured instruction replaces free play, and systematic teaching can be started. Failing to achieve method and competence, the child may develop a sense of inferiority. His capacities and anatomy may seem inadequate for the tasks at hand. These feelings may originate in the home, and the school may not provide enough challenging and successful experiences to overcome them. The school curriculum should provide a significant environment by helping children to develop work-related competencies. Learning to utilize his competencies well, the child is on the road to a sense of "identity" based on the confidence built up during the elementary school age.

Erikson has provided a frame of reference in analyzing children's psycho-social development. The school's curriculum should reflect an awareness of how each child is likely to progress through what Erikson calls "ages and stages" with maximum success. It should also minimize developmental difficulties that arise. A meaningful curriculum, supplemented by the service of specialized personnel, can do much to help each child to grow into maturity.

FAMILY FACTORS

The family in American society provides not only a child's genetic inheritance but also his orientation toward himself, others, and life. The American family does not brand a child for life with the finality found in some stable societies. However, the family's effects on behavior are so important that familial factors should be considered in planning both the curriculum and related instructional strategies. Combined with racial, ethnic, national, and personal factors, the family factors are significant determinants of a child's needs and success in school.

Balance of Influences

The school is in a delicate position if it attempts to bring about behavioral change in children that is incompatible with their home environment. It may teach values, ideas, or facts *contrary* to those of the home; however, its best approach is to teach *cultural alternatives*. This permits a child to maintain respect and affection for parents while forming his own personal and unique living styles—selected from alternatives learned at home and school.

There is difficulty in inducing desirable behavioral changes at variance with home learnings. The family makes its influence felt at a significant time when a young child is relatively isolated from other influences, is in need of intimacy and affection, and is developing his communications with other human beings. Loyal to family ties, a child may be suspicious of contradictory school teachings. He may, if resentful of parents, reject school personnel as mere extensions of parental authority. Bitter about his family, a child may accept school teachings gladly in some cases. School success or failure may even be used by children to reward or punish their parents. The significance of a family's effect upon a child's learning is largely a consequence of how the child feels about his home and school.

The family provides a child's basic social system for several formative years. To a large extent the family also determines the kinds and numbers of individuals with whom a child will interact. A child's behavior will reflect his family's neighborhood, whether crowded ghetto, spacious suburb, or isolated mountain village. In a manner comparable to the soil in which seeds are planted, a child grows and blossoms largely in proportion to his external and internal resources. A child is not an absolute prisoner of his family and neighborhood. His *perception* of his present and potential circumstances determines whether they are a help, hindrance, or challenge. A supportive, competent teacher is in a strategic position to help children attain their maximum potentialities within the limitations set by family.

Some of the family's influences are related to social development, others to intellectual development. Family background influences children in a host of ways, for example: (a) selective perception, the things a child will notice, experience, or ignore; (b) sense of security and feelings in facing new situations; (c) conceptions of the purpose of living, in relation to man and the supernatural; (d) the persons who serve as models of "success"; (e) the development of goals and degree of confidence and know-how in attaining them; (f) adequacy of self-concept; (g) patterns of psychological reactions to guilt, failure, fears, problems, and challenges.

The Family's Continuing Imprint

The family contributes the "raw materials" for a child. Then it molds the child through experiences, words, expressions, gestures, smiles, caresses, frowns, and many other verbal and non-verbal means. By what it does and does not do, a family serves as a powerful force in a child's development. Education and other experiences can modify the external man, refine him, and redirect his motivations and energies. However, on the feeling level, a man reflects the image of childhood. Only partly does a man outgrow the child stage. Successful living at the elementary school level is an important determinant of how confidently and successfully the child becomes a man—without regrets or regressions. The maturity of parents in nurturing the independence of the child likewise is an important factor for successful maturation.

In a rapidly changing world, with which the family interacts and which enters the home by means of the mass media, the family loses much of its traditional power in child development. Margaret Mead claims that a five-year-old today is more separated from his parents than persons several generations apart used to be.[27]

Even with the decreased impact, the family is still significant. There are varying degrees of family forces and children's perceptions of and reactions to those forces. The family continues to be an important consideration in planning curriculum.

CULTURAL AND SOCIOECONOMIC FACTORS

An informative comparison of American and other children has been provided by Brooks. He notes that in the United States, an eleven-year-old seems quite "normal" when he wiggles energetically, is untidy, and craves peer approval. His Japanese counterpart can sit quietly with folded hands. Some African peers are inclined to seek parental approval. To illustrate further: The average American child is expected to respond to test items related to colors, patterns, and spatial relationships. This kind of task would be meaningless to an Arab nomad child who lives

[27] Margaret Mead, *The School in American Culture,* The Inglis Lecture (Cambridge, Mass.: Harvard University Press, 1955), p. 11.

in a colorless desert world where "graven" images are frowned on, and where there are few shapes to observe.[28] (Culturally disadvantaged Americans also may have difficulties with some of the expectations of American schools!) Biologically such children would be comparable, yet their cultural environment contributes to radically different behavior and reactions.

The culture includes organized ways of doing things and reacting to them, ways of believing, and knowledge from the past. These ways are comfortable as a result of their being familiar. The school in the complex American society has been entrusted with passing on many traditional cultural values. "The American Way of Life," variously interpreted, contributes curriculum content which helps to make American schools distinctive in many ways. Rapidly changing American culture makes it difficult to select and revise specific content compatible with venerated traditions and emerging expectations.

The School Response

There are differences of opinion on the school's role in relation to cultural expectations. Some advocate school efforts to *change* the culture. Others deny that this is a school role. Regardless of the position taken, the school in our society is limited in the extent it can change the culture—both by the difficulty of altering built-in cultural values and by the elusiveness of the American culture. It is complex, changing, and variegated, and is a complicating factor in curriculum selection and design.

Within the American culture, there are a number of socioeconomic groups which both reflect and deflect the larger values. Religious, racial, and ethnic variations are intertwined with socioeconomic class. It is important to note that socioeconomic class does not inevitably produce certain types of behavior. However, class is a *major* behavior determinant. It must be considered in studying children's interests, motivations, and needs.

Class Differences

The middle class child may come to school both motivated and equipped to be successful in school tasks. He is inclined to have correct and "proper" speech patterns, travel experiences, acquaintance with reading materials and skills, intellectual interests, good manners, personal habits, and other characteristics directly and subtly compatible with those of teachers. He comes with better odds for success in American schools.

[28] John J. Brooks, in Helen Robison (ed.), *Precedents and Promises in the Curriculum Field* (New York: Teachers College Press, Columbia University, 1966), pp. 67–68.

The lower class child often has a desire to learn, for he sees "education" as a means to improvement. However, he may lack the necessary social, personal, language, and study tools. School to an extent is an alien place to many children, and learning to live there is a difficult task for them. He must learn the school-like language, how to study and take tests, and how to extend understandings of the abstract that are so common in school but not in his home.

In view of the dramatic efforts to provide effective education for the disadvantaged, it is appropriate to elaborate on the consequences of being born into a lower socioeconomic class. Instructional applications of these factors are developed in Part IV. Lower class children often have difficulties in living up to the expectations of teachers that include punctuality, neatness, cooperation, and doing work independently. The children may be deficient in those very ways which are common to the middle class. There are three approaches open to schools in planning a curriculum for the lower class: (a) The curriculum itself can be purged of purely middle class values and objectives. (b) The children can be given special experiences to compensate for inadequacies. (c) Parents can be helped to assist their children.

A Classless School

Broudy calls for a classless school. He also advocates recognition of some strengths to be found among the lower class: toughness and shrewdness when faced with difficulties, self-reliance, quickness of reaction, and inclination to enjoy life's varied experiences. Broudy recommends the combination of these characteristics with what he calls the "solid virtues" of the middle class such as thrift, industry, and dependability. The model for a classless society, Broudy claims, can be developed from the "wisdom of the ages"—from the Greeks, Jews, Christians, and from the science and literature of West and East.[29]

While seeking to become less middle class oriented, the school can compensate for some of the inadequacies of the lower class environment. It can maintain high expectations but permit individual children to grow in ways consistent with their family and class patterns. The school can exhibit respect and dignity for those patterns while presenting alternatives which may be more acceptable in the American cultural mainstream. Recently efforts have been made to intervene in children's lives to seek to break the lower class cycle of poverty, wherein poverty breeds poverty. The search will be continued to find ways to provide equal opportunities for all children regardless of their origins.

[29] Harry S. Broudy, "Schooling for the Culturally Deprived," *The Teachers College Journal,* XXXVII, No. 1 (October, 1965), p. 18.

While Broudy calls attention to the real or potential strengths of the lower class, others point to some weaknesses of the middle class, particularly when segregated in the suburbs. Suburbia is often called a private public school, where children are deprived of experiences with the varied ages and conditions of mankind. It is a carefully controlled setting for creating the kinds of values, practices, and knowledge deemed "good." For children with a reasonable degree of native intelligence, suburbia nurtures them as middle class children. The rebel, the low achiever, or the low-ability child may experience severe pressures to conform to a carefully selected environment.

Middle class values continue to be the prevalent ones emphasized in the school curriculum. In the great cities and in depressed rural areas, there should be adaptations along the lines suggested by Broudy. Where taught, middle class values should not be taught as *replacements* for values learned at home. Rather they should be presented as *alternatives* to be used in specific situations such as in a job setting which requires them. A child should not be encouraged to reject his parents' or friends' values. Rather he should learn how to be part of the larger society as well as the sub-culture which nurtured him.

READINESS AND DEVELOPMENTAL TASKS

It is important to regain perspective after the preceding discussions of the *separate* physical, psycho-social, and cultural factors which mold children's lives. The concepts of readiness and developmental tasks now will be discussed to emphasize the manner in which a unified being reacts to growth and proceeds from one stage of development to the next.

Readiness is a term used to describe the period in a child's life when he is uniquely prepared for a concept, skill, idea, or activity. It is a consequence of time, experience, capacity, and other factors. The school plans a curriculum which facilitates the development of readiness and builds on what lies waiting development. The school does not "push" readiness but rather provides an environment in which children can grow and will *want* to grow. The school is not passive to the point of carelessness in capitalizing on every opportunity to promote growth. It is not efficient either to plan learning activities prematurely or to delay beyond the point of readiness.

Developmental tasks are tasks which when completed produce a sense of satisfaction for children. The tasks are derived from physiological needs, social expectations, and psychological needs. There are tasks which have been identified for each age group, and these provide *general* guidelines in planning the curriculum. Of course no child needs precisely the same developmental tasks as have been identified for his age group.

It is desirable to *harmonize* the curriculum with developmental tasks which have been identified for various age groups and *adapt* them to individuals.

Each individual child has a unique pattern of development with variations from his peer group's developmental tasks. The curriculum should help him to attain his own developmental tasks. They are the stepping stones from which an individual proceeds. Faltering on one step holds an individual back and calls attention to the individual as a "failure." He may internalize his failure. If the faltering is temporary, the effects may be limited; if prolonged, his failure may be a factor in his life years later. Hopefully the school will provide many opportunities for success in a diverse and broad curriculum.

EXCEPTIONAL CHILDREN

Exceptional mental, emotional, or physical conditions merit considerations in general curriculum planning. In recent years there has been an extensive development of special programs, materials, equipment, and facilities for exceptional children—those with exceptional physical, mental, emotional, and social conditions which distinguish them from their peers. The number of specially prepared teachers to instruct these children has substantially increased. To an extent children who vary significantly from most children in a grade level have been assigned to special rooms in many schools and curriculum planning for these children may be left to "special teachers."

Actually even where there are some special provisions for exceptional children, the regular classroom teacher cannot abdicate responsibility for *any* child. Many schools do not have rooms for exceptional children, often for financial reasons. Even in situations where there are special rooms, efforts are made to include children in as many school programs as possible, for example, regular classes such as physical education or music, or academic classes such as reading or social studies. Exceptional children may be more similar to than different from all the children in their general age group. This generalization seems to hold for the exceptional children found in schools: the gifted, the mentally retarded, the physically handicapped, and the emotionally disturbed.

While commendable, establishment of special programs may result in a false assumption that regular classroom teachers have *no* responsibility for exceptional children. The other extreme position is that *no* special teachers are needed. A reasonable position is: (a) Regular classroom teachers and typical children have capabilities for helping atypical children. (b) Specially prepared teachers are needed to teach and to help others who share responsibilities for exceptional children. Special teachers may teach atypical children for part or most of a day all year, or they may prepare children to participate in a regular classroom for an increasing amount of the day as soon as possible in the school year.

The limitations imposed by a child's condition will determine the desirability of his being segregated into separate rooms (rarely in separate buildings) taught by special teachers. Some special teachers serve primarily as consultants and supplementary teachers who (a) provide some individualized aid for an exceptional child assigned to a regular classroom; (b) help the classroom teacher with instructional planning; and (c) consult with other school personnel, parents, and the community to provide good education for exceptional children.

Arguments for segregated classes for the gifted are couched in terms of increasing the speed, breadth, and depth of coverage of content. Since the gifted—usually classified in terms of academic strengths—are not equally proficient in all factors, it seems unwise to segregate them totally even in the most academically oriented school. Regardless of the means, it is important to seek ways to help the gifted attain their potentiality.

LEARNING THROUGH OBSERVATIONS

A small child stands in her back yard screaming, jumping, and flailing her arms. Her father, a very intelligent and loving parent, calmly states that his daughter's actions have convinced him that people are born with wicked tendencies. This is an illustration of how adults may view children. Others observing the same child might have come to very different conclusions.

Certain cautions should be remembered prior to viewing children in classroom settings:

1. We tend to have selective perceptions, that is, we "see" what we expect to see, want to see, or are trained to see.
2. We tend to over-generalize; we attach more significance than is valid to limited observations or events and we apply conclusions from them to many situations in the present and future, to individuals and groups.

While observing and studying children, you can identify certain general characteristics. Having these patterns in mind, you can determine the extent and manner in which an individual child *appears* to be deviating from generalized tendencies for his age. Some deviations from "normal" traits should be expected. Conclusions should be drawn *very cautiously*, and where possible in consultation with other professional personnel. Having a valid mental conception of what children are like, curriculum study can be meaningful. Preparation of instructional units—discussed in the next chapter—can be realistically conducted. Learning how to observe children in their rich diversity can lead to effective curriculum provisions for both individuals and groups of individuals.

PROJECTS AND READINGS

1. SUPERCALIFRAGILISTICEXPIALIDOCIOUS. A second grader drills himself at home until he can spell this "word" from the jacket of a Walt Disney record. Why do you think that he did this without any encouragement? What would be necessary in the school setting to develop a similar desire to learn?

2. A reading of a book on A. S. Neil's *Summerhill*, a most unorthodox school, provides some interesting viewpoints on the nature of man and education. Which of these viewpoints do you feel are not applicable to a public school in America? Which ones are? Why the difference?

3. "If you treat an individual as he is, he will stay as he is. But if you treat him as if he were what he ought to be and could be, he will become as he ought to be and could be." [Goethe, quoted in *Together* (January 1968), p. 62.] To what extent do you feel that this viewpoint is idealistic? Realistic? How could it be applied in the schools?

4. Some schools have established free breakfasts for needy children, health clinics for such children and their parents, social welfare programs, and a variety of other programs not directly related to teaching as narrowly conceived. To what extent may such programs limit the school's effectiveness in its *teaching role* (by spreading resources too thin, to name but one possibility)? Is there any alternative to attempting to meet the needs of the total child (for example, leaving non-teaching functions to others)?

5. There are indications that lack of enough stimulation of the brain in early years is closely related to underachievement in school. There may be few reading materials in some homes. Children may have never been in a library before using one in school. Some have never been more than a mile from their homes. What are the most significant findings growing out of the evaluation of Head Start, and related programs, which should be reflected in the elementary school curriculum?

6. With the current emphasis being placed on the disadvantaged, the academically gifted may be neglected. What are some of the important ways in which the gifted can be helped to attain their potentiality in a regular classroom? In special sections? Good sources of information and ideas are books and articles by men such as E. P. Torrance, J. W. Getzels, and P. W. Jackson. The most recent edition of the *Encyclopedia of Educational Research* edited by Walker S. Monroe (New York: The Macmillan Co.) is also a good source of information on special topics such as this.

7. "Man acts upon his ideas. His irrational acts no less than his rational acts are guided by what he thinks, what he believes, what he anticipates. . . . Every man, through 'cognitive work,' attempts to construct for himself a meaningful world . . ." [David Krech, *et al.*, *Individual in Society* (New York: McGraw-Hill Book Co., 1966, p. 17).] Granted that this is true, how far can a teacher of many children in a classroom permit an individual pupil to

find his own meanings? How does this interfere with the demands which the school district and community place upon the teacher?

8. Transfer—the application of something learned in one situation to another—is not automatic. It is more likely to occur when pupils are helped to see similarities to comparable situations, to anticipate applications, and (as noted in Chapter 3) to understand the structure of the knowledge being studied. Further, practice under varied circumstances contributes to transferability. What aspects of the elementary curriculum are so remote from applicability that transfer seems unlikely? To what extent do children's developmental tasks have transfer potential to varied situations today and in the future?

9. "There is, I am sure, a physical process at the basis of learning. In another 25 years or so, conferences on teaching–learning may well be addressed by neuropharmacologists who will propose the control of learning by drugs; brain physiologists who will be able to stimulate neural regions by control learning, and computer scientists who will have created astonishing analogues of the human brain." (H. S. Broudy, "Evaluation of Teacher Education Criteria," in an address prepared for delivery at the Conference sponsored by the International Council on Education for Teaching, University of Malaya, August 3, 1970.) What does this statement suggest concerning the many different kinds of personnel who in the future will help to develop curriculum and instructional strategies? How can teachers develop means of keeping abreast of developments in the many disciplines which are important to an understanding of teaching and of learning?

10. "If they are taught efficiently, they will learn," says psychologist Kenneth B. Clark of ghetto children (*Washington Post,* July 19, 1970). While not denying parental and neighborhood influences, stressed by James Coleman in his massive study in the 1950's, he claims that poor teaching rather than the environment should be blamed for pupil failure and advocates incentives for teachers who raise achievement levels. Which viewpoint seems more prevalent today? To what extent are both correct? What are ways of relating both positions to the curriculum?

11. Today's children and youth have been described as being anti-materialistic, anti-competitive, and anti-achievement as well as deeply concerned about societal and world conditions, injustice, and superficiality. What does this suggest about motivating learning, about aspects of today's curriculum that make sense, and about needed changes?

12. Burns and Brooks advocate practicing what we *know* concerning individual instruction, "psychologically structured learning, discovery methods, student sequenced subject matter, reinforcement, stimulus control, diagnostic techniques, learning hierachies, feedback, multisensory methods, cueing, and instruction in processes." [Richard W. Burns and Gary D. Brooks, "The Need for Curriculum Reform," *Educational Technology,* X, No. 4 (April, 1970), p. 11.] What are the major reasons for not doing this in organizing content and method as well as in preparing materials? What are the common threads in the above factors?

13. "To the now culture, history often seems to be a prison. By its insistence on comparison, it seems to them to deny the uniqueness of their own passionate existence. It is the disciplinary equivalent of their parents, speaking of other times when things were different." [Hazel W. Hertzberg, "The Now

Culture: Some Implications for Teacher Training Programs," *Social Education,* XXXIV, No. 3 (March, 1970), p. 277.] What should be done to relate the curriculum to the "here and now"? What are the probable consequences of severing emotional and intellectual ties to the past? Is this inevitable?

14. The nature-nurture issue has been revived by Arthur B. Jensen. He claims that children's genetic inheritances account for up to 80 per cent of variations in intelligence scores. A balanced understanding of Jensen's claims and the counter-claims should be developed, in relation to implications both for learning theory and social issues such as desegregation. Studies of children's inheritances and social nurture will indicate a dynamic interaction of the two forces and their significance for curriculum.

15. "The major scandal of our day." Thus Keliher characterizes the 1,000,000 American children whom she claims are neglected (migrant children, children whose working mothers leave them alone, and so forth). In addition, she is concerned about the non-poor who are deprived of meaning in their daily lives. (Alice Keliher, in a speech to the Midwestern Association for the Education of Young Children, Detroit, April 30, 1970.) How much should school personnel do to compensate for child neglect? Should schools work with existing child-care agencies or add special personnel to help deprived children? What is a meaningful curriculum for such children?

5

Designs for Teaching and Learning

Ultimately the test for effective teaching is the design and direction of experiences which will increase the learning of children. A conceptual understanding of society, of strategies for teaching, and of the learners in general is desirable and "practical." This mastery is demonstrated when you can organize pupils, materials and equipment, space, time, and other resources in a manner which helps children to change their behavior or potentialities for acting.

Organizing for teaching and learning was never a simple matter. It would be difficult enough if it were possible to teach a "class." Now that it is essential to help each child attain his maximum growth, the task becomes increasingly complex. To provide meaningful learning experiences for individuals, particularly when there are many of them, is a challenge of great magnitude. Then there are the seemingly endless expectations from the school system and the society at large, from the neighborhood to Capitol Hill and the White House.

Fortunately there are some generalizations available to guide the novice organizing learning experiences. As noted previously, conceptualizations of the teacher's role provides a degree of security. Individual pupils vary greatly, but they also progress in many similar ways. Often it is a matter of timing, intensity, or direction—variations of the generalized patterns of learning for children of a given age. A study of these generalizations will provide a grasp of what is involved in teaching. From an understanding of what generally applies, you are then better prepared to permit individual variations, and at the same time you can apply these understandings to the total group or small groups. Furthermore, an overall grasp can enable you to provide active leadership on those occasions when you encourage children, within their level of maturity, to plan learning experiences. Without a firm grasp of the task at hand, you may find it necessary to follow blindly suggestions in textbooks, in curriculum guides, or in professional books and magazines. With a firm understanding of designs for teaching and learning, you can more intelligently utilize these varied references for their worth, as *sources of ideas.*

While it is true that teaching is to an extent an art, each teacher needs to check his ideas against the ideas and insights of others. A conceptualization of teaching and learning designs must be in harmony with democratic ideals, with the needs of children, with a school's or system's objectives. Within this framework, you should be able to plan instruction which capitalizes on your unique strengths and assets. Nothing in the following sections suggests that *method* in itself is productive. Only to the extent that those ideas are interpreted and applied intelligently can they improve instruction. Fortunately for children, there are no 1000 tricks which can be put into a bag and doled out regularly, and their absence in teaching can create some insecurity in the novice teacher; it also may add a challenge. The capacity to design learning experiences is an essential ingredient in your professional preparation.

Curricular design is an effort to establish a miniature classroom society simplified and graded appropriately for children. Here the group creates much of the learning atmosphere—whether positive, negative, or neutral —both in cooperation with the teacher and sometimes in opposition to him. Under ideal conditions the miniature society is planned to help the whole child to grow, and efforts are planned inside and outside the classroom to attain the maximum development. Learning and growth can be promoted for their utility in the here-and-now, and for "transfer" into other times and other places.

As has been noted, each child and teacher brings into the classroom individual differences of an almost unbelievable assortment while the society has developed almost impossibly varied expectations. Fortunately there are generalizations which can guide you *in your search* for curriculum planning competence. Applied with discretion, some of the ideas which follow can provide a map for planning instruction which makes sense in terms of helping children become their best selves, for their own individual welfare and for that of their society.

FORMATION OF OBJECTIVES

As in traveling, to attain curriculum objectives you must know where you are going if you are going to get there. Instruction is far from a haphazard matter. While instruction in a totalitarian state is far more prescriptive, instruction in democracy is not a state of muddling through to satisfy the whims of individual teachers. Certain objectives provide flexible guidance in meeting varied expectations.

The ability to develop educational objectives with clarity and specificity is a valuable asset, and these factors are crucial if you are to be able to plan wisely and then to adapt intelligently. Planned instructional activities are means to attaining educational objectives. While teaching a unit, you can adapt plans to new circumstances that arise in teaching. Making plans and adapting them avoids two extremes: (a) complete rigidity in which the teacher bulldozes over all obstacles to carry out plans for the day, (b) teaching in which the teacher attaches himself to any interesting idea passing by and is carried aimlessly away to some unplanned destination.

In Chapter 1 we noted that there are different sources of objectives. We also noted the desirability of stating objectives specifically in terms of how pupils should live and think as a result of learning. Before extending those introductory ideas let us examine a precise definition of an objective by Mager:

> An objective is an *intent* communicated by a statement describing a proposed change in a learner—a statement of what the learner is to be like when he has successfully completed a learning experience.[1]

Curriculum goals should be developed in relation to expected outcomes. Bloom and others classify possible outcomes into three broad categories: (a) knowledge and understanding; (b) attitudes, ideals, and appreciations; (c) skills, habits, and behavior patterns. You will want to teach for different outcomes at different times and under different circumstances.[2]

Douglass suggests steps to determine which instructional objectives you may wish to emphasize. These steps may also be used to analyze and study sample units of work prepared by others.

1. Determine the objectives of education in terms of the kind of end product desired.
2. Determine for each of the characteristics of the kind of person desired the necessary or contributory information, attitudes, interests, skills, habits, tastes, concepts, principles, and understandings.
3. Select and arrange according to the pupil's interests, abilities, and

[1] Robert F. Mager, *Preparing Objectives for Programmed Instruction* (San Francisco: Fearon Publishers, Inc., 1962), p. 3.

[2] Benjamin S. Bloom (ed.), *Taxonomy of Educational Objectives: The Classification of Educational Objectives. Handbook I: Cognitive Domain* (New York: Longmans, Green, & Co., Ltd., 1956), p. 5.

> previous curricular materials that will result in the development of the necessary information, skills, attitudes, etc.[3]

In selecting objectives, certain criteria are helpful in estimating their validity and value. Several sources of objectives are available.

Legal authority sometimes sets objectives for the schools, for example, an understanding of democracy and communism. Such legally determined objectives may be decided upon by a state legislature, state education agency, or local school board. They include such diverse topics as alcoholism, smoking, drugs, humane treatment of animals, dangers of communism, and free enterprise. Sometimes the objectives are designed to encourage students to do something, in other cases to avoid something.

Science is a source of educational objectives. The scientific method is one of the means of finding self-evident truth, and its application to all areas of study is a basic objective. It is difficult to do this with the fine arts or with values.

Democratic society, as a reflection of the consensus and government of the community, is a source of American school objectives. The school, it is said, should seek out those accepted characteristics of the society and prepare students to live successfully in that society. Democracy is a major value in our society, and the implementation of democratic ideals and processes is a major objective.

Academic disciplines suggest distinct objectives. Historians, mathematicians, and other academicians particularly in recent years have studied their discliplines, selected content appropriate for different grade levels, and have suggested specific methods and materials. Content has been divided into sequence to enable pupils to build on previous learnings in earlier grades. The academicians often tend to stress the logical organization of content rather than the psychological factors of learning. They imply that children start in a school system and remain there through the years, thus securing a balanced education. They further suggest that all children learn in the logical manner of the specialists. Textbooks, reflecting this tendency, are organized along these lines and often curriculum objectives reflect "mastery" of their content.

Children's needs are a source of objectives. To help children grow intellectually, physically, socially, and morally, the school develops a number of objectives. The so-called child-centered school particularly emphasizes children as the main source of educational objectives. Their interests and needs provide excellent motivation and preparation for

[3] Harl R. Douglass (ed.), *The High School Curriculum*, Third Edition (New York: The Ronald Press Co., 1964), p. 32.

effective living now and in adult life, yet some people question what significant learnings would be neglected if only these needs and interests were used in selecting curriculum content.

Eternal truths as contained in the great books and in humanistic traditions offer objectives. Those values and ideals which have survived the test of time are thought better by some than those which may be fleeting. Opponents of the excessive use of the past as a source of objectives question the transfer of old ideas into new settings and object to verbal emphasis in place of experience. There has been some tendency to presume that there is automatic transfer of knowledge to contemporary society. Where "eternal" values provide objectives, a conscious effort should be made to help children apply those values to today's conditions, and practical as well as ideal applications should be studied. Particular care should be taken to avoid an excessive reliance upon the past. One genius of democracy has been its capacity to translate the values of the past, for example, dignity of the individual, into the present setting.

Moral authority is a limited source of providing objectives for public schools. Since the United States is a pluralistic society, the use of ethical, divinely inspired sources to provide objectives sets up almost insurmountable obstacles. It is legal to teach about ethical systems, according to the Supreme Court; it is not permissible to indoctrinate through word or dead in favor of a particular creed or religious body. School objectives do tend to be moral, a reflection of morality embedded in the society. Character education, reflecting values such as those contained in scout oaths, is broad enough to be permissible in terms of constitutional law, yet its effect upon behavior is open to considerable doubt.

Private schools may select eternal values and moral objectives. The public schools are more likely to depend on legal, scientific, societal, and child bases for selecting objectives. This does not imply that they do not support "eternal" or "moral" objectives, but that those aims cannot be the primary focus of curriculum. The school must serve all the people as long as their objectives are consistent with democracy. Establishing priorities is a difficult problem, for there is limited energy, time, and resources. To attempt to do everything is not realistic. Hence it becomes necessary to select certain objectives from among many *acceptable* ones.

Special attention should be paid to the ideals of democracy as a basic source of educational objectives. All that goes on in the school should prepare the child for democratic living today and give him varied, meaningful practice in such a way of life. In addition, the curriculum should be planned to provide for transfer into adult life. All curriculum areas should make their contributions since each can help to develop the whole man—both today and in the future.

Objectives in a Democracy

What are the objectives for democracy's schools? Obviously they vary, but certain ones seem to persist. One is a faith in a free search for the truth. Bruce indicates that there are two fundamental attitudes in a democracy—free sharing and continuous search.[4] With the increasing numbers of societies in which the search for truth is curtailed by centralized policy makers, it is important to assert democracy's basic faith in free inquiry. Thomas Jefferson caught the spirit of free men when he wrote:

> I am not an advocate for frequent changes in laws and constitutions. But laws and institutions must go hand in hand with the progress of the human mind. As that becomes more developed, more enlightened, as new discoveries are made, new truths discovered and manners and opinions change, with change and circumstances, institutions must advance also to keep pace with the times.[5]

While the American society has changed from that envisioned by Jefferson, an effort has been made to keep the individual as the cornerstone of democratic society. The Citizenship Education Project,[6] old in years but fresh in spirit, notes that certain conditions should prevail: (a) Each person has worth, and his well-being is important. (b) Each person should have maximum freedom as long as it does not endanger the general welfare. (c) Each person should be judged on his individual merit. (d) Each person has rights and liberties equal to every other citizen. The Citizenship Education Project writers further claim that each individual has "basic social guarantees" (religion, inquiry, speech, press, and public education). Certain rights to life and liberty, to a fair trial, and freedom from unjust laws are guaranteed or implied. At the same time, the democratic tradition stresses *responsibilities* as well as rights. These responsibilities are to self, others, and nation.

The rights certified in the Bill of Rights and in other sources are generally applicable to all citizens, although they often are not observed for children. *Due process,* rather than arbitrary rule enforcement, should prevail in democracy's classrooms. Children do have rights and responsibilities. You as a teacher are entrusted to guide children to an internalized understanding and practice of both. *Democracy is a way of living.*

[4] William Bruce, *Principles of Democratic Education* (Englewood Cliffs, N.J.: Prentice-Hall, Inc., 1939), p. 73.

[5] Written at the age of 73 in a letter to Samuel Kerchaval from Monticello, July 12, 1816. Engraved in stone at the Thomas Jefferson Memorial, Washington, D.C.

[6] Adapted from Citizenship Education Project, *Basic Premises of American Liberty* (New York: Teachers College Press, Columbia University, 1952), pp. 1–5.

Organizing the classroom as a living laboratory of democracy is one of the most important contributions you can make in attaining democratic objectives.

The teacher is the official leader of the classroom miniature democracy. This is partly a contradiction since it suggests that the classroom is not a pure democracy. The larger society has *designated* an official leader, in the assumption that full citizenship rights must be delayed until an individual has lived a certain number of years, usually 21, and hence the teacher is expected to *train* children and to teach about democracy. There is often more of a tendency to indoctrinate children concerning the facts of freedom rather than to enable them to experience living it in a democratic classroom.

Dangers of Indoctrination

When does teaching about democracy become indoctrination? How much indoctrination can be permitted before democracy is undermined? These are perplexing questions in a world filled with ideologies in which the truth is promoted through every means available in modern technology and organizational techniques. Democracy does have its intellectual and ideological bases—can it trust children (or adults) to find these bases through experience? If the answer is yes, at what ages does this experience meaningfully begin? At what point, if any, should the teacher impose his will and his ways upon pupils?

It is easy to rationalize teacher domination and force with the idea that the teacher knows what's best for children. The temptation is to *tell* children about democracy—as a faraway goal, years in the future. Democracy is seemingly a fragile instrument for developing the uniqueness of individuals. It is nurtured in a carefully designed classroom laboratory where it can take roots and blossom. The vegetable gardener does not force growth; he provides the conditions. He prevents damage to his garden plot. He waters and feeds, in the faith that under the right conditions predictable growth will occur. We see that the democratic *nurture* of children must begin during the formative years and continue throughout maturity. The involvement of children should be genuine and honest dealing with real issues for which children have both interest and responsibility.

It must be emphasized that it is unlikely that anyone can cultivate democratic values and practices in a totalitarian setting. It is more likely that you as a mature, competent teacher can exercise certain prerogatives of the larger society without totalitarian methods. It is appropriate to increase the range of pupil decision-making to be consonant with democratic principles. The *individuality* and *dignity* of each child must be preserved. You can apply democratic yardsticks to all planned activities and you can select activities that will help each individual live up to his best, which includes making his fullest contribution to his fellow man. Democracy is, after all, a way of living with others.

UNIT AND LESSON PLANNING

A unit of work is a careful design for learning. It reflects your best judgments on what should be learned by pupils; what can be learned; and how learning may be promoted by a careful use of words, materials, equipment, time, and space. The initial design is called a "resource unit." A "teaching unit" is then developed, and is broken down into "daily lesson plans." These levels of planning are discussed in detail in the following pages.

Resource Units

Resource units are plans for teaching a particular, related set of knowledge, skills, attitudes, and appreciations. They contain general objectives, appropriate questions and concepts, methods of teaching, and materials suitable for many kinds of students and for you as a teacher. In a sense, resource units include generalized plans for teaching. They contain ideas for resources from which you can draw in planning a teaching unit which is specifically planned to provide *particular* learning experiences for a particular group of pupils with *unique* needs, motivations, and strengths and weaknesses.

Resource units are adaptable blueprints for designing curriculum and they contain far more than can be *taught*. There are many sources of ideas and completed resource unit plans. Without a collection of such resource units, you would find it necessary to spend time and energy both in preparing for and organizing your own program of fundamental ideas and in modifying plans to your teaching situation. Of course, resource units developed by others should be adapted to your own teaching style. The teaching unit derived from prepared resource units must be extensively adjusted to meet classroom and community needs. Resource units can be started during college days and summer vacations since they are a *resource*. They should be periodically cleaned out to eliminate dated, poorly written, or ineffective materials, or to reflect your own growth.

Topics which are considered appropriate for different subject areas for various elementary grades can be found in courses of study, curriculum guides, or textbooks. While the exact extent to which a topic is studied or the grade in which it is studied varies greatly, the topics themselves are fairly common.

Resource units are organized sources of ideas and teaching suggestions from which you can select *specific* ideas and suggestions contained in a teaching unit—a unit for a particular group of children. To plan a teaching unit *before* you know something about a group of children in a particular setting is undesirable. Teaching unit plans should be made in relation to specific learners in a particular community.

A resource unit, like the teaching unit, includes ideas and information which can help children begin certain kinds of learning; expand and secure other learnings; and pull together those final insights, ideas, and information which are significant enough to remember and apply in a variety of situations. A series of opening learning activities is needed to attract pupil attention and interest and to help each pupil identify his interests and capabilities. It also helps the teacher to analyze individuals and the class group in terms of what the present situation is and what should be done to bring about desired objectives.

The initial content and activities then are enlarged and broadened in the light of what happened during the opening of the unit. In this intensive developmental stage, they should be selected to capitalize on and extend interests, overcome weaknesses, and increase strengths—sometimes for the total group, other times for small groups, and, whenever possible, for individuals.

The good unit has sufficient variety to meet the unique needs of individuals and groups of children. The resource unit should have enough ideas from which to select to meet the varied conditions which prevail during a teaching unit. Activities can include talking, listening, making things, dramatizing, role playing, creating through art, singing, playing games, seeing and listening to audiovisual materials, and many other learning processes. *Specific* activities should be selected for their value in teaching those facts, skills, appreciations, and understandings defined in the objectives section of the unit. Some are creative, some are drill, some are passive, while others are active—all should be significant and not merely time fillers.

Even when units create much interest and promote much learning, there is need to bring them to successful conclusions. There is that psychological and logical moment when it is time to stop one unit and make a smooth transition into the next. Some teachers plan to use tests as the concluding activity. Indeed, many tests can extend learning, especially those that require more than simple recall of memorized masses of materials. Successful conclusions may also include the applications of unit learnings, such as dramatizations, murals, dioramas, panel discussions, brief reports, bulletin board exhibits, or service projects. Discussions of unit learnings are appropriate to bring out the most significant applications.

Time pressures often make it necessary to secure resource units or parts of resource units from others. It is desirable to utilize others' ideas, yet much time is needed to carefully select content and activities compatible with *your* objectives and competencies. Certainly there is need for careful choice to insure that those resource units selected are those which can be adapted to particular children, are democratic in orientation, avoid indoctrination, are feasible, and fulfill other requirements. Several sources of units should be examined for ideas. There are teachers' manuals of textbooks, locally prepared courses of study and curriculum guides, materials printed by national subject matter associations, histories of local communities, materials developed by special interest groups (for example, unions and corporations, the chamber of commerce, and an association of dairy products manufacturers). The examples are almost endless.

Teaching Units

The resource unit is in a sense a stockpile of ideas, information, and materials. The teaching unit in contrast is what the teacher builds according to *a specific design*—to teach something to someone in a particular classroom. Exacting analysis will help in unit planning. Children's progress and problems of last year should be considered; test scores and other indications of individual needs are also important. Generalized goals for a particular grade should be studied. In addition, general community conditions should be analyzed to determine their effects on what children know, feel, and need.

Curriculum, you will remember, is the planned school program. A teaching unit design is the specific plan of action. Lasting effects from a particular unit are more likely to occur as a result of quality rather than quantity. Planning should be careful and exacting. Intelligent adaptations should be made while teaching a unit whenever it appears reasonable and desirable. Completion of unit plans is after all a *means* to an end. The varied parts of a resource or teaching unit are shown on the outline on page 120.[7]

Daily Lesson Plans

Resource units provide selected plans for the teaching unit. It is then necessary to translate this unit into daily lesson plans. The teaching unit is a plan for learnings for a period of days or weeks. The daily lesson plan is a guide for what should happen on a particular day when a par-

[7] Adapted from an unpublished outline developed by C. Lawrence Beymer and one by Kenneth L. Husbands, *Teaching Elementary School Subjects* (New York: The Ronald Press Co., 1961), p. 431.

An Outline for a Unit
(Applicable to Both Resource and Teaching Units)

I. *Identifying Data.*
   A. *Title*—often stated in a question or to provide sharpness of focus.
   B. *Estimated time*—estimated in terms of weeks, adaptable to conditions when translated into a teaching unit and daily lesson plans.
   C. *Probable position in school year*—estimated placement within school year (time of year or month), adaptable to conditions.

II. *Objectives.*
   (Stated in terms of what pupils themselves are most likely to want and need and also in terms of what the teacher thinks they should want and what they probably need for the present and for the future. Stated in terms of how pupils will be expected to think and act upon completion of the unit.)
   A. Concepts and understandings
   B. Knowledge and information
   C. Habits and skills
   D. Attitudes and appreciations

III. *Scope and Sequence.*
   A. Content to be taught, including an outline.
   B. Outline of sequence, in terms of estimated number of class sessions to be devoted to the different parts of the unit.

IV. *Activities for Attaining Unit Objectives.*
   A. *Opening of unit*—creation of interest, diagnosis of pupil strengths and weaknesses, extent of present mastery of unit objectives, setting the foundation for further activities, and involvement of pupils in planning for the development of the unit.
   B. *Development of unit*—extension and development of unit objectives, including activities for total class, small groups, and individual pupils of differing achievement levels and interests. (This is the major part of the unit in terms of time required.)
   C. *Concluding of unit and assessment of learning*—pulling together the significance and interrelationships of the varied activities in terms of most important objectives, including review activities; some new but related activities to strengthen growth started in previous stage; assessment activities, including specific test items designed to test the varied kinds of learning developed in the unit; possible applications of learnings in classroom, school, and community.

V. *Transitions.*
   A. Plans for relating unit to future units.
   B. Plans for relating unit to other subject areas.

VI. *Resources.*
   (Varied and numerous resources from which to choose on the basis of conditions prevailing when *a teaching unit* is being developed.)
   A. *Teacher bibliography*—to strengthen teacher background and to use in teaching unit.
   B. *Student bibliography*—divided into lists available in the room, school library, and other places, also keyed as to appropriateness for low,

average, and high achievement levels, and for boys and girls (in same class).

C. *Audiovisual aids*—divided into lists available in room, in other rooms, in central depository, and through other sources.

D. *Specific questions and discussion outlines*—for different parts of the unit.

E. *Other aids to learning*—resource materials, resource persons, field trips, and others.

VII. *Appendices.*

A. Outlines

B. Forms and samples

C. Other handouts

ticular content area or activity is scheduled. It includes plans for obtaining *some* of the objectives for the total unit. Time for the lesson will depend on children's maturity, lessons planned in other content areas, and the logical and psychological time to begin and end. Since content can be taught only under reasonably favorable conditions, the lesson plan should be altered to meet changing circumstances. Each day's plan should reflect the previous day's lesson. The children should have clearly in mind what was accomplished at the end of a lesson (and what was not). Children should be helped to anticipate the next day's learning activities and specifically what they, as individuals or in groups, should do to prepare for them.

The content of a lesson, its skills, attitudes, and its ideas are important; the *process* of learning how to learn, evaluate, and plan for subsequent steps is also a significant learning process in day-to-day efforts to attain the larger objectives of the teaching unit. The curriculum structure for the year is composed of daily building blocks. The best curriculum planning can be useless when unit plans are inadequately translated into day-to-day lesson plans.

The lesson, then, is a culmination of planning which started with the development of resource units and was further refined into a teaching unit (that plan for a particular class), then to the lesson plan, and finally to the lesson itself. Only when there is consistency in planning based on how teaching and learning occur can there be adequate learning outcomes. Planned, written teaching units and daily lesson plans can help to develop a mental image. It is then possible *while teaching* to adapt realistically to pupil responses and learning conditions. *Planning is thus conceived as a practical and dynamic process.* Teaching is conceived as a science (with precision in planning) and an art (with flexibility developed by interaction and learning patterns). Much of the discussion in this chapter could be labeled "classroom management"; since curriculum should be thought of in terms of results, it is difficult to provide a clear distinction.

ORGANIZING PEOPLE, TIME, AND RESOURCES

Pupil–Teacher Planning

The democratic principle in unit and lesson planning is that individuals who will be affected by a decision should participate in making it. Pupils can learn both from the planning which succeeds as well as from that which fails partially or completely. Pupils who help to plan, to conduct, and to evaluate learning activities can improve all three processes. If you accept this premise, you are in effect demonstrating your belief that school should be a place where children can make mistakes without suffering too serious consequences as a result. This hopefully will enable them to make fewer errors in adult life where mistakes may have serious consequences. Learning how to learn is a significant aspect of curriculum. Long after many of the facts and ideas learned in school become obsolete, *learning as a process* will retain its importance. You should retain an active role, particularly with young children. If you cannot help children themselves to see that their activities are nonproductive, you occasionally may have to redirect learning processes. There is a tendency to do this too rapidly.

Other Members of the School Staff

Other members of the school staff affect and are affected by what goes on in each classroom. The principal, as instructional leader for the school, should be an active participant in instructional planning. He has the responsibility for the total curriculum for the school and he should help teachers to guide children in securing new learnings and strengthening old ones. He should encourage learnings which are in harmony with the specific curriculum objectives of the school and with democratic ideals for both the individual and the society. He should participate in a *helping* relationship at all stages of planning. He has ideas, resources, and skills which place him in a key role for designing and carrying out a sound curriculum.

Patterns in Grouping Children

Grouping plans obviously reflect curricular objectives. Grouping does not guarantee success in attaining objectives; it merely facilitates or hinders the task. A plan itself is of little worth unless there is a commitment to it and the necessary human and material resources. No matter what the plan, provision should be made for each child's growth. Each of the following plans should be seen as a means of helping the teacher to manage the many tasks growing out of the diversity of pupils and objectives. Each is worthy of extensive study.

Individualized Instruction. Historically there has been a number of efforts to plan learning on an individual basis. The Dalton Plan provided for pupil contracts for individualized assignments. Supplying a tutor is not feasible in most schools, except on a very limited basis. Hence most individualized plans are for one teacher and many pupils. The teacher helps each child to plan his work for a specified length of time. Periodically each child checks with his teacher to determine whether his progress is satisfactory.

Ungraded Plans. Heralded as a means to provide for continuous progress, such plans provide for a series of steps in mastering content. The ungraded primary is the most common level but there are also ungraded programs for upper elementary and secondary grades.

There are several basic aspects to ungraded plans. Individual pupils proceed through a series of levels, typically in reading but sometimes in other subjects. When a child or several children are ready, it is possible to move on to the next level—regardless of the time of year. Several levels may be completed in a calendar year. "Failure" is abolished; extra time is provided if children have difficulty on a particular level.

Strengths are numerous and flexibility is a major asset. Continuous progress in mastering subject matter proceeds according to each individual child's learning rate. The plan provides for frequent assessment—involving teachers, parents, and pupils—before a child moves into a new level. Dividing the content into relatively brief levels appears more manageable to many children than does the system of traditional semesters or a full year.

Graded Group. Children of a given age are placed with a teacher who then attempts to meet individual and group needs. Most self-contained classrooms have a wide range of individual differences, but they can be organized to include only children of comparable capacities and achievement. Most textbooks are graded to meet the average child's level.

Homogeneous Grouping Across Grade Lines. In the case of extreme differences in children, groups may be set up to include those from several grades. Special sections for low achievers, mentally retarded, or academically talented children may then be organized.

Split Grade Grouping. This system is used primarily when there are too many children in two or three grades but not enough to require another section of each grade. There may be insufficient rooms or funds to set up as many graded sections as are justified. Since children on a particular grade level vary significantly, it is relatively easy for the teacher to establish small learning groups without regard to children's grade level. Such groups might include children from two or three grades. Records of grade levels are kept for administrative purposes. The curriculum for split grades includes elements from the grades involved yet some teachers persist in attempting to "cover" the content of two or three grades by holding class in all subjects.

Departmental Grouping. In this plan subject matter is divided into graded levels, and subject matter specialists are assigned to their content area. Children then proceed from one subject specialist to another (or in some cases different subject matter teachers rotate from room to room).

Organizational Patterns of Teachers

There are different ways of identifying and arranging content to be learned, and there are likewise different ways of organizing teachers.

In the *self-contained classroom,* one teacher is given basic responsibility for the total curriculum of children. He may, and often does, have assistance of specialized teachers who either come into the classroom or who schedule children to visit another room. It is common for specialized teachers to teach music, art, physical education, and other subject areas. The teacher of the self-contained classroom at times supplements that instruction since it is claimed that only he can coordinate learnings and capitalize on the insights of children to plan an integrated series of experiences uninterrupted by bells or changes in class schedules. Advocates of this position further claim that "transfer" is more likely when the same teacher can relate learnings from one situation to another.

An alternative is *team teaching.* In this plan a group of teachers is assigned to teach a large number of children. Each teacher does what he is best prepared to do as a result of academic specialization, experiences, and interests. At various times he may teach a large group, a medium-sized one, or a very small one. He may work with one child part of the time. Ideally, he is doing what he does best and has time to prepare well since there are few teaching tasks for each teacher. Children under this plan, it is argued, are likely to find compatibility with at least part of the teacher team. There is greater flexibility in setting up varied groups to carry out plans and in assigning children to teachers to attain varied objectives. It is claimed that the advantages of the self-contained classroom and those of having teachers teach in their own specializations are combined in this plan. Particularly if the teaching team includes some paraprofessionals or aides, student teachers, and clerical and other types of persons, there is a possibility that teachers may improve their teaching.

Some elementary schools are organized into *subject area departments.* Under this plan children are taught by subject matter specialists. These specialists may travel from room to room, or children may move from room to room on a rigid schedule. Each specialist tends to plan his curriculum without reference to the other subject areas.

The flexible school staff will need to analyze strengths and weaknesses of the varied plans described previously. Decisions should be made on the basis of objectives and resources. It is possible to use varied plans; none of their weaknesses or strengths is absolute. Intelligent selection of an organizational plan will capitalize on the strengths and interests of teachers and reflect the best interests of the pupils.

Teacher aides have become a common means to free teachers to concentrate upon teaching roles and provide individual pupil attention not otherwise possible. The teacher's task, it is argued, is to direct professional tasks for which the non-professional is unprepared. It is said that if the teacher is freed from such tasks as helping children put on coats, checking papers, and recording test scores, he can then spend more time planning the curriculum, developing instructional strategies and materials, and strengthening his professional competencies.

Often where aides are used there is also a "master teacher" who supervises a differentiated staff of teachers and aides. Group planning of curriculum then becomes essential, to develop the potentialities of shared insights, ideas, materials and equipment, and personnel.

Ghetto residents serving as aides do more than save time for the teacher. They know neighborhood objectives, speech patterns, and motivation factors. They may be able to bridge the gap between home and school by helping teachers to understand the school neighborhood. They also become better equipped to understand and interpret the school to their acquaintances. The job may also provide needed income and self-pride derived from a constructive task. Some aides ultimately may become professionally qualified to teach, while others may remain on the nonprofessional level.

The Community in Curriculum Planning

The community school concept has been discussed for many years. It has undergone considerable revision, particularly in the large cities where parents are securing the right and responsibility to determine curricular goals and to select the staff to carry them out.

Parents should be involved in planning as far as is feasible. They can interpret and reinforce school objectives if they understand them and have an emotional commitment to them. They can provide materials and other resources. They can create a community climate wherein the schools receive the kind of support needed. Parents can be included in curriculum discussions related to the classroom curriculum and to the school system itself. They might suggest that a foreign language be added to the curriculum. After staff and citizen discussions and study, the board of education should decide whether or not to include a foreign language. The *staff* should determine how to implement the decision. The *community role* in curriculum planning is that of determining *what* shall be taught, to whom, when, and where. The *professional role* is that of participating with the community in making such decisions and determining how best to design teaching and learning activities. The professional teacher and the community both share in the important role of evaluating the effectiveness of the curriculum.

Community laymen may assist in instruction, suggest facilities to be visited, discover materials to be secured, and create the interest and support necessary to maintain good schools. Community resources include official, semi-official, and private agencies and organizations, and individuals with no obvious status in the community. The school is both a part of the community and apart from the community, with walls for some controlled isolation to provide a special learning environment but also with open doors and windows when involvement is desirable.

The school system has a major responsibility for community relations. Ultimately, you as a classroom teacher contribute to major community feelings and actions relative to schools. You deal on a person-to-person level with children and neighborhood adults, and it is on this level that the quality of relationships is determined. Curriculum reflects that quality.

Scope, Sequence, and Articulation

Scope. With knowledge expanding at fantastic rates, the school is faced with the continuing task of selecting content to teach. An overly simple process is to adopt textbooks and permit their breadth to determine the extent of the school's program. Each school should reject this process and instead study its community, its children, its staff, and its total resources to determine what should and can be done.

Since each school has a different set of conditions, it is not possible to have a uniform scope of design for a particular subject area or grade level. In addition to textbooks, assistance in determining scope may be available in local curriculum guides, studies of the subject fields, and studies of how children learn. You will probably have decisions ready-made by your school system during your early years of teaching. Within established guidelines of your school, it is necessary to determine the general range of your classroom curriculum. How much can and should each child learn during the period of time you are responsible for his learning? This is the question of scope that is directly applicable to the classroom.

Sequence. After a decision has been made concerning the breadth of content to be taught, the sequence must be determined. This provides a reasonable degree of continuity for children in learning. The sequence of content within a given year is affected by what has gone before and what will come afterward in the next grade.

There are *logical factors* which suggest a particular sequence for content in some subject areas. In other words it is desirable to have children learn some things before attempting to learn others. There are *psychological factors* such as a continuity based on the order which is most interesting to children, proceeding from simple to complex, and so forth. There are *maturational factors,* such as the physical and social, which suggest placement of learnings at a particular point in the child's life. There are *incidental factors* in which the teacher capitalizes on current events which create interest and concern in a particular topic normally taught at another time. It is desirable to make use of an unusual learning resource such as a special visitor or instructional movie. There are *chronological factors* such as studying certain aspects of the reproduction cycle during the spring or the relationship of a holiday to historical phenomena. Sometimes sequence is crucial in terms of learning. At other times it is a matter of convenience. At still other times, it will be a matter of fitting in content which does not have to be placed at a specific point within the school year.

To advocate planning for sequence implies that children tend to pass from grade to grade in the same school system. Nothing could be further from the truth in our highly mobile society. The mass media, extensive travel, visits to museums, and involvement in other learning situations create great diversity in the sequence with which children learn school-related content. An example of how sequence can become scrambled is the American child born in Germany. As a first grader he may have considerable sophistication about his world. Traditional content sequence is largely invalid for many such children.

There is considerable continuity of sequence from school district to school district, from one part of the nation to another. Textbook publishers influence the total nation's grade placement of content. Teachers tend to be affected by the same professional societies, curriculum study groups, and teacher education practices which tend to be voluntarily national in character. Of late, federal legislation, nationwide foundations, and large-scale educational corporations are affecting placement of content throughout America. Consequently, while a child moving from one district to another may find differences, there is a likelihood that children in his new district will be studying similar content at approximately the same level.

Articulation. Just as it is desirable to have a reasonable amount of planning for sequence, it is desirable also to have articulation between the major segments of a school system. The growth of preschool nurseries has accentuated the need for planning for children who have had a nursery school experience. Their kindergarten program should be different, and there is evidence to suggest that programs such as Head Start lose some of their initial effectiveness if the primary grades are not adjusted to reflect such experiences.

In those areas where kindergarten is not available, first grade should begin with activities normally planned for kindergarten. Children in the fifth and sixth grades should be helped to anticipate adjustments needed for success in junior high school.

You should not develop an obsession for preparing children for their next grade level. It is important to relate this year's learning program to what has gone before and what is to come. Each year's curriculum should be taught as part of a unified structure of content and activities.

Patterns in Organizing Content and Activity

Educational objectives tend to be sufficiently varied to require specially designed organizational patterns, planned to attain certain goals. An examination of curriculum guides will reveal that these objectives may be ignored in practice. Several patterns and variations may be utilized in schools to attain diverse aims and reflect unique conditions.

Subject-centered Patterns. Instructional matter and processes in this pattern are selected and planned to encourage study consistent with the logical, chronological, or historical nature of content. The content may be planned in advance and some adaptation is possible to permit children to cover the material at different rates. Some children may even be permitted individualized study. The teacher's role is to motivate children to be interested in subject matter and to help them understand it and relate it to their needs where possible. Particularly if transfer of learning is consciously planned, it is assumed that children can apply learnings to other times and places. There is an orderly process of determining what content is significant and dividing it into grade levels, units, and lessons. Children may be permitted to participate in planning how to study the materials selected, but it is the teacher who represents authority of those who know "what is best."

Subject matter organizational patterns may be varied. They include *separate subjects,* for example, history, geography, reading, and spelling.

The subjects may be *correlated,* wherein separate subjects are taught concurrently under titles such as social studies where American history and geography are taught in a coordinated fashion to fifth graders. Subjects may be *fused* into a combination of social studies and language arts. In an attempt to teach a period of history, a social problem, or a geographical area, subjects may be integrated into *broad topics* with content from several subject areas. One broad topic would be the Westward Movement, wherein history, geography, literature, spelling, and other subjects are used to explain the settlement of the West.

Advocates of subject matter patterns presume that children left to their own interests will not learn all that is necessary to live in a changing and complex society. It is also assumed that children would waste time. It is the teacher who is seen by subject matter advocates as the one who knows how to cover as much valuable content as is possible in the best interests of the society which entrusts him with power over children.

Child-centered Patterns. There are organizational plans in which children's interests and presumed needs are central. Since children are actively involved in planning learning experience, detailed advance planning is limited. Children are helped to solve problems both on an individual and group basis. The curriculum is a way of *learning to live* rather than a means of learning content. Content is viewed as a changing means to an end rather than an end in itself.

The teacher in child-centered programs must be broadly prepared as well as flexible. This enables him to capitalize on children's interests and to extend them. In the apparent confusion of children's activities he can find ways to help them in their growth. Equipment, facilities, and materials should be varied. This permits children to find outlets for their varied interests. These may be transitory, or they may develop into long-term interests which lead to learning in depth. The teacher assists the pupil in planning experiences which are personally meaningful. There is structure in this kind of curriculum, but it evolves from pupil–teacher interaction. There is content, and there are skills taught when necessary to further the interests and needs of children.

Organizational plans should be looked upon as means to an end. There are strengths and weaknesses in the plans themselves. Some serve specific teachers and children better than do others and some require materials, equipment, or facilities which are not available. In some cases certain plans may be incompatible with instructional goals or so contradictory with community aspirations that they would produce misunderstanding and division if put into effect. The basic point is that there must be the means to use organizational plans effectively. They must fit particular (and changing) instructional goals, and they must be supported by those affected by them. There is no magic in a plan. Organizational plans are only a *part* of the overall design in curriculum.

Management of Materials and Physical Facilities

Varied materials are important if children are to have those kinds of experiences which make learning meaningful. Often, appropriate materials can be secured and organized ahead of need. At other times, at an unexpected "psychological moment" for learning, it is very helpful to have a well-organized classroom materials file. Sometimes a needed material is in another classroom, in the library learning center, or in a school system or state depository. In all of these cases an index file of resources, wherever stored, is a significant tool for good curriculum planning. Lacking resources or being unable to secure them severely restricts the kind of curriculum which can be planned.

Obviously you will find some schools more richly endowed than others. You and your colleagues should make sure that materials are indexed and stored in a form which permits rapid retrieval. Children's interests may appear to be like butterfly flights. Having *appropriate* materials available when they can capture children's interests is important in developing a rich and varied curriculum.

Textbooks on audiovisual materials describe in detail the strengths and proper utilization of learning aids. They can provide both direct and vicarious learning. They can assist you in efforts to avoid verbalization when direct experiences are needed. Used properly they can build the foundation for the abstraction and generalization necessary if the child is to enlarge his here-and-now world.

While textbooks for elementary subject areas are carefully graded for the average child in specific levels, other books may not be. It is therefore important to analyze word difficulty, effectiveness of illustrative materials, the level of concepts used, extent of appealing layout and use of color, and strength of the narrative. Part of careful curriculum planning is making an inventory of materials on various reading levels for specific interests of particular children. Different types of instructional materials have their place, but only when used to help each child attain maximum learning of the potential of a unit.

Physical space is another vital determinant of how well a carefully planned curriculum can be put into effect. Poor lighting and ventilation may create fatigue and uncomfortable and rigidly arranged seating can limit the kinds of learning which are possible. It is obvious that curriculum plans should provide for full utilization of classroom, multipurpose room, halls, playgrounds, and community space of various kinds. The space that is available should be as clean, pleasant, and functional as possible.

Research has increased receptivity to school use of air-conditioning; bright colors; varied kinds of chalk, pegboards, and bulletin boards; carpets; comfortable furniture; proper lighting; and other aspects of good physical facilities. For many schools it is difficult to provide more than bare essentials. Imagination is a vital ingredient in making physical facilities an integral part of a good curriculum.

PROJECTS AND READINGS

1. Many different individuals are advocating changes in the school curriculum. You may find it worthwhile to examine a course of study or curriculum guide from a school system for the grade you would like to teach. To what extent and in what ways does the guide provide for the following objectives: "to make urban life rewarding and satisfying, to prepare people for the world of work, to discover and nurture creative talent, to strengthen the moral fiber of society, to deal constructively with psychological tensions, to keep democracy working, to make intelligent use of natural resources, to make the best use of leisure time, to work with other peoples of the world for human betterment"? (Forrest G. Conner, in *AASA Convention Reporter*, Highlights of the convention of the American Association of School Administrators, February 12–16, 1966–taken from an AASA publication entitled *Imperatives in Education.*)

2. You may find it useful to attempt to develop objectives for each of the above "imperatives," stated in a manner compatible with the approach suggested in this chapter. Which imperatives are most difficult to write in behavioral terms? Why? What kinds of learning activities are most likely to develop pupils who can *live* the imperatives?

3. You may wish to secure and critically review a prepared unit related to one of the "imperatives." How could it, in your estimation, become more compatible with the ideas presented in this chapter? What are the ways, in your opinion, in which the unit is more desirable than one compatible with this chapter?

4. *Elementary Evaluative Criteria* (or some other criteria for elementary curriculum) is useful as a means of sensitizing yourself to the many aspects to be considered in the different subject areas. It will also summarize the many factors outside the classroom which affect the curriculum. *Elementary Evaluative Criteria* is a publication of the Boston University School of Education. See also *Profiles of Excellence*, National Education Association, 1966.

5. Children of the lower socioeconomic classes probably desire the benefits of a good education. Which aspects of the elementary school curriculum do you feel are the most meaningful for a resident of the ghetto? What changes need to be made in the curriculum for the grade in which you would like to teach to increase its meaningfulness to a slum child?

6. What objectives and learning activities do you find in elementary curriculum which are not related to the intellectual growth of children? On what basis would you feel that they should be retained or removed?

7. The Project on Instruction, National Education Association, has a number of publications on curriculum. *From Bookshelves to Action* (Washington, D.C.: National Education Association, 1964) is one which includes a number of guidelines for decision-making in the elementary classroom. The booklet

also includes a number of questions concerning each guideline and is an excellent supplement to this chapter.

8. If you chart the strengths and weaknesses of varied organization plans, their similarities and differences will be clearer. Then if you delineate varied curriculum objectives, you can determine which plan is most desirable. In such an analysis, you will need to look at the plans in terms of pupils, teachers, administrators, and society at large.

9. *Articulation* is the process of providing an orderly, sequential unfolding of learning from week to week, month to month, and year to year. A careful examination of a curriculum plan and curriculum guide will enable you to consider ways to provide for articulation and to meet pupil and societal needs. What differences in articulation provisions would you expect between lower and upper elementary children? How can teachers concerned with a particular group of children work together "informally" to provide for articulation while maintaining day-to-day attempts to relate their efforts to children's interests and needs?

10. "Most students (perhaps over 99 per cent) can master what we have to teach them, and it is the task of instruction to find the means which will enable our students to master the subject under consideration." [Benjamin S. Bloom, *Learning for Mastery,* I, No. 2 (May, 1968), p. 1.] Later (p. 4), Bloom claims that 75 per cent of students can learn at a high level of mastery if enough time is provided and proper means are used. This suggests the need for a high degree of individualized instruction. Faced with large classes, what are the problems in using varied means for providing such instruction?

11. Although developed primarily for teacher educators, the nine Comprehensive Elementary Teacher Education Models are stimulating sources of ideas and information on organizing the curriculum. The models constitute the largest effort to restructure the preparation of elementary teachers. There are many publications on the models. *A Reader's Guide to the Comprehensive Models for Preparing Elementary Teachers* has an extensive footnoting and indexing system to enable the reader to turn to the original models. [Joel L. Burdin and Kaliopee Lanzillotti, eds., *A Guide* (Washington, D.C.: ERIC Clearinghouse on Teacher Education and American Association of Colleges for Teacher Education, 1970), 316 pp.] In reading the *Guide* or the models, some critical questions should be asked: (a) To what extent should the federal government stimulate change along specific lines? (b) What are the potentialities and limitations in installing plans and ideas prepared nationally into a particular college or school district? (c) Can change be instituted locally on a comprehensive scale by adapting a model, developed by persons who know the nature of the nation and world but not of the local community?

6

Evaluation

Evaluation is a most important component of any sound curriculum. In today's modern school evaluation is becoming increasingly important and necessary. With the Congress allocating many billions of dollars to the nation's public schools, its members want proof, not only that the money has been wisely spent but that the school curriculum has been improved by such funds. Local taxpayers too are rightly asking whether the classroom teacher, who often receives more in salary per year than the average citizen in the community, is truly effective and is developing a learning atmosphere conducive to efficient and valuable learning. The parent, whose most precious belonging is the child, wonders if that child is learning through adequate teaching. Community leaders, wooing new industry or selling the area's advantages, will place good schools at the top of the list of local assets.

Then you might ask, How do you measure or evaluate teaching? How can you tell a good teacher from a poor one? How can you estimate what a child is learning, how much he has learned, how effective are his learning behaviors? How can you determine if a curriculum is purposeful to teacher and child?

But in order to measure one must know what he is measuring. What is teaching? What is learning? What is a curriculum? What is the difference in meaning between evaluation and the term "measurement"?

THE CURRICULUM

In Chapter 1 you are told that sources of understanding concerned with the teaching and learning process, combined with knowledge of the self and the society, enable the teacher to plan a program of instruction, that is, *the school curriculum.* Measurement or evaluation is the instrument or instruments which determine how effectively the objectives of the curriculum have been achieved within the prevailing form of organization and procedures. "To say it another way, schools have organized a special variety of feedback concerning the curriculum, which is blended with basic purposes and converted into decisions for the improvement of that curriculum." [1] This feedback is called evaluation.

NEEDS FOR EVALUATION

You will be asked many times during your teaching career by many children, "Why do we have to have tests anyway? I can learn much better without them." And you will hear the comment from teachers, "The curriculum works okay. Why does it need to be evaluated?"

This is the day of rapid change. New programs, new materials, and new methods are descending upon the schools in ever greater abundance. Some effort must be made to determine what is and what is not suitable for your children and your curriculum. This can only be done by trying out, testing, and evaluating the new to determine how effective and efficient is the change. Evaluation also helps teachers to understand directly how successful the curriculum is in its total operation. Do the children who graduate from your curriculum become student leaders in the junior and senior high schools? Does the reading program so stimulate children that they are increasingly taking books home from the library? Thus an evaluation of your curriculum helps you teach with greater precision because you have data on what is working and what is not. Finally and probably most essential, evaluation helps teachers and administrators assess whether the objectives of the curriculum have been adequately achieved. A stated objective might be "to help the child achieve self-discipline." Then one might well ask, "How do children behave and conduct themselves in the cafeteria, in assembly, on the playground?" "Do the children continue their learning involvement in the classroom when the teacher is suddenly called to the office?" The process of evaluation will give an understanding of how this objective has or has not been achieved.

With such an assessment of the curriculum, parents and teachers will be in a much wiser position to make more effective fundamental decisions about changes in that curriculum as a whole or in parts of it. Questions which teacher and parent may have had for months (or years) will be openly voiced, and there will be evidence at hand to answer them openly

[1] Association for Supervision and Curriculum Development, *Evaluation as Feedback and Guide* (Washington: The Association, 1967), p. 3.

and with confidence. If curriculum objectives are kept clearly and constantly in view, efforts and energy to improve the curriculum will be purposeful and scientific.

WAYS TO EVALUATE THE CURRICULUM

In evaluating the effectiveness of your curriculum, you will want to know something of the quality of the child's learning and the adequacy of school facilities and instructional materials. There is no precise measuring instrument to secure such knowledge. But to reduce wild speculation and increase sound judgment of the needs and efficiency of the schools, there are particular criteria which will serve you in much the same manner as a direction finder helps the navigator. The curriculum can only be improved if you, the teacher, understand how effective it is.

There is a basic criterion around which you should organize your evaluation of the curriculum. *Are children involved in learning experiences which are pertinent to modern societal needs?*

Communicating

Children are involved in the art of communication. There is a need to develop a reading program which is related to the entire curriculum and permeates all age levels. Reading is not a skill taught in isolation but is based on the needs of individual children.

There is a concern for legibility, but not a uniform style, in all writing activities. The chief objective of cursive writing is the expression of ideas.

Children learn to spell with meaning and applicability, and to speak clearly in acceptable English. They are given opportunities to listen effectively so they can react with meaning and logic.

Children learn to think and communicate with mathematical symbols and to discover relationships and meaning in mathematical terms.

Cooperating

Children acquire the skills of social behavior and learn how to work effectively as a group. They are placed in many problem-solving and activity situations in which they develop the skill to find, organize, and use facts and information. The individual child secures a sense of accomplishment through working in a task suited to his maturity and ability. The child is given individual attention, beginning with a preschool program throughout his school days. The evaluation of his learning and development is continuous. Many techniques of evaluation are used that serve as just one set of tools in aiding to guide the child.

Participating in Group Activity

The child learns to participate in group activity and to cooperate in discussing and making group decisions. A concern is developed for the welfare of the individual through an atmosphere of generosity and kindness, honesty, and integrity.

He begins to comprehend the role of the family and of the school in society. He grows in knowledge and appreciation of how American society has developed and how it is changing. His interest is extended beyond the local area and setting. He begins to view with understanding those current affairs and issues suited to his ability and maturity. The child's action is based on reason. He begins to realize that for a group or a society to survive there must be law and order.

The children are given opportunities to visit centers of human activity such as stores, factories, farms, churches, and public buildings, and to see their function and purpose in a community.

Developing Knowledge

The child is made aware of the conservation of human and natural resources. The child begins to understand how particular academic disciplines are organized and how knowledge is secured to enlarge truth.

He begins to acquire an understanding of economics and sociology, of history and political science, of geography and mathematics, of the physical and life sciences.

Such academic disciplines are used as the vehicles by which the child studies and develops the techniques and procedures of scientific inquiry.

Developing Mental Health

Opportunities are provided to develop good mental health, as well as to develop strong and well coordinated bodies. The principles of good nutrition and personal hygiene are taught and practiced. There is sufficient provision for recreation, while competition is not stressed unduly. Personal and social safety are emphasized for pedestrians, bicycle riders, automobile and school bus passengers, children on playgrounds, people at home, and occupants of schools and other public buildings.

Carrying Out Creative Activities

Creative experiences and instruction are provided in art, music, dramatics, writing, and the dance. Children are given opportunities to use clay, wood, and other media in handwork. The activities of the children

—as hallway exhibits, assembly programs—are given a central place in school organization. Children learn to appreciate the creative activities of others and to share their own.

Respecting Others

Children learn to respect individual differences but also to identify common interests. They learn to think before acting and to evaluate before making choices. Their selections should be based on acceptance of self and sympathetic understanding of others which involves giving and receiving. Changes in human relationships are hard to measure, but they are important in evaluating the worth of the curriculum.

It is difficult to secure a standard against which to make judgments. Because no one has the same education, experience, and interests it is impossible to establish one criterion. People with a wide background should have a good base for making comparisons. During the faculty study, every effort should be made to extend backgrounds through the use of such devices as university consultants, pertinent reading, interschool visits, and discussion groups. In educational research, a large sample increases the validity and reliability of a study. A wide background produces more accurate marks, notes, observations, and recommendations, thus increasing the usefulness of the self-analysis.

Here are some determinants that will help you decide how effectively the children are learning in the curriculum setting: [2]

The closed door: The traditional classroom, one teacher all day, every day, facing silent rows of children has been discredited. Primary children need to move around and chat, as kindergarten children do; their classrooms, therefore, require soundproof floor coverings. The concept of fitting the education to the child, rather than the soul-breaking reverse, means there must be small-group mobility within the classroom. In most schools, desks are movable, but few are moved. Children can take field trips into the community, well-briefed for visits to construction sites, farms, police stations, mental hospitals, airports, and hotels.

Curriculum: Beware of the school that sticks to one textbook per year per subject, and never swerves from the schedule. In such cases, usually only two or three children in each class are learning—the rest are floundering or are bored. A good teacher fragments the class into groups, with children arranged differently for each subject; there'll be no punitive streaming of a solid block of bright students and a number of dolts. The entire class should be having all-day access to a well-stocked library, and the

[2] June Callwood, "What Do Mere Parents Know About How Schools Should Be Run?" *Maclean's Magazine,* LXXXVIII, No. 3 (March, 1967), p. 31.

teacher should be training children to research for themselves and to pursue tangents, wonder out loud why the curriculum is so crowded, and if it is relevant. Look at the textbooks. Some schools use textbooks copyrighted in 1948. The world has changed a lot since then.

Floating teachers: All schools need them, but they are rare. Extra teachers are the least expensive answer to the savage problem of overcrowded classrooms. They can circulate from room to room, releasing the regular teachers to give special attention to fast and slower learners or to visit other schools using experimental methods. The best learning and teaching situation is a classroom with some 25 children.

The principal: He runs the school to suit himself with little outside influence. Find out about him. If he's a martinet, he'll cause good teachers to leave, rigid ones to flourish, and the entire student body to detest school. If he's stimulating and relaxed, he'll attract and liberate creative teachers.

Training to read: This is most important in the child's education and can't be overlooked. A good school encourages the child to enjoy books, practice conversation, express ideas, develop vocabulary—and if he is small, to listen to stories. Kindergartens and even nursery schools are essential whenever a home situation cannot provide these activities.

Failures: When a school fails a child at the primary level often the school is at fault and should be overhauled. Psychologists say failing a child causes lasting damage; educators realize that it is ineffective and unnecessary.

It is important to be able to conceptualize what factors contribute to a good school and which ones weaken the school curriculum. Studying the effectiveness of your classroom and of the total school curriculum should be a basic, personal responsibility of every teacher. There are a number of evaluative devices which can contribute to an understanding of how well curriculum objectives are being attained. No one can attain all goals, especially if they are adequate and comprehensive. Teaching and learning are too complex to enable a teacher to do everything he sets out to do. Likewise, no one can attain the level of excellence suggested by the evaluative criteria you have read in this chapter. However, the materials incorporated here and elsewhere in this book do have the potentiality of broadening your understanding of what teaching and learning involve. Hopefully, these evaluative materials, checklists, and conceptual models will challenge you to strive to attain a high level of professional competence necessary to manipulate and organize the many facets of teaching.

You must remember that the worth of a curriculum cannot be expressed as easily as that of services and goods valued by the criterion of dollars, although such a quantitative expression is often attempted. To determine the real worth of a curriculum you must collect, interpret, and report evidence on changes in pupil behavior as such changes are related to the instructional program.

What instrument is used for evaluation? Some schools make a self-study to estimate the curriculum. Its purpose is to bring about changes in programs and services with resulting benefits to children. This, however, will not be achieved unless great care is taken in initiating and implementing the process. Success will depend on the commitment, energy, interest, and sincerity of all the teachers, the organization of the self-study activities, and subsequent action upon the recommendations.

MEASUREMENT OF CHILDREN'S LEARNING

You may have looked at the curriculum and decided it has a high rating in structure and opportunities. But then you may question how effective it is with children. It was explained in Chapter 1 that children want to learn and grow; that they exhibit determination, perseverance, excitement, and enthusiasm in a task in which they feel involved, interested, and pertinent. A child is learning when he connects attributes to objects, situations, or experiences. For example, Vygotsky beautifully describes how a child learns a word:

> The word to the child is an integral part of the object it denotes. Such a conception seems to be characteristic of primitive linguistic consciousness. We all know the old story about the rustic who said he wasn't surprised that savants with all their instruments could figure out the size of the stars and their course —what baffled him was how they found out their names. Simple experiments show that pre-school children "explain" the names of objects by their attributes. According to them, an animal is called a "cow" because it has horns, "calf" because its horns are still small, "dog" because it is small and has no horns; an object is called "car" because it is not an animal. When asked whether one could interchange the names of objects, for instance, call a cow "ink" and ink "cow," children will answer no, "because ink is used for writing and the cow gives milk." An exchange of names would mean an exchange of characteristic features, so inseparable is the connection between them in the child's mind. . . . We can see how difficult it is for children to separate the name of an object from its attributes which cling to the name when it is transferred, like possessions following their owner.[3]

Learning gives the child knowledge which is basic to "know-how," and education furnishes him with the tools to utilize it. You can never really evaluate or measure the child's learning. Actually you can only test his use of the books you have given him for learning. One author describes it this way:

[3] L. S. Vygotsky, *Thought and Language* (New York: John Wiley & Sons, Inc., 1962), p. 129.

Education, as such, is perhaps the most intangible possession one may have. Education can only be measured by other educators who can only produce measurements by which they were measured by some other educator who was measured by still another.[4]

Achievement Tests

Nonetheless, there are some valid and reliable tools for measuring or evaluating a child's know-how. Probably the most common measurement used is the achievement test. These commercial tests are used widely over the country. They give some indication of how your children compare generally in reading, arithmetic, language arts, science, and social studies with children in the same grade throughout the nation. Suppose Beth, in your fourth grade, has a score of 3.5 in reading achievement. This means she is reading like the majority of children who have been in the third grade for five months. However, such scores should not be slavishly interpreted. They can help you to: (a) appraise at regular intervals the progress of children in relation to their measured abilities, (b) diagnose strengths and weaknesses as bases for corrective instruction, (c) help you, as a teacher, to evaluate and strengthen your instruction for individuals and class groups, and (d) assist you to help particular children understand themselves and plan for the future in the light of that understanding.

There are a number of achievement test batteries available for use in the elementary school. You should remember that some curriculum areas are combined in several of the test batteries. For example, in the Metropolitan Achievement Tests some study skills are included in the language and social studies tests. On the other hand, the Iowa Tests of Basic Skills and the Stanford Achievement Test have separate tests in this area, while the California Achievement Tests and the Iowa tests do not include social studies and science as such. Fewer curriculum areas are sampled by these batteries. Batteries also differ in the areas included at different age levels. More specific areas are added as the level of the test advances. For example, the Primary 1 Battery (last half of grade 1) of the Metropolitan Achievement Tests includes four tests: Work Knowledge, Word Discrimination, Reading, and Arithmetic Concepts and Skills. Spelling is added to the Primary II Battery (grade 2); Language and Arithmetic Computation are added to the Elementary Battery (grades 3–4); and Social Studies Information, Social Studies Skills, and Sciences are added to the Intermediate Battery (grades 5–6). The tests also increase in difficulty as level advances.

[4] A. A. Rockwell, "Is Education Knowledge?" *Education,* LXXXVI, No. 4 (December, 1965), p. 226.

You should examine the context of any achievement test in detail to determine whether it measures the learning emphasized in the curriculum of your school. Some tests are primarily designed to measure broad educational outcomes. For example, the Iowa Tests of Basic Skills are designed to measure Vocabulary, Reading Comprehension, Language Skills, Work–Study Skills, and Arithmetic Skills in grades 1–9.

The norms supplied with achievement tests allow you to compare the scores made by the children for whom you are responsible with the scores for similar groups of children. You can compare the achievement of your class with the national average. The standardization of scores may have been secured by grouping children according to age, sex, or grade, and may represent the nation at large, urban groups, rural groups, etc. The validity of the comparisons will depend on how well the sample used in standardization represents the specific group it claims to represent. For example, if a set of scores for fourth grade reading achievement is based on a small group of children or on one that does not represent other factors affecting reading achievement (such as sex, socioeconomic status, and intelligence) then comparisons in scores may be inaccurate and you would be misled if you attempt to interpret a child's achievement as above or below that of the average fourth grader.

Too, the group used in standardizing a reading test may be different from that used in standardizing an arithmetic test. Both tests may have sets of norms for fourth graders, but there may be much uncertainty in comparing a child's achievement in the two subjects. You cannot say that a child who has the same standing on the norms in these two tests really is on the same level in the two subjects. Tests are valid if they are of the same quality and form as those whose norms were established at the same time and under the same conditions and with the same types of children and schools. Only then can you use the test scores to indicate differences in individual children from year to year and from subject to subject.

Not all achievement tests meet these requirements. You cannot compare tests that are independently constructed and standardized on different groups under dissimilar conditions. The Stanford Achievement Test has been standardized so that comparisons can be made from one subject to another. A child's score on reading comprehension can then be compared to his achievement in arithmetic reasoning.

Some of the achievement tests most commonly used in schools are the Metropolitan Achievement Tests, the California Achievement Tests, the Iowa Tests of Basic Skills, and the Stanford Achievement Tests. You might like to examine these different sets of tests to determine: (a) which have been most recently revised; (b) which, in your opinion, are more suited to the children of your areas; (c) which cover a wider range of material in each of the subject areas; (d) which are easier to administer, grade, and interpret; (e) which would be more useful in diagnosing children's achievement.

The real place for an achievement examination is at the beginning of each school year. This is when you need a diagnostic test to discover the state of progress of each child and to help him continue his growth from that point. The great majority of achievement tests used in the elementary school, however, are of the survey type which test several areas of the curriculum such as mathematics, science, reading, language arts, and the social studies.

Achievement test scores can help to give an overall view of your classroom program, spot weaknesses, help improve your teaching, identify needed curriculum revision, and provide comparison with previous years. However, perhaps their real purpose is to help motivate and direct a child's learning. Achievement tests can function as learning exercises and the process of taking a test can have direct educational value. Test scores in themselves have no such virtue.

EVALUATION THROUGH ACTIVITY

You will find that many children in your classroom, because of great differences in learning speed and ability, simply can't measurably improve their performance when they face the demands of a continuously ongoing curriculum. Too often they leave your classroom at the conclusion of a school year "with long exposure but little tan." [5]

You might help the children to evaluate their own learning by having them participate in one or both of the following two highly organized activities in which they work at their own pace, receive immediate reinforcement, and proceed sequentially toward well-defined and attainable objectives. Through activity organization the child is allowed to perform and the teacher to evaluate.

Success Booths

Nine to twelve children who are "ticket takers" sit at two rows of paired desks in front of the room waiting for customers. Signs on these desks indicate what each child has to sell. One sign might read "We sell Math Problems"; another "We sell correct spelling words." One pair of desks might sell "Adventures in Social Studies." Each booth would include a variety of exercises with easy to difficult material.

[5] Donald Zimmerman, "Evaluation Without Formal Testing," *Education,* LXXXVII, No. 7 (March, 1967), p. 402.

To operate their booths the children who are checkers can use specially prepared, permanently mounted questions, problems, and sentences. To be successful at a booth, the other children must correctly solve every problem or answer every question. When mistakes are made, they may try another booth or make a second attempt. The children soon discover which booths are just right or too difficult or quickly completed. Of course the children will linger at those booths which they find comfortable until the teacher suggests they try more difficult and exciting booths.

Each child should keep a record of the booths he has passed correctly. The teacher can quickly check such a record and tell how many success booths the child has accomplished. The child who is checking interacts with the child who is checked; both benefit from the oral response and the performance.

Testing Game

You can evaluate children's learnings by a method very much like the textbook or workbook exercises which are acted out. It might be called the Testing Game. You, the teacher, can appoint three or four children who are doing well in the classroom as checkers. Then each child in the class might take a problem, for example, a mathematics problem or a social studies question. It would be completed or answered and then given to any of the checkers who, with the aid of permanently mounted answer sheets, could check the child's work. The checkers look at each paper, not only for the correct answer, but also for any mistakes the child might have made in punctuation, sentence structure, penmanship, or other aspects of the lesson.

When the checker finds an error, he could tell the child only the category (for example, spelling or a factual error) in which the error has been made. Then the child should locate and correct his mistake. When checkers make mistakes, they receive a "strike," three of which in a class period result in their dismissal. The teacher should continually supervise the checkers, or he himself might operate a booth. His principal responsibility, however, is to observe closely and to evaluate student performance and behavior. It is as important to evaluate social skills as it is to appraise academic skills.

Both of these evaluation methods allow children to express behaviors, acceptable and non-acceptable, which the teacher might otherwise never have an opportunity to appreciate, reinforce, and, if necessary, control. In addition, the child can secure immediate results from his test and have the opportunity to correct his test errors. He can interact socially. The teacher can observe student performance and can spend that time and energy usually devoted to the grading of tests to construct pertinent activities.

SOCIAL LEARNINGS

As a classroom teacher you are concerned with whether the child has acquired any information or knowledge which is essential to function effectively as a citizen. You also are interested in whether a child is learning to work with others, and if he is developing social behaviors which will be of benefit not only to himself but to others as well.

At the beginning of the school year, you could give a simple test to ascertain what is the relationship and rapport between children. This test should not be administered until the children have spent two or three weeks in your classroom during which you have come to know them, and they have come to know you. You then might set up a real situation. You could tell the children it might be wise to change their seating arrangement, and ask them to write on a sheet of paper the person beside whom they would like to sit. On the other side of the paper they might write the name of the person with whom they would like to walk on a forthcoming field trip or with whom they might have to hold hands as they cross a dangerous intersection. Then you could take these papers home. In one column you list the names of all the children in your class; each time a child has been selected to be a seat away or as a walking companion, he receives a mark beside his name.

Tom 1111111111
Susy 11111
Bill 0

The child who is continually chosen is a leader or star. The child (Bill) who is never chosen is an isolate. Thus, as the teacher, you would have some indication of those children who may be given some responsibilities to develop their leadership potential and those who need guidance and direction to become more integrated into the social group.

As the school year develops you may wish to know the relationships between groups of children. A sociogram may help you determine what children should work together on a committee or in a social group. You could write the name of each child in the class on the blackboard so that there will be no confusion as to spelling and no embarrassment in asking the teacher for information. The children could write, unobtrusively, on a slip of paper their first, second, and third choices for class president, student council representative, or committee chairman. These choices could then be charted into a sociogram. Circles represent girls; triangles represent boys. The chart might resemble the one below (taken from a fourth grade):

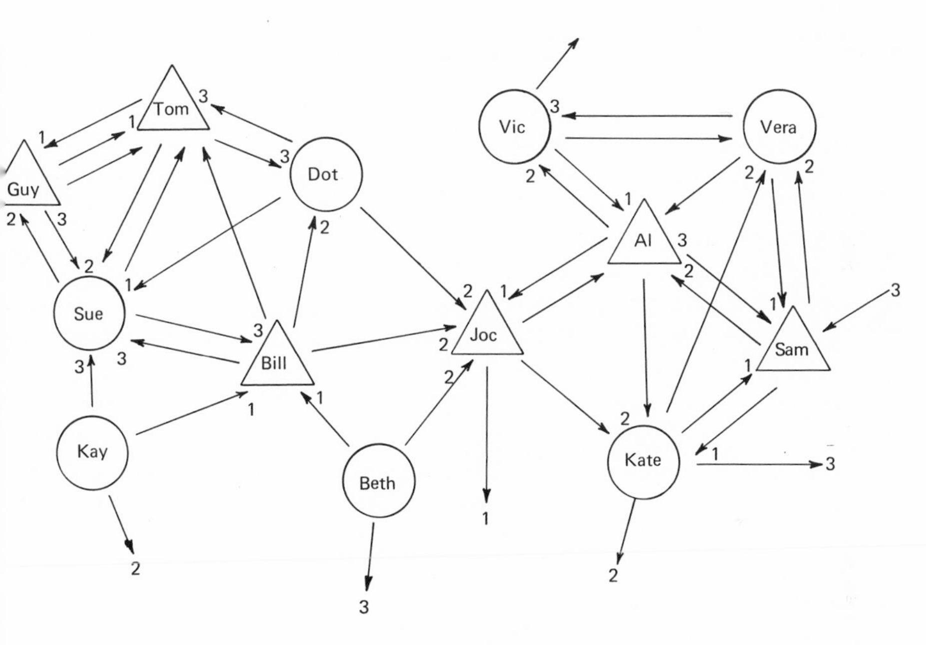

In this sociogram you have rather definite social groups which can function as a committee with designated leaders. Beth, whom no one has chosen, is the child to whom the teacher should give special attention.

INCIDENTAL RECORDS

On a day when your program is particularly well organized (for example, when you will be visited by a school system consultant who can help you with your classroom procedures), you might take a dated sheet of paper, write a particular child's name (Beth), and jot down observations concerning that child during the day. Entries might include:

1. Left the room twice
2. Requested repetition of directions three times
3. Asked if might be excused from playground activities
4. Couldn't find pencil but failed to ask to borrow one

At the end of the day this could be read and then placed in the child's personal file. Another such incidental record might be made the following week. You could also place in the folder samples of classroom work (compositions, pictorial illustrations, and so forth). Beth's folder could be used when you diagnose her problems and progress. You would thus have evidence to use in a discussion with Beth, her parents, principal, or special school personnel such as a psychologist.

This incidental record should give some indication of your observation concerning the following habits (or behaviors) of a particular child.

1. *Work Habits*
   Makes good use of time
   Takes pride in neat and accurate work
   Listens to and follows directions
   Organizes and completes work
2. *Social Habits*
   Works well with others
   Respects rights and opinions of others
   Respects public and private property
   Accepts responsibility
3. *Personal Habits*
   Accepts criticism cheerfully
   Is growing in self-control
   Practices fair play

INTELLIGENCE TESTS

There are at least 10 types of tests used by schools and other agencies. These may be grouped into three fairly broad categories: (a) measures of ability and aptitude, (b) measures of achievement in broad fields and specific subjects, (c) instruments designed for appraisal of interests and personality. The first two kinds tend to be substantially correlated. Intelligence is the amount of learning ability one has. Intelligence tests, supposedly, measure this ability. It is also assumed that the more learning ability one has the more knowledge he will acquire. The amount of knowledge one has assimilated is measured by an achievement test. If a child secures a high score on an intelligence test, in all probability he can also secure a high score on an achievement test.

One is born with a certain amount of native intelligence or ability, but how it is used and developed will be determined by the environment. The child's environment may change and, as Hunt says, "the abilities of man can be seen to be developed and become differentiated through learning or through organism–environment interaction." [6] Many schools give intelligence tests to children early in the first grade, again in the third and fourth, and finally in the sixth grade. Some schools, however, have little confidence in intelligence tests and do not use them.

[6] J. McV. Hunt, *Intelligence and Experience* (New York: The Ronald Press Co., 1961), p. 303.

Such tests, however, can help you to determine what potentiality to expect from an individual child or from an entire class. The scores from intelligence tests can give you guidance in selecting materials and methods for your children, as well as assistance in determining the teaching pace you should set, the enrichment you should provide, and the type of classroom environment you might organize. They do give you valuable information if you realize that "a single early measure of general intelligence is not used as a basis for a long term decision about a child." [7]

The intelligence test is referred to as "academic aptitude" because educational psychologists have indicated that there are at least three kinds of intelligence: academic, mechanical, and social.

There are at least four main types of academic aptitude tests. One type gives two or more scores. The California Test of Mental Maturity gives a score on language aptitude, one for non-language abilities and then a total score. On the other hand the Kuhlmann-Anderson intelligence tests give a mental age and an intelligent quotient. The Otis Quick-Scoring Mental Ability Tests and the Otis Self-Administering Test of Mental Ability give an intelligent quotient only. The Science Research Associate Tests of Primary Mental Abilities give scores in such areas as motor skills, perceptual speed, quantitative skill, verbal meaning, and space for boys and girls between the ages of five and seven. For children between the ages of seven and eleven this test gives scores in perception, number reasoning, verbal meaning, and space.

Some non-verbal tests are culture free, individual, non-verbal, or based on performance. Examples include the Davis-Eeels Test of General Intelligence or Problem Solving Ability (Davis-Eeels Games), International Pupil Aptitude Test, Culture Free Intelligence Tests, Lorge-Thorndike Intelligence Test, the New Revised Stanford Binet Scale, and the Wechsler Intelligence Scale for Children. These are but a few of the academic aptitude tests available for the elementary school.

REPORTING THE RESULTS OF TESTING

If you have evaluated the learning of children, using the best tools at your command, then such results should be communicated to those most deeply concerned—the children themselves, the parents, and the administration.

The parents may say to the child, "What did you learn in school today?" and the child may answer, "We played." Such a statement often disturbs the parent. If the parent understands that when the child was playing

[7] Benjamin S. Bloom, *Stability and Change in Human Characteristics* (New York: John Wiley & Sons, Inc., 1964), p. 88.

with four trucks and four cars he was learning addition and subtraction, there would be less distress caused. The parent–teacher conference type of reporting has become increasingly popular to provide for meaningful interpretation of a child's progress.

Preparation for Good Conferences

In preparation for the parent–teacher conference some teachers take slides of the children in the school and distribute large explanatory booklets illustrated with rough Gestetner-printed photographs of the children. Whatever your method, your conference with a parent should never be rushed; plan on an hour to explain the child's work, to answer such questions as "Why doesn't my little one have any homework?" But more important, it takes time to establish rapport in order to share with the parent your understanding of how the child is progressing within the curriculum.

Such rapport can only be secured through adequate planning before the conference. Such preparation includes:

1. Assembling a file of pertinent samples of the pupil's work
2. Reviewing the anecdotal record you have made of the child and underlining significant observations you wish to discuss with the parent
3. Looking over sample work you have placed in the child's cumulative folder
4. Checking recent test results in light of the child's classroom performance
5. Talking to other teachers who have contact with the child and asking for their observations
6. Talking to the child himself, before the conference, if this will give the conference more meaning

However conscientious you may be in your preparation you may do considerable harm during the conference unless you handle it skillfully. These guidelines may be of assistance: [8]

1. Attempt to secure a friendly atmosphere with the parents and try to keep the conference free from interruptions.
2. Try to be positive—begin and end the conference with favorable comments about the child.
3. Be honest with the parents but avoid bluntness.
4. Ask for constructive suggestions as to how you might be more helpful.
5. Try to secure an understanding of the parents' conception of the child as an individual.

[8] Louis Romano, "The Parent–Teacher Conference Can Be an Effective Means of Reporting," *NEA Journal*, XLIV, No. 9 (December, 1959), p. 21.

6. Remember you are a professional person, and information given to you by the parents is confidential. By your poise and attentive listening, the parents should understand you do have professional ethics.
7. In explaining the child's school work keep your vocabulary simple. You may have to explain such terms as discovery, inquiry, or reading level.
8. You may find it helpful to take notes during the conference, but you should review them with the parents.
9. Invite the parents to return to some school function.
10. Your judgments should be based on facts; and, if there is a problem, more than one solution should be suggested.

GRADES AND MARKING

Your grading and marking of the child may be quite difficult whether you indicate this through a parent–teacher conference or on a report card. Grading indicates the child's level of attainment on the educational ladder. Marks are symbols to show the quality or degree of achievement on a particular test or for a particular period of time.

Grades as a measuring device are very unreliable, because children differ so greatly and in so many ways. You will learn that a standardized test given to a fifth grade class will show one child reading on a third grade level but on a sixth grade level in mathematics. Another child measures seventh grade in reading achievement but fourth grade in mathematics. Thus, in any grade level you will find many variations among children, due as much to differences in traits within each individual as to differences among the indivduals of the group.

To think that you are teaching a fifth grade class is a mistake. It would be much better to describe your class as a group of 10- and 11-year-olds, because there are very few fifth grade classes where the boys and girls are all achieving at that grade level in every subject area.

Marking, too, has its pitfalls. Does a "B" have the same meaning to a child who puts forth little effort as compared to the child who puts forth a great deal of concentration and work in the same subject area? A mark assigned by one teacher does not have the same meaning as the same mark given by another. Sometimes, too, a teacher will assign a different mark, under the same circumstances at another time. Does an "A" in art have the same meaning as an "A" in mathematics?

Many teachers use descriptive comments on the child's papers and on his report card. One teacher writes on a child's papers comments such as, "John, this is a much better paper. You made only four mistakes. Watch your division. You are not subtracting correctly." To the child perhaps this has more value and meaning than a "C" or "B."

Report Cards

The methods of reporting a child's school progress to his parents are of many varieties and forms. They range from a very formally organized report, giving the percentage scores the child has secured in particular subject areas to the most modern of subjective ratings where the child's progress is recounted in descriptive sentences, or in letters to the home. Many report cards resemble little books with their attractive covers and bindings.

Today, many report cards are colorful, ranging from a soft pink to a vivid green, with photographs and illustrations to heighten interest. Each grade level within a school may have its own type or method of reporting to parents. A great majority of the new report cards stress work habits and attitudes rather than achievement in particular subject matter areas, and the scale of rating takes one of the following two forms.

E—excellent	P—poor
G—good	U—unsatisfactory
VH—very high	A—average
H—high	L—low
M—medium	VL—very low

These symbols were based upon how the child had improved in relation to self or in relation to citywide (or in some cases nationwide) norms for his particular age level. Reporting on the whole child—his health, social development, problem-solving abilities, as well as his personal attitudes and work habits—is a common practice in elementary schools.

Most report cards use two symbols only in evaluating the kindergarten child and five for grades one to six. These symbols are explained and interpreted for the parent on a particular sheet of the report card. Generally, it is the homeroom teacher who determines the child's grade in every reporting area; in some schools this is done four times a year and in others six times.

Some sample report cards are given in Figures 6–1 to 6–3.

EVALUATING THE TEACHER

Once you have examined the curriculum for strengths and weaknesses and attempted to evaluate how effectively the children are learning, you should also determine how you measure as a teacher. "Teaching is a system of actions intended to induce learning." [9] Thus to measure teach-

[9] Herbert F. LaGrone, *A Proposal for the Revision of the Pre-service Component of a Program of Teacher Education* (Washington: American Association of Colleges for Teacher Education, 1964), p. 16.

GROWTH RECORD

Grades One and Two

l's Name____________________ Grade______School____________________

her____________________ Principal____________________

Parents,
During the school year you have been asked to come to at least two conferences with your child's teacher to discuss and plan with her for your 's school progress. This final report is a brief summary of these conferences.
This growth record lists important aims and goals for the maximum development of the children of these grades. Since no two children develop or at the same rate, we are trying to describe your child's progress in the light of these aims. There is no attempt to compare your child with children of his class.

Alvin T. Stolen, Superintendent of Schools

NERAL CHARACTERISTICS: (Those checked are descriptive of the child's behavior as observed by the teacher.)

dependable	aggressive	industrious	self-controlled
adaptable	friendly	courteous	truthful
responsible	leader	cooperative	attentive
self-confident	follower	obedient	follows directions

CIAL HABITS, WORK HABITS, HEALTH AND SAFETY:

HOLASTIC GROWTH:

Reading **Arithmetic**

Reading level____________________

Art **Music** **Physical Education**

ECIAL INTERESTS AND ABILITIES:

DITIONAL COMMENTS:

tendance Record: Days present____________ Days absent____________Times tardy____________

Report next year to grade____________Date____________________
Month Year

Fig. 6–1. Growth Record for Grades 1 and 2—Duluth Public Schools.

PROGRESS IN HABITS

Following is our rating of certain important social and work habits of your child:

SOCIAL HABITS	REPORT PERIOD I	II	III
Is polite and kind			
Works and plays well with others			
Respects the rules of the school			
Offers good ideas			

WORK HABITS	I	II	III
Works well by himself			
Takes care of materials			
Follows directions			
Works in a neat and orderly manner			
Completes work on time			

ATTENDANCE RECORD

Only your child's illness, or other unusual causes, should prevent prompt and regular attendance.

	I	II	III
Days Absent			
Times Tardy			

EXPLANATION OF MARKS

A Excellent — C Fair — F Failing

B Good — D Weak

PROGRESS IN SKILLS

The following marks indicate your child's rating according to his ability.

	REPORT PERIOD I	II	III
Reading			
Arithmetic			

The work in other subjects is satisfactory unless otherwise stated.

* * *

PRIMARY GRADE PLACEMENT

Since abilities differ, a child may receive satisfactory marks in reading and arithmetic and yet progress slowly through the grades.

There are three steps in each grade. The red line indicates your child's progress to date.

GRADE	1B	1A	2B	2A	3B	3A

FIRST REPORT PERIOD

TEACHER'S COMMENTS

ATTENDANCE

	1	2	3	4
Days Present				
Days Absent				
Times Tardy				

Citizenship

Citizenship—a summary of personal habits, social habits, study habits, and conduct as observed in school.

2—Above Average 3—Average 4—Below Average 5—Unsatisfactory

	1	2	3	4
Citizenship				

Scholarship Report

The number opposite the subject name indicates the child's rating in relation to the rest of the group.

2—Above Average 3—Average 4—Below Average 5—Unsatisfactory

S—Satisfactory U—Unsatisfactory I—Improving shows the child's progress in relation to his own ability.

	1	2	3	4
Arithmetic (Group Rating)				
In relation to the child's own ability				
1. Knows number facts				
2. Works accurately				
3. Reasons well in solving problems				

Art (Group Rating)				
In relation to the child's own ability				
1. Shows originality				
2. Developing workmanship				
Health (Group Rating)				
In relation to the child's own ability				
1. Understands necessity for good health habits				
2. Applies these habits to personal living				
Language Arts (Group Rating)				
In relation to the child's own ability				
1. Expresses thoughts clearly in speech				
2. Expresses thoughts clearly in writing				
3. Learns new spelling words each week				
4. Spells correctly in written work				
5. Writes plainly and neatly in all written work				
Music (Group Rating)				
In relation to the child's own ability				
1. Shows an appreciation for music				
2. Is learning to read music				
3. Sings in good tone quality				
Reading (Group Rating)				
In relation to the child's own ability				
1. Understands what he reads immediately				
2. Reads well orally				
Science (Group Rating)				
In relation to the child's own ability				
1. Has an understanding of subject matter				
2. Shows an interest in experiments				
Social Studies (Group Rating)				
In relation to the child's own ability				
1. Takes part in class discussion				
2. Is able to find and use material				
3. Applies material to the present				

Fig. 6–3. Pupil Report for Grades 4, 5, and 6—Cheyenne, Wyoming, Public Schools.

ing is to evaluate one's actions, particularly those which produce changes in children. To a great degree the teacher who produces desirable changes in children in most aspects is a good teacher.

You might measure your actions as a teacher by the use of several tools. Make tapes or secure photographs of your teaching and then examine the recording or film, asking the following questions:

1. Do I question the children so that I stimulate thinking? Are my questions so worded that I challenge the children to be creative and original? Too many questions asked by teachers require only a yes or no answer, or seem to suggest Guess what I'm thinking?
2. Do I respond to the children in a positive manner and encourage them by the tone of my voice and by my actions? Do I often say, "That's good, now why don't you try it another way," or "I think you can do much better than that."
3. Do I distribute my attention among all the children? Have I spoken to or given some attention to each child during the day? Some teachers focus all their attention on the bright children or to the slow learners.
4. Do I talk too much (or too little)? Is my voice expressive, do I change its pitch or pace? Do I talk too loudly or too softly, too fast or too slowly? Do I pronounce my words correctly and clearly? Remember that your voice is your most important tool.
5. Do I move around the classroom too much? Have I developed habits which detract from my teaching? (Such as biting chalk or rolling chalk between your fingers). Do I give the children the feeling of poise and confidence?

You may ask a supervisor, your principal, or a colleague to observe your teaching and to look for the following behavior.

1. Do you motivate the children, hold their interest, and encourage them to complete an assignment or a project? This might be measured by the interest that you yourself display, by the organization of your lesson, by the clarity of your directions, and by the amount of your involvement with the children.
2. Does your general appearance give an impression of neatness, confidence, and self-assurance? This might be measured by noting any nervous habits you have acquired, by the amount of close attention the children give you, and by their eagerness to participate and become involved in the lesson.
3. Do you distribute your attention among all the children? Do you speak to or commend each child during the day? Do you balance your attention among all children, whether bright or dull or average?

It is not expected that your observer will find answers to all of these questions in any one period; rather one or two types of teaching behavior will be noticed during any given observation visit. You might request your principal or supervisor to arrange for you to watch a teacher who excels in the particular area under consideration and you might notify this teacher of the specific points you are interested in observing.

No observation is complete without a careful and thorough followup through discussion and interpretation. Only in this way can you learn to analyze and evaluate your own teaching proficiency.

Some teachers request the children to evaluate their teaching. Such a technique is practical in the third, fourth, fifth, and sixth grades. Written (or printed) unsigned comments are effective. The questions given the children should be positive and require constructive suggestions. The initial question such as "What do I do best as a teacher?" should set the tone for the evaluation. To the question, "How might I be a better teacher?" one little fellow replied, "Get a job at the dime store."

If you wish to improve your teaching, you cannot be overly sensitive; you must be willing to receive suggestions and recommendations and to realize that there is always room for improvement. You can become a better teacher only by evaluating your teaching. "The teaching act can only be analyzed through observation. Observation plays its proper role in evaluation on teacher effectiveness when an attempt is made to gain insight into the nature of effective teaching." [10]

EVALUATING TEACHER BEHAVIORS

Several conceptualizations of teaching and learning are reported elsewhere in this book (see especially Chapter 2). Classroom "climate" is also discussed in that chapter and in Chapter 8. To an extent teacher effectiveness can be evaluated through the use of checklists based on researchers' studies of teaching behavior and classroom climate.

Certain aspects, such as verbal behavior, can be assessed. It is more difficult to evaluate the *direct influence* of single aspects of teaching behavior upon children's growth and behavior. Conceptualizations of teaching and learning, such as reported in this book, should be used with extreme caution. Teaching and learning are sufficiently complex to make it difficult to evaluate either one comprehensively or objectively. More important, perhaps, is the fact that conceptualizations can be useful in helping administrators, other personnel, and individual teachers to assess others and themselves to provide information needed to improve teaching and learning. In other words, evaluation could become largely a matter of cooperative efforts to appraise certain aspects of teacher and pupil

[10] N. L. Gage (ed.), *Handbook of Research on Teaching* (Chicago: Rand McNally & Co., 1963), p. 249.

behavior. Using objective as well as subjective data could provide *clues* as to how the learning environment could be improved.

Information and insights about behavior can be made available in a way that is acceptable and in a form that is understandable. Opportunities to utilize or act out these insights can be provided. Our own ability to accept information is complex, but it helps if we believe the assessment information is objective, valid, and given in an effort to help rather than hurt. Your understanding of this information will depend a great deal on your ability to organize it and use it for your improvement. However, openness to improvement requires freedom from threat and embarrassment.

It is only through the assessment of your teaching philosophy and method that you can determine whether the learning process for children is bearing desirable fruit for them individually—and for the society they should be able to serve effectively.

Evaluation for teachers, as well as for pupils, should be a means of improving educational effectiveness. It should be part of the growth process for teachers. A positive environment will promote an assessment by the individuals affected by the teaching–learning processes.

Too often evaluation is conducted for purely administrative or grading purposes rather than for the purpose being assessed. It should be part of the total effort to help each person—teacher and pupil—to understand his assets and liabilities as well as to discover ways in which to improve them. An assessment program should have as its principal purpose the improvement of curriculum for the best possible learning environment.

PROJECTS AND READINGS

1. The basic resource book for testing is Oscar Krisen Buros, ed., *Mental Measurements Yearbook,* Sixth Edition (Highland Park, N.J.: The Gryphon Press, 1965). This volume is the tenth in a series. Its purpose is to assist test users in education, industry, psychiatry, and psychology to locate, choose, and use tests with relative ease and discrimination. The sixth edition covers the period from 1959 to 1964 and supplements earlier volumes in the series. It consists of three main parts: the test section with test reviews, the book section with book reviews, and the indexes. All volumes in the series are designed to be used in conjunction with another Buros publication, *Tests in Print* (a 1961 publication by The Gryphon Press). This volume is a comprehensive bibliography of tests for use in education, psychology, and industry. It is designed to serve as an index to the contents of all the *Mental Measurements Yearbook* volumes. This volume presents listings of all tests known to be in print as of June, 1961, and title listings of all tests that are listed in a *Mental Measurements Yearbook* but out of print. How could such a publication be of assistance in selecting tests which would be most appropriate in evaluating progress consistent with your curriculum goals? Who are other members of a school staff who could be most useful in assisting you to use the *Yearbook?*

2. *Making the Classroom Test,* a 1961 publication prepared by the Evaluation and Advisory Service, a division of Educational Testing Service (Princeton, N.J.), outlines several basic rules for test-making:

a. Have the purpose of your test clearly in mind. To what extent are you trying to measure how well your students have learned a particular unit of study? To what extent do you hope to rank your students accurately according to their abilities? How highly diagnostic of the strengths and weaknesses of individual pupils do you want your test to be?
b. Make a careful plan for the test questions. Unless your test covers a limited unit of work, the plan should be written. Most plans for tests are not so simple that they can be kept firmly in mind. Furthermore, when you examine the written plan, you are better able to recognize its strengths and weaknesses.
c. If your test is mainly diagnostic in a basic skill area, you should prepare at least 10 questions—preferably more—for each sub-test that you use. These sub-tests should yield separate scores on the various elements needed for mastery of the skill.
d. If you are trying to find out how well your class has mastered a particular unit of study, you should make a test which parallels the work in class. Generally speaking, this test should not be too difficult and the commonly accepted figure of 70 per cent for a passing score is probably appropriate for many classes.
e. When the major purpose of your test is to rank a selected group of students in order of their achievements, the questions should be on "critical" points of learning. These are the points that go beyond the superficial and obvious. They are critical in the sense that is necessary to understand them for truly high-level achievement. Questions on critical points often require understanding implications, applying information, and reorganizing data.

Can you add a sixth rule which would help you to determine how effective you are as a teacher?

3. One of the chief means used by educators in evaluating the effectiveness and qualities of teachers is the so-called rating checklist. On this rating list a two to nine point scale may be used as the basis for evaluating the strengths of teachers. In one school system an administrative officer may rate a teacher "satisfactory" or "unsatisfactory." Another system may use a five point scale of "excellent," "good," "fair," "poor," or "not observed." What are the strengths of the rating form shown below (see also page 457)?

EVALUATING TEACHER EFFECTIVENESS IN THE ELEMENTARY CLASSROOM *

Directions for Use of Check Sheet

The philosophy of this revised form is that:

1. Classroom activity is worth observing.
2. The activity is the matrix for learning.

* Hugh M. Davison, "Evaluating Teacher Effectiveness in the Elementary Classroom," The Pennsylvania School Study Council, 1965.

Evaluating Teacher Effectiveness in the Elementary Classroom†

Important: The observer should consult the Directions for Use of Check Sheet before working with this scale.

Class observed ____________

Teacher ____________

School ____________

Date ____________

	1	2	3	4	5	6	7	8	9	Score
A. Pupil Learning	Few influenced by the class activity		Many responses indicate lack of understanding		Instruction generally understood		Some excitement for learning		Feeling of high importance for learning	____
B. Teacher's Plan for Learning	Without objective		Vaguely organized		Useful with several lapses		Good understanding of topic and/or content; good methods used		Deep insight into content, and method well-organized	____
C. Pupil Preparation	Little		50% prepared		75% prepared		90% prepared		All ready with complete assignments	____
D. Pupil Vocabulary	No noticeable gain		Used a few new words of assignment		Used words of assignment or lesson		Added related words of assignment or class activity		Noticeable verbal use related to all learning	____
E. Pupil Creativity (in area)	None		Trace of creative activity		Occasional creativity noticed		Creative use of ideas by 25% of class		Used own (many—50%) initiative in creating	____
F. Learning Process	Rote learning; no discussion		Workbook method predominately		Teacher directed text-book-type; some free discussion		Teacher encourages individualized work materials beyond text		Individual research done for written and oral work	____

Interpretation of Total Score

43–54 Superior 30–36 Satisfactory
37–42 Good 18–29 Problems
6–17 Discouraging

Total Score ____

____
(Signature of Observer)

3. The observation of the child is the key to assessing the learning he acquires.
4. Learning is a positive modification of behavior.
5. The success of the teacher depends on:
   a. Pupil involvement
   b. Guidance of learning activity
   c. Planning for learning to take place

Purpose of Form:

The purpose of this form is to evaluate teacher effectiveness within the elementary classroom in terms of the plan for pupil learning and the responses made by pupils which are indicative of desirable learning.

The evaluation scale has been used extensively on an experimental basis and is believed to be a valid and reliable instrument. Administrators, supervisors, or those personnel responsible for evaluation should study the form carefully in order to understand its full implication in diagnosing the strengths and weaknesses within the classroom.

The elementary classroom evaluation form is believed to be more than a subjective check list based on value judgments of the teaching–learning situation; and when properly used, it is an objective coverage of many activities which are considered important in appraising teacher effectiveness.

Use of Form:

There is a score for each activity from numbers one (lowest) through nine (highest). The score for each item should be recorded on the far right side of the scale in the space provided. Intermediate points or fractions may be used and a profile drawn. The individual scores for the six activities should be added and the sum placed in the blank space marked "Total Score." (For interpretation of "Total Score," see equivalent non-numerical quality rating at bottom of sheet.)

4. The following publications are good soruces of additional information about assessment.

   a. Walcott H. Peatty (ed.), *Improving Educational Assessment and an Inventory of Measures of Affective Behavior* (Washington, D.C.: Association for Supervision and Curriculum Development, NEA, 1969), 164 pp. This compendium presents a delineation of numerous measurement purposes in the educational enterprise, of procedures for structuring and conducting an evaluation, and of the place for emotion in schooling plus a catalog of measuring instruments.
   b. R. Douglas Savage, *Psychometric Assessment of the Individual Child* (Baltimore, Md.: Penguin Books, Inc., 1968), 117 pp. Savage aims to help teachers become aware of the specific types of information of a practical nature which they should receive in understandable language from school psychologists and other diagnosticians.

5. Should teachers, students, or laymen be held accountable for poor achievement or failures? How is learning progress to be assessed and improved? In March, 1969, the Education Commission of the States began a "National Assessment of Educational Progress" to determine the achievement levels of a 100,000-person national sample of several ages: 9, 13, 17, and 26

to 35. The $3.5 million project is funded for a three-year period and is expected to produce data on several curricular areas. Several questions should be asked: (a) Will the questions be fair to all races, classes, and geographic areas? (b) Will preparing for such assessment become a major teaching goal? (c) Will apparent school failures be used to undermine public confidence in and support for the schools? (d) Will the tests neglect learning objectives not easily measured?

PART II

Dynamics of Curriculum Study

Curriculum is a dynamic process. It involves the complex interaction of people in the classroom; the school building; the school system; and local, state, and national levels. Increasingly, curriculum is influenced by international events and conditions. Not only is it affected by present conditions at home and abroad, but it also bears the imprint of the past and projected future. It is in part the work of teachers and administrators, and in part the expectations of school boards, other school officials and pupils, parents, and general citizens. The capability to relate relatively small curriculum decisions into the larger picture is a major challenge which faces you. Being able to do this is an important means of planning and implementing a relevant, dynamic curriculum to meet the needs of each individual child and his society.

7

Organizing Study of Entire System

POTENTIALITIES AND PROBLEMS

Study and improvement of the planned learning experiences for children are integral parts of your teaching responsibilities. Curriculum study may be defined as: (a) a planned effort on the part of those affected by a phase of curriculum to evaluate objectives and means of attaining them; (b) decision-making to implement the curriculum planned; (c) continuous appraisal and adaptation where needed to produce the type of learning significant for the child, the teacher, and their society. Since curriculum is affected by funds, materials, equipment, facilities, and responsibilities —both within and outside a particular classroom—it is necessary to work cooperatively in a curriculum study to bring about the most good for the most people. The individual teacher is affected by, and in turn affects, decisions related to diverse curriculum questions.

The need for cooperation in curriculum study is suggested by Ragan's emphasis upon the school's *planned* learning environment:

> The curriculum is concerned with providing an environment that will help each child achieve self-fulfillment and at the same time prepare for social service by acquiring useful information, skills, and attitudes. The school curriculum is a specialized rather than a chance environment. Instead of being as broad as life itself, it is an environment that has been simplified, systematized, and edited.[1]

[1] William B. Ragan, *Teaching America's Children* (New York: Holt, Rinehart & Winston, Inc., 1961), p. 96.

Curriculum study proceeds in a purposeful way when there is an atmosphere of *mutual trust and support.* Where such conditions prevail, there is a desire to help others to improve the quality of the educational output —the learning of boys and girls—which has both immediate and long-range importance. In this atmosphere it is possible for professional and lay people of all ages, as well as pupils, to contribute willingly to the extent that their education, experience, and maturity permit. It is possible to make errors in the curriculum study itself and to admit mistakes made in teaching and learning. It is possible to openly seek best ways of bringing about desired learning experiences. Persons willing to work on curriculum studies need to have assurance that their ideas will be respected, considered, and practiced when supported by group consensus and where feasible in terms of school resources.

Advantages of Wide Participation

Many advantages of wide involvement could be listed, but a sampling will suffice to stimulate further consideration of the point. First, there is increased effectiveness in looking at broad curriculum issues when persons have experienced productive curriculum study. Second, involvement contributes to the understanding with which the teacher and others can put curriculum decisions into practice, for involvement clarifies the objectives and the means of attaining them for a particular phase of curriculum. Third, there is increased interest for both teacher and pupil when a meaningful curriculum evolves from efforts of those affected by it. Fourth, there is increased status for education and professional educators when the school is converted into a place where pupils, teachers, and laymen find challenging activities occurring. Finally, there is increased support when involved people understand what is going on, have a voice in the determination of policy and procedures, and are convinced that the school is indispensable to individual and society.

As success is tested and found to be to everyone's liking, there is a greater willingness to tackle profound curriculum questions and increased competency in organizing curriculum studies to solve problems which are now perceived with more clarity. This statement of advantages is obviously optimistic. Success is relative and varies from situation to situation. At least one can conclude that there are *possibilities* for worthwhile outcomes when many persons are involved, are assisted in becoming productive in curriculum study, and are given extensive support in developing objectives and means of attaining them.

If there are many advantages of group participation in curriculum decision-making, why would anyone question or resist the group approach? Group participation offers no guarantees. It opens up certain *potentialities* to be sought that can be developed after certain problems are met realistically. They should be considered as challenges rather than insurmountable barriers.

Barriers to Effective Participation

Before participating in group processes or striving to attain them in your situation, you should consider the following potential barriers. Some persons in your group may be relatively *indifferent* to curriculum questions as a result of a variety of factors, including a desire to concentrate upon classroom routines, preoccupation with personal and family concerns, or short-term plans for remaining in teaching. There may be personal factors: *fear* of exposing oneself to the questioning and thinking of others, *shyness* in group situations, and a degree of *incompetence* in the art and science of effective participation and curriculum study.

The individual who has a status in things as they now exist may oppose change since it may decrease his position, outdate his instructional plans and collected materials, or force him to reorganize his objectives, methods, and materials. There *is* a certain security in the status quo, which in jest has been called a rut or a grave open at both ends. Insecure persons need help in facing uncertainties which proposed changes might bring; they need assurance that their contributions will be respected and recognized. Relatively inexperienced teachers should empathize with the veteran teachers before attempting to push change too rapidly.

Tiredness or excessive responsibilities may have the effect of discouraging extensive, in-depth curriculum study. The teacher who has diverse responsibilities such as working on a graduate degree or raising a family may reject responsibilities beyond those of classroom teaching. Systems may attempt to overcome this problem through released time (where children are sent home early from school to provide time "on school time"), through provisions for substitutes while selected teachers are involved in curriculum study, and through paid summer work on curriculum projects. It should be clearly understood that none of these devices in itself is likely to provide the total amount of time needed to conduct intensive and continuous curriculum study, for there are too many aspects of curriculum that change too rapidly. The point is that the genuine gesture goes a long way in telling the teacher that his time and energy are valued and that curriculum study is an important contribution. Parenthetically we assert strongly that all the gestures in the world cannot overcome a school system's neglect of either the individual teacher or the curriculum.

Large numbers of persons involved in groups may result in a degree of *inertia*, for it does take aggressive, energetic effort to get action designed to accomplish curriculum improvements. People may feel that they are going in circles, by returning to their original point in discussion or curricular practice. There are individuals in a faculty group whose past experiences lead them to anticipate little progress in discussions and study or to assume that after group study their recommendations will be neglected or ignored. Unfortunately teachers, like children, are manipulated in some instances. They are led through *outward manifestations* of democratic procedures, when in actuality administrative decisions have been made earlier. Democratic leadership is genuine and honest; it respects group processes and their results without abdicating responsibilities delegated by a board of education and state regulations.

The basic point is that group processes may be either productive or futile. You should neither ascribe magical qualities to group processes nor assume that they are doomed to failure for reasons noted previously (or for other causes). It is possible both to utilize large numbers of teachers in studies and also capitalize upon the leadership abilities or subject matter competence of administrators and curriculum consultants. Administrators and consultants should have time and resources for helping teachers to improve learning.

Certain questions should be answered in curriculum study, according to Sowards and Scobey. Answering these questions leads to several steps in curriculum study, shown in the right-hand column:

What shall we teach?	The selection of subject matter.
How shall we teach?	The determination of method.
When shall we teach?	Grade placement and continuity.
How shall we organize for teaching?	Overall curriculum design.
How shall we know how well we have taught?	Evaluation techniques and procedures.
How shall we improve all of our efforts?	Research and development in curriculum planning.[2]

TYPES OF CURRICULUM STUDIES

Involvement of Pupils and Teachers

The classroom is the place to begin to study efficiency in stimulating and guiding behavioral changes—the goal of effective curriculum. If important changes do not occur, teacher and pupils should be encouraged to seek meaningful learning alternatives since they are the ones vitally affected. This teacher–pupil capacity will not develop easily, especially with pupils whose backgrounds are limited. Slow progress in assuming personal responsibility for self-learning is better than no advance at all.

[2] G. Wesley Sowards and Mary-Margaret Scobey, *The Changing Curriculum and the Elementary Teacher* (San Francisco: Wadsworth Publishing Co., Inc., 1961), p. 67.

Involvement of pupils in curriculum planning is a controversial topic. Little is utilized at the secondary level and almost none at the elementary level. We believe that teachers *can* involve children in curriculum issues, within their level of maturity and communication patterns. We claim for elementary pupils, to a degree, the same advantages as proposed for involving secondary students:

1. Teachers need help from pupils in interpreting the pupils' natures, including their interests and needs.
2. Teachers need help from pupils in discovering the learning activities in school and out that will in fact stimulate learning experience.
3. Pupils are likely to become lifelong learners—an essential in a society characterized by rapid, continuous change—if they learn how to identify learning needs and how to select from the environment those elements that help them to achieve that learning.[3]

Classroom Research

Implicit in involving teachers and pupils in curriculum study is an acceptance of some failures or limited successes. Effective study procedures can decrease failures. Interest in classroom curriculum study can be increased by experimenting with various curriculum objectives, content, and procedures. This is called "action research" and it stresses that classroom teachers seek alternatives for felt concerns and problems. Anderson and Gruhn summarize several steps in action research. These have been liberally adapted in the following discussion.

1. A teacher feels that a problem exists or results are not as significant as desired.
2. A teacher discusses the problem with others, establishes hunches about possible reasons and solutions—the "hypothesis"—and devises plans for testing ideas.
3. Information is collected as the experiment is conducted, to provide means of comparing previous results with those achieved under experimental conditions. This information may be collected through tests administered before and after the experiment, through observations conducted by trained observers, or through other means. The significant factor is that care is taken to draw conclusions only from factors related to experimental activities themselves rather than from conditions unknown to the experimenter carrying on the research.
4. Information collected is then organized into a form which objectively shows changes in results to be an outcome clearly of the condition in the experiment. Care must be taken to draw conclusions accurately. Often it is desirable to secure aid from someone trained

[3] Harl R. Douglass (ed.), *The High School Curriculum,* Third Edition (New York: The Ronald Press Co., 1964), p. 40.

in research methods since many teachers are not adequately trained in this area.

Action research may be conceived as a means of seeking answers to problems in instruction felt by an individual teacher, or a group of teachers. Since the number of persons involved in research of this kind is often small, it is important to view conclusions as tentative and limited in validity. Nevertheless, action research is a good type of curriculum study, for it does add to an individual's knowledge of curriculum results and may set the groundwork for extensive research conducted under more valid research conditions than a single teacher or a small group can manage.[4]

You will want to develop an internal security and professional competence which will free you to carry out action research and enable you to participate in more formal types of research with careful research designs on what you teach and how. This may mean that an observer will be in your classroom for scheduled times to provide objective means of assuring valid information. From action research and more scientific investigations can come a curriculum which is valid in terms of goals and outcomes. You will accept a role in promoting both action and formal research-type curriculum study as a significant part of professional activities.

The classroom is a valid point of origination for both kinds of research. It is a place where research findings should be put into practice and revised as needed and it is a place for teamwork involving pupils, their teacher, and other teachers with comparable problems and goals.

Single School Studies

Groups of teachers, in cooperation with administrators and curriculum specialists, may work effectively together in curriculum studies. There are several types of such cooperative studies. Teachers of the lower grades in a building may have a common concern to study. Teachers of several grades in a building may work together on mutual problems. The advantages for using *an individual school faculty* as a basic unit in curriculum study are numerous: (a) reality of shared problems, (b) relative ease in implementing recommended changes, (c) face to face communications, (d) minimum wastage of time in getting participants together for meetings, (e) possibility of practicing and appraising ideas under comparable conditions and thus providing data to be used in evaluating outcomes. The assumption here is that persons with common con-

[4] Vernon E. Anderson and William T. Gruhn, *Principles and Practices of Secondary Education*, Second Edition (New York: The Ronald Press Co., 1962), pp. 472–74.

cerns start with a motivation to get a needed job done. Studies in a typical elementary school can involve most teachers while remaining manageable in size.

School System Studies

Some curriculum study and experimentation should be conducted by groups drawn from different buildings. Such groups may have some potential advantages over building studies: (a) minimized tendency to concentrate upon fairly trivial concerns for extended periods of time; (b) more effective leaders; (c) more money, released time, and expert resources available to do an adequate job. Inter-building groups may maintain greater objectivity, avoid extended discussions of teacher or pupil personal problems, and have more impetus to complete studies as a consequence of their being more "visible" and more difficult to convene.

There are problems when a school system proposes that inter-building study findings be inflexibly applied system-wide, regardless of local conditions. Recommendations developed by a relatively large, impersonal committee may not be widely accepted and applied in individual buildings and classrooms unless a two-way communication system is developed to secure ideas from individuals for study committees and also to feed committee ideas and progress reports to individuals. It is important to stress the need to use system-wide studies only when there is a particular reason for so doing. When curriculum studies are made on such a basis, building staffs and individual teachers should be encouraged to adapt relevant studies to local conditions. Hopefully this freedom will result in curriculum practices which are in harmony with the needs of particular teachers and neighborhoods.

Combination of Approaches

Actually a combination of classroom, building, and system-wide curriculum studies and experiments probably will be needed when the curriculum is analyzed and alternative study procedures considered. When a harmonious atmosphere prevails, it is possible to conduct studies and experiments on the most appropriate level.

Lacking this atmosphere, individuals may become overly concerned with defending their positions and suspecting those of others. In a negative atmosphere, an individual may assume the position that he who is not with me is against me. Curriculum study may then become a series of meetings and reports in which those with authority summarize what already has been decided administratively. If this approach prevails, it is relatively unimportant whether the authority figure is a building administrator or a central office official, for the concept of meaningful involvement is lost.

Teacher Group Involvement

The relationship of curriculum study groups to local professional associations or educational labor unions is varied. The teacher groups may be completely ignored, partially integrated into a system's study, or substantially involved. Teacher groups should make contributions to the growth of boys and girls. Involvement of teacher groups in curriculum studies should result in a better understanding of total system needs, not only of teachers' salaries and fringe benefits but also of facilities, equipment, and materials which affect curriculum.

Teacher group policies may affect curriculum study groups, for example, when recommendations are made to provide salary differentials to encourage teachers to work with the disadvantaged or to change assignment policies which place inexperienced or less competent teachers in slum schools. It is difficult to generalize other than to advocate teacher group involvement to the degree that it is feasible and productive. Cooperative studies of school system–teacher group may be established, representatives of the teacher group may be included in official studies, or curriculum recommendations of the teacher group may be accepted and put into effect by school officials.

Inter-System Studies

A *supplementary* type of curriculum study may be conducted on an inter-school system basis. Area-wide cooperative studies may capitalize upon certain advantages: (a) stimulation of contrasting viewpoints and practices from different school systems, (b) availability of extensive and expensive materials and consultation services, (c) availability of the best leadership from a broad area, (d) an objective emphasis upon the problems at hand rather than personal illustrations of them, (e) availability of sufficient numbers of persons to study specific aspects of several curriculum problems concurrently which a small staff may not be able to do. The negative aspects of area studies are somewhat similar to those cited for system-wide studies, perhaps intensified by distance, differences in school schedules, and varied administrative policies.

"Outside" Influences

Although the topic is treated in more detail in Chapter 9, a word should be said about the relationship of state, federal, and other non-local influences. They affect local curriculum efforts in increasingly significant ways, for example: (a) Local personnel attend state and national conferences where they are stimulated to consider curriculum changes. (b) Supplementary funds provide the means to innovate. (c) Research by a university professor is conducted in local schools. (d) Outside groups conduct research or innovative programs which are incorporated into instructional content and materials. (e) Pressure groups may induce local districts to include some content and materials or eliminate others. (f) The state education agency or legislature may require certain content in a particular subject or grade level. (g) Certain guidelines may be established by a federal agency which force changes before federal funds may be used locally. (h) A national organization of subject matter specialists may recommend that content previously taught in junior and senior high schools be taught in the upper elementary grades, thereby upsetting the continuity of content in the lower grades. The listing of outside influences could be continued almost indefinitely.

These outside influences often are positive in their impact. Local curriculum groups may place major emphasis upon minor issues indefinitely and so study committees must take outside influence into account, both from local groups of state–national organizations and also from the state and national groups themselves. *When outside recommendations are incorporated locally, they should be adapted to particular local conditions.* When outside consultants are used by local study groups, they should be heard critically yet openly as potentially vital supplements to local professional opinion. It would be tragic if curriculum becomes provincial or narrow or if it is abdicated to unknown persons in the state and national arena. America is too large and too diverse to standardize curriculum; education is too significant for national survival to leave it solely to local practitioners. Professionally minded people are the keys in developing a curriculum which is vital to *particular* children who share a common heritage and future as Americans.

Parental Involvement

Some of the previous generalizations may be applied to the issue of parental involvement in curriculum. Hand has developed a guideline on lay responsibilities which is helpful; the layman has important or ultimate responsibilities in determining *who* shall be educated, *when* education shall begin and end, *where* education shall be conducted, and *what* general content shall be included.[5] Official responsibility for lay control over these usually resides with the local lay board of education, acting as the

[5] Harold C. Hand, *Principles of Public Secondary Education* (New York: Harcourt Brace Jovanovich, Inc., 1958).

local arm of the state. The board desirably (and usually) involves administrators in policy decisions and delegates responsibility for administering policy to professional school administrators. Representative teachers should be involved in policy formulation in an effort to incorporate as many perspectives as possible. After the four w's are cooperatively established, the professional staff should have primary responsibility for the *how* question: how to bring about the desired results.

Thus far we have delineated official community responsibilities, carried out by local school boards. How extensively should laymen other than board members be involved in matters related to curriculum? There is considerable value in the two-way communication of ideas, facts, and goals when large numbers of citizens are involved in curriculum studies. Critics personally and responsibly involved in curriculum studies may find that their criticisms are partially invalid; educators may find that laymen can see ways to improve the present curriculum. All must develop a mutual respect that will lead to an ability to disagree agreeably.

The board of education should carefully plan for citizens groups. Some crucial aspects are: (a) objectives for the citizens group, (b) representation which draws not only from organizations but also from citizens in general, (c) plans for sub-committees and a coordinating committee, (d) date on which reports are desired by the board of education, (e) date when the group should cease to function. Both large and small communities can benefit from involving the board of education, citizens, and staff in curriculum studies. Building study groups can also be stimulated by citizen involvement.

SPECIFIC IDEAS FOR CURRICULUM STUDIES

From generalizations we now turn to specific recommendations:

1. Informal curriculum discussions can be fruitful, during a coffee break, during informal drop-in visits to other rooms, and in other casual situations where you can share curriculum concerns and ideas.
2. You may wish to develop a moderately structured plan in which you meet regularly for a period of time, with specific goals in mind, with teachers who teach the same general grade level or who share a concern for particular curriculum content in all grades. The cooperative planning of the total faculty will be needed if study time and mutual aid are to be available. A chairman and recorder may be helpful to keep discussions moving forward.
3. You should become involved in building studies which affect the total staff's plans for helping boys and girls grow. The principal

has a direct responsibility for the curriculum, but he should encourage faculty leadership and initiative.

A building's faculty council may be useful in planning cooperative studies and activities. The council may help the staff to coordinate the use of faculty and pupil time, facilities, equipment, and materials. If too many individuals and groups attempt to study and innovate concurrently, energies may be dissipated and conflicting plans may emerge. The council may be largely advisory and may function primarily as a communication center for a two-way flow of ideas and plans. It may become a calendar scheduling group, wherein plans are made to schedule curriculum study activities which are reasonable in terms of time and resources. It should be small, especially for staffs of less than 20, but large enough to provide representation of divergent viewpoints on the faculty. Adequate reports should be filed with the council, but not to the point where they restrict free communication by becoming cumbersome. The essence of records is the who, when, where, what, why, and how to enable the reader to determine what has been done and what should be done next and by whom.

Some building committees are semi-permanent. The council itself and study committees concerned with pupil health and safety or with special observances and programs are in this category. Others may last two meetings or two years depending upon their clearly stated original objectives. The objectives should be attainable within a reasonably brief time, or be planned in stages to enable the group to enjoy success and be stimulated by it.

Your minimum degree of participation is in those activities of the total building faculty. Some principals may require participation in other types of curriculum studies although there is some question about the extent to which involuntary participation restricts and contaminates constructive discussions.

PROCEDURES AND BENEFITS

Let us turn now to some specific details of how a school system with a few or many buildings may attain the *potential* benefits of large-scale organizations. You as an individual teacher will be, or are, affected by system-wide philosophy, procedures, and studies. You can capitalize upon the potential assets and utilize them in your room and building curriculum endeavors. The school system to a very great extent determines climate for change and innovation, and its resources restrict or free you in your efforts. A school system is largely a service rather than a regulatory organization. Since school systems are political and taxing entities, *some* uniformity may be practical and necessary.

Steps in System-wide Studies

Certain steps should be followed in developing a point of departure for curriculum studies in the system. The individual building faculty then should adapt the published documents which evolve from these steps.

First, a philosophy of education should be written to set the general tone of efforts to establish a curriculum which will bring about changes desired in your particular building and system. To name but one example, if your main goal is development of fundamental skills, such as reading and mathematics, your curriculum content and procedures will be quite different from those of a system which feels that social skills are most important. The philosophy of education becomes a basic determinant of what is included and what is excluded in deliberations of study groups and selection of content by the classroom teacher.

Writing a history of your school community is a helpful first step in understanding which community resources are available and which aspects are so controversial that they may be divisive. It is good public relations to utilize persons in studying the community, and it is good instructional practice to relate classroom instruction to community experiences of children. The history can also increase awareness of changes, those past and those that are occurring, which should be reflected in the curriculum. An example is a community which has changed from a Caucasian middle class community into a Puerto Rican lower class community. An up-to-date history does not guarantee that the curriculum will reflect major changes, but it does increase the likelihood that there will at least be an awareness of change. If meaningful historical studies are conducted prior to writing it, a history, however brief, can be utilized to enrich social studies by teachers and pupils through just the mere process of their composing it. The final written history may be typed, duplicated, mimeographed, or printed, depending upon the number of copies desired and funds available. In whatever way it is reproduced, there should be plans for periodic revision.

Another step in studying curriculum, for both system and individual building faculty, is to study the *characteristics of particular children* for whom curriculum is being planned. Printed studies of children at various ages are available, and while they are useful they cannot be expected to apply to the specific types of children found in a neighborhood school area; even studies of the children served by your school do not apply completely. Lists of traits of children will not help you to know how *specific children* behave and learn. Studies of characteristics of children at different ages can serve as a *starting point* in studying individual children, and they can help in clarifying the manner and extent a particular child deviates from others of his general age group. Perhaps the basic value of these studies lies in their ability to aid you and other teachers to look squarely at what will help the children. The studies should not be used to brand an individual child who may differ from his peer group.

A review of psychological, sociological, physiological, and other factors which affect what, when, and under what circumstances children most effectively learn can be a helpful process in curriculum study. To cite an extreme example, a curriculum study group could recommend that highly competitive intervarsity football be included in the fifth grade physical education curriculum, only to find that physiologically and emotionally the child at this age would benefit from a different kind of program. Without studying sociological factors, a study group could recommend a highly academic program assumed to prepare children for college even though most children of a particular area may not now (or probably in the future) be attending college.

Curriculum should not proceed in a vacuum without insights from several academic disciplines. Proceeding without these insights, you would be likely to write curriculum proposals which are largely meaningless in that they would not be designed for the children to be taught. Nothing is less useful than a curriculum statement which applies to no particular group of children. Vague generalizations can be expected unless the insights of various disciplines are utilized to sharpen understandings of the children to be served by a particular faculty.

Initiation of Curriculum Proposals

An individual, whether a teaching or administrative member of the staff, should have both the right and the responsibility to suggest the need for a study which seems purposeful to him. A building screening committee and a system committee are necessary to encourage studies which are valid and systematic. Without these qualities, conclusions derived from a study will probably be weak.

When an individual or group of individuals propose a curriculum study, the proposal should include most or all of the following information: (a) title of proposed study; (b) specific goals of the study; (c) summary of research, literature, trends, opinions of experts, and so forth, derived from a preliminary study; (d) summary of anticipated time, cost, problems, and other specific details; (e) tentative date when the proposed curriculum change could be put into effect if the study shows that the change is desirable; (f) dates when progress reports and final reports can be expected by the coordinating committee. With studies of a fairly simple nature, the details can be simple; as the studies become more significant in terms of energy and effects on large numbers of persons the details and planning become increasingly detailed. Unless careful planning is carried out, there is a danger that curriculum studies may be a hodgepodge of trivial generalities. Careful initial aim at a particular target for curriculum study is likely to be worth the effort.

A coordinating committee, whatever its name and scope, should carefully consider a proposal from a particular individual or group in the light of overall needs of children, resources, and plans. A reasonable amount of coordination between each elementary grade and between elementary and secondary levels should be attained. Certainly the financing of different curriculum proposals should be balanced, to avoid using disproportionate amounts of funds and resources for strengthening limited portions of the school programs. The procurement of instructional materials, equipment, and personnel should be in harmony with instructional goals, which in turn should reflect the needs of children and society.

Implementation of Change

Teachers may appropriately participate in setting priorities for revising the curriculum and selecting materials, but the actual implementation of changes appears to be an administrative responsibility. Curriculum studies should be supplemented as soon as feasible, and it is the duty of the administrator to use his time and his perspective to implement curriculum proposals which have been developed cooperatively.

The selection of basic instructional materials, particularly textbooks, is the main concern of many curriculum studies. The choice of means, mainly materials, should follow the determination of end products desired, that is, the type of behavioral changes hoped for as a result of certain instructional activities. Following this important step, certain additional measures are appropriate: (a) securing sample materials from reputable companies for careful examination and (where possible) use by pupils; (b) studying the materials systematically, through the use of a standardized guide which brings out important aspects of the materials, provides a means of comparing them uniformly, and assigns a numerical score to the strengths of each material; (c) making specific recommendations to the appropriate school officials. Both teachers and administrators should participate from the beginning in the overall study and help the study group to select materials which "make sense" in relation to the benefit of the pupils and teachers affected. Since it is often necessary to use instructional materials for a prescribed number of years, selection processes should be undertaken seriously. A schedule of replacement of teaching materials is desirable if adequate time is to be available before a decision must be reached and sufficient funds are to be available. Neither rushing nor delaying is justifiable since instructional materials have great impact upon what goes on in the classroom.

An adequate system should be developed to keep the total staff and community informed of the changes being studied, or of those which have been approved by appropriate groups, and the short-range and long-range schedule for their implementation. All proposals should be dated and coded in such a way that the staff can keep curriculum guides updated. A looseleaf notebook is useful for this purpose.

The completed study should be summarized in a concise guide which provides basic information on the content for each grade level. A suggested form follows:

1. In the upper right hand corner of all pages: general curricular area (for example, reading), inclusive grades for which the content is designed, and the date when the curriculum content and materials became official (for example, when approved by the Superintendent of Schools).
2. In the first section of a guide for a particular subject area: a listing of approved instructional materials to be used in carrying out curricular objectives, including the titles, publishers, date and edition of material used, and grade or class in which the materials is to be used.
3. In a second section of the guide: the general design for a particular subject area for a particular grade level (for example, the general content in reading for grade two). Sometimes the listing of content will be derived from the table of contents of the textbook used, but the content should be selected specifically for the community's children.

Study of Individuals or Small Groups

Replacing instructional materials and implementing changes in content, method, or organizational patterns for instruction need not occur simultaneously in all classes of a building or in the total school system. While a certain amount of administrative uniformity may make the life of the administrator simpler, this should not be the ultimate criterion as to whether changes should be implemented on a limited or extensive basis.

Changes brought about by the teacher or small group can be cited. One teacher may be interested in and competent in organizing individualized reading, and in cooperation with his principal, may teach reading this way and evaluate the results. A group of teachers in a building or in a school system may be interested in teaching science experimentally and, in cooperation with administrators and science consultants, may work out experiments together and thereby gain confidence. A number of teachers and administrators may study together to determine ways in which the curriculum can best be adapted to meet the needs of disadvantaged children. A group may wish to experiment with creative dramatics. Examples could be discussed almost indefinitely.

Teachers working on an individual project or together on a mutual concern are more likely to benefit than if they are working under compulsion. A reasonable amount of coordination is needed in a school building and system, since facilities, equipment, materials, and personnel must be shared. Some types of instructional plans affect many persons, for example, if an ungraded primary plan is being adopted, so that total faculty planning is necessary. Perhaps the oversimplification is that the individual teacher should be encouraged, within reasonable limits designed to produce good studies, to seek out his own unique ways of organizing instruction for his unique pupils.

Freedom for Curriculum Studies

You probably will find increased freedom to experiment with your curriculum as you become proficient in analyzing its present effectiveness; considering alternatives; cooperatively selecting the best alternatives; "tooling up" with needed materials and equipment; putting new ideas into practice; interpreting the changes to parents, pupils, and fellow teachers and administrators; and evaluating and altering plans. It is best to begin with relatively small changes to demonstrate your care in effecting changes.

There seems to be a burden of proof upon the individual who wishes to change things. At least this is the impression the beginning teacher may get, particularly in a school where most of the staff have been there for some time. You may feel that this burden should also be upon those who seek to maintain things the way they have been. However, organizations tend to be conservative, and the relatively inexperienced teacher will need to demonstrate that he does not seek change haphazardly and that he will carefully select changes which can improve the present situation rather than alter it drastically. If you plan carefully and interpret sensibly you will find that other faculty, parents, and pupils are quite willing to see *some* changes made.

It is wholesale and rapid changes, particularly when made with new terms or new and emotionally-tinged slogans, that bring about demands that change be slowed or stopped. This is fair enough, for all changes are not for the good and those which have much good in them may produce enough negative results to justify caution. Certainly changes cannot be justified merely because they have worked elsewhere or are generally recommended by experts. A "good" change has little chance for success if undertaken in an atmosphere of mistrust, doubt, and suspicion—whether among staff, citizens, or pupils.

Beginning teachers should take enthusiasm, flexibility, and professional competence into a job. They should be encouraged to implement change where needed *and when feasible.* A caution is that the teacher new to a given teaching situation may appear to have contempt for what has been if he proposes changes too rapidly.

We have suggested that curriculum studies are an important role for teachers. Anderson provides a concise summary of potential benefits of curriculum studies:

Help us to develop skills in planning together as teachers, administrators, supervisors, pupils, and laymen.
Make us anxious to work with parents or with the school.
Encourage us to seek for the causes of children's behavior and to learn how to study children.
Cause us to demand a chance to take an active part in the program.
Cause us to analyze the experiences we are providing for children in terms of the purposes we have in mind.
Result in our attuning the curriculum to changes of behavior.
Create good rapport between us and our colleagues.
Create a desire for us to try out new ideas, to read, to question.
Result in the improvement of children's experiences in the schools: experiences in being successful, in being understood, in being creative, in living with other children, in understanding the world about them, in understanding themselves, in gaining skills.
Make a difference in the lives of children.[6]

A FICTITIOUS CASE STUDY

A fictitious, and to a large extent ideal, case study may further help you to conceptualize the curriculum study and innovation process on the local school level. It describes how a new principal and staff gradually changed curriculum processes in a school. Elements of the process described below are experienced in schools with vital curricula.

From Teacher to Principal

The telephone message is brief. "Call Mr. Hamlin at your convenience." When the pupils in the sixth grade class leave after school, the teacher calls Mr. Hamlin. Mr. Hamlin asks the teacher—Mr. Johnson—to come to his office. He indicates interest in Mr. Johnson as candidate for the principalship at the Pleasant Acres Elementary School where he has taught for the last three years. A. O. Cratic, the principal there now, has secured a position as director of elementary education in a nearby school system. "I'm definitely interested," Mr. Johnson tells Mr. Hamlin. "My graduate work has been planned with administration in mind," he tells the superintendent.

[6] Vernon E. Anderson, *Principles and Procedures of Curriculum Improvement*, Second Edition (New York: The Ronald Press Co., 1965), p. 168.

Mr. Hamlin indicates faith in Mr. Johnson's ability to look over the situation and make changes where needed. "I want you to feel free to develop the kind of program best suited for Pleasant Acres. You have worked on the system's curriculum guides and know their values as a unifying influence, but I think that some principals place too much faith in them." Mr. Hamlin goes on to explain his hopes for more decentralization and greater local building initiative. "You have several things in your favor. You have a pleasant building and a staff with a good experience and academic background. You know what the community and the profession are trying to achieve."

A need for clarification comes to Mr. Johnson's mind. "To what extent do you want me to carry out educational goals the way they are being carried out in the other schools in the district?"

Mr. Hamlin is very emphatic in his reply. "I certainly expect a reasonable degree of consistency, and I believe that your regular meetings with the administrative staff and work with system committees will help you keep in touch with the best thinking of our staff. You can expect the teachers also to keep abreast of what is needed for the children. Of course, this is only if you really believe in them and turn to them as part of the team. Confidentially, I think this is a weak aspect of Pleasant Acres School."

As he leaves the conference, Mr. Johnson is quite certain that his job next year will be that of principal. A contract two days later confirms this. Mr. Hamlin has discussed the position with the teachers at Pleasant Acres. They indicate support for Mr. Johnson—the support he *earned* as a teacher. There is great potentiality for productivity in the position.

The Present Situation

The staff has been known for being rather contented concerning the curriculum. This is especially true of those teachers who feel that their only responsibility lies in the classroom. They welcomed the small number of meetings, the briskness with which the previous principal, Mr. Cratic, handled them, and the certainty of instructions which he gave during meetings. Many numbers of the staff liked the security offered by Mr. Cratic: that is, they liked knowing where they stood with him.

The more intelligent members of the staff resented the subtle manipulation which lay back of the friendly smile and warm personal interest displayed in each teacher. The staff responded to the orderliness and organization for which Mr. Cratic felt real pride. They displayed *his* elaborate handbooks, curriculum guides, and procedure books in a prominent place. (These publications produced uniformity or conformity, depending upon one's point of view.)

The staff is quite intelligent and academically respectable, but its inability to display initiative in decision-making is apparent when the principal is away—it becomes a group of confused individuals. No one was willing to assume leadership, for such an act could boomerang.

The pupils reacted to the principal rather affectionately, for he took a paternal interest in their lives. He decided upon their disciplinary patterns, modes of dress, extra-curricular activities, and relationships to their teachers. As long as they did not question his methods, he was indeed a "good Joe" type of principal. They have long been accustomed to going to his office for all but routine class matters. He immediately gave them positive answers and definite procedures. He sincerely believed that he was doing what was best for them.

The community had high regard for Mr. Cratic. They liked the way in which he authoritatively described goals, methods, and results of the school program. They compared his sureness with the uncertainty of the teachers concerning school goals and results. He was known as a good citizen, for he was active in church, civic, and benevolent organizations. These contacts afforded him many opportunities to speak formally and to converse informally about school issues.

Curriculum practices stressed narrowly defined "fundamentals" and American history. In fact Mr. Cratic proudly served as a judge in local oratorical contests designed to promote student pride in democracy. He chose textbooks and workbooks that emphasized fundamentals and skills. Teachers were expected to rely on the curriculum guide whose content was minutely delineated by grade level and subjects. They were told to follow the guides rigidly so that pupils would be "prepared for junior high" (and uphold the good name Pleasant Acres pupils had when they entered junior high).

Mr. Cratic believed that his job required strict evaluation of personnel and pupils. He carefully used achievement tests to prepare comparisons of pupils in each class and comparisons of different rooms. There was just as rigid an evaluation of teachers based upon a carefully devised rating scale which emphasized conformity in teaching and detailed routines. Since he believed himself to be *the* educational expert in the building, he confidently used his standards to evaluate teachers and pupils. If they did not measure up, he determined what they needed to do to meet his expectations. Failure in Pleasant Acres School meant failure to meet the clearly defined philosophy, procedures, and goals of Mr. Cratic.

Mr. Johnson's August Preparations

Osmosis is a word that comes to Mr. Johnson's mind as he sits in the office. It is easy to think in a quiet office. Soon the quietness will be broken by the chatter, largely of female voices, as the staff begins to arrive for preschool conference.

As he sees it, osmosis is an important preparation for their arrival. He wants to reorient his thinking from that of a classroom teacher to that of an administrator without losing a sense of communication and common purpose with the teachers.

There's the Curriculum Guide, partially familiar—at least the fifth and sixth grade portions of it. He plans to stick with it as a general instructional guide for the school until the group feels secure enough to make it more flexible and compatible with the real needs of children. It could be used as a point of departure for those four new teachers.

And there, neatly filed in file number 23, are the teacher's reports filled out during the rush of last year's hectic closing days. He recalls the warm weather, pupil inertia, reports to be filled out, thoughts about summer plans, and all the host of problems which crowd the last days of school. In several reports there are very similar ideas with only slightly varied wording. How can a new principal develop real democratic participation and diffuse the influence of the clique which has secretly developed an informal but "practical" program for Pleasant Acres School for this year? What are the real teacher needs and interests in the hidden meanings of these formal reports? How can the staff cooperatively develop a continuous evaluative process to eliminate these end-of-year reports?

Also in file 23, there is a very thick folder of Supervisory Reports, Form Number 5, which Mr. Cratic used when he wanted to get an individual to do something. He certainly had a way of letting teachers know that he had a lot of "information" about the way they did things—a not too subtle way of pressuring people! Mr. Johnson plans to examine these reports and attempt to sift out the real educational implications without getting in the mire of detailed trivia. He resolves also to keep a folder, but not like this. Mr. Johnson's folder will summarize group discussions and decisions, and will note who prompted them, who assumed different responsibilities, and who helped to evaluate them. Also he wants the folder to contain brief notations of informal discussions. By next year at this time, he is more likely to know the real concerns of the group. Personal considerations will be included in the folder, for he knows that teachers do not work in a vacuum. While he finds the teachers' job applications helpful in supplying background information, he wants to supplement this with other materials as he discovers them.

As he looks through the files, Mr. Johnson is amazed at how often Mr. Cratic held the spotlight. Chairman, recorder, discussion leader, master of ceremonies, editor, organizer, expert—it is no wonder that many stood in awe of him. But then Mr. Johnson recalls the many fine teachers who silently withheld their varied skills and ideas from the group. After all, their leader basked in his glory. It was simpler to "stick to the classroom."

Preschool Conference Sets the Tone for Interaction

Behind the smiles and the good-natured ribbing about the "new" principal, there seems to be some uneasiness. There is insecurity for everyone during times of change. At the opening coffee hour Mr. Johnson attempts to be himself. After all, these are people that he has known for a long time. He does find himself guarding his comments, toning down his teasing, and avoiding statements that might seem to indicate that he has made inflexible plans during the summer. The real stage setting for the new year comes during the planning sessions. He emphasizes changes which have been dictated by the board of education and legislative enactments. Then he asks the group to fill out an open-ended questionnaire on curriculum developed from reports from past years and comments from different teachers.

He finds it hard to avoid appointing committees to find answers. Instead he asks for nominations for a committee composed of a few relatively new teachers and several of the veteran teachers to analyze the questionnaires, summarize them, and present them to a faculty meeting later on. He suggests that this same group might also think of some other questions that the total faculty might want to consider later.

As soon as he senses some signs of inattention and cynicism showing, he switches to something "practical" such as pupil policies, lunchroom and playground assignments, opening-of-school procedures, and other such items. These are details that the group can not only discuss but also make decisions about. The cynics are not without some basis for their cynicism. They have gone through endless discussions, made recommendations, and have seen them ignored. They seem to be surprised that the appointment as principal has not made Mr. Johnson an "expert" on everything.

At first the ideas are repeats from last year. Then a beginning teacher openly suggests a change. Mr. Johnson doesn't blink an eye at the suggestion, and even asks if there are other possible suggestions. The recorder lists the alternatives on the board. As the discussion moves back and forth, there seems to be some jelling of the group. Some teachers, as well as Mr. Johnson, realize with some surprise that there is not a single vote taken. The staff agrees on school routine!

On the third day of the conference the group seems to be getting into real issues. For example, the fourth grade teachers are quite concerned about supplementary science books. The coffee break discussion centers around supplementary science books, a shortcoming which has been recognized by many members of the staff for many years. Mr. Johnson offers to drive over to the Instructional Aids Center at State University. "Would anyone like to come along to see what is available?" (He silently notes that there is a great deal of interest in science. With some encouragement, the staff might be interested in delving deeper. He controls the temptation to suggest this, for he doesn't want to involve the group in something until it recognizes this need as vital.)

An afternoon coffee break in a home gives the staff a chance to establish closer ties and such periods are bridging the gap between different cliques and personalities. They are learning to share ideas and disagree in an informal, nonpressure setting. This relationship can be carried over into decision-making situations.

The First Week

The first week passes rapidly. The staff carefully follows past procedures without attaching unique emphasis to them. Mr. Johnson asks questions which hint at alternatives. He meets with grade level groups to get group consensus on immediate problems. He makes suggestions when the group reaches an impasse. He continues his resolve that the group will grow in self-direction as time passes.

There is a perceptible change in the atmosphere of Pleasant Acres. Teachers seem to feel more confident to take some initiative. This is reflected in the beginning of some pupil–teacher planning. The pupils themselves seem to be more relaxed, within the orderly confines of safety and thoughtfulness to others.

The stage has been set for the faculty, pupils, and community to start some real examination of what is being done and what should be done. The relaxation of tensions does not turn into chaos and licence in the name of "freedom" and democracy. It is orderly and efficient group democracy in operation.

A Look at Group Process

Vacations are good since they give the principal and teachers a chance to think without having to handle requests for assistance, or telephone calls, or dozens of other pressures. The cheerful wishes for a pleasant vacation exchanged the last day of school prove that there is a "*we* feeling" at Pleasant Acres. It is surprising how much is learned about the lives, hopes, and fears of a staff in a free and supportive atmosphere.

Mr. Johnson's initial goal of getting the group process underway has been partially achieved. Now there is a need to deepen it. He encourages the staff to flip through textbook indexes and tables of contents to look for notations on group process, curriculum dynamics, and similar concepts. He records some of the most important concepts and leaves space for evaluating the present state of affairs and further evaluation at the end of the year.

Getting the Group To Form Group Activities

The preschool conference questionnaire is only the beginning step. It is no longer necessary to solicit ideas. The faculty council assumes a major responsibility for developing studies and setting up agenda for meeting. What Benne and Muntyan call the "human relations structure" is informal but active in operation. The different members of the staff function as official leaders as the need for different types of leadership arises. Mr. Johnson sees his primary task as helping the group select its problems and decide upon the most productive ways to solve them. "Having problems is permitted" is the way Benne and Muntyan decribe it.[7]

The Principal's Role in Group Discussions

Increasingly the principal succeeds in avoiding the two extremes Haiman mentions: "overshadowing" and "idea eunuch." He has learned that the group expects him to participate as a *member* of the group. It seems to be more important for him to remember how to participate rather than exactly what to say.

Freeing the Teacher for Better Participation

It appears that teachers at Pleasant Acres are interested in curriculum improvement provided that certain factors are kept in mind:

1. Group processes take time. The staff has secured Board of Education approval to have pupils released 60 minutes early once a week for in-service training activities.
2. Several members of the staff can assume leadership roles and recorder roles. With definite goals related to group needs, there is an interest in in-service training and assumption of responsibilities.
3. The faculty is a professional group. It is capable of setting up its agenda, coordinating the curriculum, evaluating instruction, and making policy recommendations to the superintendent and Board of Education.

[7] Kenneth Benne and Bozidor Muntyan, *Human Relations in Curriculum Change* (New York: Dryden Press, 1951), pp. 84–98.

4. In cases where an action affects only part of the faculty, a subcommittee can be appointed. Discussions and decisions are kept in the hands of those most immediately affected. There is need to keep the energies of each staff member directed toward real situations. There is no time to waste on irrelevancies.[8]

Utilizing the Total Resources Available

On some occasions the faculty council feels that it needs to look beyond Pleasant Acres. One such occasion involves the system's science program. The faculty council invites the superintendent of schools to attend its meetings. Generally he doesn't make it, but he does come when there is a definite reason for his being there. The staff feels that he is an integral part of its operations. Since Mr. Johnson does not give the impression that Pleasant Acres is "his" school, the staff feels free to bring in the superintendent, the coordinator of instruction, system consultants, and specialists from State University and Department of Public Instruction. Quite regularly lay citizens who have unique contributions to make feel free to make them. The older citizens particularly are able to work with pupils on special projects. There is a functioning neighborhood coordinating council which quite often brings together the best thinking of lay citizen, teacher, pupil, and principal in a mutual search for the best education possible. As the group works together, there is a good understanding of what the total staff and community are doing and hoping to do. This is coordination of the highest order.

Effects on Instruction

The children find Pleasant Acres a better school. The ultimate goal for all group process is to improve the way school affects pupil thinking, living, and growing. The children seem to be more secure and happy, for they reflect the reactions of their teachers. They find that their teachers take more initiative in creating a climate for living and growing which minimizes problems. When difficulties do arise, the teachers feel free to work directly with pupils, thus giving the teachers more status in the eyes of pupils, who are in turn more receptive to continue teaching. It seems to be natural for the teacher to plan with pupils now that teachers experience cooperative staff planning. There is no longer what Florence Stratemeyer calls the false dichotomy of teaching about democracy from a book and not practicing it in daily relationships.[9] Lewin stresses the

[8] Arthur J. Lewis, "Staff Utilization to Improve Learning," *Educational Leadership*, XVIII, No. 7 (April, 1960), pp. 410–15.

[9] Florence Stratemeyer, *et al.*, *Developing a Curriculum for Modern Living* (New York: Teachers College Press, Columbia University, 1947), p. 392.

idea this way: "The character and cultural habits of the growing citizens are not so much determined by what they say as by what they live.[10]

Democracy "Holds Up" in Operation

Group process has been in operation for several months but it has been maintained, even "under fire." There have been crises and there have been problems. However, the atmosphere is free from bitter personality clashes. There is willingness to discuss issues rather than personalities. There is emphasis on what is right rather than who is right.

With security and individual worth recognized within the framework of group process, there is a desire by most individuals to make their maximum contribution. There are still times when old patterns return, but they are decreasing under steady and quiet group pressures to carry out the goals established by the group within specified time limits.

The thing that really counts is the children. They are relaxed and growing in self-control. They are being brought into more and more pupil–teacher planning for instruction, activities, and goals. Their motivation is increasingly based on the excitement that accompanies real learning. Report cards still are used, but the faculty council is working with the staff on ways to make reports to parents more interpretive.

The staff does many challenging things together now. Techniques of group process will increasingly make it more and more productive. There appear to be few practical limitations to its potentiality.

Wiles's suggestions for democratic leadership are applied by the principal and staff: "(a) To increase group unity, (b) to encourage the experimental approach, (c) to enrich the group's thinking, (d) to build the security and self-confidence of the group, (e) to help the group see clearly the boundaries of its authority, (f) to increase interaction and sharing of experience, (g) to extend the opportunities for leadership."[11] These concepts of democratic leadership make group process at Pleasant Acres real and vital to children, teachers, and community.

PROJECTS AND READINGS

1. Several steps are needed to bring about a successful adoption of new practices in a school system, according to James E. Allen, Jr., "Shaping Educational Policy–Role of the State" (*The Teachers College Journal*, XXXVII, No. 4 (January, 1966), pp. 154–55). The steps are: (a) It must be "identifiable, describable, and reproducible" under conditions prevailing in the system.

[10] Kurt Lewin, "The Dynamics of Group Action," *Educational Leadership*, I, No. 4 (January, 1944), pp. 195–200.

[11] Kimball Wiles, *Supervision for Better Schools* (Englewood Cliffs, N.J.: Prentice-Hall, Inc., 1955), p. 33.

(b) School personnel must be aware of the proposal to establish a new program. (c) Visitation must be available in a situation where the new program can be observed. (d) Support for the new program must be obtained, particularly from administrators. (e) Support and endorsement must be secured from the public and its board of education. (f) Legal restrictions must be removed. (g) The local district must arrange for necessary additional financing. (h) Physical facilities must be planned where necessary. (i) Allocations of time—day, week, or year—must be planned. (j) Needed materials and equipment must be made available. (k) New teachers entering the system after the establishment of the new plan must be oriented and prepared. (l) Practice of new kinds of teaching must be planned, including provision for supervisory and consultant help while the new program is being established. (m) Testing programs must be planned for the new program. Thus it can be seen that change involves a series of coordinated plans. Which of the above steps appears to have the most significance in terms of the classroom teacher?

2. A school system often has a number of curriculum-related committees. Effective service on committees requires considerable time. What, in your opinion, are the pros and cons of service on committees in terms of effectiveness of classroom teaching and of a building's instructional program, and in terms of personal and professional growth? To what extent do your answers hold for a new or inexperienced teacher if he is requested to serve on a system-wide committee?

3. The National Association of Elementary School Principals, Association for Supervision and Curriculum Development, and American Association of School Administrators have good publications on curriculum on both the building and also the system-wide level.

4. An old but stimulating publication entitled *Curriculum Development as Re-education of the Teacher* presents a basic message: Teachers ultimately are the implementers of curriculum change and therefore should be included in decision-making. Involvement is time consuming. In your opinion, are there circumstances where a school superintendent, curriculum director, or principal should make a major curriculum decision without involving classroom teachers? What are likely to be the consequences, positive and negative? What, if anything, can speed up the involvement processes? George Sharp, *Curriculum Development as Re-education of the Teacher* (New York: Teachers College Press, Columbia University, 1951).

5. School systems, particularly large, urban ones, often are faced with great community pressures to develop non-segregated systems. One approach is to develop an education park (or parks) which draws students from such a large area that the school complex serving that area is likely to be integrated. What are the consequences if a school system does (or does not) respond to pressures? In the case of a school park, which could bring as many as 20,000 elementary and secondary students into one location, what are some educational advantages and disadvantages to all students? (Journals for school administrators and school board members are likely to have articles on this very pertinent issue.)

6. A good basic curriculum reference, which has both curriculum recommendations and bibliographic references is *Planning and Organizing for Teaching* (Washington, D.C.: Project on Instruction, National Education Association, 1963).

7. School systems should develop broad statements of purposes and guidelines for their attainment in individual school building and classrooms. How, in your opinion, should a system attempt to translate into local terms a publication such as *The Central Purposes of American Education?* (Washington, D.C.: Educational Policies Commission, National Education Association, 1961).

8. Some guidelines for "strength and vitality" in a school system have been identified by the Dean of Education, Ohio State University, Luvern L. Cunningham: (a) organized ways to analyze goals; (b) more interest in the present than in the past; (c) methods for combating vested interests determined to maintain the present; (d) an environment which is hospitable to different kinds of individuals; (e) means to carry on constructive self-criticism; (f) ways to avoid tendencies to become trapped by its own procedures; (g) capacity to solve problems; (h) capacity to evaluate ideas on merit rather than on the source of ideas; (i) flexibility to enable individuals to work together in different ways for different purposes; (j) "motivation, conviction, and morale by people who care." [From a speech given in Chicago, on November 17, 1967, to the joint meeting of the Illinois Association of School Boards and Illinois Association of School Administrators; reported in *The Newsletter* (Ohio State University), XXXIII, No. 4 (January, 1968), p. 3.]

9. An example of community planning is parental participation in the selection of principal and teachers, the curriculum, and other aspects of control previously reserved for the school board and administrative staff. Particularly in large cities there are proposals that schools be turned over to local, popularly selected neighborhood governing boards which would receive school district financial aid and almost complete autonomy. How do you feel about lay control on this level? What professional prerogatives would remain? If you investigate the topic, you will find several prestigious proponents of local control. To what extent do you agree with them that this is the only way to gain a sense of local responsibility for making education relevant and effective? How can local control of curriculum and school administration be established without fragmentation of the American people? Or is this an unlikely prospect? What are the prospects that organizations such as the Parent–Teacher Association could assume a more active role than they have in the past?

10. The Center for the Study of Instruction, National Education Association, has prepared a series of publications based on the broad theme of "Schools for the 70's." The publications include position papers and annotated bibliographies. They are recommended reading for serious students of curriculum. To what extent should every teacher be expected to read such materials, and to what extent should in-depth thinking be left to educational leaders? Can teachers be held accountable for curriculum progress and problems until they become serious scholars of education?

11. There may be as many as 93 new kinds of jobs in the schools by the 1980's, according to Shane. See Harold G. Shane, "Designing Changes in Teacher Education Through Future-Planning: The Role of Systems Theory," an address presented to the AACTE Dissemination Project Workshop–Seminar at the University of Missouri-Kansas City, November, 1969. With differentiated staffs doing the many tasks assigned to the schools, many organizational patterns will emerge. What does this suggest to you about your pre- and in-service preparation? What attitudes and competencies can you develop to facilitate your taking advantage of new kinds of job opportunities in the future?

12. Instructional activities organized by students and the faculty in a school without a building. This describes the Parkway School in Philadelphia. This small high school is composed of students and faculty who want to organize a new kind of meaningful program. Philadelphia itself is the curriculum. Materials are secured from the organizations, agencies, and enterprises which provide space and many volunteer teachers. Tutorial groups are organized when needed to develop "basic" skills. In your opinion, how sound is the concept? To what extent could it be applied to elementary education? What factors are likely to be most important in either blocking or facilitating the idea?

13. Massive changes dictate comprehensive educational planning. The "systems approach" must be used increasingly to update curriculum continuously in the light of new knowledge and conditions. This approach requires (a) an analysis of the society and of the learner, (b) an identification of the parts of the large picture which must be observed in decision-making, (c) specification of performance levels to be sought (objectives in behavioral terms), (d) delineation of various solutions to educational problems, (e) selection of best alternatives, (f) implementation of those alternatives, and (g) assessment of their effectiveness and change as needed to attain objectives and retain relevancy to the changing needs of society and of the learners. Granted the efficiency of the systems approach to large-scale problems, how can schools maintain their concern for individuals? How can the curriculum demonstrate the validity of rational problem-selving?

8

Human Relations and Group Dynamics

THE CLASS—A GROUP OF INDIVIDUALS

The term used to describe a group of pupils assigned to a particular teacher for a specific period of time is deceptively simple. Whether "class," "level," "5–b," or "Miss Halmer's class," there is an implication that a word can describe a group of pupils. Let us examine a definition to provide a focus for this chapter:

> Although social psychologists have theoretical disagreements as to the nature of a group, most would agree with substance of the following definition: "A group is a social unit which consists of a number of individuals who interact with each other, who hold a common set of values, and who are interdependent." [1]

Depending upon the unity of a classroom of children and their adult supervisors, an elementary group meets this definition. The complexity of a group is a challenge of great importance, for it is commonly accepted that when you teach, you teach something to someone, both individually and collectively. The group has great influence on individual reactions to the curriculum.

Individuals in an Impersonal World

To avoid looking at a class as a mass of pupils it is necessary to examine why each child is unique. Several factors contribute to individual

[1] Louis M. Smith, *Group Processes in Elementary and Secondary Schools, What Research Says to the Teacher Series,* No. 19 (Washington: Association of Classroom Teachers, A Department of the National Education Association, 1959), p. 3.

differences and each child is affected by them at a given time. The fluctuating influence of these factors should prevent you from categorizing a child at the beginning of the year and assuming that he will behave in particular ways all year (or for that matter all day, all week, or all month).

When holding class was the accepted teacher role, emphasis upon *ruling* the class with an iron hand was valid. Indeed survival as a teacher dictates that to an extent you probably will enforce discipline rather uniformly until reasonable order prevails. Curriculum, as we have suggested, is essentially what happens in the classroom; it is unlikely that constructive learning can occur under chaotic conditions. Democratic group processes are the ultimate goal; they are arrived at only through understanding, skill, and patience. They are ultimate rather than immediate practices.

The teacher of today is not expected to "pound some sense into children's heads." The pressures now are for influencing present and prospective pupil behavior through rationality, worthwhile instructional activities, and constructive human relations. Contemporary conditions make this difficult. Pupils are largely removed from an intimate involvement with the social, economic, and political order. As a result, the curriculum may have little relevancy to them; and the teacher may be viewed as part of the impersonal social system. In a ghetto child's view, his teacher seems to exploit him. A middle class child may view a woman teacher as driving him mercilessly; he may even, as a result of his view of his teacher, subrogate his father's authority to the point where he identifies his father's roles with those of his mother. Many children view their teacher as someone who violates childhood; they desire to play, to be gay, to be noisy, to be physically active, and to change activities when the present ones become uninteresting. The teacher is expected to bring forth out of the classroom's many forces not only order but also *learning*.

Additional complications arise from the separation of school from community which is a common but not inevitable situation in modern society. Parents and citizens without the type of contact common in the days of the one room school may feel either disinclined or incapable of interpreting the school curriculum to children. They may agree with the children that the curriculum is irrelevant. Involvement may then be limited to formal relations such as parent–teacher groups, advisory councils, or other committee approaches by the relatively few parents who identify with the school. These approaches may be limited to superficial discussions of education in general rather than the education of a particular child. Parent–teacher conferences and report cards are helpful but are not adequate in establishing strong home–school bonds. The news media are only one-way vehicles.

Elements of Diversity

Large-scale, impersonal education does not produce understanding, supportive adults who pass along similar attitudes to children. As a teacher you are viewed as a "system" official until you demonstrate that you are a unique person as well. Even if the community situation is ideal, there is a bewildering diversity of children's reaction to the school curriculum.

Ethnic differences, even in the American melting pot, contribute conflicts and suspicion. Good human relations practices have to be supplemented by facts and appreciations concerning the contributions of the many groups which have built America. Curricular materials should be objective and comprehensive. (For example: avoid reading materials which rarely include Italian characters or those that depict them only as organ grinders with the ever present monkey or those that give stereotyped presentations of all groups, even the White Anglo-Saxon Protestants. The history of America is one of upward mobility. Ethnic groups found their promised land and made it promising. Each group has to an extent found it necessary to struggle, physically and emotionally, to become an integral part of its new homeland. Good human relations practiced in the classroom should complement what is included in the curriculum.

Religious tolerance has become increasingly the accepted mode. There are greater tendencies to accept with constructive interest the differences and similarities of religious groups. The study of religion is accepted under U. S. Supreme Court rulings which banned sectarian instruction in the public schools. Cooperative relationships between public and private schools have been developed under the Elementary and Secondary Education Act. Under ESEA provisions the public school systems hold *title* to facilities, equipment, and materials but share them with private and parochial school children. Out of these cooperative arrangements may come some improvements in religious group understandings. It is possible to consider instructional implications of religion if there is a healthy community climate in which to accomplish this. An example would be a study of the difference in motivation which may prevail between Protestant, Catholic, and Jewish children.

Racial factors are a predominant concern in many American school districts. Indians, the earliest Americans, were not Caucasians; but they were soon outnumbered and after bitter conflict relegated to lands and locations not desired by white Americans. They have been insulated from the mainstream of American life in separate schools and have been a source of direct concern for relatively few teachers. There is a challenge to develop instruction to improve the understanding of this important group of Americans and also to insure positive attitudes toward all peoples. Presently there are serious questions about both the quantity and quality of instruction concerning American Indians.

Comparable points could be made concerning other racial minorities. Asians often are neglected in curriculum materials. American blacks constitute the major racial group currently seeking its place in the sun. Aided by massive coverage in the mass media and a sense of national urgency, changes are taking place in the curriculum to provide for better understandings of the rich diversity of America.

Typical discussions of racial factors dwell upon the races previously mentioned. There is need to consider the human relations factors for Caucasians. It is easy enough to assume that they have an adequate sense of dignity and worth. The poor white child of the city or rural slum has some advantages over Negroes, yet his skin color doesn't help him overcome all the forces which seem to hold him down.

Racial relations should be studied as *human* phenomena. The capacity to develop constructive human relations among the races stands out as a basic national challenge. No American problem is more striking; consequently no curricular concern is more vital.

Socioeconomic factors contribute some problems and divisiveness in the classroom. The haves and have nots may develop some suspicions and resentments which interfere with effective learning. The contributions of all socioeconomic classes should be stressed to help children develop a sense of dignity and worth so necessary for good human relations.

Individual differences themselves may contribute some tensions and conflict. Differences may arise between the more healthy and less healthy, the physically large and agile and those who are not. The bright and not so bright sense their differences and respond to them. The emotionally disturbed and imbalanced bring their problems into their relationships. Those poorly adjusted in social relationships present difficulties for the teacher and the class. These individual differences in themselves do not necessarily contribute problems. Learning to accept and even to encourage differences can become a vital learning experience with lifelong values. The challenge is to provide the atmosphere, the experiences, the knowledge, and the personal security which enable children to live with their own uniqueness and that of others.

You should examine carefully your irrational likes and dislikes. Experiences with different kinds of people and knowledge can help you to accept or reject an individual on his personal merit. Equally as significant, you can find out about yourself and develop that maturity, that sense of dignity and worth, so important for those who guide immature, often troubled, children seeking to find their humanness. Without your professional help, many children may be swept along with the tides of hate and fear and may be deprived of healthy and constructive human relations.

The *society of children* is a powerful force in classroom human relations. It exists side by side and within the official school society controlled by adults. Pupil leaders may influence the way in which children will react in the classroom, on playgrounds, and traveling to school. They can help individual children to find their true selves. On the other hand peer leaders can add frightening and negative dimensions to the lives of those children not accepted by the child society. If they perceive you as a helpful and competent person, these peer leaders can provide learning motivation for many children.

The childhood society has its own curriculum, some of which has been effectively passed on orally for hundreds of years (games, chants, jokes, ideas about teachers and parents). It can be related to the official curriculum and you can even use some of its teachings in motivating children to learn.

The Controlling Adults

The more commonly recognized society is that of adults. In the school setting, the significant adults are teachers, and administrators (usually one principal in smaller schools), plus assistants and consultants who visit several schools. Children sense the *quality* of relationships between those adults. It is hard to believe that a school can be effective in its formal instruction unless constructive human relations are practiced by the staff.

Children deserve to have adults who can resolve differences and conflicts in an open, frank, and realistic manner. This does not suggest an artificial atmosphere where all adults force smiles and agree with colleagues all the time. The total staff—as well as children and parents—should be treated with dignity and respect.

The principal sets the basic atmosphere. He should respect the right of each child and adult to have unique opinions, competence, and differences. He can help those under school dominion to make curriculum and other decisions within the limitations of school board regulations, civil laws, state regulations, and community norms. He should not pretend that anyone is helping to formulate decisions if he has already made them. Neither should he abdicate responsibility and permit anyone to follow personal whims. The democratic atmosphere is one where individuals practice rights and responsibilities.

A brief word needs to be said about some adults who serve several schools. Sometimes they are called *supervisors*, other times *consultants*.

Titles are less significant than their roles. If they are seen as *helpers,* they add a constructive dimension, a link between school and neighborhood and the larger community.

Teacher aides are somewhat difficult to place in the school society. Clearly the addition of another adult in a classroom changes its atmosphere. The aide can provide added affection, attention, and assistance; or he can become a source of conflict and hostility. The aide also may decrease the intimate teacher–pupil contacts which often create rapport.

The use of teacher aides is only one aspect of changing relationships in the elementary school. *Teams of adults* assigned to a group of children may include "master" teachers, other teachers, student teachers, teacher aides, clerks, and other types of personnel. The human relations factors that prevail when a team teaches a group of children are quite different from those that arise from a situation where there is one teacher assigned to a group of children.

Community Input

The general community of adults reaches into the school in many ways. In large measure it determines the quality of education and the general atmosphere of the school. It sets the minimum and maximum limits through provisions for staff, materials, equipment, and facilities. Equally significant is the community influence on attitude, motivation, and other intangible building blocks in school achievement. The hopes, objectives, and dreams of the community are taken into the school by both pupils and adults.

The School Outreach

The school need not be a passive recipient of influence. It can reach out with service—helping the neighborhood make its most vital decision, how to educate individuals of all ages. It can demonstrate concern for *individuals.*

The school can also bring citizens into the school to interpret pupil progress and problems and to share skills and teaching materials. What human being has nothing to share? What human being does not want to help his children or his neighbor's children?

The citizen who knows the staff as people can begin to understand the multiple roles of the teacher and, in his own way, may encourage children to benefit from the school curriculum. There are serious obstacles in creating bonds of respect and support between school and community. This may be particularly true in those neighborhoods—such as ghettos—that need these bonds. What is lived and learned become more mutually supportive and enlightening where good relationships prevail.

The school is a special type of society, set apart to provide some control over the learnings offered to children and yet hopefully a part of the community which nurtures it. Each person who has a role in the school—pupil, teacher, secretary, custodian, parent, general citizen—must sense a dynamic, creative environment and feel not only a right but also a responsibility for what goes on. Each has a unique role. The teacher is a part of the group, a vital key to helping each person attain his potential.

CLASSROOM HUMAN RELATIONS

The interaction of the individuals in the classroom with each other—and with others in the school and those connected with it—constitutes a social system of considerable complexity. While it would be interesting and worthwhile to study group processes in detail, this section will focus on those pertaining to the classroom. In the last analysis here is where the hopes and objectives of those inside and outside the classroom converge. This is where the effectiveness of the education system is decided and where the verbalized and published curriculum either comes to full realization or failure.

An Analysis of the Setting

In the school situation, conflict may undermine conditions needed for learning. Williams, in an old but useful publication, cites general group conditions conducive to conflict. Illustrative classroom examples of his ideas have been added parenthetically: (a) frustration and insecurity (academic failures and fear of failure), (b) continued contacts and competition for power and for that which is both scarce and desirable (peer prestige or teacher approval), (c) complexity of society (children and teachers with extreme diversities), (d) efforts to prove superiority (disadvantaged children emphasizing physical strength), (e) free floating hostilities (middle class child seeking a scapegoat for frustrations arising from middle class pressures at home). Williams himself did not discuss conflict in the school setting, yet his ideas seem to contribute to an understanding of classroom conflicts.[2]

There may be conflict in classroom decision-making when neighborhood, classroom peer group, teacher, or the norms are too diverse and rational decision-making has not matured. While a group may develop conflicts, it also offers advantages to members. It provides a means of attaining goals efficiently which one person might find difficult. Individuals with special group roles develop a sense of identity; even the child

[2] Robin Murphy Williams, *The Reduction of Intergroup Tensions* (New York: Social Science Research Council, n.d.), pp. 52–60.

who is the butt of ridicule may like his group role better than normally being a "nobody." Individual children will vary in their tendencies to cooperate with, resist, or ignore the group.[3]

Smith notes several unique features of a classroom group: [4]

1. The freedom of a school group is affected by imposed objectives, learning, and other kinds of growth.
2. The individual classroom is part of a school building and school system which establish certain expectations for children in particular grades.
3. The classroom group has a designated, official leader—the teacher—with certain rights and responsibilities, and certain expectations as to how he should, and indeed must, behave in his relations with children.
4. The classroom group is a captive group, since neither children nor teacher normally can leave during a specified school term. The children who fit best into this system are rewarded with praise, marks, and other means of approval. The children who do not fit may become increasingly hostile (or withdraw into their own dream world) which brings them into increasingly severe conflict with authority. Smith notes that generalizations drawn from research on the nature of groups should be applied with caution to those of the classroom since the school groups are unique in many ways.

Improvement of Classroom Relations

The teacher can improve the climate for good human relations. The child placed in successful situations with those who accept him can then build toward achieving acceptance by others. Each child has something to offer to the group; often that something is difficult to discover. Some children are effective in writing reports, others at speaking. Some are artistic or musical. Some can bring things, others build things. Some are followers, others leaders. Each classroom has a great diversity of pupil resources. Finding each child's group contributions requires spending time with each child. It means looking for the meaning of what a child writes, says, and does for trends and hints concerning his behavior. It then requires patience to accept failures and regression, along with successes, in the realization that a child's behavior patterns have developed slowly and can only be altered slowly.

It is important to be able to diagnose the type of interaction prevalent in a classroom. Gibb has provided some symptoms of two basic types

[3] Adapted from Everett M. Rogers, "The Communication of Innovation in a Complex Institution," paper presented to the National Conference on Curricular and Instructional Innovation for Large Colleges and Universities, East Lansing, Michigan, November 6–11, 1966.

[4] Smith, *op. cit.*, pp. 4–5.

of group behavior. First, he notes the following "signs of dependency and lack of participative movement":

1. Domination by either teacher or certain students favored by the teacher.
2. Dependence on limited numbers of students in class discussions.
3. Stabilization of individual roles (rather than having them shift with changing conditions).
4. Rebellion against authority, particularly that of the teacher.
5. "Disruption and breakdown" when the teacher is out of the room.
6. Evidences of "semi-reverence" for the teacher.

Second, there are signs which point to what Gibb calls "participative or interdependent movement" in the group:

1. Spontaneity within the group.
2. Difficulty in ascertaining leadership roles. (In other words, a few are not dominating the situation.)
3. Difficulty in predicting who will assume leadership in a given situation (since leadership is shared and varied with the situation).
4. Support for decisions made by the class.
5. Evidence of felt responsibility for group decisions.
6. Tendency for students to be at ease whether teacher is absent or present.[5]

In the participative situation, you should be able to secure frank, constructive reactions from pupils concerning the curriculum. You will be able to discuss and plan curriculum where you have this option; or if there are required contents, you can plan with pupils, within their maturity and experience level, the when, who, and how questions, and ultimately the how well done question. In the dependency situation, there will be a tendency for some pupils to accept blindly what the teacher wishes to have done regardless of personal meaning or understanding. There may be a tendency to reject or to rebel. Pupil responsibility for making the curriculum effective would then be unlikely.

To help children assume a sense of responsibility for their instructional objectives and procedures is a long-range goal. Ultimately, helping the group to overcome its weaknesses after it has analyzed them will in itself become a learning experience and should open the way for group planning of additional learning experiences.

Group skills should be developed through planned activities and whenever they arise incidentally. The following factors should be considered.

[5] Adapted from Jack R. Gibb, "Sociopsychological Processes of Group Instruction," in Nelson B. Henry (ed.), *The Dynamics of Instructional Groups,* Fifty-ninth Yearbook, National Society for the Study of Education, Pt. II (Chicago: University of Chicago Press, 1960), p. 121.

Your attitudes toward yourself, the pupils, and other adults concerned with the school should be examined. Knowing your prejudices, assets, and objectives—those that comprise the real you—will enable you to recognize the basis for many of your actions.

You can cooperatively study the atmosphere which prevails in your school and neighborhood. Does it exemplify the best in democratic human relations? What steps should be taken to improve it? How can available resources (people, equipment, materials, space, and time) be better utilized? What additional resources should be secured as soon as possible?

Action should be planned next. There should be planning for improvement, organizing for it, and evaluating what has been done and what must be done next. The democratic principle is that those affected by decisions should share in their formulation. Even young children have good perspectives about their own problems but they need to grow in the ability to solve them. Pupils and staff can discuss, seek alternatives, and plan ways to bring about needed changes. Parents and other citizens can also be involved. Both formal organizations (for example, a faculty committee and a genuinely representative student council) and informal methods (coffee hours for parents and impromptu teacher–class discussions) can be utilized.

Pupils can role play (act out real situations) success and failure, conflict and harmony, love and hate. They can role play races, ages, social class, and roles other than those with which they are familiar. They can learn about others through biographical and fictional materials. They can study about themselves and others in social studies, literature, creative writing, and other curriculum units. Most importantly perhaps, the general atmosphere of the school must continually reflect genuine respect for everyone (even those who seem least likable, for they especially need it). Open signs of disrespect, such as derogatory names and intentional embarrassment, should be strongly discouraged. Staff and pupils should exert group pressures against anything which undermines human dignity. In the constructive environment, formal instruction in human relations, incidental discussions, and organized activities all have a chance to bear fruit.

Efforts to improve human relations must be genuine; superficial attempts are readily sensed by children as well as adults. A student council with no real role may create contempt for democracy. A faculty committee expected to rubber stamp the principal's prior decisions is a farce. Children and adults do not feel that they must be involved in minor decisions. They are more likely to desire participation in major policy decisions and see a responsible person carry them out. They recognize that they do not have the right to make policy about some things, but they want to understand when and to what extent this is true. They want to know what the legal and official policy limits are—the real ones and not the artificial ones.

Discipline in Human Relations

Discipline is a reasonable aspect of a democracy; there could be chaos without it. There are some persons who need some external restraints: the immature, the maladjusted, those driven by irrational fears or frustrations, the greedy, those who undermine the freedom and dignity of others. While efforts are being made to help them to grow into more acceptable behavior, the rights of all individuals must be protected.

The curriculum should include content and activities designed to improve an understanding of how rights are inseparably paired with responsibilities. Democracy is an orderly process in which some restraints are applied when necessary to protect the rights of others. You as a teacher have the somewhat unpleasant responsibility of restraining pupils who endanger anyone's right to grow, to learn, and to enjoy opportunities in the classroom. Primarily you are a guide who helps the classroom group to set norms which increasingly free each pupil to grow into his best self.

There is a temptation for the novice in teaching to seek advice on what to do to control pupils. This leads to a search for physical or psychological means to restrain children, or academic methods—such as extra homework, tests, lowered marks, or a host of other efforts—that ultimately will evolve into ways to punish or subdue children.

It is appropriate to stress that purposeful learning activities—in a beneficial environment guided by mature, thoughtful, helpful, and competent adults—are a major contributor to constructive discipline. Positive discipline, like other objectives which should be included in the school curriculum, is a means to an end. It is always *in process*, rarely achieved. Constructive group processes can contribute to individual attainment of self-discipline. As each child and his group learn to live together in the democratic tradition, curriculum plans can become translated into meaningful terms. The plans will be made to benefit each, yet all can participate in adapting and implementing the curriculum to fit real needs.

Applied Human Relations

In the following section there are numerous specific suggestions for applying the principles of group processes to the subject areas. While there is a place for formal pupil study of group processes, they will learn them primarily while involved in instructional activities.

FULLY FUNCTIONING INDIVIDUALS

The "Whole Child" Concept

We have emphasized inter-relatedness: (a) Effective group relationships contribute to learning and other kinds of growth. (b) Effective learning should strengthen human relationships. The human being as an effective "whole" can contribute more to the group than can one who is fragmented by fear, suspicion, and hostility that may burst out indiscriminately and unpredictably. The cohesive group can add collective wisdom and insights to the individual. The mature, secure individual in such a setting can develop his own uniqueness as long as it does not infringe upon the freedom and dignity of others. Curriculum for fully functioning individuals and human relations includes knowledge, attitudes, values, and practices. It is carefully planned, and it capitalizes upon incidental learnings which arise in a free and dynamic group.

The school should be an individual and group laboratory wherein the democratic tradition is combined with the best insights of learners and school staff. Efforts cannot be superficial and limited to platitudes and shallow discussions. The learning should be real and exciting for both children and adults. Problems, goals, and needs of the individuals attending a particular school are the meaningful content in human relations. As growth in rationality and critical thinking proceeds, there will be growing realization that there are resources at hand in books, in the minds of others, in the community, in the traditions of a free people which can enlarge individual and group perceptions and practices. Individuals are after all the basic resource in helping others.

The "Helping Relationship"

Let us examine in more detail the idea of a helping relationship which prevails in a dynamic, democratic school. Rogers writes extensively on this subject [6] and the following summary reflects his concepts. Practicing these suggestions can contribute to the individuality of each person in a group.

1. We should be what we are at a given moment. Others see us for what we are rather than what we say we are.
2. We should communicate our true sentiments with clarity and feeling.
3. We should feel free to *experience* deep feelings. This will not undermine others' acceptance of our professional competence. We

[6] Carl Rogers, in Peter T. Hountras (ed.), *Mental Hygiene* (Columbus, Ohio: Charles E. Merrill Books, Inc., 1961), pp. 441–56.

should be further prepared to accept others' inability to express their deep feelings without resenting their apparent non-response.
4. We should be willing to know ourselves adequately, to protect others from our smothering people for our own purposes, and to accept others' unwillingness or independence of us without resentment.
5. We should be strong enough to permit others their uniqueness and should be glad when they are able to become increasingly independent of us.
6. We should grow in the ability to see the world through others' eyes without the temptation to impose our own "correct" perceptions upon them.
7. We should improve our capacity for seeing others as they are, without condition.
8. We should be able to react to others without implying threats which can limit others' capacity to expose their true selves to us.
9. We should enable others to proceed with self-analysis and openness by removing evaluation of their acts.
10. We should accept others as being in the process of becoming, rather than regarding them bound by their past or ours. We should stress their potentialities and encourage them to accept what they might become. We should avoid anything which might confirm others' low esteem of themselves.

Rogers was discussing the helping relationship as applied to counselors. Individual variance from norms can be accepted with greater ease for a counselor than is possible for a classroom teacher. The classroom teacher with 20 to 50 pupils often requires greater restraints as a means of maintaining reasonable order.

A hypothesis is that the secure, mature teacher can communicate acceptance and understanding while imposing restrictions for the sake of the group. Children perceive what you *are*. If you are a person who identifies with others the children will sense this and accept reasonable restrictions. You will need to experiment to determine how much freedom a particular class can live with, and how much restraint must be imposed until the immature achieve democratic maturity.

The Teacher's Leadership Roles

You as a teacher are the key to the development of discipline and the formation of democratic individuals and groups. "Discipline" can turn into authoritarianism with preordained leaders thinking for everyone. "Democracy" can turn into a chaotic pursuit of whatever happens to capture the whims of the moment. True demcoracy is a way of life, and the teacher is potentially the only person in the elementary classroom with adequate grasps of democracy's challenges and complexities to help children to understand democracy and practice it as a way of living and being. This guidance, purified of selfishness or hidden motives, should help each child and his peer group to grow into both self-reliance and unselfish co-operation.

The teacher must remain in the leadership role. He is with, but not of, the childhood society. No matter how much he may admire the spontaneity and apparent simplicity of childhood, he cannot return to childish behavior. The children want and deserve far more than that.

The teacher who helps to create effective group processes while maintaining individuality has achieved a major objective of curriculum in a democracy.

PROJECTS AND READINGS

1. "Three criteria of interpersonal competence are: (a) the awareness of the problems; (b) the solution of these problems in such a way that they remain solved; and (c) the accomplishment of both without deteriorating the problem-solving process within or among the individuals involved." The problems noted here are those which the individual can control. See Chris Argyris, *Explorations in Human Relations Training and Research,* Number Three–1966 (Washington: National Training Laboratories, National Education Association), pp. 4–5. Argyris notes that group processes are improved when a group encourages ". . . its members to be open, to experiment, to be responsible for the effectiveness of the group, and to delegate the leadership function to the person who can best fulfill it, thereby rotating it as the group goals change and different competencies become highlighted." Some people claim that these points relate to human groups in general, while others would maintain that a group of children is so specialized that Argyris' generalizations do not apply. Which generalizations do not seem applicable to a classroom of elementary children? Why or why not?

2. The following answers were most frequently given by 429 high school teachers to the question, "What do you wish that you had known about human relations before you became a teacher?":

How to handle deviant children.
Understanding of individual differences—intellectual, emotional, socioeconomic, religious, racial, ethnic.
Understanding of the problems faced by the adolescent.
Understanding of the negative aspects of the teaching profession—politics, apathy, narrowmindedness.
How to deal with parents.
Better knowledge of the behavioral sciences.
How to teach for individual differences.
How to deal with administrators and co-workers.

It was also noted that "Many wished that they had had broader practical experience in human relations situations." [North Central Association of Colleges and Secondary Schools, *Human Relations in the Classroom: A Challenge to Teacher Education* (Chicago: North Central Association of Colleges and

Secondary Schools, n.d.), pp. 15–16.] How are these human relations applicable to elementary schools? Which ones do you feel the most need to think through further?

3. Human relations, group dynamics, group behavior, and behavioral engineering are some terms used to describe topics discussed in this chapter. Such words can be used as guides in seeking journal articles and books.

4. "Experimentation: Unless there is opportunity to try out new patterns of thought and behavior, they never become a part of the individual. Without experimental efforts relevant change is difficult to make." ["Reading Book," Twenty-first Annual Summer Laboratories in Human Relations Training, 1967 (Washington, D.C.: National Training Laboratories, National Education Association), p. 10.] Do you feel that a teacher can permit each individual child to experiment with different kinds of behavior? What positive and negative consequences would you predict, in terms of various kinds of learnings? In the "Reading Book" (page 26), there is a description of what human beings avoid, and what lowers self-esteem: "being manipulated," "dominated," "pushed around," "determined by others," and "to be misunderstood." How can some children be permitted to experiment with behavior without seriously damaging other children's self-esteem and dignity? (The papers from which the above notes were taken were originally prepared for theory sessions at NTL's laboratories.)

9

Outside Influences on Curriculum

TRADITION OF LOCAL CONTROL

The traditional control of American education by local communities results from omission of a specific federal education role in the United States Constitution and delegation of authority to local agencies by most states. The Tenth Amendment in effect leaves education a state function; yet at the same time the general welfare clause (Article I, sections 8 and 10) implies justification of the existence of wide federal roles if needed. In recent years national defense needs and the availability of extensive funds have created an acceptance of increased federal educational roles.

This chapter will focus on those forces beyond the control of the local school district which significantly may affect what is taught, when, and with what materials and equipment, and indeed in what facilities. The classroom teacher can plan his own curriculum only to a *limited* degree. He is restricted directly by the local school district in which he teaches and at the same time is affected directly and indirectly by other influences —legal, quasi-legal, and private—that are beyond the limits of local district control. Elementary teachers are increasingly influenced by outside forces that include actions affecting elementary education as well as those aimed originally at secondary schools that now have impact upon elementary schools.

The little red schoolhouse has largely disappeared as a physical manifestation of very local operation of education. Its spirit is dying since people live mainly in metropolitan areas where they are beset by problems of such magnitude that local (and even state) resources become inadequate. The implications and applications of education have become so widespread that education is now conceived as a nationwide concern and responsibility. The President and the Congress have recognized this and have responded with a wide assortment of federal educational programs. Examples include the National Defense Education Act, Elementary and Secondary Education Act, and Education Professions Development Act.

This shift of responsibility—support and control—from local to state and national governmental as well as private bodies produces advantages and disadvantages. As with most significant issues, there are gray areas instead of black and white ones, alternatives rather than clearcut solutions, strengths and weaknesses, advantages and disadvantages, choices and necessities. The issues are so complex that it will be years before current shifts in opinions and patterns become clear enough to allow us to see exactly what has happened to the control of education in post-war America.

THE STATE: CHANGING ROLES

According to the Constitution powers not assigned to the national government were to be delegated to the states. Although deeply committed to education, the Founding Fathers nevertheless placed it among the delegated powers. Within the states themselves, authorities reflected their concern by writing into state constitutions and statutes provisions for education. The typical pattern was to entrust responsibility to *locally elected* state school officials.

School officials were relatively independent of other local and state governmental officials. Sometimes they were appointed by the local government. They were empowered to raise funds, set budgets, and select officials and staff if autonomous; otherwise they were dependent upon the general municipal budget along with the other government units.

Inequities of educational opportunity within the states encouraged them to provide funds and leadership for making education more effective throughout. Otherwise it was possible that some districts, blessed with a major industry or other source of rich revenues, could provide for education with slight effort while nearby ones often were hard-pressed to provide even a minimal educational program. With the advent of increasing state funds the necessity arose for fiscal accountability. Since education usually has been a legal, state function it was relatively easy to increase the amount of state control.

In some cases traditions of local control have been persistent, as when small districts resist state consolidation plans or a religious group objects to programs for sending children to schools removed from local influences. (The Amish are an example of the latter.)

Contrasts in State Leadership

State domination is a potential pattern. The state could assume extensive and excessive decision-making powers over budget, subject matter, grade placement of content, materials to be used, and so forth. It could require local educational boards and administrators to secure approval for any deviations from its programs. The state could administer achievement tests to determine how well local schools are helping pupils to meet state standards for particular grades and subjects.

Strong state control prevails in varying degrees in several states. With good leadership and adequate financial and moral support, there are potential advantages. There could be massive improvements within a whole state; good leadership, both fulltime and voluntary, may be attracted to larger challenges. State resources, derived unevenly from within a state, can be spread over the entire state to the benefit of all. There may be fiscal economies resulting from larger administrative units.

It is a matter of continuing debate as to how much state control can be exercised without weakening local support and involvement. If local citizens, school officials, teachers, and pupils sense that most decisions are made elsewhere, they may lose a sense of initiative and responsibility for educational improvement. They may feel that it is futile to seek that school organizational plan, that method, those materials, or those facilities which are particularly suited to their situation. There is a unique educational plan needed for each classroom, each school, and each school system, and nothing should be done to endanger local efforts to secure that plan for a community's children.

Even with rapid communication and transportation, remoteness from the local scene—*people*—can result in a sense of detachment by state capitol officials. This detachment may lead to either objectivity or indifference. Continuing experimentation is needed to determine the right mixture of state and local leadership, control, and involvement. Neither state or local control is "good" or "bad"; both have their place; both need mutual support; both need improvements. Federal funds are now available to strengthen state departments of education. Many federal programs for local school agencies are channeled through state education agencies. These and other developments may result in more power, prestige, and effectiveness for state education programs in the years ahead.

You as a classroom teacher are probably most interested in the more direct ways in which state educational policies and procedures will affect your teaching. You can see that the state in a dominant role would affect many of your teaching activities. The state in a primarily *supportive* role can also affect your instructional program and by acting in such a role, it can do several things to improve instruction. It can:

1. Provide general and special financial aid to individual and groups of districts, both for basic and also for special programs and services.
2. Convene study groups which can present the best thinking available on various topics at meetings and in written reports.
3. Provide consultants to aid local groups to work out their own solutions.
4. Sponsor conferences of laymen and professionals, both on local and regional bases.
5. Focus attention to the needs of schools and seek local and statewide support for education.
6. Facilitate, through legislation and leadership, new combinations of arrangements which capitalize on private and public resources of individual and groups of districts.
7. Provide professional analyses of materials, equipment, and facilities and share information with teachers and school officials.

The state in a supportive role does not abdicate responsibility for providing supervision of state educational funds spent locally. Neither does it assume that local control in itself provides good education. It sets up a system of checks and balances wherein both local and state officials work cooperatively with all those concerned with education.

Orderly processes of decision-making and support for education can involve both local and state levels. Primary responsibilities under such arrangements would be designated according to resources and type of roles, for example, finances through statewide resources; curricular decisions on the local level, where decisions can reflect the objectives of a relatively small group of citizens. Local decision-making should be influenced by citizen participation to a very great degree.

THE AWAKENED FEDERAL GIANT

The federal government always has been involved in education through direct and indirect financial assistance, through educational activities supported by many governmental agencies, and through direct operation of educational programs. The trend is away from *activity related to specialized needs*—for example, the education of Indian children—to *the total educational program involving millions of persons.* Examples include Head Start programs, financing of innovative plans in elementary and secondary schools, and fellowships for college students. There is now a common tendency to believe that education is a national source of solutions to economic, political, and social problems and hence federal programs have reflected this national consensus.

Increased federal involvement occurred for some of the same reasons noted for increased state action. Money is not always where educational needs are. A mobile nation and a complex and integrated economy can not endure poor education in certain states. It can not live up to its democratic concern for the individual unless it seeks educational gains through which each individual everywhere can attain his maximum potentiality. In terms of national survival, which was the original basis for enlarging federal aid to education, the Congress has recognized that the nation can not tolerate spotty educational efforts. Federal funds for education amounted to $1.3 billion at the beginning of the Kennedy administration; now the funding is several times this level, supported by both political parties (which differ on philosophy and procedures but not on the need). Funding is likely to increase in the future.

The total federal government has been effecting massive educational changes. The courts have forced integration and the Congress has included non-discrimination clauses in its education acts. The Executive Branch has enforced laws compatible with its objectives, and it has funded public and private groups inclined to develop programs compatible with the enlarged and powerful federal educational bureaucracy. The curriculum of the school has been drastically affected by what the federal government has done or has failed to do. The Congress, which functions to an extent as a national "board of education," is now seeking to assess the positive and negative effects of present programs.

With the dramatic increase of federal involvement in education, numerous issues have arisen. The questions below should be seen as a means to encourage discussion; they do not imply criticism of either state or federal programs.

1. A major question is whether federal aid should be *general* or *categorical.* If general, federal funds would be disbursed to state or local officials who would then decide how to spend the money within general guidelines established by the federal government. If categorical, funds would be dispensed for very specific purposes and within specific guidelines on how the moneys could be spent. *Opponents of general aid* charge that funds would be absorbed into present programs and would not make dramatic breakthroughs needed to meet today's needs; they further claim that state and local officials in the past have not demonstrated either the willingness or capability to take drastic actions to change education. *Opponents of categorical aid* object to the control of educational programs from Washington, since such specified funds distort local programs to include those for which funds are available rather than those which appear to local officials to be most needed.

2. There is the question of *how to disburse funds.* Should they be distributed directly to local school districts by the federal government, or should funds be channeled through state education agencies? Can state education agencies be sufficiently strengthened to enable them to assume such a role? Would they promote educational programs needed for contemporary conditions? Is the record of either the state or federal educational bureaucracies sufficiently outstanding to justify disbursing all funds through either level?

The current mood of the Congress seems to be toward favoring increased state responsibility for disbursing federal education funds.

3. While bureaucracies are not in themselves bad or good, they may tend to favor those who agree with their objectives. Specifically, will the federal educational bureaucracy favor (with funds and recognition) the practitioners who advocate programs compatible with those advocated by federal officials? Will funds distort the kinds of varied and balanced research and inquiry needed in the educational community, in favor of those for which large sums are available?

4. Since they are dependent upon others in the executive as well as the legislative branch, is it possible that excessive attention will be given to carrying out the wishes of federal personnel and too little to the needs of the total society, children in particular? In other words, are federal education officials too vulnerable to federal pressures?

5. Now that federal funding has reached major proportions, are too many discretionary powers being placed in the hands of a relatively few federal officials? Are there adequate checks and balances established to make sure that the general public is heard before major decisions are made? Is there adequate assessment of federal programs by objective personnel?

6. With the proliferation of massive federal programs, many noneducators have assumed major posts in the federal educational establishment. They include fiscal, legal, systems, public relations, and legislative personnel. Is it possible that such individuals, even with the best of intentions, may cause American education to take courses which historically have been proven unsound? Will noneducator personnel accept sufficient advice from practitioners? Are adequate checks placed on their decision-making processes and programs?

In the years ahead, federal programs will likely be evaluated critically and enlarged to permit local and state agencies to develop broader educational programs. At the same time, categorical aid—for limited, specific purposes—probably will be continued as a means for stimulating massive innovations to solve pressing problems.

BUSINESS DISCOVERY OF EDUCATION

Expenditures for education in this nation have reached a sum exceeded only by that for national defense. It is not surprising that many big firms have "discovered" what small and medium-sized businesses and certain large companies discovered 100 years ago: Education requires very large purchases of materials, equipment, facilities, and services. The schools are the largest business operation or among the largest in most communities. In recent years, as funds have been increased on the local, state, and federal level, traditional types of expenditures have correspondingly increased. There has also been a dramatic change in the kinds of school expenditures, to include new kinds of bookkeeping equipment, language laboratories, programmed books, teaching machines, and others. The extent of the involvement and investment suggests that big business is in the market to stay. This involvement of the industry in education has far greater implications for the curriculum than did its past activities.

It is well to look first at the positive *potentialities* of the large "learning corporations"—those who cater to educational needs. Business brings to complex and extensive educational problems competencies and long-range financial strengths needed to research educational needs of the changing society. Ultimately they have to put their research into practice. They claim to have the capability for designing and bringing about the in-service education of staff in order to utilize effectively curriculum packages—complete sets of related printed materials, audiovisual aids, equipment, teaching suggestions, tests, and so forth. Business also claims to have flexibility in planning innovative educational activities, for it does not have individuals with emotional involvement in traditional programs. Further, under pressure to ultimately show profits, business claims that it must plan and produce products, materials, or ideas which are marketable and which will be marketable only if they meet contemporary and anticipated needs. There are now in existence curriculum packages for most subject areas.

The complete package concept (requiring varied business resources) has led to mass mergers of traditional publishers of textbooks, manufacturers of "hardware," and corporations whose products are ideas—"software." The new companies or those branches of old companies specializing in educational services are thus in a position to sell to schools a prepackaged curriculum which can be installed with a minimum of effort timewise, and they provide an enterprise capable of selling ideas and materials to school staff, school board, and the community at large. These companies claim that the changing and enlarging educational needs of America are so complex that traditional methods of bringing about curriculum changes will not work. They assert that only the know-how and resources of business giants can master the gigantic problems facing American schools and other educational agencies and enterprises.

It has always been recognized that there is an educational role for business. That new types of business enterprises may be needed is a readily acceptable fact. However, there are some questions and cautions. A continuing search for suitable checks and balances in dealing with educational business enterprises is needed in view of their considerable present and projected roles.

Presently business is making educational decisions without direct responsiveness to public policy. It is questionable that independent school districts scattered throughout the nation can exert much pressure on business policies. While the consumer may be "king," the producer is "ruler" since he has the means of creating demands for his product which may become irresistible to local educational authorities.

Business is largely organized to produce things and may overemphasize materials and equipment in the curriculum packages developed. The teacher hopefully will select those materials and that equipment which further his educational objectives. It is easier to obtain such materials than it is to use them wisely and effectively.

Businesses have relatively few persons with teaching backgrounds on their staffs. Persons educated and experienced in non-educational fields may overlook and ignore the experiences of those in the educational enterprise. While there have been educational failures in the past, it would be erroneous to reject all or most educational philosophy, practices, and products of the past and present educational community. Communication lines between business and practitioners are rather tenuous at present and should be developed to a greater degree.

Once business has a large investment in a "packaged" curriculum, it may be tempted to continue its sale even though its value has been diminished. Often value is diluted by changed conditions or proven unworthy of continued use. The buyer does indeed have the option of stopping use of the package, but he may hesitate to do so in view of his large investment in the plan and the larger investment of time and money needed to replace it and prepare staff for a new curriculum package. This suggests a limitation of the packaged curriculum: Cost and time commitment may be so extensive that the package continues to be in use long after it has outgrown its usefulness.

Private corporations maintain that public scrutiny, by public agencies and mass media, should be limited. Therefore, decision-making, production, marketing, and evaluation procedures are largely closed to public inspection.

Business has a tendency to standardize in order to simplify production and thereby increase profits. Thus one curricular package is likely to be developed for a particular subject and grade level. While a teacher may select and adapt other instructional products to it, it takes imagination and skill. The package must be used as a package, regardless of the best of intentions of the producer. To encourage intelligent use, the producer may build in several options which lend themselves to adaptations to specific, local situations. Technology makes it increasingly possible for business to provide many options in curricular objectives and tools and perhaps eventually to design a curricular package for *a specific pupil in a specific grade.* Standardization may then become an insignificant problem; presently it is a latent problem at a time when the schools should be searching for means to individualize instruction to bring out the potential of each pupil. (See especially Chapter 11.)

The involvement of business in education has had a long and largely honorable history. On the local level business has supplied schools with needed services, supplies, equipment, and facilities. On the national level business, particularly the publishing business, has provided valuable tools for educators. Business on all levels has provided much of educational financing through taxes. It is a partner with educators in carrying out the huge educational task at hand. There are rich potentialities in business for bringing to the classroom carefully designed curriculum resources. There are likewise some problems, present and potential, which must be carefully considered. As a citizen and professional, you should look critically at business, as with all those involved in the educational enterprise, to determine what is best for children.

STATEWIDE AND NATIONWIDE INFLUENCES

Earlier it was noted that teachers may feel a loyalty to the profession at large rather than to the local school system (see Chapter 1). This is but one example of how organizations outside the local school and school system affect internal relationships. Organizations functioning on statewide and nationwide bases appear to have increasing influence in determining content, materials, and methods. As with most issues, there are several "sides" which should be studied. Different types of groups will be discussed in the following sections.

Professional Organizations and Teachers' Unions

In recent years the distinction between professional organizations and teachers' unions has decreased for various reasons. Under pressures from teachers in urban areas, where more and more teachers work, both types of organizations have become increasingly militant in asserting their rights, not only those pertaining to "welfare" items such as salaries and sick-leave provisions but also those relating to curriculum decisions. Teacher groups on all levels have become pressure groups. They interact with citizen groups of various kinds, as well as with administrators, and school boards.

It is most appropriate to discuss curricular implications of educational organizations in a book of this kind. Their role includes recruiting prospective teachers, recommending content and learning experiences for teacher preparation programs, orienting new teachers, and promoting inservice growth. Organizations have the potential for affecting the attitudes, objectives, and competencies of teachers.

Previous examples mentioned activities in which organizations cooperate with legally constituted officials. The organizations carry on several types of activities in their own right which often relate to curriculum: (a) sponsorship of conferences; (b) publication of journals, books, and monographs; (c) commissioning of study groups to develop curriculum recommendations; (d) conduct of research or sponsorship of research on campuses; (e) relationships with government officials and others in a position to affect education. The typical classroom teacher attends some conferences, reads some organizational materials, and participates in other organizational activities.

Professional organizations tend to be of both general and specialized nature, with local, state, and national components. The National Education Association, the largest professional group in the nation, includes administrators and teachers of all subjects and grade levels (nursery through higher education). In addition there are departments for specialists in education, for example, the Department of Elementary, Kindergarten, and Nursery Education (EKNE). There are groups that are not related to the NEA but which have teacher members, for example, the American Association for the Advancement of Science (AAAS). Organizations tend to have diverse concerns, including many with curriculum implications.

In a rapidly changing society and profession, the organizations to which you belong may be your major source of continuing information and ideas. In addition, contacts available through organizations are a source of inspiration, release from frustration, and organized strength in dealing with the general public and school boards, plus a variety of other functions.

Curricular Roles. What *instructional* roles do the professional associations see for themselves? The views of Arthur Corey, Executive Secretary of the California Education Association, provide one viewpoint which is summarized as follows:

1. The profession should help extend profesional education *started* in college. In a changing society, professional education must be continued throughout the teaching years.
2. The profession should cooperate with officials responsible for curriculum in recommending curricular objectives and in assessing the effectiveness of curriculum. The professional organization should *not* attempt to administer the curriculum.
3. The profession should cooperate in defining policies under which instructional materials are selected but not administer the selection process.
4. The profession should help to define but not administer policies on grading, pupil placement, evaluation of teachers, reporting to parents, and in-service education.
5. The profession should have a competent committee on instruction which will keep up with research, trends, and ideas on the local, state, and national levels. The state and national units should pro-

vide consultative assistance, materials, conferences, and other means to keep the total profession alert to changes and responsible to them.

Corey cautions that bargaining or negotiating on these matters should be a last resort in instances where continuous cooperative arrangements break down.

You should note that Corey emphasizes that professional organizations should participate actively in development of policies but not in their administration. The cliché is that a committee cannot run anything. Hopefully you will be among those whose advice and participation are sought during the policy-making phases of curriculum. What and how you teach in the classroom are vitally affected by curricular decisions made in the school system, as well as in the larger arena of state and nation. Organized groups are among the most effective ways of objectively seeking the best answers to curriculum questions.[1]

The position of the American Federation of Teachers on matters related to curriculum has become increasingly crucial now that it has won the rights to represent teachers in many large school districts. One AFT state executive secretary has claimed that not only is his organization bringing about changes directly where it functions as the bargaining agent in school districts, but also that rival "professional" organizations, *sensing competition,* are becoming more active.

The instruction-related concerns of a teachers' union may be determined in part from the reading of a contract, such as the following one from Detroit.[2] Board and union rights and responsibilities related to curriculum include agreements to:

1. Utilize textbooks and curriculum materials which reflect the contributions of Negro and other minorities and which include comprehensive histories of all parts of the world.
2. Use federal funds under the Elementary and Secondary Education Act to reduce class size in inner city schools to a minimum of 25 and also to decrease enrollment in special education classes. Adopt a calendar for reducing class size in other schools.
3. Increase the use of special services in inner city schools, both during regular school terms and summer schools.
4. Develop in-service programs designed to increase teacher competencies in working with disadvantaged persons.
5. Make an effort to eliminate achievement tests which have cultural biases and schedule tests when they are least "disruptive."

[1] Arthur F. Corey, *The Responsibility of the Organized Profession for the Improvement of Instruction* (Washington: National Education Association, Center for the Study of Instruction, n.d.), p. 13.

[2] Board of Education of the School District of the City of Detroit and the Detroit Federation of Teachers, Local 231, American Federation of Teachers, AFL–CIO, *Agreement* (September 18, 1967–July 1, 1969), 57 pp.

6. Make efforts to secure integration and compensatory programs as a means of minimizing educational effects of disadvantaged conditions. Plan free summer schools for those who fail a grade.
7. Prohibit teachers from being assigned outside their area of certification.
8. Pay tuition for post-bachelor's degree course work, under guidelines included in the contract.
9. Make provision for teachers to serve on committees designated to select instructional materials. Analyze textbooks every five years.
10. Provide for the use of teachers on committees reviewing and developing curriculum guides and material lists.
11. Provide for in-service workshops and meetings prior to putting new curricula into effect.
12. Provide for the dismissal of school for parent–teacher conferences. Make provisions for early closing of schools for regularly scheduled weekly faculty meetings.
13. Establish a calendar showing days when school will be in session and closed for various reasons.
14. Provide for preparation periods for elementary teachers.
15. Develop policies in discipline considered necessary for teaching and learning.
16. Provide for aides to release teachers from non-instructional duties.
17. Prohibit anyone from changing grades assigned by a teacher.
18. Provide for the improvement of school facilities.
19. Provide for a large number of other professional, administrative, and welfare clauses which have direct and indirect effects on teacher behaviors and feelings—ultimately bearing upon classroom instruction.

The impact of teacher union growth is somewhat unclear. Until recently teachers' unions had few members and relatively little influence outside of major metropolitan areas. Teachers' unions use collective bargaining on a host of demands, including those with curriculum implications, and it appears that teacher involvement in curriculum is likely to increase.

The Uncertain Future. The future of professional organizations likewise is somewhat uncertain. Formerly stereotyped as part of the "educational establishment" comprised of older teachers and administrators who stand for the status quo, professional groups in recent years have become more militant. The implications of this militancy on curriculum are not clear. Teacher influence is being felt more strongly now than it was in the past. Curriculum will continue as a concern of teacher groups, but other issues related to teacher welfare may assume higher priority.

It is difficult for the objective observer to assess the significance of the differences between professional organizations and unions. There is often a discrepancy between goals and methods that are verbalized and those that are practiced. It seems appropriate that you participate in organizational activities designed to improve educational conditions; such activities should serve members, pupils, and the community at large. These are years of decision which will determine whether professional associations or teachers' unions will be the major organized influence.

Certain criticisms have been leveled against curriculum change instituted by nationwide professional and union organizations. Wann notes four objections. *First,* the studies which lead to change are on a subject-by-subject basis and may upset balance in content when used in the local curriculum. *Second,* their comprehensiveness may encourage districts to incorporate the "packages"[3] without adequate in-service education for the staff or to include plans for assessing the value of the new materials for local conditions. *Third,* there is the possibility that creative approaches to teaching and adapting of the package to local learners will be neglected. *Four,* the packages are organized in the assumption that present organizational patterns of school semesters, hours, and so forth will continue (and may indeed help to freeze present patterns beyond their usefulness).[4] It should be noted that these are only potential problems; they can be eliminated or at least minimized with careful planning.

You should know enough about the curriculum packages which are available for several academic fields to render some judgments on their significance for elementary teaching. Elementary and secondary teachers should plan for reasonable continuity in the total school program. The need is most crucial when the total curriculum is affected by a massive change inherent in adoption of a system-wide program for a subject area. Sometimes the curriculum package developed by a national group includes materials and methods for elementary grades; at other times the elementary grades are affected when a new curriculum is adopted for the secondary grades.

The Educational Establishments. In discussing the organizations of educators, it is appropriate to mention the "educational establishment"—variously defined, but which usually includes full-time educational practitioners and teacher educators, as well as those who cooperate with them. The establishment is criticized for impeding progress, for being too exclusive, for being administrator dominated, and for many other things. It

[3] A "package" is a complete curriculum design and the means for putting it into effect for the number of days needed. Packages may include suggested objectives, unit plans, printed and audiovisual materials, test materials, bibliographies, and other aids.

[4] Kenneth D. Wann, in Helen Robison (ed.), *Precedents and Promises in the Curriculum Field* (New York: Teachers College Press, Columbia University, 1966), pp. 13–14.

is probable that there are some groups of persons likely to have ideas in common and who act with considerable harmony in their own areas and in some cases on a state or national basis. Since they are often together and have common interests, it is not always necessary for them to *formally* plan cooperative actions.

At times they may make formal pronouncements, plan concerted action, and share information. The point here is that the educational establishment is to a large degree an informal arrangement based on mutual concerns and continued contacts. There are similar "establishments" in other professions and endeavors.

Other individuals constitute an establishment of sorts. At times the "in" people are in a particular political party, labor or management group, foundation, journal staff, or professional group or teacher union. It is very important to realize that an *informal* grouping of individuals may wield influence. Examples include an accrediting team (such as the National Council for Accreditation of Teacher Education), professors, and the staff state education associations. State legislators, while not members of the educational establishment since they are not professional educators, have considerable authority, as do local boards of education. Nevertheless the members of the educational establishment, in the job fulltime, have many ways of getting their wishes implemented. They should reflect a reasonable degree of flexibility and willingness to involve others interested and concerned with education. At best the establishment represents those who are deeply involved, committed, and qualified to carry a disproportionate responsibility in their fulltime educational roles.

Other Education-oriented Organizations

There are many education-oriented organizations composed exclusively or primarily of laymen. The American School Boards Association, the National Congress of Parents and Teachers, and citizens' councils for schools are examples of such groups. They have varying influence on the curriculum and are worthy of some study. When involved in serious curriculum study, community organizations offer a channel for desirable citizen involvement. They should not be the exclusive means to involve parents, for often formal organizations are not representative of the many individuals who are not "joiners."

Churches

Churches have a long history of involvement in education, reaching back into early American history when they often operated the only schools. Today, churches may operate major parochial school systems, attempt to influence public schools to include and exclude certain curriculum content, or seek to influence school policy development. Church groups also may exert pressures: (a) to include or exclude school observances of religious holidays, (b) seek "released time" from school hours during which children can secure religious instruction (not on public property, in keeping with U.S. Supreme Court rulings), (c) promote a study of religion's influence in various aspects of life, (d) seek character education emphases in the curriculum. Whenever church leaders participate directly in school activities, care must be taken to avoid sectarian indoctrination and to balance the involvement of leaders from different groups.

You will be wise to work within the guidelines established by your board of education, which were hopefully enacted in cooperation with local religious and community groups. Under no circumstances can you promote, by what you include or exclude, either sectarian viewpoints or an anti-religious position. The Supreme Court has made it clear that it finds sectarianism rather than religion objectionable. There is no "safe" approach to religious aspects of the curriculum, and there are weaknesses in arguments for including or excluding religion and character education in the curriculum. It is an issue worthy of considerably more attention than is given here.

Service, Social, and Patriotic Organizations

Service, fraternal, social, and patriotic organizations often have educational interests. They may conduct educational programs on their own in the schools, or in cooperation with the schools. They may pressure schools to include some curicular content and exclude others. They and their state and national counterparts may influence legislative policies which affect curriculum.

The classroom teacher should not be expected to make decisions with potentially powerful community groups. Decisions will be made by school authorities, in consultation with the total staff, on which of the many valuable organizational programs and materials have a place in an already crowded schedule and curriculum. Materials should be used only when they are needed and when they harmonize with school objectives. The school can provide children with many enriched learning experiences, both in the school and in the community itself, as a result of the educational interests of organizations.

Local Outside Influences

It is difficult to know just how to categorize local outside influences which exert an effect on schools although not constituted to do so. In a sense local agencies, groups, and individuals should not be considered outside the school's network of relationships; hopefully they are included in early stages of school policy development.

We will characterize as local outside influences anyone or any group other than the staff and children of a particular elementary school or system. The following types of persons are outsiders only in the sense that they function largely outside a particular school:

1. Parents acting as individuals or in a group who seek to influence the school curriculum, on the basis of personal factors, national or international conditions, or political convictions.
2. Persons who seek to maintain the status quo, who often oppose curriculum changes.
3. Persons or professional staffs of secondary schools who want elementary pupils to be "prepared" for junior high, senior high, or college.
4. Persons concerned about a particular segment of the school population, whether the gifted, deprived, or some other identifiable group of children.[5]

You may disagree with outsiders in some cases. Their involvement *may* create support. At least it provides a legitimate avenue for citizen participation in curriculum.

Pressure groups are often organized for both short-term and long-term purposes. Even in a relatively small city there may be a few hundred organizations. Local units of state and national organizations actively write letters, make telephone calls, distribute literature (as part of a national distribution running into the millions of pieces), contact influential persons, and work through political parties. There is considerable difference of opinion on the effectiveness of their efforts. At the minimum it is likely that they are able to capitalize on current interests and affect community sentiment and actions on specific curriculum issues.

There are thousands of local or state affiliates of national trade associations—a sizable number with many constituents. The labor unions are concerned with education, since it is a vital means of securing "upward mobility" for children and youth. Farmer groups, while representing a decreasing proportion of the people, are well-organized for promoting a curriculum important to rural interests. Groups which are particularly active in many communities include the local chamber of commerce, League of Women Voters, service clubs (Rotary, Kiwanis, Lions, and so forth), and American Association of University Women. Community groups are as diverse as they are numerous.

[5] Summary derived from a mimeographed report on the Arrowhead University Elementary School Conference, November 23–25, 1958, sponsored by the University of California at Los Angeles. Not dated.

Pressure groups should be welcomed in curriculum discussion and planning. The book *Balance in the Curriculum* includes some cautions on group involvement. Pressure groups should be permitted and encouraged to participate if:

1. Results do not endanger the general welfare or welfare of pupils.
2. Efforts are not based on "ego-satisfaction" of groups or individuals.
3. Changes sought are not for financial or economic advantage.
4. Changes are not sought for social or political gain.
5. Efforts are not made to diminish effective curriculum.
6. Changes will promote a free society and learning for each individual.[6]

Whenever local school authorities seek advice from groups, the tasks for such groups should be clearly stated, a deadline for completion of their study defined, and the ultimate legal responsibility for decision-making by the board of education stated. It is also important to remember that organized groups speak in a limited fashion for only part of the people. Many individuals are members of many groups, some of which have conflicting objectives and viewpoints. Many are not influenced by organized groups in any significant fashion. Citizen groups should include influential persons who claim to represent no one but whose word is important to large numbers of citizens.

Mass Media

Another crucial outside influence is the mass media. The press, radio, and television staffs in the local community should naturally be considered as an integral part of the community. Your local system should establish completely honest relationships with the mass media—on a continuous basis. Much of what goes on in the school is not newsworthy, but the news media reporters appreciate being kept informed. Reporters have a right to know what the schools are doing. They will attempt to do their best to report objectively and fairly, and can become a most valuable ally in promoting good education in the community.

On the state and national level the mass media play a vital role in interpreting education. As dramatic curriculum changes have occurred, the media have attempted to give better coverage to education. They have created greater public interest in all phases of school activities. You will find it to your advantage to read regularly such periodicals as *Saturday Review*, *Newsweek*, and *Look*—and certainly other publications of this quality—to find what information the citizens are getting and also to note the excellent background they provide. Newspapers and journals

[6] *Balance in the Curriculum* (Washington: Association for Supervision and Curriculum Development, 1961), p. 165.

provide information on what has happened. The media also lay the groundwork for acceptance of, pressures for, or rejection of curriculum proposals.

The mass media are in themselves an up-to-date resource for classroom use. They are vivid and stimulating and their writing is professional. They are usually available.

Foundations

Foundations exert great influence on what is taught and also on teaching methods, materials, and media. Foundations by the hundreds have been established by the living and by the dead to maintain certain individuals' influence. In some cases they are concerned with limited programs, and in others they are involved with broad aspects of the society. Foundations may be viewed as supporters of worthy causes, or as a dangerous means of perpetuating the influence of a few men; there are advocates of both positions. That they are largely removed from public control is a source of concern for those who question motives and programs. Yet this is a source of satisfaction for others who feel that there is need for private groups to examine the society detached from public pressures.

Foundations, some say, are dangerously distorting the curriculum by making money available for prestigious groups to promote limited curricular objectives. Others claim that the foundations are properly prodding the educational establishment.

The foundations are capable of molding public opinion and promoting changes. Regardless of how you feel about foundations, you will find that your school's curriculum has been influenced by national curriculum study groups promoted by foundations, foundation-financed writers (for example, James Conant), or legislation initiated by programs given a "trial run" by a foundation-financed project.

Foundations speak authoritatively; they are widely heard and respected; *they are influential.* They are among the most vital forces in American education. Their actions are powerful and their influence is beyond estimate. Reactions to foundations tend to become value judgments concerning whether foundations ought to do what they do and ought to carry as much influence as they apparently do.

THE COURTS

The American system of government provides a unique system of checks and balances. This system is designed to prevent any part of the government from securing disproportionate powers. The courts are supposed to provide for individual rights guaranteed under the Constitution and since education is considered a right in American society, the courts actively engage in making decisions which will affect education.

The Supreme Court has been particularly active in setting aside the "separate but equal" doctrine by which many states maintained separate school systems for Caucasian and Negro pupils. Partially as a consequence of Court actions and partly as a result of legislation, there have been marked changes: (a) use of instructional materials which include multiracial characters and situations, (b) adjustments in the curriculum to compensate for deprived children, (c) human relations emphases in the curriculum. The Court has stimulated a major re-examination of American education.

The state courts have concerned themselves with upholding state constitutional requirements for using public funds only for public schools and with necessity for providing such funds, the separation of school funds from other state funds, and the provision of a uniform state system of public schools and its ultimate supremacy over local educational authorities.

Some state constitutions have been rigid to the point of preventing needed adjustments to changing conditions. Recently revised state constitutions often delegate administrative decisions to a board of education responsible to the people and empowered to keep the state's educational system relevant and viable. The state courts then serve as a balance by providing the means through which citizens can challenge those decisions. The legislature maintains its influence through its control of appropriations and its ability to pass laws. The executive branch is responsible for implementing decisions or is an influential factor in developing educational policies and procedures, as well as proposing legislation.

EMERGING PARTNERSHIPS IN CURRICULUM

The ultimate in simplified local control was a one-room school controlled largely by its patrons. It was—and is in those cases where such schools have been maintained—a simple matter to select objectives, content, and materials. In today's complex society, consolidation of rural schools and centralization of urban schools have created a complex series of relationships between the many individuals, agencies, organizations, and enterprises affected by and interested in education.

On the national and state level, influential officials, industrialists, and other important individuals speak and act decisively in curriculum matters. Educators now are only a part of the team of decision-makers. The involvement of non-educators in curriculum decision-making brings attendant strengths and limitations. This new partnership is being forged as a result of a national consciousness of the urgency to secure the best education possible.

On the local level, various kinds of influential people are being joined by the "common man" in seeking to influence—sometimes dictate—educational policies and practices. There are networks of officials, quasi-official, and unofficial arrangements. Curriculum is public business, and the public (actually several publics, often hostile and competing) is making curriculum its business. Reading newspapers and magazines, as well as listening to television and radio newscast, reveals diversity of interests and depth of concern. The pressures are for decentralization to enable all kinds of people to participate in decision-making. Your curriculum decisions now must be made in collaboration with various professional and nonprofessional "partners."

The new partnerships undoubtedly will create tensions, frustrations, and fears. New patterns take time to develop. Ultimately involvement can create a constructive environment for a desirable curriculum: (a) contributions of individuals with varied competencies and insight; (b) moral and financial support derived from understanding and involvement; (c) increased respect and support for the professional teacher who demonstrates an ability to help the community to attain its recognized, important objectives; (d) increased interest in learning by pupils who can see the recognized values of education. Out of present uncertainties concerning the new partnership in education may well come a local to national resurgence of interest in and support for education. The schools belong to the people. The task of the professional is increasingly becoming that of helping the community, and the nation, to develop its most important resource—its children.

PROJECTS AND READINGS

1. Sputnik may have been the most important development of the past few decades to influence American education, according to J. Myron Atkin, in "The Federal Government, Big Business, and Colleges of Education," *Educational Forum,* XXXI, No. 4 (May, 1967), p. 391. Atkin notes that Sputnik contributed to an atmosphere in which large-scale federal educational programs were approved. Do you feel that the response to Sputnik was reasoned and balanced? What are some other examples in which American education is influenced by international events and situations? What curriculum changes have you heard about in several subject areas?

2. On the home front, there are many outside influences. An old but still good reference is *Forces Affecting American Education* (Washington, D.C.: Association for Supervision and Curriculum Development, 1953). What are the changes in these pressures which you believe have occurred since 1953?

3. Paul R. Hanna has proposed a broadly representative national commission to develop alternative curriculum designs from which state and local officials

could choose on the basis of their needs. Could such a voluntary group influence American education sufficiently for the pressing needs faced by the nation? Will the federal government be increasingly inclined to apply pressures to secure rapid change?

4. "The state is uniquely equipped to formulate policies, conduct research, make decisions, and take action on a scale not so limited as to be fragmentary, transient, and localized; nor so vast as to be remote, impersonal, and conducive to the development of a bland, mechanistic conformity." [James E. Allen, Jr., in *The Teachers College Journal,* XXXVII, No. 4 (January, 1966), p. 152.] How realistic do you believe Allen's analysis is? What are some of the strengths and weaknesses which you find described in other publications?

5. If you can arrange to talk with someone in a leadership rôle of a community organization, it might be informative to determine how his organization seeks to influence education on the local, state, or national level. It is also possible to get comparable information by following newspaper accounts of organizational efforts to influence educational policies and practices. Which of these efforts appears to be oriented to the needs of most Americans, and which efforts appear to be rather narrow in outlook and purpose?

6. Wann claims that most recent curriculum changes have occurred as a result of influences *outside* the school system: foundations, academicians, prominent writers, and others who are conscious of the social setting of education and have called for education capable of responding to those conditions. (Kenneth Wann, in Helen F. Robison, *op. cit.,* p. 20.) What are the positive and negative aspects of having curriculum changes brought about by non-educators? To what extent do teachers appear sufficiently aware of emerging conditions to change the school curriculum?

7. Arthur S. Fleming, former secretary of the Department of Health, Education, and Welfare, is reported to call for more teaching about religion in the schools. The Supreme Court ruling on religion in the schools did not prohibit such instruction. [*Phi Delta Kappan,* XLVIII, No. 6 (February, 1967), p. 277.] What content, if any, is appropriate in the public schools? What methods would be effective in teaching about religion? How could various religious and secular groups be involved in planning for objectives, methods, and materials? How do you feel about shared time as an alternative to including instruction in the public school program?

8. Some good references on the changes which affect education are John Goodland (ed.), *The Changing American School,* Part II, Fifty-sixth Yearbook, National Society for the Study of Education (Chicago: University of Chicago Press, 1966); Project on Instruction, *Education in a Changing Society* (Washington: National Educational Association); and Project on Instruction, National Education Association, *Schools for the 60's* (New York: McGraw-Hill Book Co., 1963).

9. With more than 90,000 elementary schools in the United States there is much diversity. To what extent do local pressure groups accelerate differentiation of curriculum? What groups promote similarity (and perhaps even conformity)?

10. The concept of parity is widespread in educational thinking today. It holds that different kinds of citizens and professionals have unique contributions to make about decisions such as curriculum. Interactions between layman and practitioner are to be carried on the basis of equality. The older

viewpoint was that professionals made decisions and told laymen the nature of good curriculum. How can citizens be involved in curricular decisions without undermining the professional role in the "how" questions of instruction? What are current indications of the kind of curriculum that emerges when parity prevails in school–community interactions? How are the best interests of the nation at large maintained when community control prevails?

11. In the Texarkana Dropout Prevention Program the federal government has contracted with a commercial firm to improve academic performance. The firm's income is based in part on tested improvements in pupil achievement to a pre-determined level. Tangible incentives for both pupils and teachers are provided when progress occurs. Other cities are adopting similar plans in which firms contract to hold themselves accountable for prescribed pupil performance. Should teachers be paid on the basis of accomplishments of pupils? What are the strengths and weaknesses of financial and other tangible rewards for academic achievements?

12. Should parents receive money with which to send their children to any public or private school? Would "competition" lead to curricular improvements? Those who advocate an "education vouchers plan" claim that it would result in more relevant schools and point to the "G.I. Bill" as an example of how successful this approach can be. The National Education Association, among opponents, claims that the plan would weaken public schools and could lead to racial, economic, and social isolation and divisions.

10

Effects of Past and Present Factors

CHANGING OBJECTIVES FOR SCHOOLS

Curriculum is the organization of learning experiences for children over a period of time. These learning experiences must have a goal. The curriculum of the public school in the United States has had three main objectives in its long history. Immediately following the Revolutionary War the school was to develop American citizens, to create an educated populace which could function effectively in the infant democracy. The school was to instill loyalty to the young republic and prepare its citizens to develop and expand it. This goal is very pertinent to the school curriculum. The War Between the States almost tore the young nation apart.

Following this great national upheaval America was almost swamped by vast numbers of immigrants from all areas of Europe. Again the public school took up the challenge to heal the wounds of war; to unite the nation; and to prepare thousands of young Irishmen, Italians, and Central Europeans to understand and participate in American democracy.

Today the public school has been given a third challenge: to integrate the culturally disadvantaged child into the mainstream of today's technical society to prevent the separation of American society into those who are fully educated and prepared to participate in the space age and those who are not.

The majority of American taxpayers have great faith that young people who receive an education will have more of an opportunity to achieve success than those who are uneducated. Too, in a truly democratic society, the vast majority of its citizens must have the knowledge, intelligence, and wisdom to participate in that society. Only an educated person can become a responsible citizen.

By 1976, if the population projections are at all accurate, 60 per cent of our population will be 18 years of age or under and some 50 to 60 per cent of the population between 18 and 22 will be in some kind of college. This means roughly that some 75 to 80 per cent of the population between ages 6 and 22 will be under the direct physical control of the nation's educators. Presently the men and women who teach in all schools, public and private, make up the largest single segment of the national work force—three million people. There are more teachers than farmers.

Now what type of curiculum will best serve so many young people? This is the persistent question that countless educators are continually asking. It has been answered in different ways at different times in our history. The type of curriculum experiences which American children should undergo is still a matter of vigorous and angry debate. This debate seems to evolve about two main issues.[1]

1. What kind of curriculum experiences will promote maximum freedom for all individuals?
   a. Should the curriculum stress social understanding or purely intellectual studies?
   b. Should the curriculum emphasize the "3 r's" only?
   c. Should the curriculum stress learning by direct experience or by reading books?
   d. Should there be one curriculum for the intellectually gifted and another for the less able child?
2. What type of curriculum is the most efficient to a free society?
   a. Should the curriculum be constructed by teachers in the local schools or by curriculum experts?
   b. Should the curriculum be of a national scope or be indigenous to the local area?
   c. How much commonalty should there be between the curriculum of the public school and that of the parochial school?
   d. Should the curriculum of the elementary school be an entity unto itself, or should it be a preparation for the curriculum of the high school and college?

The answers to these questions have bothered American educators since colonial days.

INHERITANCE FROM COLONIAL DAYS

The British crown was the source of governmental authority for 175 years of colonial rule, and each colonial government was given jurisdic-

[1] R. Freeman Butts, "Search for Freedom," *NEA Journal,* XLIX, No. 3 (March, 1960), pp. 33–48.

tion over education. However, each colony handled the education of its children differently.

The exemplary colony in its concern for schools was Massachusetts. The legislature of that colony passed a general educational law in 1642 which was to apply to every section of the colony. The law indicated that all parents must be responsible for their children learning to read, understand the law, know the catechism, and learn a trade. Town officials were to enact this law. A second law, passed by this colony's legislature in 1647, obliged all towns of 50 families or more to hire a teacher for an elementary school and pay him a salary out of public funds. This teacher was responsible for seeing that children learned to read and write. This same law required towns of 100 families or more to hire a secondary teacher. Thus, very early in our history the curriculum of both the elementary and secondary schools was of primary concern to both colonial (or state) and local governmental authorities.

It was not until the eighteenth century that colonial governments began to allow different religious groups, small groups of businessmen, or landowners to establish their own schools. The educational charters which these groups were granted allowed them to incorporate as a board of trustees, build buildings, appoint teachers, and admit students. These private schools could be run for profit; the public school on the other hand could not. It was controlled by a government agency which could set the fees or establish the taxes and employ the teacher. The type of curriculum and the achievement of the children were also determined by a government agency. Too, through the years the public school became more and more nonsectarian. As people moved out into unsettled areas of the nation, they built and managed their own local or district school, removed from a central state control.

Of course not all children attended school, but the principle was established that all children should learn to read, write, recite the catechism, and possibly do some arithmetic. This was the essence of the curriculum for the colonial school, and this essence became part of the public school's curriculum heritage.

CURRICULUM IN THE EARLY REPUBLIC

It was determined early in our national history that a democratic government requires that the people who elect that government, hold office, make laws, enforce laws, and consent to be ruled must be educated as responsible citizens. John Adams insisted that "The whole people must take upon themselves the education of the whole people and must be willing to bear the expense of it."

The common school was given this heavy responsibility. It should teach in English all the children of all the people to live together and govern themselves. The government should control the common schools since it was only through the government that all would be served. To keep these schools close to the people, the state and local governments should control the schools. To keep the school free from political prejudice, policy for that school should be determined by a local board of education, subject to but separate from the executive, legislative, and judicial branches of government. The local board, as a policy making body, could determine the local curriculum needs. These curriculum needs revolved around the provision of basic information, as well as literary and moral teachings required for every free man.

However, the principle was established early that each school district could determine the structure of its own curriculum. There was to be no nationally controlled curriculum as was prevalent at the time in many European nations. The American state exercised its authority in making schools available and also in insisting that children actually attend school. Massachusetts passed its compulsory attendance law in 1852. Thus all the children in the same area would experience the same curriculum. The United States built a universal system of free elementary schools with local curriculum determination sooner than any other country in the world.

The earliest essentials of the curriculum consisted of reading, writing, and arithmetic to give the basic tools for acquiring knowledge. Many new dimensions were included in the school program. History and geography were thought necessary to instill loyalty and pride of nation while subjects such as bookkeeping and directed work experiences could help a student to earn a living.

CURRICULUM AFTER THE 1860's

In the decades following the 1860's, the curriculum of the elementary school began to evolve as a sturdy native development. The provoking ideas of great European educators influenced and vitalized that curriculum, but the product was an American brand. Pestalozzi, the humble Swiss teacher, stressed instruction in geography and the study of nature. Froebel, the father of the kindergarten, placed nature study and school gardening in the school. The rapid development of technology and the resulting industrial changes brought the manual arts into the elementary school curriculum.

After the war great streams of immigration flowed into our country from across the Atlantic and Pacific oceans. Since the children of these new citizens had to be given an understanding of the American way of life and its governmental structure, civics was added to the elementary curriculum. It was believed, that by adding this course to the curriculum, a repetition of the tragic events of the 1860's would be prevented.

The period from 1860 to 1900 witnessed great industrial growth in this country, the beginning of the westward movement of population, the rapid growth of cities, the impact of science and technology, and the vast improvement of communication and transportation. The curriculum of the elementary school was designed to prepare children as citizens for this new society. The year 1860 brought the kindergarten, manual training, and domestic arts into the elementary school as a consequence of the destruction of the old type home, and the virtual disappearance of the apprenticeship system of training.

The American people looked forward to a great political and industrial future. Early American leaders early realized that the advance of scientific method made it necessary that the child himself should be studied with the exactness of the physical sciences. Education could not rest on untested general impressions. The American child study movement arose from such generalizations.

The Child Study Movement

The pioneer in this child study movement was Granville Stanley Hall (1846–1924). In 1883 he made an inquiry into the schools of Boston which he published in *The Contents of Children's Minds on Entering School.* Then he began to explore the mind of the child and the adolescent in a long series of studies which provided much of the material for his great book on adolescence, published in 1904. Hall was the pioneer and initiator of the child study movement. By the end of the nineteenth century the scientific study of the child had become an accepted aspect of modern educational activity. Such inquiries into child development opened up new vistas of knowledge which could be applied to curriculum innovation. The school program could thus be made more adaptable to the child's abilities, interests, and needs.

John Dewey, the great American philosopher (born 1859), had much in common with G. Stanley Hall. Dewey founded the Laboratory School at the University of Chicago in 1896. This school was to prepare the way for the school of the future. The ordinary schools, Dewey claimed, had not kept up with the great social changes brought by the Industrial Revolution. The schools had served earlier generations well enough when the nation had been primarily rural, but these same schools had not changed sufficiently to serve an ever-expanding industrialization and urbanization. The self-sufficient rural family had broken down, and the country village as an entity was disappearing.

The American child of a century ago was a rural child. In his own home he might watch the shearing of the sheep and the working of the loom. To secure illumination, his mother fried animal fat, twisted wicks, and then dipped candles. The child shared in all the work of the home, and perhaps without any consciousness of effort he built up mind and experience. The child of the industrial age is surrounded by manufactured goods and has little idea of how they were produced. He rarely sees milk until he drinks it from a bottle, nor wool until he puts on his mittens. His home is heated by gas, oil, or electricity; and he has rarely chopped a log to be used for fuel.

Dewey took a close look at the schools. The fixed, unvarying desks presupposed passive children absorbing what the teacher had prepared for them. There was little opportunity for children to learn through activity. The classroom was arranged to allow the children to listen. The curriculum was so organized that children could be dealt with in masses and not as individuals. Social education can only be secured through participation in the common aims and objectives of a democratic society, but little was done in this area. Dewey saw that "in the schoolroom, the motive and cement of social organization are alike wanting. Upon the ethical side, the tragic weakness of the present school is that it endeavors to prepare future members of the social order in a medium in which the conditions of the social spirit are eminently wanting." [2]

Examining the school curriculum at the turn of the century, Dewey indicated four main problems that were pressing for solution:

> (a) What can be done to bring the school into closer relation with the home and neighborhood life? (b) What can be done in the way of introducing subject matter into history and science and art that shall have a positive value and real significance in the child's own life? (c) How can instruction in reading, writing, and arithmetic, the formal subjects, be carried on with everyday experience and occupation as the background, and made interesting by relating them to other studies of more inherent content? How can adequate attention be paid to individual powers and needs? [3]

Dewey divided elementary school life into three psychological periods: (a) the play period from four to eight years of age, (b) the period of spontaneous attention from eight to twelve, and (c) the period of reflective attention from twelve onwards. The *play period* is characterized by directness of social and personal relations. The child is beginning to emerge from the narrow limits of home life and is making his first acquaintance with the social world beyond the home. Thus the central

[2] John Dewey, *School and Society* (Chicago: University of Chicago Press, 1900), p. 28.

[3] *Ibid.*, p. 116.

them of the curriculum for this stage of the child's life is the life and occupations of the home.

The *period of spontaneous attention* is the period of technique. The child is now both able and willing to acquire different forms of skill because of his growing sense of the possibility of more permanent and objective results. Proper history with America as its subject now takes the place of the general treatment of the occupations and their evolution. The aim is to give a knowledge of social processes used to secure social results by showing how human purposes are achieved under a variety of typical conditions of climate and locality. The curriculum should be directly practical.

Dewey indicated that the *period of reflective attention* comes when the child has sufficiently mastered the methods of thought, inquiry, and activity appropriate to various phases of experience to be able to concentrate upon distinct studies and arts for technical and intellectual aims. Now the child is able to raise problems for himself and to seek solutions for them.

Dewey insisted that educators must secure a clear view of the dominant directions of learning activity at successive periods in a child's life. Once this is obtained through a scientific study of the learning process, there must be achieved through experience and experiment a selection and a grading of the material suitable for the curiculum at each level of development. Dewey was the dominant influence in curriculum development for half a century. Since the mind is essentially social, the curriculum should focus on social development, according to Dewey.

In restating the essential purpose of the curriculum in terms of the child's individual experience, Dewey transformed the whole character of the teacher's work. Subject matter in itself seems to be ill suited to develop a child's growing mind; it might be an empty symbol without meaning. What has to be learned is not fixed and ready-made outside the learner's experience.

Subject content should satisfy a child's needs and interests so that it becomes a move from the child's present experience into organized studies. What the child learns then becomes an integral part of his conduct and character in organic relation to his present needs and aims. Once an interrelationship is secured between child and curriculum, motivation for learning is achieved. There is no necessity to make the memory do the work that should be done by reason.

By the turn of the century the process of providing free, universal education was almost complete as a framework. Several states had no compulsory school attendance laws, although the first of these state laws had been passed in 1852. Powerful groups in every state opposed compulsory, free public education. They argued that compulsory education was unAmerican and interfered with the personal liberty of parents. The state, it seemed to some, was assuming unjustified powers. Yet, state by state, the logic of requiring school attendance as essential to the welfare of both individual and state eventually prevailed. The last state enacted compulsory attendance laws in 1918.

However, in 1900 public education was a pale counterpart to what is accepted as good schooling today. The average pupil probably attended school less than four months a year. The national average length of schooling was less than four and one half years. At least 10 per cent of all Americans over 10 years of age were illiterate. These comparisons indicate how drastically educational conditions have changed during the past 60 years.[4]

CURRICULUM FROM 1900 TO THE 1960's

Piaget and Bruner: Leaders of a New Curriculum

In 1900 about half of the children aged 6 to 13 were in elementary schools, but by 1960 over 99 per cent were in attendance. In this century both quantity and quality in education have been keystones in the elementary school curriculum. Since 1900, nowhere else in the world have so many people been so concerned about the elementary school curriculum so much of the time. Many educators are dissatisfied with the status quo of the elementary school curriculum today.

The elementary curriculum has long started with six-year-old children. Today a vast number of schools have kindergartens, which were first started by Friedrich Froebel in Europe in 1870. Most American cities have established nursery schools for two- to four-year-olds.

Since 1900 the elementary school has broadened its curriculum. Drawing and the arts, the social studies, science, language arts, health, and physical education have been added to the basic "3 r's." Units, work projects, audiovisual aids, handicrafts, gardening, laboratory experiences, and bus excursions also have replaced the slavish drill from the textbook or notebook. The general quality of the curriculum, for a great majority of American children, has been improved; and zest and vitality, interest, and comprehension have been added.

However, in the late 1940's and early 1950's the cry was raised that Dewey had made the schools soft, "fun palaces with an emphasis on social adjustment." The launching of Sputnik by the U. S. S. R. in 1957 resulted in a cry that the Russians were ahead of us in preparing children in mathematics and science as well as foreign language. New curriculum

[4] Taken from Robert A. Marshall, *The Story of Our Schools* (Washington: National Council for Social Studies, 1962), p. 18.

designs were launched by leading physicists, mathematicians, biologists, and chemists. The academic scholars then became interested in the curriculum.

Various learned societies searched for methods of establishing contact between leading scholars and educators in the schools. The National Academy of Sciences, for example, encouraged a closer relation between scientists in universities and science teachers in the schools. Educators and psychologists, too, closely examined the curricula and explored new teaching methods. The two outstanding leaders in the new revolution to improve the curricular in the schools are both psychologists primarily: Jean Piaget, director of the Jean Jacques Rousseau Institute in Geneva, and Jerome S. Bruner, professor of psychology at Harvard.

Piaget's Theories about Children. For Piaget the crucial issue for today's curriculum is to help the growing child adjust himself to the world in which he lives. He has tried to understand how a child thinks by attempting to get inside the child's mind and see how the child looks at the world. Piaget believes that there are four major stages of child growth, three of which have significant curriculum implications. His "stages" are summarized below.

The first is the sensory motor stage which lasts from birth to about two years.[5] During this stage of development the child discovers his muscles and senses, and learns by establishing habits how to handle realia.

The second stage is the pre-operational or representational stage which extends between the representative ages of two to six years. The child now learns to label with words the external world about him and to express his own feelings through language. He learns to adjust to the world about him through trial and error and to make intuitive judgments.

Between seven and eleven years the child passes through the third stage called concrete operations. Now he can move things around and make them fit properly with developed fine motor skills. Now he can attack physical problems.

The final stage in the child's development is that of formal operations which prepare him for adult and mature thinking. This stage develops between 12 and 15 years. Now the child can set up hypothesis, reason through the possible process of a logical solution, perform a controlled experiment, and come to some possible conclusion.

The child's intelligence, says Piaget, is born of action. Patience and time are necessary for growth. Intelligence is put into effect through operations. Thus the task of school curriculum, argues Piaget, is *not* to

[5] Frank G. Jennings, "Jean Piaget: Notes on Learning," *Saturday Review*, L, No. 18 (May 20, 1967), p. 82. For another interpretation of Piaget's work, see J. McV. Hunt, *Intelligence and Experience* (New York: The Ronald Press Co., 1961), chaps. 5, 6, and 7.

create individuals capable of understanding everything in the history of ideas or capable of repeating history but rather to focus on forming individuals who are capable of inventing—of finding new answers and new solutions. The child should be helped to go beyond the present. The curriculum should allow the child to be active, to be inventive, to be unique.

Bruner's Contributions to Curriculum. Jerome S. Bruner is particularly interested in how a culture is transmitted—its skills, values, styles, technology, and wisdom. Further, he wonders how in transmission it produces more effective and zestful human beings! Bruner claims that the school curriculum is divided into subject matter, an invention of a highly literate society.

Each subject matter has a particular way of thinking and it is from the curriculum then the child should learn that method of thought. A curriculum to Bruner is balanced to include a particular subject area that meets the needs of the child as well as the standards of the academic discipline from which the materials have been derived. Another factor is the need of the teacher trying to stimulate patterns of thought with the children.

The principal curriculum aim should be the development of children capable of using their potential powers to achieve a good life and make an effective contribution to society. This is accomplished through a curriculum which helps each child to master himself, discipline his taste, deepen his view of the world, and learn that he has value and pertinency.

The curriculum may be made up of separate sets of ideas. The child must be helped to achieve a sense of their interaction and how they have brought reason into the world. This is accomplished first through contrast, second by stimulation, and finally by participation. Bruner claims that it is much more interesting for a child to learn facts after he has tried to figure them out for himself. The child must master the art of securing and using information and then learn what is involved in going beyond given information and what makes it possible to take such leaps.[6]

Thus a good curriculum should help a child to become self-conscious about his strategies of thought by giving him the tools of thought. He should be given the experience of trying out a theoretical model with some sense of what is involved in becoming aware that he is trying out a theory. Children need not discover all generalizations for themselves, but they should be given some opportunity to develop a decent competence at it and some confidence in their ability to operate independently. The curriculum should be organized to give children a respect

[6] Jerome S. Bruner, *Toward a Theory of Instruction* (Cambridge, Mass.: The Belknap Press of Harvard University Press, 1966), p. 149.

for their own powers of thinking and for their power to develop good questions. They should be encouraged to try out some informed guesses in which they are interested. Bruner would have the curriculum more amenable to the use of the mind rather than to mere memorizing.

According to Bruner's thinking, curriculum is not a course to be run as much as it is an involvement in the mastery of skills to be achieved. This in turn leads to the mastery of still more powerful abilities, which will establish self-reward sequences. One of the principal objectives of learning, says Bruner, is to save us from subsequent learning. For example, if the principle of addition has been grasped in its deeper sense, then it would not be necessary to learn multiplication, since in principle, multiplication is only repeated addition. In Bruner's curriculum multiplication would not be another unit. Learning for the sake of learning is not enough; learning must have sequential organization potentialities.

A good curriculum should include questions about the unknown. Obtaining knowledge then becomes an active process, and thinking becomes the reward for learning. A curriculum should be judged on how well it can enable children to leap the barrier from learning to thinking.

To Bruner a curriculum has six major characteristics.[7] *First,* it helps a child gain increasing independence of response from the immediate nature of the stimulus. He should learn to become free from the textbook in making his decisions. *Second,* he should be given the opportunity of selecting experiences from the school environment and internalizing them into a storage system which will correspond to the complete social and physical environment in which he has his being. *Third,* the curriculum should stimulate that intellectual growth which involves increasing the capacity to communicate to oneself and others by means of words or symbols what one has done or what one will do. *Fourth,* the curriculum should allow systematic and incidental interaction between teacher and child. *Fifth,* since teaching efficiency is greatly increased through the medium of language, which is a means of exchange and the instrument which the child can use for himself in bringing order into the environment, language development is the focus or heart of a curriculum. *Finally,* a curriculum should be so organized that it allows the child to increase his capacity to deal with several alternatives at the same time, to focus on several sequences simultaneously, and to give the appropriate time and attention to these multiple demands.

Three Thinkers' Views on Curriculum. You can see that Dewey, Piaget, and Bruner—three great curriculum thinkers of this age—have several beliefs in common. They believe that:

[7] Jerome S. Bruner, *The Process of Education* (Cambridge, Mass.: Harvard University Press, 1961), p. 5.

1. A curriculum should allow the child to be active in exploring his social and physical environment and to bring order out of chaos in that environment. The child should experience an "active" curriculum.
2. The curriculum should be so organized that there is a sequential development in the child's learning which will teach him to think efficiently. The real purpose of any good curriculum is to help the child develop a method of efficiently collecting information from which he can reach his own conclusions.
3. The curriculum should be concerned primarily with giving the child the tools with which he can understand, comprehend, and improve his environment.

Dewey's and Bruner's thinking have accelerated the evolution of American education. Piaget's classic research on the learning of children is now beginning to influence American education to a major degree. New methods, new processes, and new subject areas are entering the curriculum.

The new curriculum has changed the classroom. In it the teacher is a friendly, helpful guide while the children are absorbed in teaching themselves. Dewey and Bruner claim that children remember best what they find out for themselves and least what they are told about. Educators call it the Discovery Method. It seeks to build the child's self-respect and encourage his curiosity. It emphasizes individualized teaching, continuous progress, and uncensored discussion periods and teacher evaluation rather than end-of-term examinations.

An Example of Modern Curriculum

Mrs. Helen Bumphrey's second grade class might be an example of one kind of contemporary curriculum.[8] She helps the children to devise their own curriculum. She collects hundreds of books—from parents, from other teachers, from the local libraries. She allows her 31 seven-year-olds to use the books. She realizes that a child or two in her classroom reads on a fourth grade level, a few read at the lowest grade-one level, and the remainder struggle between the extremes.

Beginning in September, Mrs. Bumphrey tests her class thoroughly. She is a highly professional person and knows what she is doing with batteries of tests, phonics diagnostic tests, and a few tests she has developed herself. Using the knowledge derived from the tests, she begins to make suggestions to individual children. The advanced children are nudged towards books that will stimulate them. Under-achieving boys

[8] June Callwood, "Why Good Teachers Don't Teach Anymore," *Maclean's Magazine,* LXX, No. 5 (May, 1967), p. 58.

are encouraged to read books with high interest. Books for slow readers often are profusely illustrated and have a high interest but a low vocabulary. Then the children begin to read. There are no book reports or questions about what they have read.

The children form committees with children acting as chairmen and talking about what they have read. One group may become interested in the study of bees, another in dinosaurs, another in sea life. The children are given a great deal of responsibility in handling their own education. For example, there is no formal spelling program in Mrs. Bumphrey's room, but the children keep a list of all the words they find useful. One little girl admires the words "miscalculate" and "alphabetical" and teaches herself to spell them. A boy, at six, discovers to his indignation that some books he reads state that the shark is not a true fish, while others say the opposite. He checks through the encyclopedia and eventually gives the class his considered opinion: not a true fish, since it doesn't have a proper backbone. His next project is to assemble a list of authors who could be believed and a list of authors who could not. Bruner would say these children have caught the passion of learning.

At some time during the day, Mrs. Bumphrey puts an arithmetic problem on the board, teaches about it briefly, and then invites all those with an inclination to meet her at the back of the room to discuss the problem further. Arithmetic is learned through number games, flash cards, and such hilarious projects as measuring the school corridor to determine if a brontosaurus would fit. The children learn that mathematics is a tool and a means of communication.

It is difficult to detect, but in Mrs. Bumphrey's classroom there is much skilled professional teaching. Each child in rotation has a five or ten minute private chat with the teacher—three or more times a month. The children call it their conference time and await their turn eagerly. They schedule their appointments in the timetables they plan for themselves every day. Mrs. Bumphrey calls it evaluation and puts the results in her records. If remedial work is necessary, the child receives it immediately, or later in a casually assembled small group with a similar problem. Educators claim that children can accept a self-directed education program at two periods in their lives, the first and best in the early school years and the second in their adolescence.

Some of Mrs. Bumphrey's ideas for her classroom curriculum are taken from John I. Goodlad's concept of non-grading.[9] First, the school has no rigid grade level standards. Instead there are realistic goals expecting

[9] John I. Goodlad, "The Changing Curriculum of America's Schools," *Saturday Review,* XLVI, No. 45 (November 16, 1963), p. 87. Also "Nongraded Schools, Meeting Children Where They Are," *Saturday Review,* XLVIII, No. 12 (March 20, 1965), pp. 57–59.

each child to do his best. Secondly, there must be continuous progress on a broken front. Finally, meeting individual differences is not so much covering the same material at different rates of speed as it is providing alternative programs for different children. Out of such a curriculum might grow the following program.

The Pooling Period or Planning Period. This usually follows opening exercises and is the time when the children plan their activities for the work period which will follow. It may be 15 minutes or perhaps only two or three minutes in length. At this time interest groups are organized, new books introduced, and temporary groups are established for remedial instruction. The teacher assigns seat work to those who need it, and sometimes there may be a short teaching lesson. Here is an example of one child's plan for a work period.

9:15– 9:30—Bring my record book up to date. Put my interesting words into my dictionary.
Check in the library books. [This child was a classroom librarian.]
9:30– 9:40—Pick my books. (Try to get *The Curious World of Snakes.*)
9:40–10:15—Work on my report on Brachiosaurus.
10:15–10:30—Read a Dr. Seuss book with Tammy.
10:30–10:40—Have a conference with Mrs. Bumphrey.
After recess—Watch a film.
If I have time—Do page 32 in my Phonics book.

The most important part of the pooling period is an individual schedule or plan that each child makes for himself.

The Work Period. This is usually about 60 minutes in length. The length of the work period will vary from day to day as this block of time must be used flexibly to allow time for children to pursue their interests, to interact with each other, and to feel free to express themselves creatively. A rigid timetable often inhibits creative expression.

At the beginning of the school year the periods are kept very simple. Later, when the children develop more self-management, there might be many different activities. The teacher must help the children to realize that they may engage in many kinds of activity. In collaboration with the teacher, they are responsible for working out a balanced program and engaging in positive learning activities.

Such a classroom might at first be rather confusing; many children would be out of their desks with the teacher nowhere to be seen. But each child would be busily reading, writing, creating, discussing, or building something he feels is important and interesting. One interest group might be discussing a topic around a table. Children might be sitting on the floor in pairs reading to each other. Some might be watching filmstrips on film viewers. As the child librarians return books to the shelves, some children may stop their work and select their new reading material. In one corner a group of children might be playing word games. Other children may be quietly writing book reports, letters, or stories at their desks.

Much of the silent reading and written language, and some of the oral reading, is done in the work period. Subject word lists and individual dictionaries assist the children in their writing. Each child also keeps a record of the books he has read although no premium is placed on the number of books a child reads.[10]

The Evaluation Period. These short periods are sometimes held following sharing periods or work periods. The children are guided in self-evaluation although group estimation is done in a general way. Evaluation is based on the child's progress in relation to himself rather than in relation to any predetermined standard.

The Sharing Period. A teacher might have two planned sharing periods each week. There will also be many informal discussions following work periods and incidental kinds of sharing experiences in the pooling period.

For the planned sharing period the teacher usually chooses the participants. Each participant will have handed in or prepared some piece of work, the best that he can produce.

There may be a lively discussion during the sharing period. The teacher may withdraw into the background, but she is prepared to take advantage of "'teachable moments." She may bring a shy child into the discussion, or she may ask for further explanation and deeper reasons. She selects and emphasizes worthwhile ideas, attitudes, and questions.

This sharing period helps children to extend their thinking horizons and provides much motivation for further reading, probing, and investigation. It is an excellent opportunity for the child to develop oral language skills, to organize and express his thoughts and have them evaluated on the spot.

Self-selection. This is the heart of the program. This kind of curriculum demands a large supply of books, filmstrips, magazines, and other reading materials. They must include a wide range in theme, style, and difficulty; and they must be so organized that they are easily available to children.

Construction materials, rolls of butcher paper, paint and crayons, paste and scissors, clay and building blocks, colored paper, and varied colored

[10] Helen Bumphrey, "Learning Is Fun," *A. T. A. Magazine*, LXI, No. 9 (May, 1967), p. 15.

yarn must also be convenient to the children's use. Space in which to spread out, and the freedom to move easily and efficiently from place to place in the room are essential to the success of the program.

This kind of program may provide the following advantages to children. *First,* there may be an increased interest in learning; children may stop thinking of the curriculum as subjects to be covered and as the bases on which they are to be judged by the way they handle these subjects. *Second,* there is an opportunity for critical thinking to be developed. *Third,* the schoolroom environment allows children to broaden their horizon of interests. *Fourth,* the children may secure an awareness of and respect for methods of organizing knowledge. *Finally,* and probably most important, the children may learn to become more independent workers.

How different this classroom program is, influenced by Dewey and Bruner, from that found in the majority of elementary schools a decade ago. The extent to which this kind of program can be found today varies greatly within a school building and school district. Individualized instruction is one of the most dramatic efforts to develop a meaningful curriculum for each child. This plan, implemented by a competent teacher, provides a means of applying much of what is known concerning teaching and learning processes. Even if not *fully* applied, its concepts are valuable when applied to varied instructional patterns.

Creative Teaching—Creative Learning

You, as a teacher, must have time to be creative; time to indulge in your own area of interest and excitement. It is almost impossible for you to be creative if you must spend most of your time looking for lost mittens, trying to balance the lunch-money account, collecting picture money, and doing all the other jobs that still fall to the lot of teachers in many schools.

You also need time to meet with other teachers as well as a place for those meetings. Usually the most exciting classrooms belong to teachers who have worked with other teachers. When teachers are given the opportunity to share their classroom experiences, the resulting cross-fertilization of minds creates enthusiasm and excitement which are contagious.

Probably more important, you must help each child understand and respect himself as a human being. You can help the child build a positive self-concept by allowing him to participate in learning and discover the excitement of developing his own thinking abilites.

An Example of Discovery Learning. One day when first graders come into the room, they might find a big tub of water with some heavy rocks around it. Of course the children won't be able to resist dropping rocks into the tub and splashing water all over. The next day the tub is still there, but this time there are pumice stones around it. Now when the children drop the pumice into the tub much less water splashes out, and the pumice floats. Next the children might place a plastic spoon and a metal spoon in the water. One will float; the other will sink.

From such observations the children are discovering scientific principles within the realm of their experience. But they must now talk about what they have learned, draw pictures, or write about it. Otherwise there will be little understanding and less learning. Children learn to communicate by talking about what they have observed and experienced. They learn to record by drawing what they have seen or by dictating words for the teacher to write.

One child might pick up the metal spoon and discover that it is like a mirror. But the image is right side up on one side of the spoon and wrong side up on the other. The child is intrigued. You, the teacher, suggest that the child look for other things that act the same way and encourage him to talk, draw, and write—and thus learn. You set the environment for learning by arousing the child's curiosity. Then you guide and direct that curiosity toward a goal and help him to think about it through some sort of structure or organization. A flexible curriculum provides an environment for individual pupil growth.

CURRICULUM FOR A CHANGING SOCIETY

This is an age of confrontation. Conflict besets almost every aspect of our society, and education is not immune. There are loud arguments on the educational scene about the who and how of decision-making, the dimension and design of relevant instructional programs, and the unique role of the school. Student is pitted against administrator, black against white, parent against parent, teacher against teacher.

This is also the era of great changes within our society. It is inevitable that such changes must affect the school's curriculum. The school must prepare a child for the realism of society. Change is like the activity of a pot of thick soup on a hot burner. The soup is the curriculum, and society the hot burner. The bottom layer of the soup, reacting to the pressure from above and the heat from below, attempts to rise when the fire is too hot and the mixture too unyielding; the surface is forcibly breached and things splatter all over. But, if the mixture is of reasonable consistency and is stirred occasionally, the layers mix. Nothing is irreparably scorched, and the soup is reasonably palatable for all concerned. Thus it is in the school curriculum.[11] Change must be consistent with that taking place within the society itself.

[11] Betty Nickerson, "Unshackle Our Youth," *The B.C. Teacher*, XLVI, No. 7 (April, 1967), p. 309.

Technological developments, particularly in communication and transportation, have created new situations and new awareness. Adults are still adjusting to speed and contact, but children are different. These things were on the scene when they appeared; they cannot imagine life otherwise. They live with a different mental picture of time and space than do adults. Their concept of man is different from that of their parents. The curriculum suitable for their fathers is not suitable for the modern child.

It takes courage to change a curriculum. Educators tend to have strong vested interests. Social pressures are found in every school and are brought to bear against the innovating teacher. The advocate and adopter of anything new may expect some loss of social status, reputation, position, or public acceptance. Anyone who introduces something new into the classroom may become an isolate, at least temporarily. Of course, educational change is "the thing to do" in some school settings. Change should be promoted within the context of a particular setting.

You can discuss daring changes and softly utter sentiments about education. If you are to make an impact on the curriculum, if you really intend to accomplish something, you may expect some problems and some anxiety. Significant changes never come by default or accident. They are caused by teachers who make a conscious commitment and have courage to apply their ideals. The curriculum will have to change in the coming years if it is to serve adequately the educational needs of a changing society.

The first step you must recognize is that curriculum change is a problem worthy of attention. The second step is to ask what kind of human beings you wish our schools to produce. The third is to help determine what school resources are available to assist each child to attain his full educational potential. It will be necessary to question everything that is accepted in the present curriculum. Of course some of the present curriculum will be found to be sound; but it must be examined, manipulated, and applied. Nothing can be *assumed* to be valid in today's world for today's children simply because it was useful yesterday.

Critical questioning should lead to essential changes and improvements of all sorts within the curriculum. These changes will be far reaching; they will affect the structure, content, teaching methods and materials, physical plant and equipment, child–teacher relationships, and administrative arrangements. They should aim at raising the quality, efficiency, and effectiveness of the curriculum. Some will cost more; others will save money. Curriculum changes are essential in their own right, but they are also tactically necessary if the school is to justify its claims to larger funds.

Children today comprehend the world in light of its more recent developments. They are more mobile, less inhibited by the past, and more flexible in their thinking. They mature earlier than did previous generations. They are stronger, are healthier, and know more than children of past decades. The curriculum for the children of the space age is not the same as that curriculum which reflected what the social machine needed and was then designed to turn out products that matched those needs. Schools once provided a common base of knowledge and skill and then gradually prepared the child for that specialization which the society needed. That age has passed. To be relevant, the old curriculum patterns must pass into history.

THE NEW TECHNOLOGY

Individualized Instruction through Technology

Technology may free the curriculum from its lockstep structure. Children may now be educated in ways which make sense to them as well as fit their own individual needs and interests. Educational technology is based on two major premises, both of which have been validated by research. Children learn at different rates. Age and grade level are in no way guides to the appropriateness of a learning task. Second, learning is incremental. In most instances the child builds his learning block by block, like a wall.

> The biggest news of our time is coming from research in the institutions of higher learning—new scientific discoveries, new ways of putting together the webs of past and current history, new means of apprehending and enjoying the stuff of sensory input, of interpersonal relationships, of involvement with life.[12]

The long-distance means of communication such as television and telephone make it possible for children to have the entire world at their fingertips.

Many teachers believe that human personal relationships, such as they are, will be lost in schools where machines are used widely. But, the word technology does not refer necessarily to machines; it implies any practical art using scientific knowledge. Wise users of educational technology are not as interested in presenting information and knowledge as they are in developing each child's capacity to learn and in his ability to carry forward his own education.

Teaching machines, sometimes called self-instruction machines, are only one facet of the new technology. The machine itself is just another mechanical gadget and is not even essential in many learning situations.

[12] Marshall McLuhan and George B. Leonard, "The Future of Education—The Class of 1989," *Look Magazine*, XXXI, No. 4 (February 21, 1967), p. 86.

It is the programmed material, which can be presented to the child with or without benefit of machine, that is important. This programmed material is adapted to the rate of training of each child. He proceeds from one lesson to the next only after he has mastered each step. This material may have many aspects of a game and can add interest to rote learning. It allows learning to continue outside school hours. Thus children can go as far and as fast as they please in many areas of the curriculum. Self-education is now possible within the curriculum. The use of machines can relieve the teacher of drill work to assume the role of guide and leader.

Computer-assisted instruction is a planning tool based on electronic data processing The computer may bring individualized instruction to the classroom. It allows the teacher to monitor the responses of individual students. The educational environment of the classroom may be so enhanced that better outcomes are provided for the children, as well as more rewards and more satisfaction.

The computer offers the teacher immediate access to a wide range of highly relevant information about any single child. Such information can aid the teacher to an early assessment and provision for appropriate responses to behavior problems and educational difficulties, as well as for attitudinal or motivational problems. The computer can be used as a finely sensitive tool available to support the kinds of relationships that are necessary if each student is to be treated as an individual human being.

The computer might become the equivalent of a "master instructor" which is responsive to the learning needs of a particular child. It can be used as a tool which may make learning an exacting and welcome experience for every child in the school system. It can allow him to engage in individual learning games and respond directly and immediately in harmony with his own temperament and learning style. Computers also provide opportunities for accomplishing significant research on human learning in the classroom and school environment. The computer is a valuable tool which can be used to investigate the fundamental questions of how children learn.

A few classrooms have been installed with consoles which are linked to a centrally located computer. Children use the consoles, which look like typewriter keyboards, to interact with the computer when studying specific topics. Thus the computer shares the instructional responsibility with the teacher. The computer in the classroom may also assume the role of an information retriever. A number of classrooms or schools are linked to a computer which has been programmed with selected social science, or mathematical, or language arts information. Here the children will use the computer as a data source or a calculation aid during the study of designated topics.

An Example of Computer Utilization

At the Pennsylvania State University, course content in elementary school mathematics is programmed using Coursewriter, a computer language developed by International Business Machines Corporation's Thomas J. Watson Research Center. The program is stored and relayed by a computer, located at the university's Computation Center. Course materials are processed over telephone lines for presentation on an IBM student terminal—a modified electric typewriter, random-access slide projector, and tape recorder unit.

Each student relays his response to the computer which evaluates it, provides knowledge of results if correct, and then either shows a slide, plays a tape, or types out the next question. If the answer is an anticipated wrong answer, a specific clue is provided and the student again responds to the question. For anticipated wrong answers the computer either types out a series of clues or the reason for the correct answer, or "branches" into a series of small step questions. Coursewriter allows for partial answer-processing on such factors as key words or spelling. Branching decisions are based on particular answers, on an accumulated error count, or on student decision. Several advantages have been noted for computer instruction, in comparison with other programmed devices and approaches.

Advantages of Computer Use

The computer carefully controls the learning sequence of each child and requires the child to comprehend each frame. The computer can judge constructed responses for accuracy. It may offer a more stimulating learning situation than is sometimes provided by programmed texts. Background information can be utilized on each child for constructing learning sequences and judging responses. The computer is more versatile than a programmed text. It can teach a wider variety of tasks and employ a wider range of auxiliary stimulus presentation equipment. Presently there is a great deal of interest in the use of the guided discovery approach in many areas of the curriculum. The author of a program which is to be utilized in a computer is able to use the same type of guided questioning that is typical of directed discovery patterns. This program may have an advantage over a guided discovery discussion since each learner must respond to each question, experiencing discovery *himself*.

The computer can offer data on the entire learning session as well as summary information. These data can be useful in revision of a programmed sequence as well as for school records and research purposes.

Children can use their "type outs" for individual study. The child's computer record can also be very useful in analyzing the thinking pattern of students.

The computer may be a long-term curriculum investment which may have a variety of uses and purposes. It may, in the final analysis, be less expensive and less space consuming than programmed texts.

SIMULATION

Simulation is another new curriculum tool. The simulation game provides a child with a vicarious environment which, although it is somewhat artificial, gives the effect of realism in which the child may participate. Bruner believes that active participation in the learning process can be gained "particularly by the use of games that incorporate the formal properties of the phenomena for which the game is an analogue. In this sense, a game is like a mathematical model—an artificial but often powerful representation of reality." [13]

There are several simulation games available for the classroom. There is the "Democracy" game, a composite of eight different games which simulate the legislative process. The "Life Career" game presents a simulation of certain features of the labor market, the "education market," and the "marriage market," as they now operate in the United States and as they may operate in the future. The "Community Response" (disaster) game presents a simulation of a community hit by a localized natural disaster, while the "Parent–Child" game simulates the relationship between a parent and a child in respect to five issues important to both. There is also the "Consumer" game which is a model of the consumer buying process involving players in the problem and economics of installment buying. An "Economic System" game simulates the interrelationships of a competitive economic system with nine owners, manufacturers, workers, and farmers' market. An effort is made to produce and consume goods while trying to make a profit and maintain a high standard of living.

The distinction between games and simulations as two separate techniques might be explained by the following diagram:

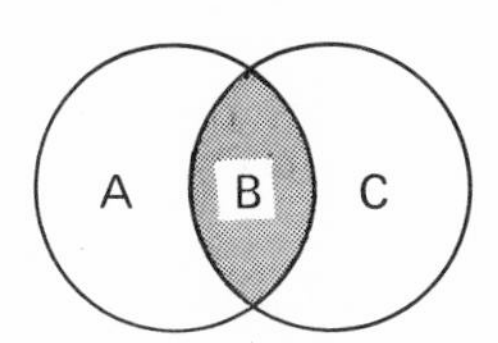

[13] Bruner, *Toward A Theory of Instruction, op. cit.,* pp. 92–93.

Circle A, excluding the shaded portion, is representative of competitive games with a set of rules that all players must follow and with a means of determining a winner or winners. Likewise circle C, excluding the shaded portion, is representative of simulations in which participants take roles which reproduce certain features of real-life social processes. The coincidence of these two techniques, that is, simulation-gaming or the creation of games with simulated environments, is represented by the shaded B portion of the circles.

Politics, both national and international, has been a popular subject for simulation games. Three games to teach economic principles at the upper elementary levels have been developed by the Board of Cooperative Educational Services in northern Westchester County, New York. All use computers to simulate the economic environment, whether it be a prehistoric society, a newly emerging African nation, or a retail store. The Nova High School in Fort Lauderdale, Florida, has developed the Nova academic games project which has as its goal the integration of games with the regular course work at all grade levels and the introduction of interscholastic competition.

There may be a major curriculum trend in the development of simulation for educational purposes. It suggests a possible curriculum direction for the future.

INQUIRY APPROACH

In the future the child's principal curriculum activity may be inquiry and investigation into the structure of knowledge. Bringing some order out of chaos is the chief function of any school curriculum. The inquiry or discovery approach to the curriculum helps children to perceive and experience the process of organizing facts and content in the testing of a particular hypothesis. Thus they discover a pattern or structure of operation. Several prominent scientists confess that their interest in science resulted from early participation in research. Surely the curriculum might be so organized that it can give children the opportunity to experience early the thrill of discovery.

The inquiry or discovery method in the curriculum attempts to teach children how to ask empirical questions concerning the environment around them. This may lead to hypotheses which in turn can be tested by collecting appropriate facts. The very process of inquiry should progressively help the children to understand the organizing concepts of knowledge. Hence children who perceive their ability to formulate rules or conclusions from a series of concrete observations or experiments will come to realize that the environment can be predicted and controlled.

To use the inquiry method effectively, children and teacher must resolve a concrete problem which serves as a focal point for study and investigation. Suppose a class of third grade children are to study Alaska; the teacher, to stimulate interest, has displayed pictures of Anchorage after the earthquake on Good Friday, 1964. The children can be encouraged to ask questions. How far is it to Alaska? How would we get there? Is it safe to go to Alaska? Why does Alaska have earthquakes? Out of such questions a well-defined and immediately intelligible problem must be resolved. For particular children a meaningful problem might be, "How must we prepare to make a visit to Alaska?" Each question in turn opens up a whole area of investigation—What are the land, the people, the animals, the food, and the recreation like in Alaska? The children begin to realize that they must investigate or study Alaska before a trip there can be planned or an understanding of its earthquakes can be secured. Too many teachers rush this introductory phase of the inquiry method. The children should be given time to think, to contemplate, and to trim and sharpen questions and consolidate them into a pertinent problem. In a three week unit, three days are not an excessive amount of time for asking and consolidating questions, discussing them, and refining the problem.

Once the problem has been organized and thoroughly understood, the classroom environment should include information necessary to solve the problem. Each child must act on his own responsibility to obtain, organize, and interpret the data. This is not possible with one textbook and no globe. Suitable trade books, atlases, wall maps, brochures, newspapers, periodicals, recordings, films and filmstrips must be so organized and located in the learning environment that each child can gather, with a minimum of tension and frustration, the essential facts and information for the solution of his problem.

This is where the inquiry method often breaks down and becomes self-defeating. Materials on Alaska may not be available at the moment of need. The chief responsibility of the helpful administrator is not only to assist in the organization of teaching and learning materials, of which there is great abundance, but to make certain that they are available in the classroom when required. The collecting and organizing of specific materials is not the responsibility of the classroom teacher alone. The librarian, a district helping teacher, a teacher aide, and the principal must assist in the survey and search of such materials as soon as the children begin to formulate their questions about a particular problem.

Children's Role in the Inquiry Approach

Once the materials are efficiently available and organized, children may search for answers to their problems individually, in pairs, as groups, or in committees. The teacher should give guidance and direction to the children in the search for information: "This atlas is a good one to find how many miles it is to Alaska from San Francisco." "This might be the best way to write down the things you've learned." Teacher guidance is most important in the children's successful investigation and coordination of information necessary to the solution of the problem under consideration. If a group of children seeks answers to the question, "What animals will we find in Alaska?," the teacher can help the children to discipline themselves in the search for material on *that* topic, rather than on the subsidiary topics of fauna, climate, or topography.

Screening still must take place once the facts pertaining to a particular topic have been gathered. Information collected may not be completely pertinent to the problem or to the individual child involved. One child may decide to emphasize or specialize on bears. Then, his notes or outline may concern bears although he may share information he has found on foxes or seals. The child must be taught not only to keep before him a fairly accurate picture of what he is attempting to explain, but also to focus on only those facts which are relevant or essential. Group verbalization is one of the best methods of testing, selecting, and organizing the information concerning a problem.

Once facts have been acquired, the child should apply them to a particular project or activity. The child might prepare a diorama or mural of wild animals in their Alaskan environment, or a scrapbook of pictures with a written description of animals in their habitat. Here the child structures the information into a hypothesis which can be tested and integrated. The hypothesis might be that the Alaskan animal population is large because of vast open places where few people live. This can be organized and illustrated in the child's project, explaining the conclusions the child has reached.

Thus the child is given an opportunity to do real thinking, about real events, built around a problem suitable to his ability and maturity. He has actually imitated the scholar's method of investigation—he asked questions about a problem that interests him, gathered quantities of relevant information, and has been given the opportunity to build ideas out of that information. He has been encouraged to check his ideas with those of other children and with the authorities pertinent to his problem. Finally, he has synthesized his ideas into a solution or conclusion in the form of a work project or display.

Although the inquiry method in the curriculum is not a tested and proven pedagogical method, it can be used as effectively as skillful expository teaching. It prevents the use of facts without a goal or purpose. Most important, though, is that it teaches the children how to utilize the methods of a particular science or discipline.

BASIC QUESTIONS

The curriculum of the elementary school and its objectives are under searching examination. Educators are carefully examining today's curriculum, and countless school districts from California to Pennsylvania are experimenting with new approaches. What guidelines or criteria might you use to evaluate and judge a new curriculum?

Is the curriculum so constructed that its focus is the involvement of children? If the essence of the curriculum is expository or descriptive, it is not new or different. It should allow the child to initiate self-discovery on his level of maturity and interest into the reality of his immediate environment. The curriculum should be organized to enable the child to set up an hypothesis and then collect the evidence to prove or disprove his assumptions. True, he may not make revolutionary discoveries in his search for evidence, but the program should give him the opportunity to organize that method of attacking a problem which is the most efficient for him.

Is the new curriculum expandable? In other words, can it be adjusted to a particular group of children in a particular geographic area? Many of the new curricula, particularly those developed in the universities, are geared for the college-bound student or for the gifted child. A curriculum developed for Hawaii may not be suitable for Texas, no matter the amount of adaptation.

The program should contain sufficient suggestions concerning activities, topics, and problems from which the teacher might select those which will initiate the curriculum at his level of competence and preparation and at the socioeconomic and ability level of the children. The curriculum should not be so rigidly structured that it does not provide for the individual differences of teacher and children.

The goals and objectives of the school's curriculum must be the total goals and objectives of all individual teachers. A good elementary school curriculum helps the teacher to recognize the separate entities and aspects of curriculum, to classify them, and describe them for himself. No curriculum should be so structured that teachers must accept and follow it unflinchingly.

Does the curriculum contain issues and concepts which the child can comprehend? It must contribute useful ideas, attitudes, and frames of reference which are pertinent to today's child in today's society. The curriculum must have some measure of utility within the culture as it is presently operating. A large majority of today's elementary school children will live as adults in an urban setting. It seems pertinent that many aspects of the curriculum be concerned with city living. The child must be given some understanding of the present tumultuous change in society and be equipped with some help to meet this change. The curriculum must include some emphasis on the future for which the child is being prepared.

Is the curriculum objective? Curriculum scope and sequence should not be derived completely from emotional patterns and feelings. The curriculum must be so organized that careful and objective consideration can be given to the complexity of the intellectual tasks at hand.

The amount of honest inquiry engaged in by the child will be in direct proportion to the amount of objective material the curriculum contains. Under these circumstances the child can go beyond present skills and knowledge to produce creatively new and different applications and interpretations. Even in its simplest form, a curriculum which allows only subjective judgments cannot help the child to develop new perceptions or to make new discoveries.

It seems essential that a modern curriculum prepare the child effectively for the space age. Facts and information are important, not only for their inherent value but also for the manner in which their content exemplifies or illustrates important basic concepts essential for the twenty-first century. The child must be allowed to investigate ideas which are pertinent to the new age. Otherwise, as Marshall McLuhan indicates, the school curriculum will be a desert in an oasis rather than an oasis in the desert.

PROJECTS AND READINGS

1. Increased science, technology, and industrialization over the earth continue to pull mankind together. However, growing nationalism tends to keep societies of men apart. Today, there are well over 100 nations, each claiming complete sovereignty. Each nation seems to believe that it is the center of the universe. Each nation teaches its children that its institutions, values, and military and political leaders are superior to those of other nations. This conditioning is systematic in the schools. How can the elementary school curriculum foster an international attitude with children? To what extent do you believe that an international attitude *should* be taught? In relation to an international viewpoint, how would you define constructive patriotism?

2. America's capacity to produce for war has been aptly demonstrated. There seems to be no inherent reason why the productive capacity attained in wartime cannot be applied in peacetime to an improved standard of living for every American. The impediments to an improved society are not, strictly speaking, economic. They are to be found in the absence of a clear purpose to produce for an improved society. Should the elementary school curriculum be concerned with attempting to change the goals of society and the various means of implementing those goals? How, and by whom, should decisions be made concerning which goals are desirable and how to attain those goals?

3. Education is a form of action—a means of influence and control of a particular society. It always expresses a definite social philosophy, involves

certain types of behavior, and demonstrates conceptions of well-being and moral viewpoints. What do you believe is the social philosophy, the social behavior, and moral preconceptions which influence the direction of today's elementary school curriculum? Do you believe it is consistent with American society? To what extent and in what directions do you believe that it should change?

4. In 1938 the Reich Ministry of Education prepared a manual of directions for all Nazi teachers. Following are some statements from this document entitled *Education and Instruction,* Official Publication of the Reich and Prussian Ministry of Knowledge, Education, and Culture (Berlin, 1938).

a. The school hands down the cultural content of one period to the next, but in National Socialism it follows the decisive transformation of its cultural philosophy.
b. It is not the aim of education to educate scholars nor to produce intellectuals.
c. All educational agencies have one common goal, the education of the National Socialist Man.
d. One of the important aims of education is to train students to submit to authority, and that authority emanates from the Party.
e. In its origin the National Socialist system of education is not a result of educational planning but of the political fight and its laws.

In what ways would you feel that educational goals for a democratic society would differ from those of a totalitarian state? To what extent do you feel that American elementary school objectives are consistent with the objectives of the American way of life? What five educational objectives would you write for American elementary schools?

5. These sources will give you a fuller understanding of how the past has affected today's curriculum.

a. Robert Bendiner, *The Politics of Schools* (New York: Harper & Row, 1969), 240 pp. This book is an attempt to assess the usefulness of school boards as a practical means of dealing with basic public policy issues related to education.
b. William Glasser, M.D., *Schools without Failure* (New York: Harper & Row, 1969), 235 pp. This book offers insight into methods for making the process of education a participatory one and to make classroom teaching a more successful experience for the teacher as well as for the child.

PART III

Issues and Trends

Elementary school curriculum ultimately is converted into subject and learning activities. Part III begins with efforts to stress the importance of developing a curriculum which makes sense in terms of both child and society. Subject matter selected and learning activities carried on are means to an end—to develop the total child for meaningful living in a democratic society. The content chapters in Part III are a sampling of some basic issues: *content, method,* and *research.* The chapters are similar but not identical. Issues raised in one chapter may not be dealt with in subsequent chapters, or may be raised in a different manner from one chapter to the next. The issues in these chapters have sufficient implications and applications to justify major treatments. We hope that you will find additional sources which provide systematic and comprehensive discussions of the various subjects taught in the elementary schools. Part III is a continuation of previous efforts to combine both general and specific issues and trends. It should provide considerable concreteness to some of the abstractions discussed in earlier sections of this volume. This book closes with a personalized epilogue—our person-to-person conclusion which we hope will be a stimulant to a fruitful study of elementary school curriculum that should span your lifetime.

11

Maintenance of Individuality

INDIVIDUAL AND HIS SOCIETY

Generally, Americans are known for their energetic activity, for their drive. This activity drive may grow so strong *that it engulfs the person who has it and those who come in contact with him.* Such an individual may consume others by compelling them to yield to his drive. Americans are prone to heart attacks, ulcers, and asthma partially as a result of their excessive drives.

The United States is unique as a society in that it is propelled by its productive forces to constantly spiraling expansion and change. The vast natural resources of the United States, coupled with the energy of its people, have brought about great industrial development through technical creativity. Creative activity in the laboratory results in new discoveries and inventions which produce more changes. How can an individual use his active energy to achieve and satisfy the drives thus engendered to some kind of self-realization within a rapidly changing technical society that frowns on non-conformity? How can the school curriculum meet this dilemma? How can you as the teacher understand this dilemma and help prepare children to adjust to or solve it?

What are the factors which characterize our modern world? As has been emphasized, one chief characteristic of our society today is change. More subtle than the physical variations and perhaps far more important are the changes in the temper and spirit within society itself. It is this social variation and flux which you will, perhaps, have difficulty in incorporating into the curriculum. The acceleration of the tempo of change in the world generally has created an explosion of knowledge, particularly in the realm of science. There is about 100 times as much to know now as was available in 1900, and by the year 2000 there will be over 1,000 times as much.

While this change has been going on in the realm of the intellect, revolutions have come about in other equally important areas, especially within the past 10 years or so. Political, social, and economic upheavals in every part of the world have brought about the emergence of new nations, with a new nationalism (as opposed to internationalism and the concept of collective security). Other changes include new economic concepts, the affluent society, new conflicts between the haves and have-nots, new concerns for human and civil rights, planned attack on poverty, and increasingly critical confrontations between democracy and communism. A world in flux has also become a world in crisis. And over all the shadow of The Bomb is cast. What has caused this dilemma?

Individuality and the Threat of War

Technology has advanced at such a rapid pace, particularly in relation to the weapons of war, that the world is directly threatened by nuclear weapons. Considering the destructive powers of present nuclear weapons, life seems to lose much of its meaning.

It has been the classic responsibility of a nation's government to guard the security of its citizens. Taxes are paid, powers delegated, and a military establishment maintained by the government for this purpose. Technological breakthroughs have decreased the effectiveness of security by military means. The accumulated tonnage of nuclear explosions has been doubling every three years, since July, 1945, when the first atomic bomb was set off in New Mexico.

How does a government protect its citizens from modern technological war? It may do so by "herdening," that is, direct protection against physical damage. It may use concealment, including subterfuge and, as in the case of the Polaris submarine, missile mobility. The most straightforward and certain method is numbers, that is, presenting more targets than the attacker can possibly cope with. For a crowded nation this is also the easiest because it can attain absolute superiority in numbers.

One of the great challenges that technology has brought to the individual then is to find a place, a voice, and a fulfillment in a world threatened with massive destruction.

Affluence through Technology

Technology also has brought affluence to the industrial nations of the earth. The United States is the most highly industrialized nation. Such industrialization has brought extensive economic development. The people of the United States live better than those in other countries. The have-nots are more conspicuous in the United States than they are in much of the world. The United States has approximately one-fifteenth of the world's population and about the same proportion of the world's land area and natural resources. Yet the United States:

1. Produces about one-half of the world's manufactured goods.
2. Has more than one-half of the world's telephone, telegraph, and radio networks.
3. Has more than three-quarters of the world's automobiles.
4. Has almost one-half of the world's radios and consumes more than one-half of the world's coffee and rubber, over one-half of the steel, one-half of the coal, and nearly two-thirds of the crude oil.

While 30 per cent of the U. S. population and 20 per cent of England's population are statistically non-urban, it cannot be reasonably argued that farming is a way of life. The farm has become a factory. Television and radio broadcasts reach the most remote hamlets, as do electrification, central schools, hospitals, national newspapers and magazines, social security, super-highways, and the like.

Poverty and the Individual

On the other hand there is mass poverty in the underdeveloped nations as well as disease and illiteracy. The income gap between developed and underdeveloped countries is vast and is continually widening. In fact in recent years the development of the average per-capita income in the underdeveloped nations has begun to slow down. Food production in these nations is lower per head than it was before World War II and in recent years it has not kept pace with the population increase in Latin America, Asia, and Africa—where the present world population growth is occurring. The food supply in these nations will have to be more than doubled in order to preserve the *present* grossly inadequate standards of nutrition. A doubling of the present food supply will be needed by 1980 to feed the increasing population and achieve a very modest improvement of nutritional levels throughout the world generally.

Every minute dozens of persons die from the effects of malnutrition. Every hour of the day the world's population will increase by some 1,770 persons—the difference between total births and deaths. This means there are some 170,000 additional persons for breakfast each morning.

The population of the world increased by 400 million in the decade of the sixties. It will grow, on the best estimates available, by about 500 million, outside of China, in the seventies. According to the United Nations, if present trends in food production continue, more than half of the people living on earth during the seventies will be malnourished and therefore vulnerable to disease. Predictions by military authorities indicate that the present $200 billion the nations of the earth spend each year on military arms will double by 1980. Resources must be diverted to increasing food production and to birth control education if man is to survive the seventies.

The industrialized nations have come to realize that it is both inevitable and desirable for the rest of the world to enter the modern era as rapidly and as painlessly as possible. It seems far better to assist than to frustrate the process. If modernization can be achieved with the full cooperation of all parties concerned and with the best interests of the developing nations at the forefront, then the chances of minimizing international conflicts will be markedly enhanced. However, if nothing is done, or if not enough is done, there may be little hope of maintaining a world environment in which free societies can prosper to nourish free individuals.

This growing separation in basic production between the haves and the have-nots on the international scene can be duplicated within the United States itself. It is true that few Americans are starving although it is estimated that hundreds die each year from diseases caused by malnutrition. There are 32 million poor people in our country which breaks down to one out of every six Americans. The upper limits of poverty in the United States, which constitutes an annual income of $3,130 for an urban family of four and $2,190 for a farm family, would mean comfort in most parts of the world. In our affluent society these amounts insure only minimal subsistence. Life below this poverty line means nonparticipation in our consumer society.

The have-nots in our nation are cut off by their inability to compete for housing, transportation, medical care, and legal help. They are denied credit, political power, and often a livelihood. The poor in our society are alienated. They often are locked out by geography, by age, and commonly by race. Feelings about self are affected by exclusion from the total society. The faceless urban poor submerge their individuality.

Individuality in Urban Areas

Chase, the economist, indicates:

> Survey after survey shows American cities rotting at the core surrounded by widening areas of urban blight. One of every eight New Yorkers lives in almost incredible squalor. Some tenements are packed with as many as 10 persons to a rat-infested room. Much of the city is a jungle where no one is

safe after dark. Even inside some public schools, teen age girls walk in pairs as protection against rape. Urban renewal and public housing are unable to offset the galloping deterioration. Great sums must be invested if cities are to be made fit to live in.[1]

Adlai Stevenson's words reaffirm Chase's conclusions:

> While our cars have grown longer, our TV screens broader, our washing machines grander, our kitchens brighter, at the same time our schools have grown more dilapidated, our roads more crowded, our cities more messy, our air more fetid, our water more scarce, and the whole public framework on which private living depends, more shabby and worn out.[2]

Some claim there is no technical or economic reason for the existence of the modern city.[3] The acceleration in the transport of ideas and things eliminates the need of large centers for administration, finance, culture, and entertainment. Automation and computerization permit the decentralization of skilled labor pools; and, except for service work, the need for unskilled labor is almost non-existent. Various branches of technology such as climate control, nuclear fuel and hydroponics, and cryogenics make convenience to a seaport, fresh water, power, or even a decent climate unimportant. The single reason for the existence of the city, some sociologists claim, is social. The same sociologists also maintain that it is a disaster to live in a city, except for the fortunate few who can escape its fetid embrace when it pleases them.

The city in the mid-twentieth century has become a megalopolis which von Eckardt explains as "a huge string of central cities, suburbs, and satellite areas that stretch along the eastern seaboard of the United States from north of Boston to south of Washington and is the largest, wealthiest, and most productive region on earth."[4] This conglomeration creates one vast complex of industry, commerce, financial power, and high population density. It concentrates skills, learning talents, job opportunities, schools, affluence, and institutions. It also creates despair in its unemployed and low income people, its blighted areas, its need for more schools, its lack of adequate housing, its increasing tax burden, and its maladjusted (those who have not become urbanized).

The modern city has a rapid, intense pace complicated by the forces of technology. Its culture has seen great physical and social changes. Crowding people into limited space results in such increased demands as

[1] Stuart Chase, "Can We Stay Prosperous?" *Saturday Review*, L, No. 6 (February 11, 1967), p. 22.

[2] *Ibid.*

[3] Percival Goodman, "The Decay of American Cities: Alternative Habitation for Man," *New University Thought*, V, No. 4 (1967), p. 21.

[4] Wolf von Eckardt, *The Challenge of Megalopolis Based on the Original Study of Jean Gottman*, 20th Century Fund Report (New York: The Macmillan Co., 1964), p. 5.

for public utilities, traffic regulations and movement, police protection, parks and other recreation centers, civic centers, schools, libraries, public transportation, fire protection, health and welfare measures, and housing. There is not a single American city that is not faced with needs for physical improvements as well as growing attendant social problems.

President Johnson said in his State of the Union Message of 1965:

> I propose that we launch a national effort to make the American city a better and more stimulating place to live . . . an educated and healthy people require surroundings in harmony with their hopes. In our urban areas the central problem today is to protect and restore man's satisfaction in belonging to a community where he can find security and significance. The first step is to break old patterns. . . .

ESSENTIALS FOR TODAY'S SCHOOLS

John Dewey at the turn of the century foresaw the problems of an industrial society. He was alarmed that Americans were becoming slaves to technology because they were not sure of how to cope with a modern industrial society. The important problem for the school curriculum, he believed, was to help people remain free in that industrial society. The focus of education, for Dewey, was the development of a scientific method which could help children to understand the industrial world and provide training in democracy to enable them to utilize the abundance of a technical society wisely and profitably. He proposed a system of learning by doing which some have called progressive education. Children would learn to comprehend the machine civilization through the scientific method, and they would learn the process of democracy in an increasingly controlled society by learning how to operate the community of their own classrooms. These were the two basic lessons which a good curriculum should provide in the education of the American child, said Dewey. Thus the three prime lessons of progressive education were democracy, the learning of science by practicing it, and permissiveness for animal spontaneity.[5]

Many children in the ghetto schools by the fourth grade have become cynical and disillusioned about school, themselves, and life in general. These children are hostile, rebellious, and bitter. Some belong to gangs, some use drugs, and some even have police records. They are hyperactive and constantly in motion. A democratic, rational manner of living is difficult to attain in a confused, hostile classroom climate.

The inner city children's physical and intellectual worlds are quite limited. Many have never been more than a few blocks away from home.

[5] Paul Goodman, "Mass Education in Science," The 33rd Annual Sir John Adams Lecture (Los Angeles: University of Southern California Press, 1967).

Many do not own a single book, nor do their parents. Almost all come from broken homes. Many live with a grandmother or a guardian who is burdened with more children than she can care for. A few literally take care of themselves. The home environment does not and in many ways cannot prepare the children for school or encourage them to do well. The school is often remote and alien to their lives. They seem to have low self images; most have experienced failure throughout their school careers; they seem to be frustrated and defeated easily. They live difficult, chaotic lives and do not come to school with the curiosity, interests, and controls that the middle-class-oriented school expects, demands, and uses as an assumption for much of its curriculum.

The child of the inner city may require a particular curriculum which goes beyond the curriculum suggestions given by Dewey for a technical urban society. However, there are some pertinent attributes necessary to any curriculum in developing the full potential of each individual in our machine-oriented social environment.

CREATIVE BEHAVIOR

Our democracy is dedicated to perpetuating a nation of thinkers who are unique and creative. The environment tends also to favor a nation *of dependent, conforming citizens.* If the society is to be characterized by freedom of thought, freedom of action, and the freedom to express unique ideas, then the school curriculum must be fully dedicated to fostering and facilitating each child's creative abilities. Within the school curriculum opportunities should be provided for each child to discover, express, and use his own ideas, as well as his imagination, his hunches, and his insights and experiences.

Creation of a Creative Atmosphere

To free such creativity you should first set up a classroom atmosphere in which children have the liberty to explore—a classroom in which the child becomes stimulated to express himself not only orally but through work projects as well. The following procedures will help to develop such an atmosphere.

1. Invite children to share in the planning.
2. Make it clear to the children in what areas of classroom management they may share authority.
3. Allow the children to participate in as many classroom decisions as possible.
4. Make group and committee organization as flexible as possible and subject to change when group evaluation indicates such is advisable.

5. Help children to understand each child and each committee as part and parcel of the entire class.
6. Organize a small planning committee to work out a policy for the classroom procedures. This committee should report its decisions to the entire class. A representative of each working group might be a member of this planning committee.
7. Encourage each child to become self-directed when the appropriate situation arises.
8. Be sensitive to the mood of the children, and play a dominating or recessive role as the classroom climate demands.
9. Refer your suggestions, as well as those of the children, to the entire class for discussion and decision-making.
10. Use the word "we" and "our" rather than "I" and "mine" when working with the children.
11. Never forget that one learns through failure as well as through successes. If the results will not seriously harm anyone, allow the class to make mistakes.
12. Frustration is the pathway to problem solving. Do not be alarmed if children experience frustration.
13. Use praise often and continuously. But use negative evaluation if it is necessary for progress.
14. Be slow in supplying the answers to problems; rather suggest alternate solutions.
15. If disagreements arise, allow the children to settle and solve them.
16. Encourage children to evaluate their progress by concrete evidence, and to evaluate themselves continually.
17. Make it a rule to know each child well and allow children to become acquainted with each other.
18. Allow the children to occasionally organize social affairs. Encourage them to plan class projects.

Children in the elementary school, regardless of their backgrounds, have different experiences in space and time. Each child attempts to orient himself to his natural physical environment; he seeks security. He uses all his senses to take in data and responds by direct physical action to such data. The child is continually attempting to give form to the content of his world. He does not do this once and for all time. He continually structures and restructures his world as he receives new experiences. He is constantly involved in a search for pattern. This groping for an interpretation of the environment is the essence of every child's sense of creativity. You can find your greatest delight, as well as your greatest challenge, in fostering this essence of creativity in every child, regardless of his background. Igniting creativity in children may be your most valuable contribution to society. Galbraith says:

These are the days when men of all social descriptions and all political faiths seek the comfortable and the accepted, when the man of controversy is looked upon as a disturbing influence, when originality is taken to be a mark of instability, and when in minor modification of the scriptural parable the bland lead the bland.[6]

Stimulation of Creative Thinking

To help children break with the comfortable and the accepted will be your greatest challenge as a teacher. Here are some ideas which might stimulate creative thinking in your classroom.

1. Have a "brain storming" session with the children. Ask, "Who can think of the most pleasant, or the most wonderful thing to do? Can you tell of an exciting but dangerous trip you might take?" Help the children learn how to develop fluency of ideas.
2. Play word and number games such as: "Think of three words that sound alike and all begin with St." "What number would follow numbers 2, 4, 8, and 16?"
3. Have a group of children gather around a tape recorder. One child could begin a story; another could add to it; another could finish the story. The children could then listen to the recording and discuss how the story might be changed.
4. Have a competition to see who can think of the most beautiful word, or the loveliest phrase or sentence.
5. Secure an electric motor. Ask the boys how it might be used in the classroom.
6. Ask a child to say a word. Ask a second child to give a word of opposite meaning. Make a game of this procedure.
7. Secure used milk cartons, cereal boxes, or cans. Allow the children to use these materials to create any object they wish. Have the children outline any object they wish on the inside of an old inner tube. The outline, once cut out, can be retraced. Use a paper punch to make small holes around the edge of each cutout. Sew the two cutouts together with string or shoe laces; stuff with newspaper or cloth. The object might be a turtle, a kangaroo, or a Japanese doll and could then be painted.
8. Describe a real problem. "How might this classroom be made more attractive?" Encourage alternative solutions to the problem.
9. Have the children write a letter describing a classroom incident to their parents as well as to their best friend or a child overseas. Tell them to illustrate the incident for a local newspaper and for a Russian newspaper.

[6] John Kenneth Galbraith, *The Affluent Society* (Boston: Houghton Mifflin Co., 1958), p. 5.

10. Ask the children to draw a picture of people receiving Christmas presents in this country, in Japan, in Mexico, in a rich family, in a poor family.
11. Have the children draw cartoons of a particular incident with which they are familiar. Let them suggest different captions for the cartoons.
12. Give the children the opportunity to tell a funny story, a sad story, a real story, or a make-believe story. Ask them to make up an easy mathematics problem and a difficult one.
13. Encourage children to illustrate and compose their own comic strips. This might be an individual, group, or class project.
14. Read the children the story of a real historical event. Ask the children to tell or dramatize what feelings and what thoughts the personalities involved may have had.
15. Play a recording (something from the Beatles might be appropriate). Ask the children to illustrate or draw their feelings or thoughts aroused by the recording.
16. Have the children write their own plays or poems. Writing a class book could be an interesting project. Each child might write a chapter.
17. Let a child cut a picture, a cartoon, or a drawing from a newspaper, periodical, or magazine and make up a story about it.
18. Put a large map, illustration, or diagram on the chalkboard. Encourage the children to ask questions such as: "What country is it?" "How do we get there?" Help the children to ask good questions. Comment to the class, "Was that question clear to you? How might it be improved?"
19. Play such games as, "I spy with my little eye something that begins with B," or "I am thinking of someone who. . . ."
20. Have a quiet corner in the classroom sheltered by a screen where there is a work bench, a rocking chair, a book case—a place where children can go to think and work out ideas.

Your attitude with the children will determine how well their creative abilities are aroused.[7] You might follow these principles:

1. Treat each child's question with interest and respect.
2. Do not be surprised or disturbed when children present unusual, imaginative ideas.
3. By your attitude and comments, let the children understand that every idea has some value.
4. Allow the children the opportunity to test ideas without the penalty of grades or evaluation.
5. Encourage the children to initiate ideas, try them out, and evaluate them.

[7] E. Paul Torrance, "Creative Thinking Through the Language Arts," *Educational Leadership,* XVIII, No. 1 (October, 1960), p. 18.

6. Help the children understand how the evaluation of an idea is connected to causes and consequences.

With today's tremendous impetus toward creating new products, new ideas, and new approaches to the solution of increasingly difficult problems, it is essential that you help children develop into adults who will be creative individuals. One of the greatest dangers inherent in our technical society is standardization and conformity. It is in the elementary classroom that the future adult learns to desire to be and to be creative. The child is naturally curious. This curiosity will bud into creativity if unfettered by anxieties concerning classroom intellectual exploration. The child should be allowed to think ahead, think differently, and derive new and strange conclusions. If you feel free to encourage exploration, curiosity, and varied approaches to problems and if you provide children with an opportunity to have trial and error experiences, you will have established an environment for the development of creativity within the classroom.

INDIVIDUAL DIFFERENCES

Every year there will probably be at least one child in your classroom whom you will find difficult. If you don't have one this year, you may have two next year. A particular child may irritate or vex you. You may begin to feel guilty because you cannot force yourself to like each child. As you become more experienced as a teacher, you will learn not to expect the impossible and you will begin to face the reality that every teacher has one or many problem children. The saving grace of such a situation is to grant each child, whatever the nature of his problem, the respect that every human being deserves.

It is not necessary to love every child, or be fond of all children under your guidance. You should be sufficiently professional to be of maximum service to each child without being affected by the state of cleanliness, economic condition, or nervous manifestation of a particular child. Personal favoritism has no place in the classroom. Every child desperately needs someone who believes in him. It is not difficult to determine a child's liabilities; a teacher's responsibility is to search out each child's assets and develop them to their highest potential.

If you allow a child to progress at his own rate, you are respecting him as an individual. If you group the children according to ability, interest, and compatibility, you are allowing for individual differences. If you select materials and resources to fit the interest, ability, and maturity level of the children, you are showing concern for the individual child. If you use audiovisual aids to facilitate learning for the child who does not respond to books, you are meeting the needs of individual differences.

Ways To Recognize Individual Differences

Do not labor under feelings of inadequacy if you cannot bring about a complete transformation of a problem child. The child is in school a relatively brief amount of time. Many of his behavior patterns are set before he enters your classroom and they are regularly reestablished by home and community. You will have achieved real accomplishment if you overhear the child who dislikes school whisper to her friend, "She's the best teacher I've ever had." What can compensate for the softly spoken words "I love you, teacher," from the little fellow with whom you have been struggling the entire school year? Be realistic enough to know that there is a limit to what you can do with each individual child. However, these suggestions might help you to meet individual differences, the ultimate translation of curriculum.

Use experiences which are familiar to children. This will facilitate individual learning. A child will participate more readily—and with greater understanding and motivation—if you attempt to determine his background of experience.

An example is a second grade class involved in weather observation. A chart can be constructed on which to record daily temperatures, the amount of humidity, and the position of the sun. A field trip can be planned to a local park or some other outdoor destination. Then the children can discuss what they should wear, how they should behave if there is rain, if the rain freezes on the streets, or if the rain turns to heavy slush. What precautions will truck drivers take on such streets and what type of wares might be prominently displayed in particular shops if the weather is wet and slushy are additional questions.

Such an application of weather observation probably is much more effective than discussing the effect of rain on wheat fields, or on the rise of flood waters or on the accumulation of snow in the mountains—unless children have had meaningful experiences with such situations. Discussions might follow, after the effect of weather on the local or immediate environment is understood by the children. One child might make the comment, "If it rains, our roof will leak again." Another might complain, "If it rains, I'll probably get a cold again." Using these expressions of individual understandings, the teacher can effectively move to broader understandings of how weather affects health or housing. The child can realize that his individual contributions to the discussion are essential to a complete understanding of the phenomena under study.

Use concrete materials and real objects which the children can handle. Personal realia, as instructional materials, can help a child to realize that he is unique in his choices and preferences. Discussing particular experiences and looking at pictures is not enough. Concrete things to be experienced can stimulate a child to an understanding of his individuality, a significant curricular objective.

A fourth grade class might discuss clothing as one of man's basic needs. Some children may collect samples of silk, others of cotton, some of wool, some of synthetics. The designs may be different colors and quality. Each child could discuss why he selected a particular cloth for a particular piece of clothing. He might then design his own sweater, trousers, or pajamas. A child might select particular samples for drapes or rugs or cushion covers. The class might visit a carpet store where each child could select a carpet he would like for his bedroom floor. Here again the child has learned that he does have individual tastes and preferences and that he need not necessarily follow the tastes of the crowd. Indeed, individuality enriches the total class.

Encourage individual experiences and activities within the school environment. Children need not necessarily do the same thing at the same time. One group may work on a social studies mural, another group might conduct a science experiment, and a third could read quietly in the "cozy corner" of the classroom. It is important to encourage and develop each child's individual interests. An example of how to do this follows. A big sign on the bulletin board of a fifth grade class might read:

Contest! Contest!

Easy to enter!

Easy to win!

All you have to do is write an answer to the following question:

Which European country would you most like to visit?

Big Prizes

Free trip to the country of your choice!

The children will normally select a country in which they are interested. Then the teacher could announce that each child will have only one day in the country he chooses to visit and he can do anything he wishes during that day. One child might want to attend a bullfight in Madrid. He could read about bullfights and then tell the children about his reactions. Another may wish to paint the Eiffel Tower in Paris. She could display her painting. Another may decide to visit the Bolshoi Ballet in Moscow. She could play a recording of the music of "Swan Lake" and describe the dance. Thus each child, within the content or framework of a class assignment, can express his own particular interests and talents.

Accept children's "leads." You can learn from children. If you listen and observe carefully, you can pick up hints as to each child's individual thinking process. You may find that many children can initiate and carry out projects on their own. Your role is to clarify, supplement, and help each child to organize and bring to reality his individual plan.

A third grade class discussion might revolve around space travel. As a result one child might bring to class a clay model he had made: one round ball representing the earth and a smaller ball representing the moon. The two clay spheres may be joined by a toothpick; but the child may complain, "My moon doesn't revolve around the earth." You shouldn't pacify the child by answering, "But I think it is most adequate." Rather you could reply, "What remedy do you propose?" The child may make several suggestions. "Try them," you offer.

Finally a gleam may appear in his eye. "I think I know," he exclaims. "I'll stick a dowel stick into the earth, then I'll put the dowel stick into a spool. Then I can twirl the stick, and the moon will revolve about the earth."

You may or may not need to suggest the materials the child might use. You can accept the hint that the child wants to do something more with his model, and you can allow that hint to flourish into an individual accomplishment for the child. You can help him to make an individual discovery.

Teach each child to establish his individual study habits and skills. You can give each child under your guidance and direction the most precious of gifts—a solid foundation in study techniques that will be of inestimable value throughout his school career.

First, help each child to schedule his work. Most children and often their parents do not know the techniques of study. One child may learn to spell words orally, another by writing the word continuously, another by watching his mouth form the word in a mirror, still another by placing each spelling word on a separate three-by-five-inch card or scrap of paper.

Some children need to schedule their easiest work first, followed with the more difficult, then the most difficult, and finally taper off with a simple study assignment. Other children may find the exact opposite more effective and rewarding. A child may need to study out loud, or alone, or in a group. He may find that teaching himself is most rewarding. He may find that visualizing that which he is learning is his best study approach.

While evaluating each individual child's study methods, you can note specific deficiencies; for example, one child may need help with a particular reading skill, or be taught how to outline, or how to use a dictionary. Teach each child to study in a manner that is compatible with his special capacity and need.

In fostering unique individuals, the practices and procedures you use will be largely dependent upon your attitude and aptitudes. You should look on your classroom experiences as fields for exploration and experimentation. Your horizons will expand through the knowledge you glean from observation of children in action. You are not only a teacher but also a learner.

Uniqueness and Oneness with the Group

One of your great concerns should be to help each child make a personal social adjustment which can contribute to efficient development of needed knowledge and training skills. You should also help children to see the value and need for basic classroom routines, and train them to work and think independently. Each child needs to have a feeling of self-worth and the knowledge that his personal contributions to class life are welcomed and accepted. The individual needs to feel both his uniqueness and also his oneness with his classroom group. To foster individual differences remember to:

1. Provide firsthand experiences which seem to be most effective in terms of a child's learning. Exploratory activities such as cooking, taking trips, and working with concrete materials and sensory experiences are strongly recommended.
2. Recognize the value of play materials as tools for learning. From the first grade on, encourage children to "think things out" and to reach their own conclusions.
3. Utilize many sources to provide content for class experiences. Explore better ways in which to present content and thus encourage greater participation from the children.
4. Have many books available to provide abundant opportunities to reinforce newly acquired interests through searching and comparing. It is wise to use many and varied textbooks, as well as pam-

phlets, brochures, and similar materials, particularly in content areas such as social studies and science.

5. Introduce a variety of audiovisual materials—flat pictures, filmstrips, movies, and recordings, as well as such things as pupil-made illustrated booklets, slides, models, paintings, and drawings.
6. Gear your expectations to the children's abilities, developmental levels, and needs.
7. Involve children in class life and create good teacher–pupil relationships. Children with behavior difficulties tend to adjust more readily where such conditions prevail.[8]
8. Create a relaxed classroom atmosphere, enjoy children and teaching, recognize and anticipate children's needs, be sensitive to their feelings, personalize classroom experiences, display a sense of timing and spacing, and allow for each child's individual interest and ability. This can foster uniqueness in each child.

OPPORTUNITIES FOR THE DISADVANTAGED

Our technical society has created two classes of citizens. There are those who have received great advantages in material and personal benefits from the affluent society—these are the socially advantaged. There are large masses of people who have been bypassed by industrialization. These, along with the poor who live in rural poverty areas, are the socially disadvantaged. It is the children of this second class of citizens with which the school must be most concerned in the development and maintenance of individuality in a changing world. The children of the disadvantaged have difficulty in developing a self concept. The home and community environment is too often meager and barren, lacking the stimulation and enrichment necessary for the child's identity of self. The socially disadvantaged child needs much assistance in the development of his individual potential.

The key question is: Who are the socially disadvantaged? Havighurst [9] indicates the following characteristics in terms of the family situation, the child's personal characteristics, and the social group with which the family is integrated.

The family usually does not attempt to answer the child's questions or encourage him to ask questions. It does not help him to extend his vocabulary with words, adjectives, and adverbs. Nor does it give him a right and a need to stand up for and to explain his point of view on the world. It does not provide him with a reading environment nor a variety

[8] "Skillful Teaching Practices in the Elementary School," Board of Education of the City of New York, Curriculum Bulletin—1961–62, Series No. 12, p. 114.

[9] Robert J. Havighurst, "Who Are the Socially Disadvantaged?" *Journal of Negro Education,* XXXIII (Summer, 1964), p. 211.

of toys nor play materials with colors, sizes, and objects that challenge his ingenuity with his hands and his mind. His parents, too often, do not indicate that they believe in the value of education. They do not talk with the child or attempt to enlarge and expand his speaking vocabulary. Lacking stimulation to develop his unique perception of self in relation to environment and others, the disadvantaged child often lacks attitudes and aptitudes which contribute to school success.

The socially disadvantaged child develops particular personal characteristics. He may have inferior visual and auditory discrimination, poor judgment concerning time, and limited number and other basic concepts. This inferiority is not due to physical defects of eyes and ears and brain. It is due to insufficiently developed habits of hearing and seeing and thinking. The family environment of these children does not teach them to "pay attention" to what is being said or to the visual scene. School performance thus suffers when a child has not learned to "listen" to the teacher or to "see" the things they are shown in school. Lacking the means to succeed in school, the disadvantaged child may become a nameless face if he is apathetic, or be continuously branded a "troublemaker" if he is aggressive. In either case the disadvantaged child often is not seen as being unique and is frequently distinguished by a reputation which may become a self-fulfilling prophecy.

It is wrong to think that all children of working-class families are socially disadvantaged. The number of socially disadvantaged children is about 15 per cent of the child population. They tend to have the following characteristics that obliterate individuality:

1. They are at the bottom of the American society in terms of income.
2. They have a rural background.
3. They suffer from social and economic discrimination.
4. They are widely distributed in the United States. While they are most visible in the big cities, they are present in all except the very high income communities. There are many of them in rural areas.
5. Many are Negroes from the rural South who have migrated recently to the Northern industrial cities.
6. Some are whites from the rural South and the Southern mountains who have migrated recently to the Northern industrial cities.
7. Some are Puerto Ricans who have migrated to a few industrial cities.
8. Some are Mexicans with a rural background who have migrated into the West and Middle West.

There seem to be four outstanding principles which you should be continually aware of when working with disadvantaged children. The socially disadvantaged child is usually deficient in communication skills; this inability causes failure in other subjects. You should be willing to experiment with a broad range of teaching materials such as filmstrips, records, and television, and with administrative approaches such as team teaching and flexible programming. You should make strenuous efforts to search out and use community help such as various public health and welfare services or private philanthropic organizations and business and industry. Finally, you should create a desire to teach such children with concern, devotion, and enthusiasm—and, of course, involvement.

Urban and rural slum schools are seen as failures by many study groups, among them the 1964 President's Panel on Educational Research and Development. Authorities such as Ausubel still consider those schools failures.[10] This conclusion seems to be based on five current school circumstances: severe scholastic retardation which progressively worsens as children grow older; a dropout rate which exceeds 50 per cent; the enrollment of fewer than five per cent of this group in some form of higher education; deterioration of I. Q. scores; and a distressing picture of adolescents leaving schools without an education needed for success as an individual or citizen.

Ways To Overcome School Failures

As an elementary teacher, you can give these children the essential foundation and preparation which will help them become productive members of an urbanized, industrial society. First, allow them to become active partners in the learning process. These children need to talk and to express themselves. They should be included in the making of every possible decision in their group life. They might decide how their schedule will be arranged for the day, how the bulletin board might be arranged, and how the desks might be situated. They could form committees to plan for a Valentine party, or discuss how a resource person will be received, and what questions he might be asked. They may make mistakes and require a great deal of time to come to decisions. This is the process of learning which is relatively new to many disadvantaged children.

Socially disadvantaged children can acquire much learning from experimentation and from each other. Most of their work can be in small groups—possibly those which are permanent for the entire school year. The noise level will probably be high, for the teacher's role is that of a consultant rather than of controller of all classroom processes. The children will become more involved; they may enjoy school more, learn more, and retain more. Such a role will probably give you closer relations to the children, fewer discipline problems, and more opportunity to relax and move about the room to talk with the children on an individual basis.

[10] David P. Ausubel, *Readings in School Learnings* (New York: Holt, Rinehart & Winston, 1969), p. 202.

You should remember that the socially disadvantaged child is deficient in many everyday experiences that are taken for granted by the majority of American children. He probably has had little, if any, experiences or contact with plant and animal life. He has had few excursions beyond his immediate environment. He has had few socially organized experiences. He has had little experience with human warmth and understanding. He has received little satisfaction in the pride and success of learning. Your greatest concern with such children is to help them to learn and experience success thereby contributing to a sense of adequacy and a learning capability.

Socially disadvantaged children, to achieve maximum personal development and learning, need a classroom atmosphere that is unthreatening, fair, purposeful, and relatively unhurried. Such an atmosphere can be developed only when you set an example and expect children to deal with each other in a similar fashion. You should ask each child for *his* personal opinions and judgments. He should put himself into the classroom experiences and thus increase his self-development. In order to help the child increase his self concept, his parents' aid should be solicited. Honest conferences with parents or guardians can contribute an understanding of the child's self concept, his progress, and his limitations.

Many children arrive in school with an adequate self concept. Your task in such cases is to maintain and extend it. With disadvantaged pupils, the task often is to help a child to *develop* such a concept. Success in school may help a child to have constructive and valid perceptions of self and world.

THE SOCIALLY DISADVANTAGED CHILD

The disadvantaged child is not without a culture. If raised in an urban environment, he has experienced a limited part of the total culture. If he moves from a rural area to an urbanized center, he brings with him the culture of his former dwelling place. This culture includes a salty basic sense of humor, a value system concerned primarily with today, and attitudes that focus on physical rather than mental or rational matters. It is a culture in every sense of the word, but it is different from the middle-class-oriented school environment. It is not harmonious with his school surroundings; and it is probably not adaptable to full participation in the life of the modern, complex city.

It seems that a curriculum for this youngster should focus on helping him to adapt to urbanized, hostile living conditions. This does not mean changing the young child's values and behavior patterns, but rather helping him to adjust to the new environment when it is important for him to do so to obtain a job or some other desirable objective. The following suggestions may be of some value.

Be Concerned with Feelings

Disadvantaged children need an opportunity to learn in the affective domain. Federally supported programs for the disadvantaged and deprived have pushed, unfortunately, for cognitive development. But helping the child develop a good self concept, a good feeling about himself, is as important as learning to pronounce the initial consonant blends correctly.

Give each child a few minutes during the school day for reflection. The child may just rest if that is what he most needs at the time. In this noisy, hurrying world this child needs some buffer between himself and his annoying environment. You might do well to reserve some time during the school day for the children to pursue their own interests.

On many occasions, the culturally disadvantaged child will have more business smelling flowers than learning to read. Find a place in the day's program for the child to thrill to the beauty of a bird in full flight or to enjoy the first warm breezes of spring. Help the child to make contact with and come to respect God's firmament.

Surround this child with pleasing sights and sounds. Pin inexpensive prints of art masterpieces to the bulletin board. Surely occasional soothing music filling the classroom should violate no school rule. A messy and littered classroom will assail the sensibilities of any child.

Give this child the feedback of success. The least thing he needs is to be "put down." Try to give the child a joy in learning. Give the classroom a liberating environment by demonstrating the value of cooperation and mutual concern. The tone and climate of the classroom environment can spell success or failure for the attainment of the effective domain by the culturally disadvantaged child.

Allow the Children To Make Decisions

Ask these children what they want to study. The answers will come thick and fast and will vary from air and water pollution and the conservation of natural resources to problems of isolated groups of people and their place in the world and the conflicts of people as they interact within groups.

Allow the children to make a decision on one major area and then determine the three or four major questions which must be answered in order to understand that area. Each child could select the question he wishes to explore. Committees could be organized and a chairman selected for each committee. The chairman could report on the progress made and any material which cannot be located. You should be available to any committee "by invitation only." Individual committee members might conduct research through the following types of work: daily investigation of news stories in local daily newspapers; the use of magazine articles and pictures; taped interviews with local resource persons; interviewing parents; and reporting on pertinent television programs.

Use the bulletin board for the display of pictures, questions, and committee communications. The bulletin board can be utilized as a resource center and as a mural and also for discussion.

Encourage each committee to present reports in a unique and meaningful way. At the conclusion of the reporting, challenge the class with the question, "Since we know what the problems and their preventions are, what are we going to do about it?" Involve the children. Give them room to grow, to investigate. Give them time to think and form their own opinions; the opportunity to draw their own conclusions and try out new ideas. You are then giving the culturally disadvantaged child the opportunity to learn and understand.

Acquaint the Children with the Law

Many children from disadvantaged homes have not been deeply affected by instruction in morals or in values. They have little if any respect for the law. If you wish to help these children grow in a real understanding of laws and the basic legal principles which govern morals and values within our society, a discussion on law might be developed, particularly in the upper grades of the elementary school. You might organize the procedures as follows.

Provide an opportunity at the local level for the involvement of attorneys, the teachers in your elementary school, and administration and curriculum specialists to plan a unit on the study of law. Planning at the local level is important because it allows for the consideration of specific local educational needs. Such local planning will foster the development of personalized, meaningful insights and understandings of particular local educational situations. Educational personnel, both teachers and administrators, should gain much knowledge and appreciation of those legal principles that are significant for the elementary school child. Also, attorneys working with educators will attain a more comprehensive perspective concerning the educative process. But, more importantly, the culturally disadvantaged child will gain a greater knowledge and appreciation of law as it applies to him.

Planning must include not only a consideration of teaching procedures but also the topics and materials to be used. The content of the study might include something of the history and evolution of law, how the law is concerned with the child and his monetary responsibilities and peer commitments, and particular laws within the community and certain comparative state and national laws. This content must be related to materials and experiences which are meaningful to the culturally disadvantaged child.

You will have to continually modify and evaluate the content. You should appraise the change of attitude towards law and law enforcement by the children. You should invite legal consultants from the local and regional community into the classroom to answer questions and perhaps give expert advice.

The culturally disadvantaged child needs not only to know the law but also how to use the law. The classroom can be one source of this valuable information.

Present a Strategy for Thinking

These children need to be led into higher levels of thinking by being asked to be more persistent with the use of a definite method of questioning. You should so frame your questions that they ask for more than simple recall of factual information. You will call for facts, of course. But much more important, your questions should make the child use facts to produce new facts and new ideas. Your questioning might be organized into the following hierarchy, which begins at the lowest level.

Recount and recall questions ask for a simple testing of facts. You can look for a wide variety of answers which serve as a base for building the hierarchy. Be sure that every child contributes something, but make certain that the answers are short and concise so that a lot of time won't be spent later on haggling over just what was meant. Now the discussion can be raised to the next level of questioning.

Collocation and grouping requires the child to give an answer which makes him construct several sets of facts into a collocation. You might ask the children, "Of the statements on the board, which ones might go together?" The letter "A" might be placed before one group of statements that go together; the letter "B" before another group of sentences that go together. Arguments may arise as to whether the groupings are correct. This will lead to the third type of questioning.

Seeking explanations gets the youngsters to think about why they were grouping certain sentences together. If there is general disagreement as to whether a particular grouping is valid, the child who suggested that grouping must defend it.

Classification concerns naming a particular group of sentences, once all the facts have been placed into some collocation. Several titles might be given and debated before the children decide to name a group. It takes a higher level of thinking to classify than it does to recount and recall. You will be surprised how a few of the children who had been hesitant to react suddenly begin to participate.

Exact statement of classification forces the children to examine the statements even more closely. You might ask, "If you were to put *all* of the items in this one group into one statement, what would you say?" Here, you are lifting the children's thinking into crystal clear responses. Once the children have reached a decision that the titles are good ones and fit all the statements to which they pertain, the classifications can be written on another area of the blackboard.

Total classification is a question which attempts to secure from the children a sentence which states everything that was discussed during the period. You will have to steer the children away from giving vague and all-too-general classifications. Keep after them until they give precise answers.

The focus question requires a great deal of preparation. The children might be given an assignment to construct a chart or perform an experiment that would prove the stand taken by their particular group when they had been asked the collocation question.

Pointing to the purpose requires each reporting child to answer a "why" question that is related to the purpose of the investigation. In the process of narrowing the discussion to a fine point, you may find that many of the responses become personal. Don't be concerned, for this leads inevitably into the next probe question.

The question that involves the child attempts to secure the child's own feelings in the discussion. What are his reactions? What would he do about the situation?

Seeking a conclusion or summary is the type of question which is intended to lead to a resolution of everything that has been discussed. You might ask, "What did we learn from these presentations?" The children might indicate they had begun to wonder and want to learn more. They might say they had secured some different ideas which they want to try out.

These 10 probing questions allow the child to interpret. The children must not only recall facts, but they must also interpret them. Now they are ready for a set of questions which deal with cause and effect.

The hypothetical question asks, "What might happen if." You may have to guide and control imaginations here and move to the next type of questions in the hierarchy.

The lifting question asks, "What good things might happen?" This requires the children to think optimistically and positively.

Substantiation is the final probe question in the hierarchy and attempts to secure a logical ending to the discussion.

These 13 probe answers can be adapted to any need and any topic. They can help children to learn how to organize their thinking so that they can examine their social environment more objectively and concisely.[11]

Many "deprived" children have great reserves of energy and ambition, contrary to widespread feelings among those who do not know the facts.[12] The teacher who can tie this energy and ambition to productive learning makes a great contribution to the development of an individual worthy of the democratic tradition. All children need this kind of help; the disadvantaged particularly require guidance of the kind noted above.

INDIVIDUALITY: A MAJOR GOAL

In this chapter we have noted various conditions which tend to threaten individuality. The individual child may be engulfed by a complex, impersonal, and continuously changing world. While all children need help, disadvantaged children particularly need compassionate, competent assistance and a meaningful curriculum. They need aid in building a sturdy self concept and those "tools," intellectual and otherwise, needed for success in a changing world.

The average individual today, as he views the relations between nations and the belligerent differences between peoples, may feel completely unimportant, ineffective, and unwanted. The child, through the medium of television, may quickly come to the conclusion that human life has little value and purpose. Whether he watches actual battle scenes in some faraway place or commercial programs intended to entertain, the object lesson often is one of violence and the expendability of the individual.

The decline of our cities depresses rather than energizes the individual. The seriousness of the situation can be seen if we realize that the nation is now 70 per cent urbanized. The American city seems to become less livable and less governable each year. Its ghettos, its rising crime rates, its polluted air, its shapelessness, and other problems threaten the individual.

The American public school, through a vibrant, challenging curriculum, can create the growth of a new generation who through their individuality and creativity can meet, understand, and solve many of the problems plaguing man and his urbanized society. This curriculum should educate

[11] Ronald D. Griffin, "Questions that Teach: How To Frame Them, How To Ask Them," *Grade Teacher*, LXXXVII, No. 5 (January, 1970), p. 59.

[12] Lou La Brant, "Broadening the Experiences of Deprived Readers," *Education*, LXXXIII, No. 8 (April, 1965), p. 502.

and prepare the gifted, the socially disadvantaged, and all the children of all the people.

The following chapters, concerned with particular content areas, will stress societal emphases reflected in content areas. The chapters also stress a curriculum which is related to the perceptions, experiences, needs, aspirations, maturity, and ability of the individual child. They also reflect an awareness that curriculum often must be taught under the severe limitations imposed by crowded classrooms, busy schedules, and a scarcity of materials.

The subject areas discussed briefly and in a survey manner should be studied as a means to an end—the development of individuals who can experience a life that is productive and meaningful. The dignity and worth of each child are ultimate goals of the curricular content in our democratic society. The content areas include the insights, information, and ideas which the society holds to be important for each individual. Well organized and purposefully taught, the subject matter of the subject areas may contribute to an enriched and effective self and citizen.

PROJECTS AND READINGS

1. The dean of American organismic biology, G. E. Coghill, developed not only the principle of purposive striving in each individual but also the ultimate assumption that humans have intrinsic powers of creativity and self-direction. See Floyd W. Matson, *The Broken Image—Man, Science, and Society* (New York: George Braziller, Inc., 1964), p. 176. Coghill argues forcefully that there is no scientific ground for a doctrine of "determinism or fatalism." He believes that the human person is primarily a system of self-initiated *action* rather than *reaction*. He is the creator no less than the creature of his organic destiny. [C. Judson Herrick, *George Ellet Coghill: Naturalist and Philosopher* (Chicago: University of Chicago Press, 1949), p. 137.] Socrates, in his final words to his friends, indicated that even in the last extremity, the mind of man has freedom of action despite the incapabilities of his body. Socrates notes:

> For, by the Dog! these bones and sinews, I think, would have been somewhere near Megara and Boeatra long ago carried there by an opinion of what is best, if I had not believed it better and more just to submit to any sentence which my city gives than to take to my heels and run. But to call such things causes is strange indeed. If one should say that unless I had such things, bones and sinews and all the rest I have, I should not have been able to do what I thought best, that would be true, but to say that these, and not my choice of the best, are the causes of my doing what I do . . . would be a very far-fetched and slovenly way of speaking.

[Plato, "Phaedo," in *Great Dialogues of Plato* (New York: Mentor Books, 1956), p. 53.] Both Coghill and Plato seem to indicate that each individual is self-motivated and self-created. Each person's energy, directed toward particular goals, will shape his environment, as well as give it substance and meaning. The individual often seems moved to activity purely for the sake of activity. He is a stimulus seeker rather than one who avoids stimulus. This tendency may be used to mould the organism into conformity. See J. W. Getzels, *New Conceptions of the Learner: Some Implications for the Classroom*, Twenty-fifth Yearbook, II, Claremont Reading Conference (Claremont, Calif.: Claremont Press, 1964), p. 11. What characteristics should a teacher himself have to direct children's use of active energy toward constructive purposes? In what particular behaviors and social areas should the child be taught to conform? In what particular behaviors and areas should he be encouraged to be a nonconformist?

2. Even in the greatest of mental and physical difficulties children, like adults, have strong opinions about current issues. They will make such comments as, "We don't have any business fighting in Southeast Asia. Maybe we don't want it to go Communist, but we didn't try to help any of the satellite countries break away from the U.S.S.R." *or,* "If I was sent to fight somewhere, I would take a gun full of sleeping darts. To me killing each other doesn't make sense," *or,* "Why are we always helping other nations when we have plenty of problems at home. Other countries aren't grateful to us anyway." How would you handle such opinions in your classroom? What methods would you use to get children talking and thinking like this without causing an upheaval in the community?

3. Many of the religious orders founded during the Renaissance, such as the Jesuits, became teaching orders involved with children and young people. These orders persuaded parents that clerical teaching orders were spiritual guardians responsible before God for the souls and indeed the bodies of children. It was recognized that the child was not ready for life and that he had to be subjected to a special treatment—a sort of quarantine—before he was allowed to join adults. See Phillippe Aries, *Centuries of Childhood,* translated by Robert Baldick (New York: Alfred A. Knopf, Inc., 1962), p. 412. The public school became a similar instrument of society responsible for preparing children for adult life. Has the modern school curriculum broken the inherited purpose of preparing the child for adult life and if so, how? What is a good balance between educating for the future and for the present?

4. Jerome Davis, surveying the occupational status of the trustees of 27 institutions of higher education with endowments of $10,000,000 or more several years ago, concluded that of 659 trustees, 254 were bankers, 141 were merchants, 111 were public utilities operators, 63 were railroad operators, 153 were professionals, 22 were judges, and seven fell into miscellaneous classifications. Two could be classified in more than one category according to Ferdinand Lundberg, *America's Sixty Families* (New York: The Vanguard Press, 1938), p. 378. A principal purpose of such trustees is to preserve the status quo on those campuses which they govern. To what extent do you think that the composition of governing boards may have changed in the years since 1938? If the composition of a local school board were distributed among occupational and professional groups like those indicated, to what extent do you believe that curriculum planning focused upon helping children to be more creative and innovative (individualistic) would be supported by the board of education? What are your reasons for thinking this way?

5. These sources concerning individuality may be of interest to you.

a. John Curtis Gowan, George D. Demos, and E. Paul Torrance (eds.), *Creativity: Its Educational Implications* (New York: John Wiley and Sons, Inc., 1967), 336 pp. This book gives specific directions and techniques for discovering, fostering, and restoring creative potential in children.

b. Herbert Kohl, *Thirty-Six Children* (New York: The New American Library of World Literature, 1967), 227 pp. The author spells out creative, viable, and realistic experiences for the inner city child.

c. Mario D. Fantini and Gerald Weinstein, *The Disadvantaged: Challenge to Education* (New York: Harper & Row, Inc., 1968), 453 pp. This book describes a curriculum which is diversified, experiential, organized vertically by sequence skills, participatory, and affective.

d. Ralph A. Smith (ed.), *Aesthetic Concepts and Education* (Urbana: University of Illinois Press, 1970), 460 pp. This collection of 17 essays explains how teaching can become an intentional process of liberating children to think and to form their experience for themselves.

e. Ronald T. Hyman, *Ways of Teaching* (Philadelphia: J. B. Lippincott Co., 1969), 480 pp. This book has an interesting section on the art of questioning which stimulates individual thinking among children in a classroom.

12

Language Arts

THE THREE SIDES OF CURRICULUM

A child lives in a "world of words." He cannot function effectively in our technical urbanized society unless he can spell words, write words, hear words, read words, and speak words. Scientific evidence indicates that there is a positive correlation between the child's ability to read words and his ability to express himself orally in words. Most children enter school with the developed ability to understand words and to use them orally; but the school must teach them to write, spell, and read words. That area of the curriculum which helps the child to manipulate words is called the language arts.

Any area of the curriculum, whether language arts, mathematics, or social studies, might be said to have three components which are related one to the other, as are the sides of a triangle. Each side or aspect of the curriculum area is as important as the other two. There must be *content* in the curriculum area. This is basic to any subject field. There also must be a *method*—the best way to present skill, knowledge, or subject matter to children. The third side of the triangle consists of the *materials* which will be used to develop the method by which children may acquire those particular experiences and learnings pertinent to their education.

CONTENT

There is a trend in education to have children of elementary school age learn more sooner, faster, and better. This in turn might enable them to complete high school earlier and become scientists and mathematicians or other kinds of specialists required by the space age. Thus, many recommend that the language arts program be made much tougher and be slanted much more toward academic knowledge and skills. Some elementary schools are returning to the teaching of grammar, to regular assignments of topics for writing, and to rigorous academic standards which every child must meet at each grade level. Pooley suggests that "the best foundation for spoken and written English in the elementary school through grade six is secured without formal instruction in grammar." [1] He indicates that all evidence from research shows that formal grammar has very slight influence on children's language usage and has "little or no effect" upon skills in composition. Young children who grow up in an environment in which they are exposed to correct language usage will speak properly without knowledge of rules of any sort. Children who have access to interesting books will want to read them. If they have something exciting to write about, they will write.

In selecting content for the language arts program, you would be wise: (a) to discuss with children the ideas they wish to express and the best form for expressing them, (b) to provide children with opportunities for genuinely purposeful writing, (c) to create a learning environment in which children have meaningful experiences, (d) to assist each child in evaluating his own progress and determining how and where he needs to improve, and (e) to challenge the child to broaden his vocabulary gained through listening and reading for use in writing.

Television and Community Resources

Television is an important source of content for the language arts. It influences children's ideas and their behavior. Schramm points out that 95 per cent of children of school age see commercial TV in their own homes or in other places and that 90 per cent have the experience regularly.[2] Hence it becomes easy to see why some writers claim that the one common experience which all children bring to school is TV. A vast majority of American children acquire habits of listening, speaking, and reading from this important medium of communication. You might have children, particularly in the middle grades, plan and carry out a self survey of their own TV viewing and listening habits. An evaluation might be made of the programs selected and the amount of viewing time per week. The children themselves might make recommendations as a result of such studies.

[1] Robert C. Pooley, *Teaching English Grammar* (New York: Appleton-Century-Crofts, Inc., 1957), pp. 125–28.

[2] Wilbur Schramm, "Television in the Life of the Child—Implications for the School," *New Teaching Aids for the American Classroom* (Stanford, Calif.: The Institute for Communication Research, 1960), pp. 50–70.

The local community can serve as a source of content for the language arts. Children can explore word origins of streets, rivers, suburbs, and buildings within the immediate area. They might explore the derivation of names listed in the telephone directory. These experiences would help middle grade children not only to understand the complex problems of communication throughout the world but also to develop a sense of feeling for words.

There is a wealth of language arts content in local community happenings. The building of a new fire hall, shopping plaza, or suburb; the visit to the community of a national personality; or the progress of the local high school basketball team can serve as vehicles about which children can listen, talk, write, and spell.

Children's Experiences as Resources

Each child's own experiences in his home, on the playground, and in school can serve as content for the language arts. A child can tape his impressions and experiences of a vacation trip, of a visitor to his home, or of a game he has played. He then can listen to the recording, write a synopsis of it, and read it to his classmates.

The child, and for that matter the teacher, may speak a particular dialect in the native community. The language arts program should prepare the child for living and communicating in a national community; and, therefore, he must learn to speak and compose in a manner acceptable to society at large. The task is not to get the child to reject his family and neighborhood speech patterns; rather, the task is to help him communicate in a manner acceptable to the larger society in situations where this is desirable, for example, when applying for a job.[3]

The language arts can be the focus of the entire curriculum.[4] Suppose a third grade class is discussing the social studies problem, "Where does our food come from?" Problems which the children might consider include:

1. How is bread made?
   a. What are different kinds of bread (white, whole wheat, etc.)?
   b. How is dough made?
   c. How is bread baked?
   d. Where are the bakeries in our town?
2. What grains are used to make bread?
   a. Where is wheat grown?
   b. What is a wheat farm like?

[3] For further discussion see the chapter on dialects by Raven I. McDavid, Jr., in W. Nelson Francis, *The Structure of American English* (New York: The Ronald Press Co., 1958).

[4] Jeannette Veatch, *Reading in the Elementary School* (New York: The Ronald Press Co., 1966), p. 317.

    c. How is the wheat threshed?
    d. What happens to the wheat at the mill?
    e. How does the flour get to the bakery?
3. Do all people eat wheat bread?
    a. Why do some people eat bread made out of rye?
    b. Why do some countries have very little bread?
    c. Why is bread a good food for us?

Your problem is to fit the language arts into this social studies organization. Books must be available on wheat, on milling, on baking, and on farming, all of which the children can read. You may need to transpose materials to the children's reading level. Children can watch and listen to films on bread. They can learn to spell such words as fields, harvest, combine, and baker. They can compose and write stories, poems, and plays centered around bread. Such a selection of language arts content is exciting and adventurous; it requires much time and energy.

Children learn in a myriad of ways. They are enthralled with that which is new to them. They will ask questions, and they will investigate. They will pursue eagerly whatever topic captures their interest. It may be a party, it may be an astronaut traveling in space, or it may be a visiting soldier recently returned to his hometown. There are many opportunities to secure material for the language arts. Questions may be asked. Reports may be prepared for oral or written presentation. Reading research may be organized. Letters, poems, and creative stories may be written.

Not all learning comes from books or direct teaching. Incidental experiences that are constantly occurring on the national or international scene can be valuable sources of content for the language arts program. Children can reconstruct their ideas of these dramatic events through the written or spoken media and thus gain control over words. This can teach them to clarify their thinking and give them possession of the skills of verbal communication.

Textbook Sources of Content

Then there are the textbook sources of content for reading. The authors of most textbooks have recognized the importance of words and have attempted to provide for suitable reading experiences whether the text is in science, social studies, or mathematics. Workbooks and teachers manuals usually provide ideas for word attack skills and vocabulary building. They suggest language arts experiences within the content area. Williams categorized the reading abilities stressed in 10 textbook series and found 33 critical language arts skills, 21 of which were developed on all grade levels from first through sixth.[5]

[5] A. Williams, "Provisions for Critical Reading in Basic Readers," *Elementary English*, XXXVI, No. 6 (May, 1959), p. 325.

As an elementary teacher you will become seriously concerned with those children who encounter a considerable amount of difficulty mastering the reading content of various texts and source books in the areas of science, mathematics, and social studies. Materials for these areas of the curriculum often are written in a compact manner, constructed with a large number of unfamiliar words, concepts, and controversial statements.

You can help children become efficient in the area of content reading by having them become adept at surveying material, adjusting their reading rate, summarizing selections, and understanding the use of library facilities. You should stress vocabulary reading and reading comprehension. By giving the child assignments in silent reading, developing appropriate culminating activities, and discussing the topic to be read, difficulties in the reading of science, mathematics, and social studies can be overcome.

Many textbook series suggest language arts competencies and provide directions and instructions for teachers. In many series the teachers manual will help the teacher formulate lessons and activities designed to stimulate these skills. However, you need to add to these by helping the children to interpret or analyze a reading selection from the social studies, science, or mathematics text. Here are some questions accumulated from actual textbook lessons conducted in various elementary grades.

1. Why do you think in this book Brazil is called "A Land of the Future"? What natural resources promise a bright future? Let's read to find out what they are. To be sure we won't forget what we want to find out, will Susan write the question on the board before we begin? Now, let's read to find the answer.
2. What natural resources do you find in the picture? What use can be made of them? What will we find out if we read the page? Let's read, and as you read write down on this sheet of paper the natural resources described.
3. From the description of this science experiment in the book what do you think will happen? Write down the result you might expect.
4. Have you ever felt such pains as the book describes? Tell about them.
5. How did this story make you feel? How did the author write it to make you feel that way? Let's look for some of the words or sentences which make you feel that way.
6. Let's try to read the parts exactly the way we think the characters said them.
7. You have read the problem. Now find the key words that will tell us how to solve it.

Variety is the spicy secret of suitable content in the language arts. Russell and Russell believe that "Children live in a world of sound. They are bombarded from morning to night not only with the sounds of the physical environment but also with the words of peers and adults who want them to do something or at least want to be heard." They add that with so many directing ideas at them that they may take refuge in non-listening—listening with half an ear.[6]

A wise teacher selects language arts content from many areas—from the children's personal experiences, from popular TV programs, from text-books, and from tradebooks. Variety is not only the spice of life; it also adds welcome seasoning to the language arts program.

METHOD

It is generally agreed that there is no best method of teaching the language arts. Each child in the class might keep a language arts chart to use as a guide for individual activity and for evaluative purposes. This would result in an almost individualized program in language arts. The chart shown on page 292 contains criteria suggested by Kelner.[7]

This individual method as a teaching device in the language arts has several assets. It allows for the various reading levels found in most elementary school classes. Reading readiness is incorporated into this method since an attempt is made to improve the total background of the child. Language arts activities can be adapted to each individual pupil's interests and abilities. He may create poems, compose a social studies scrapbook, or develop an experience chart. The individual child can also develop his own steps in learning to read. He may build his own sight word vocabulary, review phonics where needed, select easy materials to read, develop content and language charts, learn how to turn the pages in a book, and determine what procedures must be followed to organize a report. Each child can make individual progress in language arts skills—from increasing reading speed and pronouncing words correctly to learning to skim, use an index, and outline. His power should grow in such study situations as reading to learn or solve a problem, selecting and evaluating information, and organizing data to present to a group. This method helps the child to refine his language arts taste. It encourages recreational reading, the development of personal reading tastes, dramatization, and the sharing of reading experiences. Each child can become aware of his own language arts needs and of his progress and this will enable him to receive help at the point of need.

[6] David H. Russell and Elizabeth F. Russell, *Listening Aids Through the Grades* (New York: Teachers College Press, Columbia University, 1959), p. 4. Reprinted with the permission of the publisher.

[7] Bernard G. Kelner, *How To Teach in the Elementary School* (New York: McGraw-Hill Book Co., Inc., 1958), p. 151.

Speed

1. Form groups.
2. Have leader time one minute.
3. Have partner ask questions on selection you have read.
4. Count number of words only in the part that you understand.
5. Mark words on graph.
6. Check partner.
7. Take another test.

Correctness

1. Form groups.
2. Work by yourself.
3. Read chapter first.
4. Answer questions at end of chapter.
5. Try at least one of things suggested in chapter.
6. Use dictionary, table of contents, and index.
7. Keep notes on 3 by 5 inch card or in notebook.
8. Check graph.

Expression

1. Select a partner
2. Select your aim.
   a. Poise.
   b. Clarity.
   c. Phrasing.
   d. Looking at audience.
   e. Bringing out important words.
3. Read to partner.
4. Complete evaluation.
5. Repeat steps to provide partner's turn.
6. Check graph.

Research

1. Work by yourself.
2. Read your assignment carefully. (What does the question ask?)
   Who—people.
   Why—reasons.
   What—things.
   When—time.
   Where—place.
   How—actions.
3. List clue words.
4. Find pages in textbooks, encyclopedias, magazines, and pictures.
5. List important words.
6. Check graph.

Learning To Read

1. Work with leader on word list.
2. Try to learn at least two or three new words perfectly.
3. Use workbook, picture dictionary, or textbook.
4. Mark graph.

There are particular methods for particular areas of the language arts. Some methods are described to illustrate the variety which can be planned.

Reading

The sentence story method is based on the principle that the words which a child learns to read are based on those which he uses in everyday conversation. They are selected from his immediate environment and from his personal experiences. Children are encouraged to talk about their feelings and reactions, their experiences and background. Such experiences are written on a chalkboard, on a chart, or in individual booklets.

Then the children read the story. Children enjoy reading about themselves; to them the content then has meaning, pertinency, and interest.

The word–phrase method helps the child identify separate words. He learns to distinguish one word from another by its size, shape, and special features. The child might learn to identify a word by associating it with a picture or object for which it stands. A child can build up a sight vocabulary by associating a particular word with its meaning by relating it to a familiar spoken word or with a picture, object, or action.

The phonic approach teaches the child a pattern of letters and understandings derived from experiences with words found as parts of meaningful wholes. Children are taught phonograms, consonant and vowel blends, structural elements in words, and how to divide words into syllables.

The Initial Teaching Alphabet (popularly called i/t/a) is a more recent and unique innovation in reading instruction. It was created by Sir James Pitman. It is an augmented Roman alphabet utilizing 24 of the original letter symbols and 20 new symbols which generally look like combinations of the original letters. By adding the 20 new symbols, Pitman's i/t/a makes it possible for each new phoneme or sound in the spoken language to be represented by a single written symbol or grapheme.

An investigation on this method was made by Mazurkiewicz in the Lehigh-Bethlehem study.[8] The purpose of this study was to demonstrate how i/t/a might be inducted into a school system over a period of time and to evaluate the long-term differences in achievement that may occur when some children are taught to read with i/t/a while others are taught to read by standard symbols (traditional orthography—T. O.). Mazurkiewicz tentatively concludes that i/t/a children who made the transfer to T. O. by the ninth month of the first year were significantly better readers of T. O. than a comparable group of children who had been taught by similar procedures but who had been taught with T. O. from the start.[9]

Reading instruction has yet another dimension: that of linguistics or the scientific study of language. Linguists believe language has two characteristics—that it can and has existed without writing, that writing cannot exist without speech, and that speech is a system of sounds which differentiates the meaning of words. There are two basic units or elements in the expression system of the linguists. There is the *phoneme* (or group of related speech sounds) or the smallest unit which differentiates the meaning of words: for example, the phonemes "b" and "p" differentiate

[8] Albert J. Mazurkiewicz, "First Grade Reading Using Modified Co-basal Versus the Initial Teaching Alphabet," U.S. Office of Education Cooperative Research Project No. 2676 (Bethlehem, Pa.: Lehigh University, 1965).

[9] For a critical review of this study see: Thomas C. Barrett, "i/t/a: A Step Forward or Sideways?," *Educational Leadership*, XXII, No. 6 (March, 1965), p. 394.

between bit and pit. Phonemes "are distinguishers only" and without meaning themselves. Then there is the *morpheme,* or smallest unit of expression that has meaning: for example, boy is a morpheme, but boys embrace two morphemes, "boy" and "s." This aspect of linguistics is called grammar, which is the study of morphemes and their combinations.

As a teacher of reading you will need some understanding of linguistics and grammar, but you need not be a linguist. In the future you probably will be using more and more of the findings of dedicated scholars in linguistics. However, most school systems today use a combination of methods. No one method is used exclusively.

Spelling

Ragan gives the following as the most commonly used procedures in the teaching of spelling.

1. Beginning in the second grade, some time should be set aside during the school day for the systematic teaching of spelling.
2. Attention should be given to spelling in connection with reading, handwriting, the social sciences, and other school subjects.
3. Pupils should be encouraged to take pride in correct spelling in all written work, to proofread their writing for errors in spelling, and to assume responsibility for learning to spell.
4. Instruction in spelling should be individualized. Some pupils may already know how to spell most of the words in the list for a certain grade; others may not be able to spell all of them by the end of the year. Individuals and small groups within the class should be allowed to progress as slowly or as rapidly as their ability and effort will permit.[10]

You might give each child a folder, containing a spelling list and sufficient writing paper, with the instructions on the top of page 295.

Each child is taught to attack directly the spelling of a new word. The number of words learned varies with each individual child. The spelling words are selected carefully. The study periods are short and managed by the children themselves under careful teacher supervision. The children use a variety of techniques. Individual spelling graphs help each child to see his own progress.

The linguistic approach to spelling may bring order out of chaos for the child who has great difficulty in learning to spell. Written language can make sense through the linguistic approach. Patterns are followed which the child can recognize and make use of in learning to spell. Within these patterns the sounds in a word determine in large measure the way it is spelled. The regular rather than the exceptional is stressed. The

[10] William B. Ragan, *Teaching American Children* (New York: Holt, Rinehart & Winston, Inc., 1961), p. 135.

Pretest (Monday)	*Drill* (Wednesday)	*Test* (Friday)
1. Leader of group reads any 30 words from spelling list. 2. Check for perfect spelling. 3. Mark list for difficult words, underlining the part that needs the most study. 4. Mark your spelling graph.	1. Study either alone or with partner. a. Work only on difficult words. b. Use dictionary for meanings and pronunciation. c. Find little words in big ones. d. Trace if necessary. e. Use word in sentence. 2. Write carefully and neatly. 3. Compare. a. Accept only perfect spelling. b. Check and write again. c. Check your spelling graph.[11]	1. Leader of group reads any 30 words from spelling list. 2. Check for perfect spelling. 3. Mark your graph and see the teacher before moving to the next group of words.

linguist approach frees the child from rote learning. He can sense the rules by which the English language is governed and discover for himself how it is organized. There is a predictable pattern for the letter "a" used to spell the sound /a/ as in "hat," the "tch" spelling for the sound /ch/ in "match," "sion" for /shen/ in permission. The child quickly learns that these sound-to-spelling relationships can be depended upon ("hat," "mat," "sat").

Speaking and Listening

Speaking and listening have become increasingly important in our verbal society. Every child knows how to talk when he comes to school, but to communicate effectively he should do more than talk. He should speak with confidence and speak with clarity; to do so he should be given opportunities to speak frequently with purpose and meaning. Listening is the handmaiden to effective speaking, and listening skills should be developed in conjunction with those related to speaking.

Children need many opportunities to speak. You might assign particular topics or encourage the child to select his own. The child might describe his favorite television program or the most exciting thing that has

[11] Bernard G. Kelner, *op. cit.*, p. 166.

happened, but he should be given some general directions. He should learn to face and look at the audience. He should speak clearly, without being too dependent on notes and without excessive rapidity. The children might take turns acting as a news announcer for a mock radio or television program. The radio microphone could be a tin can with a string attached to it; a television camera might be a cardboard box on a broom handle. A weekly or even a daily program might be organized, including commercials, news reports, a continued story, or a quiz program. Many schools have audiovisual equipment which can add realism to classroom activities.

You might collect a small box of pictures clipped from magazines. These could be mounted on 4 × 6 inch filing cards. Each child might select a picture from those placed along the chalkboard ledge. He could be given a determined time to think about what he will say before he tells the class about the picture. Techniques of stimulating children to speak are endless.

Children should learn to speak in a normal, unaffected manner. Strickland made an analysis of the spontaneous speech samples of 575 children in grades one through six. She found that children do not speak in sentences in the usual definition of "whole thought with subject, verb, etc." but rather they speak in phonological units, a unit of speech ending with a distinctly falling intonation which signals a terminal point.[12] With this in mind let them speak in the same manner they use on the playground, but teach them to give more clarity and effectiveness to that manner.

Many sounds are never heard by today's children. They are so accustomed to some of them that they simply ignore them. You might have children sit quietly for a few minutes and listen attentively for sounds. Then they might list the sounds they have heard—coughing, the wind, shuffling, sighing, and others. You might have children make a diary of the sounds they hear over a period of one day. A tape recorder can be used to collect sounds which the children are asked to identify. Children might list reasons why it is important for a doctor, a mother, or a truck driver to listen carefully.

Regardless of the means used to stimulate activity, it is wise to remember several guidelines: (a) Consider the attention span of the children. (b) Use humor to arouse interest and response. (c) Use audiovisual devices for a change of pace. (d) Ask questions about the material which the children have heard.[13]

[12] Ruth Strickland, "The Language of Elementary School Children: Its Relationship to the Language of Reading Textbooks and the Quality of Reading of Selected Children," *Bulletin of the School of Education*, Indiana University, XXXVIII, No. 4, p. 17.

[13] Sidney W. Tiedt and Iris M. Tiedt, *Elementary Teacher's Complete Ideas Handbook* (Englewood Cliffs, N.J.: Prentice-Hall, Inc., 1965), p. 123.

Written Composition and Composition Skills

Ideas for composition stem from children's experiences and their reading. After reading a story, a discussion may follow. From this discussion the children, through questions, can organize their ideas. This procedure can help them to select important ideas, stick to the subject, and say just enough. This precedes written composition. When the child writes, he should concentrate on getting his ideas on paper before he becomes concerned with the mechanics of writing. Composing the idea is the essence of composition. After he has written his story, you should suggest that he proofread it. Children can understand that in consideration for others who will read the story, it should have punctuation, correct spelling, and good sentences. They can also understand that a good story needs organization—it has a beginning, a build-up, and a good ending. Hence there will be a willingness to work on sentence structure and correct form with the help of teacher, classmates, and textbooks. Motivation for good communication is based on having something to communicate as well as a meaningful audience situation.

The following criteria could be set up for writing compositions:

1. Do I have a good beginning that makes the reader want to read the story?
2. Do my sentences follow one another to make the story grow?
3. Do my sentences begin with capital letters?
4. Have I used periods and question marks correctly?
5. Have I used run-on sentences, or do my sentences stand alone?
6. Have I spelled all words correctly? [14]

The elementary school child has a genuine and real need to communicate with people. He likes to:

1. Keep records of individual and group experiences.
2. Write letters of appreciation and invitation.
3. Write brief reports relating to class interests and areas of study.
4. Write news bulletins.
5. Write stories or verses related to ideas and impressions which have come from reading and discussing good literature.
6. Write stories related to personal experiences and observations.
7. Write original endings to stories read by the teacher.
8. Write sketches.
9. Write stories about book characters.
10. Write brief book reviews.
11. Write highly imaginative stories.

You can create an atmosphere where ideas may develop concerning the needs and backgrounds of the children. What types of magazine pic-

[14] Nancy Cary, *Teaching Composition and Composition Skills, Teacher's Encyclopedia* (Englewood Cliffs, N.J.: Prentice-Hall, Inc., 1966), p. 561.

tures, films, filmstrips, stories, and television programs are most suitable? You can stimulate children to write more extensively and effectively as a result of your unique knowledge of the pupils and of what the language arts can do for them. You should have a knowledge of what experiences are most suitable for children.

Handwriting

The teaching of handwriting is a very essential part of the elementary school curriculum. The basic essential of putting ideas on paper requires that children be able to write. Handwriting readiness is as essential as reading readiness. The child may become aware of the need for writing in the kindergarten as he watches the teacher write in print script form. The introduction of print script writing has simplified the writing process for the young child and has laid the groundwork for establishing common symbols for all language teaching, including reading.

Manuscript writing is usually taught in the lower primary grades. Cursive writing is most often introduced late in the second or early in the third grade. The change should be made only when the children are psychologically ready and after they have achieved security in manuscript writing as well as reading.

As children have more and more opportunity to write independently in the daily execution of their work, there should be less and less need for a daily writing lesson. In the primary grades there may be this need, but in the upper grades it may be reduced to a weekly lesson. Actually in the fourth, fifth, and sixth grades a class writing lesson should be kept to a minimum, used only when a *need* has been revealed in the children's written work. In the upper grades there also should be much individualized practice activities. After you return the child's work with certain errors noted and the correct form presented, he should practice writing these correct forms. The child should then work on his individual errors during the penmanship lesson while you move about the class giving individual help.

A child who is definitely left-handed should be identified in the kindergarten or first grade. If the teacher observes that the child is ambidextrous, he should be encouraged to use his right hand when he begins to write. The child may be helped to use his right hand if he is taught to sit properly. If he continually changes his pencil to his left hand and favors it in all other activities, he should be permitted to use it.

The handwriting program in the elementary school should help each child acquire a pleasing, legible, and somewhat rapid penmanship which he can use with ease in written communication.

Illustrative New Developments in the Language Arts

Linguistics and its application to the language arts program has resulted in several innovations in content, organization, and instructional procedures.

The Roberts English Series, A Linguistics Program is one of the most prominent ones which has been adapted as the language program in many elementary schools throughout the country. It is designed to be used as the total language program in grades three through nine. It is basically a text series, one book for each grade. In addition, a workbook and a record album are available to supplement each book. Two main strands run through the series, a literature or reading strand and a grammar strand. The aim of the program is to improve children's writing through sound and spelling relationships and the nature of the syntax.

The reading strand is broken into poetry and prose. In the first three books of the series, about four-fifths of the reading passages are poetry Then the proportion of prose selections increases slightly. The author believes the child's sphere of understanding should be expanded through literature and indicates in the teacher's edition that the child is "to be constantly extending his horizons, not to forever roam within them. We want to acquaint him with other items, other places, other views, and let the English lesson play its full role in bringing him into touch with the heritage of western civilization."

Too, this series has capitalized on the growing realization in educational circles that linguistics has much to offer the language arts program. The grammar strand running through the series consists of a new set of rules to be learned by the child. It is a prescriptive grammar.

The treatment of writing is limited to two broad areas—spelling and mechanics. The approach to spelling is a phonemic one which is concerned with the different letter of graphemic representations for a given sound rather than a spelling pattern approach.[15]

The University of Nebraska Elementary School Program is concerned with language, literature, and composition. It is designed to teach children (a) to comprehend the more frequent oral and written conventions of literature—formal or generic conventions or simple rhetorical conventions, (b) to control these linguistic and literary conventions in their own writing, and (c) to comprehend consciously the more frequent grammatical conventions which they can handle in their speaking and writing.

The materials for this program consist of 70 specific units for the various grade levels. These units endeavor to arrange literary works in an

[15] Paul Roberts (ed.), *The Roberts Series—A Linguistics Program* (New York: Harcourt Brace Jovanovich, Inc., 1965).

articulated sequence designed to develop the concepts essential to the literature program in a spiral fashion. However, these units which develop the literature and composition program may not necessarily be used at a particular grade level although there is a definite progression from the first grade through the sixth grade units in the complexity of concepts presented. The fable units in the first two grades introduce the child to the common devices and patterns of the simplest fables. The literary purposes of these devices and patterns are exhibited by stories in the third grade unit. The fourth grade "fable" unit and the fifth grade unit on the fables of ancient India offer a more intensive, more analytical study of the classical fable form. The series culminates in the sixth grade study of Kenneth Grahame's "The Wind in the Willows"—which introduces the children to an epic fable in a humorous, satiric, allegorical representation of the steady and gross in modern society.[16]

RESEARCH

Reading

There are literally hundreds of research studies related to the language arts of the elementary school, most of them concerned with the area of reading. Since the publication of Flesch's *Why Johnny Can't Read* there is much concern with the most efficient approach or method in teaching a child to read.[17]

Recent research indicates a close relationship between a child's vocabulary and his scholastic achievement.[18] He must have developed an adequate vocabulary if he is to make the most of his eduational opportunities. If a child's vocabulary does not permit him to express himself effectively in writing and speaking, to read or listen with understanding, he quickly develops negative attitudes toward learning. There are many materials on the market useful in helping to give the student a thorough training in word mastery techniques. An important part of your preparation is to secure competence in this aspect of language. It may be necessary for you to study and practice carefully to the point where your language competence is satisfactory.[19]

[16] "The University of Nebraska Language Arts Program" (Lincoln: The University of Nebraska Press, 1967).

[17] Rudolph Flesch, *Why Johnny Can't Read* (New York: Harper & Row, Inc., 1955).

[18] Walter L. Slocum, *Aspiration and Expectations of the Rural Poor, A Guide to Research* (Washington: Government Printing Office, 1967), p. 8.

[19] An example of the kind of material which may be useful for this purpose is James I. Brown and Rachel Salisbury, *Building a Better Vocabulary* (New York: The Ronald Press Co., 1959).

The following approaches to reading reported below are based on different kinds of research, with variations in quantity and quality of research. Summaries include major strengths claimed by the advocates of the methods, and hence should be read with caution.

A rather brief description of some of these approaches is given. The approaches are either synthetic or ideational. The synthetic approach is based upon initial study of, and drill with, letters and syllables which are combined to make words. The ideational approach rests upon the assumption that a child should initially learn whole words in meaningful reading situations. Both approaches eventually stress the study of letters, syllables, and meaning of words and groups of words.

Synthetic Approaches. Proponents of this approach argue that since words are made up of letters, the initial unit of instruction should be the name or sound of individual letters or a combination of them. Many of the phonic approaches would fall under this category.

Mae Carden System. The Carden Method was developed between 1934 and 1939 by Mae Carden, director of a private school in New York City. Before a school adopts this method, Miss Carden herself insists on introducing the method to the elementary faculty through 15 hours of in-service education. First grade children learn to say and sound the alphabet, after which the teacher introduces words that are familiar to the children. The teacher, for instance, might start with the word "kite," sound the separate syllables "kuh-eye-tuh," stress the first letter, hold the sound of the first vowel rhythmically, and add the second consonant in a soft tone of voice. After the children pronounce the word, the teacher could ask questions which help to develop a mental image of kite.

Phonetic Keys to Reading. The first grade is divided into three periods. The first period of 12 weeks is again divided into three smaller periods, one an eight-week period devoted to readiness for the pre-primer. During this first period, children are initially introduced to the long vowel sounds. Next, the short vowel sounds are introduced. Thus, in approximately three weeks, the children will have learned the long and short vowel sounds. Next, the consonants are taught. By the end of the eighth week, the vowels, the consonants, and some blends have been presented. It is assumed that the children are ready for the first pre-primer.

The Spalding System. In 1957, Romalda Bishop Spalding published a book called *The Writing Road to Reading.*[20] In it, she presents the Unified Phonics Method for teaching children correct and accurate speech, writing, spelling, and reading. She claims to have found it equally applicable to home and school use. Spalding feels that any child physically

[20] Romalda Bishop Spalding and Walter T. Spalding, *The Writing Road to Reading* (New York: William Morrow and Co., n.d.).

and mentally qualified to enter school at age six is fully able, willing, and eager to learn to write and read if he is taught by this logical approach to language. This method differs basically from other phonic methods in that it does not start with reading. Instead, the child is taught to write sounds; the child first learns the 70 common phonograms in English.

The Bloomfield System. This has been referred to as a linguistic approach. Essentially, this system of teaching reading separates the problem of word-form study from word-meaning study. First, the child is taught the upper and lower case names of the letters of the alphabet. After assurance is given that the child knows the names of these letters, he is presented with a word with an initial consonant, a vowel, and a final consonant. The material shows each letter in only one phonetic value. The basic procedure of this method is the concentration upon patterns of letters and sounds regardless of meanings.

Words in Color. This unique approach to teaching the sounds of the letters of the alphabet was introduced by C. Gattegno in 1962. Each of the 47 sounds of English is a distinct color. The short vowel sounds are introduced in the following order: "a," "u," "i," "e," and "o." The children learn to reproduce each sound, associate the sound with the color symbol, and write each symbol. The consonants, "p," "t," and "s," are introduced next as sounds made in combination with the previous vowels. The children are taught the skill of writing vowels and vowel–consonant combinations. Furthermore, they learn to decode them by reading aloud. Following this step, they begin to write syllables and words in the classroom. After the child acquires sounding and writing skills, the stress is shifted from saying words to understanding what is read. The study of phonetics and grammar of the English language leads to creative written and spoken English.

Ideational Approaches. Advocates contend that the initial unit of instruction should be the smallest meaningful unit in the English language, namely, the word or groups of words. There is evidence to support a conclusion that a majority of teachers use the sentence as the initial unit of instruction. They maintain that the child has a right to demand meaning, as early as possible from the graphic symbols we call words. Some reading systems which might fall under the ideational approach are the following:

Functional Phonetics. Ana D. Cordts introduced functional phonetics in 1953 as a phonetic aid to supplement any basic reading program. The phonetic program differs from others in that children are taught to recognize letter combinations in sight words already learned. The combinations of letters or cues in the known words are framed by pointers or marks. For example, the word "sand" is marked and "sa" is the first cue introduced and learned. Altogether, there are 85 cues presented. Cues are always presented in known words and then recognized in new words.

Phonovisual System. This system of teaching letters or letter combinations was published in 1944 as a parallel method of teaching reading, spelling, or remedial classes in reading, and as a method of developing appropriate speech patterns. The authors consider it as a supplement, not a substitute, for an eclectic method of teaching reading. The Phonovisual Consonant Chart contains 26 consonant sounds. The Phonovisual Vowel Chart, with 17 vowel sounds, is used when the child enters first grade and is beginning sight reading through the use of experience charts. The consonant sounds are used as a listening experience. The material is used as a game rather than a drill. After a mastery of the consonant sounds in beginning and ending positions, the vowel chart is introduced.

The Individualized Reading Program. Within the last decade, there emerged what is popularly called individualized reading. This is not necessarily a new concept in reading instruction. It is almost a fusion of the Dalton and Winnetka methods of organizing instruction. In the individualized approach, each child "tries on a book for size"; if he likes it and finds it palatable, he will read it independently. Thus, according to the proponents of this approach, each child can proceed at his own pace and at his own level. The teacher, as time permits, has a conference with each child so that he may assess his progress, note and help the child overcome obstacles, and give the child guidance as he strives to acquire proficiency in skills, elevate tastes, and develop appropriate habits of reading. In order to structure an adequate skills program, it is necessary for the teacher to read every book beforehand. The teacher then can be prepared to assess the student's ability to cope with the specific word recognition and comprehension skill tasks involved in the selection he has chosen.

The Basal Approach. The basal approach is a systematic attempt, using appropriately graded materials, to teach a child to read through daily instruction. It represents an attempt to teach the child all the reading skills, to develop proper habits of reading, and to elevate his reading tastes in a manner that parallels his maturational growth. It develops the essential abilities which enable the child to use books for the purpose of acquiring enjoyment, information, and guidance. A basal program is not confined directly to basal readers although they are the main ingredients in the total reading program. A good basal program encompasses trade books, teacher prepared materials, commercially prepared materials, magazines, and other materials.

The Integrated Experience Approach. This approach to reading instruction is in reality a combination of the individualized and the language experience approach. It is built upon the unique aural–oral language repertoire each child acquires during the preschool years. The springboard for this approach is the natural language patterns the child brings to school. A learning atmosphere, therefore, is created and manipulated by the teacher so that the child acquires a maturity in language skills that is commensurate with his maturational growth. Some of the unique features of this system are:

1. It involves the use of the aural–oral language facility of children with natural repetition and extension through supplementary activities.
2. The sequential introduction of skills includes the utilization of stories of pupil experiences, suggested unit techniques, and coordinated materials to maximize perceptual processes, non-verbal communica-cation, listening, speaking, reading, and writing.
3. Frequent use is made of pupil–teacher conferences.
4. Maximum use is made of trade books, supplementary materials, and teacher and pupil–teacher prepared materials.

To determine which method or approach to reading is best suited to the average child, researchers conduct many studies annually. As an example, 27 studies pertinent to first grade were sponsored by the U.S. Office of Education during one academic year (1964–1965).[21] These projects represented a cooperative effort since there was a common base for testing, evaluation, and time allotment. The results of these studies indicate:

1. No approach is uniquely effective for children who scored well on any of the pre-measures of reading competence.
2. In general, basal programs accompanied by supplementary phonics materials produce significantly greater achievement in reading than do basal materials alone.
3. Girls tend to have a greater degree of readiness for reading at the beginning of first grade and tend to read at a higher level.
4. Reading achievement, evidently, is influenced by factors peculiar to a particular school system, over and above differences in pre-reading capabilities of children. An effective reading program depends on the teacher and the school situation in which it operates.
5. Children with low readiness are more successful in a basal program where children with high readiness are more successful in a language experience program.
6. Children learn to read by reading meaningful materials, especially when they can read what they like from a great array of books.
7. Every teacher is a teacher of reading, and one who has plenty of books to use can develop a love of reading among children.

[21] Guy L. Bond and Robert Dykstra, "The Cooperative Research Program in First Grade Reading Instruction," *Reading Research Quarterly,* II, No. 5 (Summer, 1967), p. 142.

Recent research indicates the need for teaching more thoroughly—and in more detail—a much greater variety of subtle skills needed for reading in the upper elementary grades, particularly in the subject areas. The teaching of reading does not end at the second or third grade.

Almost all researchers in the field of reading since 1900 conclude that the best procedure consists of teaching *a variety of reading methods* rather than a single phonetic attack. Such research reveals that phonics should be introduced very soon after the child has started to read. Skill in handling unfamiliar words requires more than ability to name and sound the letters and the simpler phonograms. The child should know how to analyze words visually so that he may take advantage of their total makeup, detect significant features, locate familiar parts in them, translate these parts into sounds, and blend any combination of these different components.

The ability to use suffixes, prefixes, and other structural features of words is also needed. Children should be taught a variety of skills needed to work out the recognition, pronunciation, and meaning of words. This is done when a child encounters words during normal reading activities. Then the word is studied as a whole, and the parts are seen as components of the word. When a child encounters an unfamiliar word, he knows how to analyze it and find those characteristics which will enable him to recognize it. Teaching the child to dissect the whole word into helpful components and characteristics enables him to attack that word he cannot recognize on sight.

Spelling

Research has shown that it is more efficient to study words in lists rather than in context. Words that are studied in lists are learned more quickly, remembered longer, and transferred more readily to new contexts.

However, in some lessons spelling words might be presented in context when children are writing invitations, thank-you notes, letters to classmates ill at home, and in other functional situations.

Once children know the meaning of a word they have learned to spell, they are more likely to use it in their writing. When spelling words for a given grade are selected from among those most frequently written by children in that grade, the children generally will know the meanings of those words. They are likely to know the meanings of the words which they use in their own writing. When giving a test on the words in any lesson, each word should first be pronounced, used in a sentence, and finally pronounced again. However, the children should write only the word, not the sentence. The use of the word in a sentence helps children to identify the word to be spelled.

There is a great deal of research that is concerned with the best method for learning to spell a word. Findings indicate particular steps to follow. The child should pronounce each word, say the letters in sequence, and attempt to recall how the word looks. He should check the accuracy of his recall by looking at the correct spelling of the word, writing the word, and comparing the word as written with the correct spelling of the word. These steps should be repeated until the word is spelled correctly.

Visual, auditory, and kinesthetic imagery as well as an emphasis on recall are involved in these steps. Better spellers need not follow all of these steps habitually but poor spellers need special help and encouragement in using all of them. Those which provide for attempts to recall the correct spelling of a word should be strongly emphasized, since they make learning to spell a more active process. Ability to recall the correct spelling is what is most needed in writing.

Penmanship

It is only during the last 50 years that physiologists and psychologists began to analyze and record the movement made in writing. They have attempted to describe handwriting movement rather than to advocate one method over another. Such studies have shown that handwriting movements are not so simple as had been supposed. When the child writes a letter or a word, the pressure of the penpoint and of the fingers on the penholder is continually changing. These changes are very delicate and complicated; they correspond closely with the forms that are produced. The child should learn to make this complicated series of pressure changes in order to produce the correct forms. The pressure changes come to him through the kinesthetic sensation. To connect with the form, the use of these changes should be built up through a long series of trial and error. Thus, much systematic practice is necessary.

The same conditions prevail with changes in the speed of the writing movement that take place in the writing of a letter or word. The pen continually speeds up, slows down, or pauses as it makes the gentler or sharper turns. As in the case of pressure, the speed changes correspond closely with the forms of the letters. It takes much practice to learn to make those delicate changes necessary to form the letters accurately. The child's writing movement should become automatic through "kinesthetic control," which is control by the sensations of movement in the hand and arm rather than the careful inspection of the forms of the letters by the eye.

Skill in penmanship must be related to the purpose or content of its use. An adequate program of learning to write should be closely correlated to the entire curriculum. This means giving attention to the quality of writing that the child does during the school day.

Subjects closely related to penmanship are written composition, reading, and spelling. In the primary grades the child should write the words that he reads and spells. His reading vocabulary provides a wide choice of words for his writing exercise. Reading and writing should reinforce each other. The purpose of spelling is to help the child write words correctly, and writing is the principal method of learning to spell. Words used in the spelling tests should be utilized in penmanship exercises to provide cumulative practice. Clear penmanship is necessary for good spelling since many spelling mistakes are actually errors in penmanship.

Manuscript writing should be used in the primary grades. It is easier to learn cursive script and it facilitates mastery of reading and spelling since the letters are more like printed letters and easier to recognize. The letters are easier to write because the movement of writing a word is divided into a succession of separate movements. The young child is not burdened with one long complex movement in which joining letters is added to making strokes. The child will do a good deal more writing in the first two grades when he uses the manuscript style. He will use writing sooner as a mode of expressing thought.

Writing with separate strokes is easier to learn, but writing the words with continuous strokes is more efficient once it has been learned. In manuscript writing, longer pauses are made in writing the letters separately. This slows the writing down. Words are read as units and a slight departure of the form of individual letters from the ideal form does not impair legibility to any serious degree.

Careful experiments show that the child can learn cursive writing more easily in the third grade after having two years of manuscript than he can learn it in the first grade. The quality of his writing in later grades will be equal or superior to that of pupils who started with cursive in the first grade.

Listening

Research has established that more than half of a child's classroom time is spent in listening. Since the advent of television, the proportion of time a child spends in listening has been increasing steadily. Listening time is not always spent efficiently. Research shows that the average person retains only 50 per cent of what he hears regardless of how hard he concentrates. Two months later he can be expected to retain only half of that amount. However, few schools provide for listening instructions or have a listening program.

A number of studies indicate that listening skills can be taught and that listening ability does improve substantially when specific instruction is provided. Some studies show that instruction in listening produces improvement in reading and language usage. Specific ear training, during which pupils record their oral expressions and then analyze and criticize these recordings, can produce a significant improvement in language usage.

One study involving fifth grade students provided specific training in listening for main ideas, details, and inferences.[22] Significant gains were made in this ability and the skills of securing word meaning and following directions also showed improvement.

In another study of fifth graders, listening instruction included exercises in following directions.[23] In a three-month period, the experimental group showed a promised gain in listening as well as a gain of eight months on a standardized reading test. The control group—without special training —showed no unusual gain.

Another study compared three groups of fifth graders.[24] One experimental group received direct instruction and practice exercises in listening for main ideas, important details, opinions, relevant and irrelevant details, and transitional phrases. The second experimental group received indirect instruction by listening to selections and discussing their content. The control group received only the usual language arts program. Both experimental groups made significant gains in a standardized listening test. The direct instruction group showed the most significant gains. The control group showed no significant gains.

Instruction in listening not only improves listening skills but related communication skills as well. You should provide a great variety of listening situations, including many independent activities. There should be greater interest and attention when the teacher does speak if the children have been involved in many oral activities.

Recent surveys concerning the teaching of language arts indicate that teachers are teaching reading, speaking, writing, and listening as though each area were completely isolated from the other. However, recent research indicates that the amount of reading done has a more positive influence on writing ability than the amount of writing done. It may be that teachers can become more effective in teaching written composition if they assign writing tasks that are literature-centered or that involve reading assignments.[25]

To an increasing extent, research and experimentation will provide factual data on content and methods which promote language learnings. Those who produce and those who consume instructional materials will

[22] Sue S. Trisiettes, "The Effect of Training in Listening for Specific Purposes," *Journal of Educational Research,* LIV, No. 2 (March, 1961), pp. 276–77.

[23] Melvin Lubershane, "Can Training in Listening Improve Reading Ability?," *Chicago Schools Journal,* XLIII, No. 2 (March, 1962), pp. 277–81.

[24] Robert C. Canfield, "How Useful Are Lessons on Listening?," *Elementary School Journal,* LXII, No. 12 (December, 1961), pp. 146–51.

[25] Ted De Vries, "Reading, Writing Frequency, and Expository Writing," *Reading Improvement,* VII, No. 1 (Spring, 1970), p. 19.

do well to seek objective bases for their decisions. The language arts have been plagued by subjective proposals for guaranteed success. The language arts are too complex, children and teachers are too individualistic, and other considerations are too varied to permit easy answers. Content, materials, and methods will be influenced by many factors. Research and experimentation will enable you to add precision to your efforts to plan for a curriculum of language arts that is best for you and for each child.

PROJECTS AND READINGS

1. Jeanne Shall has made a study of research in the area of elementary school reading which she has described in *Learning to Read: The Great Debate* (New York: McGraw-Hill Book Co., 1968). Her study indicates that the child who begins with systematic phonics achieves early superiority in word recognition although this may not show up until after the first grade. However, more importantly, she finds no evidence that any one particular method produces better results than another in teaching the child to read. You could profit from an examination of a teacher's manual which accompanies a basal reading series. What particular suggestions are given for integrating the phonetic approach with the so called "look–say" method of teaching reading?

2. Grace Fernald has said of the child's learning to read:

> The first step in learning to spell is the development of a distinct perception of the word. . . . In reading he must associate these meanings with the symbols that represent the words. In the first, or perception stage of spelling, he starts with the symbols of the words. It is not enough to merely recognize the word as he does in reading, he must get the word in sufficient detail to make it possible for him to reproduce it correctly. In reading it is only necessary for him to get the meaning of the word when he sees it; in spelling he must get not only the meaning but every detail of the word form.

[From *Remedial Techniques in Basic School Subjects* by Grace Fernald (New York: McGraw-Hill Book Company, copyright 1943), p. 181. Used with permission of McGraw-Hill Book Company.] In what way is word analysis more closely related to spelling than to reading?

3. This excerpt selected from a first grade reader represents the "look–say" method of reading.

Something Pretty

Mother said, "Look, look. See this."
"Oh, oh," said Sally, "It is pretty."
"Yes, yes," said Jane. "Mother looks pretty."

[From *The New Fun With Dick and Jane*, Chicago: Scott, Foresman & Co., 1956.] The following, also selected from a first grade reader, stresses phonics.

The Rook

A rook
Sat hooked
To a crooked
Tree.

He shook
As he looked,
—Took an owl
For me!

[From Adele H. Seronde, *Basic Reading* (Philadelphia: J. B. Lippincott Company, 1965.] Which type of reader would you prefer to use with young children? Give your reasons.

4. Reading was first introduced into the school for religious purposes. A child was taught to read so he might use the Bible and be "stirred up dreadfully to seek God." An older generation was taught to read from the McGuffy readers which emphasized patriotism and morality. What are the basic objectives for teaching reading in the modern school?

5. Listening and reading are both receptive communication arts, as opposed to speaking and writing, which are expressive acts. Listening and reading differ primarily in the manner in which an individual receives and recognizes words. They are alike because the individual brings to both the same experience and background and employs many of the same thinking skills in each. How do these similarities and differences affect the child's use of listening and reading?

6. The terms phonics and phonetics have unique meaning. Instruction in reading dealing with letter sounds requires a unique treatment that differs sharply from that practiced in speech therapy or recorded by linguistic scientists. Speech specialists work to prevent and correct speech patterns which isolate letter sounds that do not help a child recognize words or comprehend sentences. For example, children are taught to say "buh" and "tuh" and "guh" for the letters "b," "t," and "g." The English language is made up of many other languages, and thus is difficult to organize it into a regular system of rules that can be applied when one wants to spell or read or write. However, much of our language is phonetic. Many letters in English do have a relationship between sound and name which a child can readily use in learning to read. The science of linguistics is not the same as phonics. Can you indicate how the science of linguistics has helped to make the skill of reading more efficient? How is it related to a study of curriculum?

7. In teaching penmanship the expression of meaning is an essential aspect of writing from the beginning. Periods of practice should be used to improve the form of letters and words and in the development of good posture, position, and movement. A penmanship lesson should never be merely the recording of meaningless forms on the paper. You should be careful that the meaning the child is supposed to have in mind when he writes is one that is natural for him to express. What methods can you use to be sure that writing has meaning for the child?

8. Here are some particular sources you might wish to examine to secure further understanding of the language arts program.

a. Pose Lamb (Planning Editor), *Guiding Children's Language Learning* (Dubuque, Iowa: William C. Brown Co., 1967), 362 pp. This is a collection of independent yet related chapters dealing with instruction in the language arts—speaking, listening, reading, handwriting and "creative" writing, and spelling—written by people who are specialists in each of these areas.

b. Iris M. Tiedt and Sidney W. Tiedt, *Contemporary English in the Elementary School* (Englewood Cliffs, N.J.: Prentice-Hall, Inc., 1967), 359 pp. Chapter II has a usable account of "Linguistics and the Study of Language." Chapter XXXIII gives a good description of "English for the Disadvantaged Child." There is an accompanying volume to this textbook entitled *Readings on Contemporary English in the Elementary School* by Iris M. Tiedt and Sidney W. Tiedt (eds.) (Englewood Cliffs, N.J.: Prentice-Hall, Inc., 1967), 264 pp.

c. Ida E. Morrison, *Teaching Reading in the Elementary School* (New York: The Ronald Press Co., 1968), 616 pp. Considerable attention is given in this text to the reading problems of the culturally deprived child with many practical suggestions as well as lists of books for all slow and retarded readers.

d. Delwyn G. Schubert and Theodore L. Torgerson (eds.), *Readings in Reading* (New York: Thomas Y Crowell Co., 1968). This text gives an insight into the historical development, trends, theory, research, and current practices in reading instruction. The articles selected on reading focus attention, not only on the present, but also on the writings and research of the pioneers in the field of reading.

e. Dwight Bolinger, *Aspects of Language* (New York: Harcourt Brace Jovanovich, Inc., 1968), 326 pp. This book gives the non-linguist an appreciation of what modern linguistics is and what makes up the domain of modern linguistics.

f. S. Alan Cohen, *Teach Them All To Read: Theory, Methods, and Materials for Teaching the Disadvantaged* (New York: Random House, Inc., 1969), 329 pp. The author outlines procedures for successfully teaching disadvantaged children and presents a selection of methods and materials that he has found to work well in teaching them to read.

g. Gertrude B. Corcoran, *Language Arts in the Elementary School—A Modern Linguistic Approach* (New York: The Ronald Press Co., 1970), 280 pp. This text provides a solid foundation for the linguistic emphasis on language learning and draws upon major linguistic study and research for its contributions toward helping the child discover the system of his language as well as use it effectively.

13

Social Sciences

STUDY OF RELATIONSHIPS

The term "social sciences" is now generally applied to that phase of the elementary school curriculum which deals with the relations of people to one another and to their environment. This area of the curriculum is a very complex one. If one considers only the interactions involved in the classroom itself, the complexities equal that of the atom. The social sciences are also involved with the dissemination of information, the development of social skills, and the improvement of social behavior. Materials are drawn from history, geography, economics, anthropology, political science, sociology, and psychology. Experiences from the local community cannot be properly classified within any particular social science. Not since the early days of this century have the social sciences received such a concerted and integrated investigation.

Massialas and Cox believe that the social studies in the elementary school should be the vehicle by which children critically examine values and beliefs held by individuals and groups. They maintain that a study of social sciences should accomplish the following goals: [1]

1. It should furnish the forum for the analysis and evaluation of normative propositions or value judgments about man and society.
2. It should operate within the requisites of inquiry which relate the development of hypotheses and ideas about social relationships to supporting evidence.
3. The end result of inquiry should be the production of a body of tested principles and generalizations about human relations and societies.

[1] Byron G. Massialas and C. Benjamin Cox, *Inquiry in Social Studies* (New York: McGraw-Hill Book Co., Inc., 1966), p. 24.

4. The social studies classroom should afford the student an avenue for the creative venture.

The principal purpose of the social studies program is to help children to develop dependable generalizations as the steps to be taken and roads to be travelled are outlined and analytical and intuitive processes and skills are used.

CONTENT

There seems to be a growing concern that all is not well with the social studies in the elementary school. Many believe that this area of the curriculum as presently organized and taught may not adequately prepare today's child for a complex technical society of increasing urbanization and automation. There are some who would revise and modernize the present social studies structure and advocate the same face lifting which science and mathematics were given a decade ago. Others would discard the present structure and either return to the separate teaching of geography, history, sociology, and anthropology or create a completely new type of social studies.

The "Expanding Community" Sequence

The "expanding community" sequence has been the principal foundation of the elementary social studies during the past 30 years. The child begins a study of the school and home in the first grade; moves outward to the community in the second grade; and studies the local county, the state, the nation, and the hemisphere in succeeding grades. Paul R. Hanna has organized this type of program into the model on page 314.[2]

In such a program the child will study the following scope of human behaviors as he progresses to each different community level.[3]

1. Protecting and conserving life, health, resources, and property.
2. Producing, distributing, and consuming food, clothing, shelter, and other consumer goods and services.
3. Creating and producing tools and techniques.
4. Transporting people and goods.
5. Communicating ideas and feelings.
6. Providing education.

[2] Adapted from Paul R. Hanna, Rose E. Sabaroff, Gordon F. Davies, and Charles R. Farror, *Geography in the Teaching of the Social Studies* (Boston: Houghton Mifflin Co., 1966), p. 79.

[3] Paul R. Hanna, "Generalizations and Universal Values: Their Implications for the Social Studies Program," *Social Studies in the Elementary School,* Fifty-sixth Yearbook, Part II, National Society for the Study of Education (Chicago: University of Chicago Press, 1957), p. 46.

7. Providing recreation.
8. Organizing and governing.
9. Expressing aesthetic and spiritual impulses.

Recently Hanna has organized a series of research projects that explore generalizations derived from the social sciences which can contribute to the expanding structure of the communities. "The literature of the social sciences [will be] searched for significant generalizations that could be used as a check for comprehensiveness and continuity in providing teaching–learning experiences for children." [4]

The expanding community concept for the social studies greatly influences modern programs despite critics' accusations that the communities and topics which are developed within that concept too often lead to superficial, overly broad studies.

[4] Paul R. Hanna and John R. Lee, "Content in the Social Studies," *Social Studies in Elementary Schools,* Thirty-second Yearbook (Washington: National Council for the Social Studies, 1962), p. 65.

Social Studies from Social Sciences

There is a current trend toward building the social studies curriculum on the social sciences. Some new social studies programs are based on the structure of the social sciences themselves—the concepts, generalizations, themes, and methods of inquiry that are fundamental to each discipline. This growing emphasis on the social sciences as a foundation of content for the social studies is a result of new knowledge being produced at an unprecedented rate. The social sciences, those disciplines dealing primarily with the study of human relationships, have become prominent and important in today's society. The three behavioral sciences—sociology, cultural anthropology, and social psychology—focus directly on the study of man's behavior in groups. Political science and economics are "policy sciences" because of their contributions to decision-making in the basic realms of human endeavor. Most scholars also place history and geography in the category of a social science. The importance of all these social sciences will increase in the difficult years ahead, and the demands of modern life will require the social studies to derive content primarily from them.

The Greater Cleveland Program

The Greater Cleveland Social Science Program is based on the assumption that social science can be taught in a purposeful way from the primary grades upward. The objective of this program is to present social studies in a logical, cumulative sequence, from kindergarten through grade six. The factual content and classroom materials are planned and built around basic concepts taken from the social sciences. They are more deeply reinforced each year as the child moves through the program.

This program permits a more direct relationship between elementary social studies instruction and the parent social sciences. It relies upon major understandings from the social sciences to upgrade content coverage in the elementary school; it should promote a deeper comprehension of key ideas from the social sciences.

An Economic Base. Senesh has developed a concept-oriented elementary school curriculum constructed around the discipline of economics and has established eight fundamental ideas which might be used for building a social studies curriculum based upon this discipline.[5]

1. The conflict between unlimited wants and limited resources confronts every individual and nation. Although this conflict may vary

[5] Lawrence Senesh, *Economics*, Publication #105, Social Science Education Consortium (West Lafayette, Ind.: Purdue University, 1966).

in degree at different times and in different parts of the world, it is always present.

2. Men try to lessen the gap between unlimited wants and limited resources. They have found that dividing the labor enables them to produce faster and better. If each person does one particular job and specializes in this task, he can gain in skill and increase his productivity. There are three ways in which labor can be divided: occupationally, geographically, and technologically.
3. Because there is a division of labor, people do not produce all that they need for themselves; thus they become interdependent.
4. This interdependence makes trading necessary. To facilitate trade, men have developed monetary systems and transportation methods.
5. Because resources are too limited to permit fulfillment of all wants, all societies develop allocating mechanisms that determine:
   a. The kinds of goods to be produced, for example, whether watches, textiles, toothbrushes, clothing, bulldozers, sewing machines, or cabbages will be produced.
   b. The quantity of goods to be produced.
   c. The methods of production to be used, that is, the proportions of land, labor, and machines or tools to be used.
   d. The level of production and employment to be attained.
6. In our economic system the market is the major allocating mechanism. Through it, producers and consumers find each other. It is in the producers' interest to try to sell their goods at the highest price; consumers, on the other hand, try to buy goods at the lowest price. The interaction of the two results in the market price. The rising or falling of the prices of the goods produced as well as the prices of land, materials, labor, and tools help industrial and business leaders to decide what goods and how great a quantity of them to produce as well as the proportions of materials, labor, and tools or machines that they will use to produce those goods.
7. When our society decides that certain things which the market mechanism does not provide are necessary or desirable, it may modify the decisions of the market. For example, if decisions on education were left to the market, only those who could afford a private education would go to school. When our society decided on free education for all, it modified a market decision in order to promote the general welfare.
8. Market decisions may be modified not only by public policy but also by voluntary activities. In a free society, millions of volunteers produce goods and services which modify the use and distribution of resources determined by the economic market. One implementation of this structure is discussed in "Our Working World" by Senesh.[6]

[6] Lawrence Senesh, "Our Working World" (Chicago: Science Research Associates, Inc., 1964).

The Georgia Sequence

The University of Georgia has developed a sequential curriculum in anthropology for grades one to seven which has as its specific objective the preparation of units in anthropology for these grades.[7] The units are not intended to be a complete social studies program. Each unit lasts for 25 days only and is intended to be a part of the social studies instruction at a given grade level. The grade two unit, for example, presents Indian life in five stages of cultural development and is designed to correct the stereotypes of Indians as hunters and warriors. The grade five unit presents the child with archeological methods and a brief overview of man and his culture in the total context of geologic epochs, evolutionary processes, and the thousands of years of slow cultural development.

There are many new programs in the social studies built about a particular social science discipline or an integration of several such disciplines. They are worthy of careful consideration.

Content from Thinking Processes

There is a third basis for the selection of content to provide the social studies program. Here the content serves as a basis for thinking processes which can be learned. Content can support such basic concepts as cultural change, cooperation, interdependence, differences, and causality, all of which have the power to organize and to symbolize vast amounts of information. Such a curriculum has been developed in the Contra Costa County Schools of California. In this program, the hierarchical order of the concept of interdependence—for example, as it concerns relationships of people to people—might be organized as follows:

Interdependence in People-to-People Relationships:
7th level: between governments of nations.
6th level: between levels of government.
5th level: between industries and government.
4th level: between industries and specialized workers.
3rd level: between specialized workers in services and community workers.
2nd level: between community workers and family members.
1st level: between family members.

The first grade deals with interdependence among family members. In the second grade interdependence appears on a more abstract and complex level, namely, the interdependence of services in the community. The third grade emphasizes the interdependence of members of a tribal society

[7] Marion J. Rice, "Anthropology Curriculum Project" (Athens: University of Georgia, 1966).

as demonstrated by their cooperative securing of necessities. The fourth grade curriculum stresses the interdependence between production areas in a state (for example, valleys that produce abundant food and mountains that produce abundant minerals). In the fifth grade, interdependence among the larger production areas in the United States is the major study area. Finally, in the sixth grade there is a study of interdependence among nations of Latin America and with other nations of the world.

Thus the hierarchical nature of the concepts makes it impossible to develop them fully in one unit or even on any one grade level. They must be dealt with on several grade levels. The child moving through the program reaches continually higher levels of generalizations and thinking processes concerning interdependence.

A second program which selects content to reinforce thinking processes has been developed in the Providence Social Studies Curriculum Study. This program was developed by Rhode Island College and the Providence public schools. Cultural regions and civilizations provide the framework for the organization of ideas and content.

The Providence Study is founded on the following objectives:

1. To better understand cultural patterns other than an American-centered approach.
2. To arrange content in sequence to provide for order and flexibility for children of all ages and abilities from kindergarten through high school.
3. To be concerned with the mastery of functional information leading to significant generalizations about man and his varied relationships.
4. To reflect the most important ideas, information, and insights emerging from current research and study in all the social sciences.

Classroom materials have been written and tested for the Providence Study. These materials emphasize the following concepts at each grade level.

Grades	*Emphases*
K–3	Concept of community.
4	Concept of region, with emphasis on metropolitan areas.
5	Anglo-American region.
6	Latin American and African cultural regions.
7	European, Soviet, and Asian cultural areas.
8–12	Four contemporary civilizations and one former civilization (East Asia, Moslem, Indian, Western, and Greece).

Several new social studies programs contain selected content which will shape the development of thought processes through teaching strategies. Such content serves as a vehicle to form concepts in an efficient manner.

Content Based on Citizenship Obligations

A fourth source of content is citizenship obligations. Such content usually is built about a framework of themes from which an instructional program, embodying the unit plans created to implement these themes, can be derived.

One exciting program in the Rose Tree Union School District (Pennsylvania) has been organized around five central themes: (a) man and his natural and cultural environment, (b) responsible citizenship and governmental development, (c) recognizing and understanding world interdependency, (d) economic living, (e) conflict and change. This theme approach eliminates a massive accumulation of facts, and emphasizes a limited number of concepts which transcend the increasing number of specialties within the social science field.

Taking the kindergarten level as an example, let us note for each particular theme the suggested content areas:

Central Theme—"Recognition and Understanding World Interdependency":

- Dependence on parents and friends.
- Helping others in the home and the world (UNICEF).
- Physical characteristics common among children of the world.
- Pets around the world.
- News media (learning about children of the world and pets of the world).

Central Theme—"Economic Living":

- Family members' work (for income, to satisfy needs, and to supply increased wants).
- Production. (We are all producers, and there are different ways of producing.)

Central Theme—"Conflict and Change":

- Conflict in the animal world today (food, shelter, and enemies, including other animals and man).
- Conflict among people.
- Problems similar to those of animals—food, shelter, and enemies.
- Conflict with peers.
- Conflict with adults.
- Conflict among peers and adults—misunderstanding actions, differences in beliefs, and lack of information (fear of the unknown, such as going to the hospital).

The content selected for each particular theme in the kindergarten lays the foundation for the development of such themes throughout the grades. Content may be concerned with the expanding communities of men or it may be to substantiate particular generalizations or themes.[8]

METHOD

There are several instructional methods, procedures, and techniques which provide essential avenues to effective learning in the social studies. Each has a role to play in learning. The great amount of new knowledge, devices and equipment, and audiovisual materials can greatly aid the teacher in the instructional process.

A method is a systematic approach to learning and acquiring information. It gives the teacher the opportunity to practice and develop techniques and to apply a creative approach to teaching. This can in turn foster the child's growth and development.

Expository Method

The expository method has been used in countless classrooms down through the centuries. The teacher explains, narrates, or describes content, information, experiences, and instructions in a logical, efficient organization and with a pace and manner suitable to the children's maturity, background, and ability. In this method the teacher assumes the role of expositor of knowledge while the students act as recipients. The principal materials used are sources of knowledge. The teacher's big task is to maintain the process of transmitting finished knowledge from source to recipient. The chief objective of this method is to help children to understand some previously organized system or predetermined knowledge in the social studies.

Wrightstone summarizes the expository method as it is applied to the social studies.

1. The classroom is a restricted form of social life, and children's social experiences are limited therein to academic lessons.
2. The quickest and most thorough method of learning lessons is to allot a certain portion of the school day to explanation by the teacher —often in separate subjects such as history and geography—followed by the children's taking notes, doing chalkboard work, or reading from the text.
3. Children's social interests which do not conform to the set curriculum are largely disregarded.

[8] Norris M. Sanders and Marlin L. Tanek, "A Critical Appraisal of Twenty-six Social Studies Projects," *Social Education,* XXXIV, No. 4 (April, 1970), pp. 383–447.

4. The real objective of the social studies consists to a major degree in the acquisition of content matter.
5. This method is based on the assumption primarily that knowledge of the conventional subjects of history and geography is essential in achieving social progress.[9]

This expository or narrative method in the social studies too often emphasizes only the memorization of facts in history, geography, or other subjects. The child becomes the passive listener with no opportunity to interpret, generalize, or apply the social science content under study.

Unit Method

The unit is considered by many educators to be the most efficient method yet devised for organizing this area of the curriculum. A unit may be: (a) the organization of particular content, skills, and understandings from the social studies; (b) organized about a problem, a topic, or area; (c) taught within the classroom over a definite period of time; and (d) an element into which as many allied areas of the curriculum as possible are integrated. Social studies units should be planned to provide for many approaches to teaching and learning.

Four Goals for Units. There could be four principal goals from which the social studies unit would emerge. One goal is to initiate the child into an understanding of his American heritage. This understanding should give him a sense of social continuity and an appreciation of the process by which the American value systems have evolved.

A second goal could be to give the child some feeling of rapport with, and a comprehension of, another place, people, or culture different from his own. He will need to have a greater understanding of the immediate and the familiar if he has experienced something of the strange and the unknown. The young child becomes more knowledgeable concerning his own home through the comparison and contrast with a Japanese or Eskimo home.

A third goal might be to help the pupil to formulate an understanding of his place in the immediate society. He should begin to learn his function in that society, how he can relate to it, and how he is a part of it. There are many children today who feel lost and unwanted, rejected, and insecure. Such children too often release a negative violence on their society or simply isolate themselves from it. It is most important that the social studies program help the child to develop a self concept which is integrated within the wider social group.

[9] J. Wayne Wrightstone, *Appraisal of Newer Practices in Selected Public Schools* (New York: Teachers College Bureau of Publications, Columbia University, 1935), p. 9.

Kindergarten, First, and Second Grade Unit Topics

Grade Level	*American Value System*	*Value Systems of Different Cultures*	*Building Social and Self Concept*	*Building Social Skills*
K	Principal topics might be:	Principal topics might be:	Principal topics might be:	Principal topics (and examples) might be:
	Toys I like	Toys of Japan	A playhouse	Suitable skills of place and location (direction), relation of school and home.
	Foods I like	Foods of Japanese children	A play store	Particular social skills (taking turns, sharing).
				Specific learning skills (identification, comparison).
1st grade	Treasures from our long ago	Treasures of Japan	Understanding me	Skills of place and location (homes within the community), rotation of earth.
	Homes we live in	A Japanese home	Fathers and mothers at work	Particular social skills (cooperation, assumption of responsibility).
	What Christmas and Hanukkah mean	Christmas and Hanukkah everywhere	I help at school	Learning skills (analysis and symbolism).
2nd grade	Visiting a supermarket	Things from Japan	What will I be?	Particular skills of place and location (seasons, large land masses).
	A trip to Washington	A trip to Tokyo	Our neighborhood	Particular social skills (leadership, committee work).
	Games I like	Games of Japan	Those who help	Learning skills (application and evaluation).

A fourth goal might be concerned with the learning of particular social skills necessary for the implementation of those goals already described. This goal should be integrated with the entire fabric of the social studies program and should not be isolated as a particular theme or unit. It provides pattern and fiber to the social studies program and without it no other goal has meaning or function. This goal supplies those tools and techniques which enable the child to function effectively within the entire social studies program. Reading a map or examining a hypothesis requires the child to use particular skills for maximum learning.

Illustrative Units. These goals, transferred into an operational program, must be interrelated. There must also be a relationship from age group to age group. The kindergarten program must be related to the first grade, and each succeeding grade should be correlated. The chart on page 322 contains selected unit topics for the kindergarten, first, and second grades that are pertinent to these goals. These topics have been selected to demonstrate that integration is secured not only between the goals on the particular grade level, but also between the kindergarten, first, and second grades.

Each of these suggested topics might be developed into a separate unit. This would make six units for the kindergarten and nine units each for the first and second grades. Several topics might be combined and correlated into a single unit. Others such as the kindergarten topics—toys I like, toys of Japan, and a playhouse—might be correlated into a single unit of study. However, no matter how they are organized, units should have a vertical relationship and sequence as well as a horizontal one. No matter how each goal is organized into unit topics, particular objectives should be determined and clearly stated. Such objectives might be built about Bloom's taxonomy.[10] What particular knowledge or content should be selected for each topic? What comprehension should the child acquire from this knowledge, and how should he apply it to provide reinforcement with meaning and purpose? Within the structure built about each unit topic, provision should also be made for the child to make an analysis of some values within his own culture as compared to those in another culture. He must be able to analyze a problem or a situation, particular social skills, or selected content. Within the organization of the unit topics, he should learn to synthesize content, value, and skills into a positive pattern as well as continually evaluate this pattern. This is a large task.

Let us consider the following unit topics for the first grade: "Treasures from Long Ago"—related to the goal concerning the American value

[10] Benjamin S. Bloom (ed.), *Taxonomy of Educational Objectives. Handbook I: Cognitive Domain* (New York: David McKay Co., Inc., 1965), p. 87.

Unit Topics for First Grade*

American Value System	*Value Systems of Different Cultures*	*Developing a Self Concept*	*Building Social Skills and Behavior*		
			Place and Location	*Social*	*Learning Skills*
What is our flag?	What is the flag of Japan?	Who am I?	How do we know that the earth is round and that it revolves?	How can we share in small groups (social cooperation)?	How do we express a social influence (verbally or by illustration)?
What is Thanksgiving?	What is the Doll Festival? The Kite Festival?	Where did I come from?	How do we use direction?	When should we listen to others?	How can we search for information?
How was George Washington a brave man?	Why are the Japanese so fond of Mount Fujiyama?	Who are my people?	How can we understand how to represent space and location (beginning map work)?	When do we take turns?	How can we learn to interpret materials or information?
How was Abe Lincoln a great man?	Who was Commodore Perry?	What will I be?	How can we use geographic terms—lake, ocean, mountain?	How can we take leadership responsibilities?	How can we focus on the solution of a social problem?
Who lives in the White House?	Where is the Emperor's Palace?	Who is like me?		What social manners are important?	
		Who can help me?		How do we follow instructions?	
		Who likes me?			

* Particular skills would be incorporated into those questions that are most harmonious to them.

system; "Treasures of Japan"—pertinent to the goal concerning value systems of a contrasting culture; and "Understanding Me"—relevant to the goal of helping the child to build a positive self concept. The questions in the table on page 324 might then be pertinent for each of these topics, as they are integrated into the total structure. Then you might well ask: If the topic "Treasures from Our Long Ago" is considered as a unit, what behavioral objectives would be valid for such a unit? How should children be changed because of the unit?

1. The child should know the following objectives which are fairly easy to achieve and to measure:
   a. What does our flag mean, and how was it developed?
   b. What was the first Thanksgiving like, and why was it celebrated?
   c. Who was George Washington, and what particularly brave deeds did he perform for his country?
   d. Who was Abraham Lincoln, and what particularly good deeds did he perform for his country?
   e. What is the White House, and what is it used for?
2. The child should comprehend these objectives that are somewhat more difficult to achieve and measure:
   a. What the flag means as a symbol, and how it is different from the state flag or the flag of the United Nations.
   b. Why Thanksgiving is observed and what we should be thankful for in the United States.
   c. Why George Washington is called "The Father of Our Country" and why he is remembered as a great man.
   d. How Lincoln served the nation.
   e. What the White House represents as a national symbol, and what history it contains.
3. The child should be able to apply:
   a. The idea of the flag to other symbols such as the bald eagle and the state flower.
   b. The celebration of Thanksgiving to other national holidays such as Independence Day.
   c. George Washington's service to his country to similar contributions of other famous personalities such as the astronauts.
   d. Lincoln's freeing of the slaves to the broad issue of civil rights today.
   e. The idea of the public ownership of the White House to other public buildings—the post office or the fire station.
4. The child should be able to analyze:
   a. The flag's symbolic nature—the entire flag is the nation, the stars are the states, and the stripes the original 13 states.
   b. Why we celebrate Thanksgiving with turkey, pumpkin pie, and cranberry sauce.

   c. Some of George Washington's difficulties in fighting the British.
   d. Why Lincoln freed the slaves.
   e. How the White House is not only the residence of the First Family but also a place of business as well as a place where famous people visit.
5. The child should be able to synthesize:
   a. The meaning of the flag with its proper and respectful use and with the "Pledge of Allegiance."
   b. The time of Thanksgiving with other pertinent events in the calendar—Christmas or Valentine Day.
   c. The time relationship of George Washington and Abraham Lincoln in the nation's development.
   d. The location of the White House with the nation's seat of government.
6. The child should be able to make some evaluations:
   a. The importance and use of the flag and its relationship to the flag of the UN and those of the states.
   b. The differences in the celebration of Thanksgiving between Americans today and the Pilgrims.
   c. The contributions of Washington and Lincoln to our society.
   d. The several uses of the White House and its importance. (Should it be the home of the President and his family as well as serve as his office?)

Evaluation of Success. Each of these objectives must be continually evaluated. Have they been reached? How successful is the method used? How appropriate are the materials? Have the children altered or changed their social behavior? Evaluation will help to answer these questions. To measure or evaluate the cognitive aspects of those particular objectives related to the flag, the following examples might be developed.

To measure the child's knowledge and comprehension concerning the flag, he might answer a series of multiple-choice questions and simply draw and color the flag from memory. To determine if he can apply his knowledge and comprehension, he might be asked to draw the flag, salute the flag, and handle the flag correctly in particular situations. To know if he can analyze, synthesize, and evaluate such knowledge and understanding of the flag, he might be asked to create a classroom flag or a flag for the school or the community. Such an activity might determine if he has analyzed the symbolism of the flag and thus evaluated its true meaning. It is more difficult to assess the personal significance of the flag to a child. As always, it is hard to measure some very significant aspects of a child's learning.

Inquiry Method

The inquiry or discovery method is a modern adaptation of the unit method. Its principal purpose is to help children to perceive and experience the process of organizing facts and content in the testing of a social studies hypothesis and thus discover a pattern or structure of operation. Prominent scientists sometimes confess that their interest in science resulted from early participation in research. Surely such an early interest in research can be applied to the social studies by giving children the opportunity to experience early the thrill of discovery.

The inquiry or discovery method in the social studies attempts to teach children how to ask empirical questions concerning the social heritage and environment which will suggest hypotheses that can be tested by the collection of facts. The very process of inquiry will progressively help the child to understand the organizing concepts of the social sciences. Thus the child who perceives his ability to formulate rules or conclusions from a series of concrete social observations or experiments can come to realize that the social environment can be predicted and controlled.

However, in the social studies there are inherent dangers in the unrestricted use of the inquiry or problem method. While it is true that one function of the social studies is to help the child to understand change within the culture, there is an even more important purpose—to teach the child to conserve and to protect that culture. Our first concern is to survive rather than adapt. We must be assured that new ideas do not kill us. We attempt to preserve the culture by presenting it to the child in traditional glory. To hold our culture together we sometimes believe we must cling to old ideas and thus the social studies seems always against some things and for others. The child is taught to love our American form of government and hate totalitarian regimes.

The social studies teacher seems to have little choice; he must prepare the children to live in the culture as it is. Do any social studies programs dare to teach the child to freely inquire into the pros and cons of monogamy, communistic societies, or the law of supply and demand and allow him to reach his own conclusions? Each society—our own included—establishes schools to perpetuate itself. There are limits to inquiry concerning its values. The inquiry approach used in mathematics and science may not be the same as that used in the social studies.

However, a version of this approach is most applicable and suitable for the social studies of the elementary school. There are several steps in the formulation and operation of the inquiry method for the social studies.

The child should be given the opportunity to do real thinking about real events built about a problem suitable to his ability and maturity. He should actually imitate the process of investigation of the scholar. He should also be encouraged to check his ideas against those of other children and the authorities pertinent to his problem. Finally, he should synthesize his ideas into a solution or conclusion in the form of a work project or display.

The inquiry method in the social studies is not a tested and proven pedagogical method. It can be used as effectively as skillful expository teaching. It prevents the use of social science facts without a goal or purpose. Most important, it teaches the child to think in the media of the social sciences. It is applicable for the "here-and-now" as well as the past and far-away problems.

RESEARCH

Some Pertinent Examples

Five recent research studies will be discussed that will give some idea of the direction the social studies seems to be taking. These studies seem to indicate that varied efforts have been made to secure interdisciplinary cooperation to develop a social studies program that is relevant and vital. They reflect efforts to secure objective content which can be incorporated into the curriculum and to provide experimental evidence on effective instructional procedures for the elementary schools. In addition, these studies are part of attempts undertaken to develop a social studies curriculum that will have unity and purpose from one grade to another. From the following examples it may be concluded that a social studies program can be developed along scientific lines. Derived from many social sciences and reflecting contemporary conditions, the resulting social studies program should prepare the child for living in a complex and changing world. It should eventually replace the present social studies programs which in a sense "just grew" in response to varied circumstances, pressures, and individual interests of influential leaders in the field.

The Havighurst–Caul Study. Robert J. Havighurst and Robert M. Caul in 1965, using the disciplines of history and sociology, initiated a study at the University of Chicago entitled "Interaction Between Education and Society in Chicago." Concerned with the impact of social forces since 1925 upon education in the Chicago metropolitan area, the study covered the effects of demographic changes and of social, political, and economic forces on the structure and functioning of education at all levels.

The study developed special research procedures for analyzing the interaction of the school system with business, civic, and welfare organizations as well as the communications system. The study determined efficient interaction techniques within the educational system between private and parochial schools as well as suburban and city schools.

The Lee Study. John R. Lee of Northwestern University studied "New Approaches to and Materials for a Sequential Curriculum on American Society for Grades Five Through Twelve." The study was initiated on January 1, 1964, and completed on December 31, 1968.

Through the social studies curriculum study center at Northwestern University cooperation was secured among the departments of economics, geography, history, and political science as well as with the School of Education. This cooperation brought the current research in the social sciences into closer alignment with the social studies curriculum. The center then concentrated on the problem of the currently loose, diffuse, diverse, sometimes outdated, and often duplicated treatment of American society in the social studies curriculum.

The specific objectives of the Lee Study were as follows:

1. Synthesize results of previous investigations of instruction in social studies concerning American society, particularly in grades five, eight, and eleven.
2. Develop approaches and materials that incorporate basic ideas and concepts concerning American society from economics, geography, history, and political science.
3. Ascertain—through experimental use of the new approaches and materials—the levels of ideas and concepts concerning American society most suitable for grades five, eight, and eleven.
4. Formulate a curriculum in social studies for these same grades that avoids undesirable duplication and facilitates learning in depth about basic aspects of American society.
5. Evolve means by which scholars and teachers may collaborate in the development of the social studies curriculum in order to relate more closely the social sciences and the social studies.
6. Disseminate to appropriate persons and groups the research findings, instructional approaches, and materials developed through the Center's activities.

The study itself involved several steps:

1. Preparing a critical review of presently available findings concerning learning about American society in elementary and secondary social studies, particularly in grades five through twelve.
2. Securing from appropriate social scientists an identification of basic ideas and concepts concerning American society and their sugges-

tions for, and samples of, instructional materials and guides that will facilitate learning of those ideas and concepts.

3. Securing the cooperation of teachers in appropriate grades and in a variety of school communities to experiment with the instructional materials and approaches.
4. Holding group conferences and effecting other adequate contacts between the participating teachers and social scientists developing the new materials and approaches.
5. Using what is presently available and developing additionally, as needed, evaluative procedures to ascertain the effectiveness of the materials and to serve as a basis for needed improvements.
6. Preparing, on the basis of the results of evaluation, a proposed curriculum in social studies for grades five through twelve that will eliminate undesirable duplication and promote efficient learning in depth.
7. Reporting periodically to the sponsoring agency and to concerned school personnel the feedback and the evaluation from the pilot testing of the curriculum in selected classrooms.
8. Arranging for the production and general dissemination of instructional guides and materials developed through the Center.

The conclusions and recommendations of this study are still in the process of being tested, edited, and revised.

The Fox–Lippitt Study. Robert S. Fox and Ronald Lippitt at the University of Michigan from June, 1963, through February, 1964, made a study of "The Teaching of Social Science Materials in the Elementary Schools." It is based on the assumption that scientific education about human behavior and human relations should begin early. Young children should have an opportunity to develop accurate images of who the social scientists are and what they do, just as they develop comparable images of physical and biological scientists. Of even greater importance is the fact that the solution of many of today's critical problems of teaching and learning depends on the learner's understanding and internalization of certain basic facts about motivation, learning, individual differences, human development, and the dynamics of group problem solving. The young child—immersed in a complex social culture and constantly required to interact wisely with his classmates, his older or younger siblings, his parents, teachers, and other adults—has a pressing need to develop an understanding of social processes and to perfect appropriate interpersonal skills. This need has not been systematically dealt with by the school curriculum.

The primary objective of this pilot project has been to check the feasibility of present programs and to lay the groundwork for more extensive development of curriculum methods and materials for the teaching of the social sciences in the elementary schools. The project attempted:

1. To utilize working materials created during the previous year in writing two resource units for the teaching of social science in the elementary grades. The areas selected for the two units were: "Angry Feelings" and "Relations Between Younger and Older Children."
2. To explore the need for a set of resource materials directed toward helping the classroom teacher gain the knowledge and skills needed to engage successfully in this approach to the teaching of social science.
3. To field test the resource materials in elementary school classrooms at various grade levels.
4. To carry forward in a summer day camp additional efforts in developing attitudes and skills in children of different age levels toward their relationships with others who are older or younger.
5. To develop, as a result of these exploratory efforts, proposals for basic research and for curriculum development projects to be submitted to the U.S. Office of Education Cooperative Research Branch, which will deal in a more comprehensive way with the problems of teaching social science in the elementary school.

The procedures of the study conducted by Fox and Lippitt are described in the following pages. When behavior problems arise in the classroom, they are usually handled by teacher exposition of a more acceptable model of behavior or the imposition of controls; however, relatively little emphasis is given to the scientific study of human behavior as part of the curriculum.

Using the scientific approach, the scientist works on a problem by observing the phenomenon, formulating hypotheses about it, gathering data, analyzing it and drawing conclusions, and testing these findings against reality in a variety of settings.

To encourage classroom implementation of the laboratory approach to learning about human behavior, a systematic plan for dealing with a problem has been devised. Eleven phases or stages are proposed that will serve as a framework upon which a meaningful sequence of activities can be constructed:

1. Warming up to the topic.
2. Developing a behavior specimen for study.
3. Collecting data.
4. Analyzing data.
5. Interpreting causal dynamics.
6. Evaluating consequences.

7. Experimenting with alternative causal sequences.
8. Summarizing learnings.
9. Utilizing social science resources.
10. Exploring relevance of classroom discoveries to other life situations.
11. Evaluating the unit.

This framework for teaching a unit has been utilized for the various topics explored so far. Its usefulness for children at different age levels is under examination. The extent to which flexibility in the coverage of all phases can be permitted while still retaining the basic orientation toward a laboratory approach to learning about interpersonal behavior is also being studied.

These additional units were prepared for teaching in the elementary grades:

Units with Self and Self–Other as Focus:

1. Angry feelings.
2. Friendly feelings.
3. Growing up.
4. Deciding and acting.

Units with Social Psychology and Socialization as Focus:

1. Relations between elders and youngers.
2. Relations between like-age peers.
3. Relations between boys and girls.
4. Relations between grown-ups and children.
5. Relations between teachers and children.

Units with Sociological Emphasis:

1. People and groups different from ourselves.
2. Getting work done in groups.
3. Social conformity pressures and individuality.

The above topics were subjected to the analysis of a multidisciplinary panel of colleagues for a critical review before moving beyond the developmental stage. The investigators feel that they are in the early stages of what may become an active ferment of revision of the social studies and experimentation with social education.

The Gill–Conroy Study. From June 30, 1966, to June 6, 1967, Clark C. Gill and William B. Conroy of the University of Texas worked on "Development of Guidelines and Resource Materials on Latin America for Use in Grades 1–12." This study was based on the need for the citizens of the United States to have an adequate understanding of contemporary Latin America. Our geographic proximity, our trade, and other relationships have resulted in considerable involvement of the United States in

Latin American affairs. Sometimes this involvement has been harmonious, other times it has been met with varying degrees of hostility.

The major objectives of this study by Gill and Conroy were to identify and organize, sequentially, content from the social sciences appropriate for developing proper understanding of contemporary (post-1945) Latin America, and to develop the needed resource materials for teaching about Latin America in the elementary and secondary school.

Scholars from the social sciences at the University of Texas identified major ideas essential for a basic understanding of contemporary Latin America. After current curriculum materials were examined to determine the extent to which they provide for such understandings, the project staff prepared a statement of guidelines suggesting scope and sequence of key ideas on Latin America for inclusion in the social studies in the elementary and secondary school. In addition, teaching guidelines on selected topics on Latin America that were not adequately treated in current materials were prepared, field tested, and evaluated in the schools.

The effectiveness of this project is still in the process of evaluation.

The Wing Study. Richard L. Wing of the Center for Educational Services and Research (Yorktown Heights, New York) began a study in 1964 entitled "The Production and Evaluation of Three Computer-Based Economics Games for the Sixth Grade."

One of the games developed is the "Sumerian Game," designed to teach sixth graders some basic principles of economics in operation at the time of the revolution in Mesopotamia.

The essential idea behind the second game, the "Sierra Leone Development Project," is to simulate the economic problems of a newly-emerging nation, placing a secondary emphasis on a study of the country's culture.

The educational planning for these games was accomplished by a fourth grade teacher at Katonah Elementary School, the chairman of the Social Studies Department at Briarcliff High School, and a graduate student in the social relations department at the Johns Hopkins University. The programming was done by IBM, and visuals for the project were prepared by a graphics artist. (Other personnel included a programmer and a terminal supervisor.)

Equipment used in these projects included stock 1050 typewriter terminals, an experimental random-access slide projector, and an IBM 7090 computer using a time-sharing system, so that several pupils could be taught at the same time.

The objectives of the Wing Study were as follows:

1. To prepare materials of some length suitable for teaching through automated instructional technology.

2. To program this material in the simulated environment mode.
3. To administer these programs to samples of students.
4. To measure the effectiveness of this kind of instruction with respect to achievement and speed of learning.
5. To determine differential effects of independent variables, such as intelligence and reading ability, to the extent that the size of the sample will permit.
6. To measure student attitudes towards instruction in the simulated environment mode.
7. To improve and expand the exposition of a rationale for simulation which is being written for the current project.
8. To make available a body of instructional programs with visual components in the simulated environment mode capable of being adapted at computer centers for demonstration in other geographical areas when necessary changes in the computer programs have been made.

In the search for improved methods of individualizing instruction it is hypothesized that:

1. The game mode as a type of computer-based simulation can be shown to be an effective method of teaching skills and understandings in economics.
2. The game mode will save instructional time in comparison with "conventional methods."
3. The game technique can be shown to stimulate significantly increased interest in economics on the part of students.
4. The game technique will result in greater retention of economic understandings on the part of students.
5. The game technique is an appropriate method for students at several different grade levels.

In order to assess the results of these games the following experiment was set up. For a six-month period 25 sixth grade students from the Mohansic School in Yorktown Heights, New York, played the two games at the Center for Educational Services and Research. These pupils started in some cases with the Sumerian Game, in other cases with the Sierra Leone Game, and then completed the other. Meanwhile, a control class of equal ability studied about the economics of life in Sumer and Sierra Leone under the direction of a talented teacher using ingenious but "conventional" methods.

As soon as each pupil arrived at the Center for the first time, he was shown how to operate the terminal by the terminal supervisor. Before starting the Sumerian Game, each student watched and listened to an introductory sequence of slides and tape describing the student's role as Luduga, son of the priest king in Sumer. After the orientation and introduction, the terminal supervisor signed on the program each time and remained available in case there was any trouble with the system. Each student played the game for about 90 minutes and then signed off, returning on the following school day to continue.

An anecdotal record of incidents at the terminal was kept by the supervisors and a summary was composed describing the ways in which each student reacted to the experience of working with the computer. Each student was also interviewed when he had completed both games and the post-tests.

The basic evaluation problem has been to appraise the combination of the two methodological procedures employed in conjunction with each other (the game method of instruction and the use of computer-based typewriter terminals for delivery of the games).

The effectiveness of the whole experiment was measured by several different techniques:

1. Observation of the students and interviews with them after they finish playing the games.
2. Comparison of their pre- and post-test scores on specially prepared test of economic understandings.
3. An in-depth interview technique designed to probe for understanding of economic concepts.

Before the experimental use of the terminals began, all students in both control and experimental classes were pre-tested with the "Test of Economic Principles Based on Ancient Sumer" and the "Test of Economic Principles Based on Sierra Leone" prepared for the project.

As each student in the experimental class finished one of the games, he took the post-test based on the game. The students in the control class were tested as they finished each of the two instructional units taught by the control class teacher. The same test was used for pre-testing and post-testing.

The scores on the pre-test between the two classes varied only two points on a fifty-point scale in favor of the control class. However, the variation of the post-test was fifteen points in favor of the experimental class. The testimony from the children in the experimental class indicated a much higher motivational and enjoyment factor than did the testimony from the control class.

Thus the control group learned more information—which was not surprising, since the students spent more time studying the subject. But the game players, contrary to the expectations, did not demonstrate that their attitudes were affected differently from those of the control group. The only significant change, a growth in political realism, was noted equally in both the groups.

CONCLUSION

Selection of content for the elementary social science program is an extremely complex task for many reasons. First, the scope of such a program is very broad. It draws its information and ideas from many social sciences. Second, there is need to apply the social sciences to present childhood experiences as well as to seek future applications to adult situations. Third, there is need for developing broad generalizations that will be useful even though many facts from which they are derived become obsolete. Rapidly increasing personal and social problems focus interest on the social studies. Several alternatives for organizing social studies programs are being studied and tested in the light of current and anticipated personal and societal needs. Using the content and processes of several social sciences is a common denominator for many of the proposals for revision. How to think and interact are important objectives to be added to the kinds of facts and skills which dominated the social studies curriculum of the past. The modern social studies program is important to the individual and his society, both today and in the future.

PROJECTS AND READINGS

1. Too often the elementary school child has never come to realize that the social studies area is an organized field of human inquiry. He has moved romantically from era to era and locale to locale without ever coming to grips with the rigorous method of the historian. The successful social studies teacher does give the child an understanding of the historical method through the use of several techniques which weave and knit the social studies into a historical pattern. How do you think the elementary school child might experience and be taught the historical method?

2. Controversial issues are those current event topics on the local, state, national, or international scene which have a strong emotional bias and about which the child or his family have strong prejudices and feelings. Controversial topics will vary in emotional intensity from community to community, from state to state. In one school racial integration might be a controversial topic, in others, religion, sex, labor unions, socialized medicine, communism, or federal aid to education. What ideas do you have concerning the study of controversial issues in a social studies program?

3. The constant food of television and the traveling mania of the average American family have widened the young child's horizons and carried his understanding beyond the circle of home and community. Today's child in kindergarten, first, second, and third grade is prepared and ready to receive guidance and instruction in the social world beyond his community and beyond his national boundaries. It is an educational necessity that he begin to receive such knowledge. What unit topics would you suggest for the primary grades which would introduce the child to international education?

4. There is an old fable, "The Devil's Wedge," which describes the time that Satan announced that he was going to retire from business and would sell his tools at public auction. On the evening before the sale many came to see what he had to sell. The chief tools were malice, envy, hatred, jealousy, sensuality, and deceit; in one niche lay a wedge-shaped instrument marked at the highest price. One person asked the devil the reason for the exorbitant price, and he answered, "That is apathy, the most useful weapon in all my aggregation of tools. I can pry open and get inside a man's conscience with apathy when nothing else avails." How might a teacher avoid apathy in the social studies? What would be some symptoms of apathy in the social studies curriculum? What might be the antidote?

5. "Opportunities need to be presented in the school environment whereby better human relationships can be developed among children. Good citizenship can come about only when the quality of human relationships among individuals is improved upon," says Marlow Ediger in "Social Studies in the Elementary School," *Social Education*, XXVIII, No. 4 (April, 1964), p. 201. What ideas have you for improving human relationships in and through the social studies program—both in terms of subject matter and experiences?

6. You might look at the film "Reading in Depth in Social Studies," produced by Bailey Films. Do you have any additional ideas as to how social studies and reading might be further integrated? What other audiovisual or printed examples of correlation of various subject areas can you find? What are the strengths and weaknesses of correlating different subject areas?

7. In every subject area there are large numbers of new publications which disseminate the latest thinking and research. There is a professional challenge to keep abreast with current publications. You might examine some recently published materials in the social studies area. The following are examples of interesting and up-to-date sources.

a. Bernice Goldmark, *Social Studies: A Method of Inquiry* (Belmont, Calif.: Wadsworth Publishing Co., Inc., 1968), 228 pp. This small volume describes not only the techniques of the inquiry method in the social studies but also radiates some of the curiosity and excitement that such a method evokes in the learner.

b. John Jarolimek, *Guidelines for Elementary Social Studies* (Washington, D.C.: Association for Supervision and Curriculum Development, 1967), 32 pp. This pamphlet sets forth criteria and guidelines for assessing new programs in the social studies. Sound explanations also are given as to how a social studies curriculum might be organized and developed.

c. Dorothy J. Skeel, *The Challenge of Teaching Social Studies in the Elementary School* (Pacific Palisades, Calif.: Goodyear Publishing Co., Inc., Inc., 1970), 190 pp. This slim text contains a fine section concerning several methods of teaching social studies, including problem-solving through inquiry, unit development, method from the structure of the social science disciplines, and methods of teaching the disadvantaged.

d. Wayne L. Herman, Jr., *Current Research in Elementary School Social Studies* (Toronto, Canada: The Macmillan Co., 1969), 462 pp. This book presents significant investigations that indicate how the social studies might be improved.

14

Mathematics and Sciences

THE SCIENTIFIC WAY OF LIVING

Mathematics is concerned with quantitative learning.[1] It is an exact, abstract tool of communication used in the process of measurement. Science, on the other hand, is the instrument that man has developed in order to understand the universe. Both are used as elements of the scientific method which consists of five particular aspects: (a) recognizing problems, (b) formulating hypotheses (guesses), (c) exploring and experimenting, (d) gathering information, (e) drawing conclusions. Valid programs in mathematics and science allow the child an opportunity to use the scientific method in the classroom. Both these curriculum areas present methods of problem solving. If children are to be encouraged to participate in science and mathematics at their level of maturity and development, they must have the opportunities to recognize, work with, and bring to an effective solution problems appropriate to *their* interest and background.

To use the scientific method efficiently, information and skills are necessary. The facts of science and mathematics are important, but how these facts are put together into meaningful ideas is also very important. A good program in science and mathematics helps children to understand some generalizations or "big meanings." They can use generalizations to solve problems in their environment and to help them grow in ability to solve problems effectively. They then will increasingly develop a scientific attitude and way of learning.

[1] Clyde G. Corle, *Teaching Mathematics in the Elementary School* (New York: The Ronald Press Co., 1964).

CONTENT IN MATHEMATICS

You will hear much talk of the "new mathematics." Experiments in space travel, astronauts, automation, and digital computers are important parts of the world in which your children will be living, and will be the everyday accepted way of life for them. This is why the "new mathematics" will have meaning and challenge. Its aim is to make your children think creatively and meaningfully.

As machines for computation are developed further and put into wider use, there will be less need for human experts. Automation will take care of the computation, but there will be a great need for people who can think in the realm of mathematics and who can "program" mathematical problems.

Teaching children to think creatively in mathematics must begin in the very early years of school. You cannot be satisfied with only the automatic response to number combinations and the right answers to problems. Social and individual competence as a human being rests squarely on man's effectiveness as a processor and user of symbols. Knowledge is packaged in mathematical symbols created and organized by men. The new mathematics helps the child to embark on that knowledge. It is a new field of learning to explore.

SOME NEW MATHEMATICS PROGRAMS

The Cuisenaire approach is a tool rather than a program of the new mathematics. Georges Cuisenaire, a Belgian school teacher, presented his children with pieces of wood that were one centimeter square and from one to ten centimeters in length. Each particular length was dyed a different color. The combination of color and length is the basis of the Cuisenaire rods. These rods help children to understand the relationship of quantitative concepts as they examine, manipulate, and discuss spatial phenomena. Children thus gain an understanding of numbers through concrete experiences. Usually the rods are used with children in kindergarten and the first grade, but computational operations with whole numbers, fractions, and decimal fractions have been developed for use in this program through the ninth grade. The unit size of the rods (one cubic centimeter) has a great deal of importance in Europe where the metric system is used for demonstrating and in teaching areas and volumes.

Stanford University Project

Patrick Suppes supervises the Institute for Mathematical Studies in Social Studies at Stanford University, which has developed two mathematical programs of instruction for elementary schools. One program is more comprehensive; it is called "Sets and Numbers" and constitutes a mathematical course of study for primary grade children. Suppes defines sets as a collection or family of objects. The child learns that sets may be represented concretely with real objects; semi-concretely with pictures or cutouts; and finally abstractly with words, symbols, or numerals. Brackets are the standard markers for sets, and the purpose of the sets is to enclose all the members or elements of that set. Number is defined as a "property of a set." It is used as a term to describe one of the characteristics of a set: how many elements?

Sets by no means represent the total emphasis of the Stanford Project. Principles of the number system, the function of place in establishing number values, and the importance of cardinal and ordinal uses of numbers are taught in the first two grades. During the primary years, money values and measures of length, time, capacity, and weight, as well as temperature receive systematic treatment. The use of correct terminology is also stressed and the skills of vocabulary are given high priority.

Algebra is introduced in the first half of the first year's work. Children use letters for numbers and learn to balance equations. In the second grade, children are introduced to plane geometry as well as various kinds of plane figures, perimeters, and areas. Relational symbols of various kinds are taught. You will find that the symbols ($<$) is less than, ($>$) is greater than, and ($\neq$) is not equal to, are often used in the Stanford materials.

University of Illinois Project

Another interesting arithmetic project was that directed by David A. Page at the University of Illinois. The purpose of this project is to help teachers to improve the content and methodology of instruction in elementary school mathematics. Page believes that the study of mathematics should be an exciting adventure requiring and deserving hard work. He also feels that if elementary school children grasp some of the inherent fascination of mathematics, they will be successful in further study of the subject.

Some of the characteristics of the Illinois project are as follows:

Use is made of geometric shapes such as triangles, squares, circles, and diamonds to replace literal numbers in simple equations. The children write a number in a frame to complete an open statement: $\square + 3 = 7$

Estimation is considered an important skill needed by children in expressing correct judgments about numbers. The estimation principle is used to round off fractional values. A mixed number is estimated correctly at the level of the whole integer. If the mixed number contains a whole number and an improper fraction, the estimate is given an increment of one for each whole unit expressed by the improper fraction. If an improper fraction is written without an accompanying integer, the estimate is equal to the number of whole units that are expressed by the fraction:

$$[5\tfrac{4}{3}] = 6$$

The child is encouraged to study a grid-like organization of numbers in a given sequence. A table of whole numbers might be arranged with 10 rows of 10 numbers in each. An arrow placed to the right of a number indicates that the child is to move in the direction indicated by the arrow and give the adjacent number as the arrow directs: for example 24 ↑ means move up one space from 24 to 34.

Children are expected to follow first a single and then a double arrow, and later a series of arrows pointing in various directions. In the beginning, they may trace the movements step by step; but as understanding develops they will find more effective ways of reaching the goals.[2]

The new mathematics, of which the previously described projects are only a part, is intended to improve the teaching of arithmetic. Any benefits your students derive from the new mathematics depends on *your willingness and ability to use it.* Modern mathematics employs its own language, and many of its terms may be strange to you. Introduction of new and rather difficult topics into your mathematics program may upset you. Improvements in elementary school mathematics are long overdue and although the proposals in many of the new mathematic projects come from specialists in mathematics, they have been supported by elementary educators.

Fundamentals To Be Taught

There are particular fundamentals that you should teach the child:

1. *He should learn to count not only how many, but also which one.* He should know that the cardinal number tells us how many, and that the ordinal indicates the position of something within a group.

2. *He should learn to write numbers.* There seems to be a desirable sequence for learning to write numbers.[3] In the first grade the child should learn to write numbers to 10; in the second grade he should write numbers to 100; the third grade, to 1000 and Roman numerals to 12; fourth grade, to hundred thousands and Roman numerals through 50; and fifth grade, numbers to millions and Roman numerals to 100. Finally in sixth grade the child should learn to write numbers to any denomination and in Roman numerals where needed.

[2] For an excellent discussion on "Maneuvers on Lattices" see Corle, *op. cit.*, pp. 51–52.

[3] William B. Ragan, *Teaching America's Children* (New York: Holt, Rinehart & Winston, Inc., 1961), p. 148.

3. *The child should use addition and subtraction with some degree of accuracy.* He should be introduced to these processes after he has had many experiences in counting, comparing, and grouping, and after he can read and write numbers to 10.

4. *He should also learn to understand multiplication and division.* Today in teaching these processes you should emphasize understanding, investigation, and discovery. The same procedure used in teaching counting, addition, and subtraction should be used in teaching multiplication and division. You should help the child to progress from concrete objects to pictures of objects to abstract symbols.

5. *The child need not complete the work with whole numbers before he begins to study fractions.* As he progresses through the elementary school, he should gradually discover principles that apply to the relations of fractions—such as inverting the divisor and multiplying when the divisor is a fraction, and multiplying the numerator and denominator by the same number without changing the value of the fraction.

6. *Finally, the child should learn to use the fundamental processes of mathematics in a problem solving situation.* He needs to find the solution to a problem where the operation or operations are indicated. He must also work with story problems where the quantitative situation is stated in words, and the child must decide what operations are necessary to reach a solution. Good story problems help the child to develop genuine quantitative thinking.

METHOD IN MATHEMATICS

Many educators through the ages have centered their educational philosophy on the use of provocative questions which cause children to think. Today the method advocated by Socrates and Dewey is called the discovery approach, guided discovery approach, or developmental or inductive approach. These methods place an emphasis upon allowing the child to figure things out for himself.

Ranucci presents the following illustration of discovery approaches in mathematics.

For example a square |X| contains exactly one square shape □. The child can discover for himself how many square shapes a square 2×2 contains

(in all five square shapes) $(1) + (4) = 5$.
Then he can move to a square 3×3 (which contains in all fourteen squares—one square 3×3, four squares 2×2 and nine squares 1×1 $(1) + (4) + (9) = 14$.

A square 4×4 contains 30 square shapes (one square 4×4, four squares

3×3, nine squares 2×2, and sixteen squares 1×1) $(1) + (4) + (9) + (16) = 30$. It looks as though a square 5×5 should contain 55 square shapes. He is asked to find out if this is so.[4]

Here the child discovers for himself the mathematical relationship of parts to the whole.

Mathematical facts, concepts, processes, and problems make sense to a child only in terms of how well he can fit what is new to him into the pattern of what he already knows. The more immature the learner, the more important it is to present new learnings in a setting to which he is accustomed and in which he feels comfortable.

In the discovery approach or method the development of insight is the final goal, the ultimate objective. Actually the question of whether an abstract generalization in mathematics should be wholly or partially derived by the child himself cannot be answered categorically. It depends upon several factors: (a) the extent of the child's experience with inductive reasoning, (b) the complexity of the generalization, (c) the character of the presentation, (d) the nature of the challenge in terms of the child's own perception of the problem, (e) the point of view upon which you base your total teaching–learning program. As the teacher you should judge the proportionate amount of help a child needs in these experiences as you work with him and learn about his abilities and needs.

You might find the following ideas helpful.

1. Give mathematics life. Try to correlate mathematics as much as possible with everyday experiences. The child should come to understand that the proper use of numbers can help solve real problems; for example, many games can be played in school to help a child when he needs mathematics in adding scores. There are card games, such as Rummy and Chinese Rummy, and there are ring cross games, target games, shuffleboard, and bowling (using real bowling scoring sheets or facsimiles).

2. Help the child to see that mathematics is a system. He should understand facts such as: (a) Our number system is built on 10 and each place in a number has a value 10 times as great as the place to its right. (b) Zero is nothing more than a place holder. (c) Mathematical processes are interrelated. (d) Addition is putting together; subtraction is taking apart; multiplication and division have the same relationship. A sample of a mathematical system is given on the top of page 344. Have the children explore the nature of its progression.

3. Once the child understands a process, have him practice it. Never forget that drill is not a method for teaching the understanding of mathematics. Practice has no use unless it is accompanied by meaning; it only helps the child to secure automatic recall. Drill always follows understanding, it never precedes it.

[4] Ernest R. Ranucci, "Discovery in Mathematics," *The Arithmetic Teacher,* XII, No. 1 (January, 1965), p. 14.

Facts about 9

Multiples of 9 add to 9, then 18, then 27 . . . .

$9 = 9$	$99 = 18\ (9 + 9)$	$189 = 27\ (18 + 9)$
$18 = 9$	$108 = 18$	$198 = 27$
$27 = 9$	$117 = 18$	$207 = 27$
$36 = 9$	$126 = 18$	$216 = 27$

You might give each child a number card related to the facts which are to be drilled. You could then ask the children questions like these:

Addition: "I have three (holding up a three card). Who can make it five?" (The child with a two card would then come up to join you.)
Subtraction: "I have seven. Who can make it five?"
Multiplication: "I have four. Who can make it 28?"
Division: "I have 27. Who can make it three?"

4. The most important aspect of your method should be the emphasis on discovery. Attempt to organize mathematical situations which remove children from passive roles into more active roles that provide the child with the thrill of discovery. This demands creative as well as critical thinking and creates the interest necessary for learning.

Numerical reversals are interesting to children. When the sign is changed, the answer reverses. These samples might be duplicated in a sheet of paper and the children asked if they can discover any others.

$9 + 9 = 18$	$9 \times 9 = 81$
$24 + 3 = 27$	$24 \times 3 = 72$
$47 + 2 = 49$	$47 \times 2 = 94$

A child will receive a functional understanding of mathematics if he himself discovers its structure, laws, and principles. He must conduct his own search for patterns in order to find sequence and order.

RESEARCH IN MATHEMATICS

Instead of searching the common everyday uses of mathematics for sources of arithmetic content, present day research workers are analyzing the fields of mathematics (especially number theory) and the basic principles governing number operations, algebra, and geometry. This search is for content that may be adapted, modified, or used as it is in the elementary school.

In selecting content, three factors seem to be dominant. First, it is now reasonably clear that—with the changes in objectives that have occurred in the past three decades—the field of mathematics is the major factor in the selection of content for the elementary arithmetic curriculum. The criterion for the selection of material is the determination of whether the material will either contribute to the understanding of mathematics or help to provide a foundation for further study of mathematics. Second, although usefulness in life outside the school is no longer considered as important in the selection of content as it formerly was, many experts in instruction conclude after critical study that demonstrable usefulness is a powerful motivating factor in the selection of content. The third factor is the difficulty of the concept. While it has been demonstrated that it is *possible* to teach some aspects of even very difficult concepts at any grade level (including the primary grades) it is often more practical to omit or postpone some topics because they are too difficult and are more efficiently taught in some later grade.

The introduction of new content—through new projects, as a result of an intensive analysis of the fields of mathematics, and from other recent innovations—has brought to curriculum makers new problems and practices with regard to grade placement of topics. Since most of the new mathematics has resulted from moving down or adapting mathematics content from high school and college courses, a climate especially favorable to including topics formerly thought too difficult at lower grade levels has also been fostered by the findings of research concerning practices in European schools. There seems to be a definite trend to place mathematic topics at a lower grade level.

New Methodology and Research

The new method, sometimes called "teaching with emphasis on discovery," emphasizes child experimentation and accents verification of statements and solutions. Controlled research studies comparing child achievement in programs that emphasize an exploratory type of procedure with programs of non-exploratory nature have given a slight edge to the exploratory programs. When comparisons of outcomes are made through other data-gathering means—such as observation of pupil resourcefulness, confidence, and general interest in mathematics—the results have been more definitely in favor of programs emphasizing exploration and discovery. This evidence indicates that the use of such programs would create a type of learning situation more favorable to the child for learning mathematics.

In constructing a better program, it is useful to know what arithmetic knowledge the kindergarten child possesses. Studies were designed to discover what specific number concepts children possessed when they enter kindergarten.[5] Children were selected in the public schools of Livonia, Michigan, and in the demonstration school of San Francisco State College. Two tests were used. The first was an individual oral interview requiring responses such as abstract counting by one and ten and rational counting by one and two. The second was a picture test requiring responses such as recognition of geometric figures and telling time to the full or half hour.

The data from these studies present some interesting results. All children could count by one; the mean was approximately 19 for both rate and rational counting. Approximately 25 per cent counted by 10, and approximately 20 per cent had some ability in counting by two. Ninety-three per cent recognized two items when flashed; and 21 per cent recognized eight which was the maximum number flashed. The majority were able to recognize the geometric figures of a circle and a square.

These children gave evidence of a high degree of skill in solving word problems which involved simple addition or subtraction facts. Perhaps kindergarten children should receive an inventory test and have a planned arithmetic program during the latter half of the school year. The mathematics program in the first grade could then allow for broader arithmetic experiences for many children.[6]

A wide variation in number knowledge possessed by children in kindergarten was also concluded from a study conducted at Peabody Demonstration School.[7]

A similar variance was found in grades one and two which indicated a need for a readiness program. But Banks concludes that readiness is not altogether a function of maturation. Ideas in mathematics must be translated into the language and concepts of the child and then through the relatedness of his knowledge to lead him through successive stages of development.

The following are excerpts from studies related to learning mathematics by the discovery approach.

Children learned skills better by spending less time on drill and more time on developmental–meaningful activities.

1. Through different arithmetic class instruction time, ratios did not differ significantly in computation or verbal problem solving as measured by a two-part addition and subtraction of fractions post test. However, on the retention test classes which spent from 50 to 75 per cent on developmental–meaning-

[5] Herbert F. Spitzer, *Teaching Arithmetic, What Research Says to the Teacher,* No. 2 (Washington: National Education Association, 1963), p. 18.

[6] Corwin E. Bjoneurd, "Arithmetic Concepts Possessed by the Preschool Child," *The Arithmetic Teacher,* VII, No. 7 (November, 1960), pp. 347–50.

[7] Hazel Lundberg, "Mathematics in the Elementary School," *Educational Leadership,* XIX, No. 6 (March, 1962), p. 367.

ful activities did significantly better than the 25 per cent group on computation, but no significant differences were found on the retention test for verbal problem solving.
2. On *total* performance on the retention test, pupils who had spent 50 to 75 per cent of their time on developmental–meaningful activities performed significantly better than the 25 per cent group.[8]

These studies indicated that:

1. There was a trend toward higher achievement when the percentage of class time on developmental activities was increased from 25 per cent to 75 per cent at all ability levels.
2. It seemed that more than 50 per cent of class time should be spent on developmental activities.[9]

CONTENT IN SCIENCE

Science content is the *what* of the science program; it embodies the science information which the children can learn in the classroom. Scientists and science educators agree that there is particular content which children can and should understand. This science content can be classified into three general areas: (a) the earth and the rest of the universe, (b) living things, (c) matter and energy. The five major fields of science are: astronomy, biology, chemistry, geology, and physics. They contribute content to these three general areas.

There are large numbers of new science programs available for the elementary classroom. These programs are rich in science content and provide much science information related to the children's environment. They do not have a tight, grade by grade, spiral of narrow topics. They have a more flexible open-ended pattern. Individual topics have been incorporated under broader, related content areas. These new programs emphasize *inquiry* which children should carry on in laboratory work that is genuinely investigative. They infer from their own data rather than memorize a rhetoric of conclusions; the processes and not just the products of science are emphasized. Structure is a second important ingredient of the new programs. Some programs organize the content so that a topic is taken up three times during the kindergarten through grade six period: once in grades K–2, a second time in grades 3–4, and a third time in grades 5–6. Other schools take up a science topic just twice: in grades K–3 and again in grades 4–6. Still other programs have no regular

[8] Albert Shuster and Fred Pigge, "Retention Efficiency of Meaningful Teaching," *The Arithmetic Teacher,* XII, No. 1 (January, 1965), pp. 24–31.
[9] Donald E. Shipp and George H. Deer, "The Use of Class Time in Arithmetic," *The Arithmetic Teacher,* VII, No. 3 (March, 1960), pp. 117–21.

pattern; they may take up a topic two, three, or even four times, depending upon the amount of science content entailed.

Hoffman believes that the best science education is one which emphasizes the concepts of the various fields of modern science in a unified way and at a level and style befitting the intelligence of the students.[10] A good science program introduces the fundamental concepts of energy and matter and then relates these concepts to man and to the world in which he lives. Such concepts presented as problems may come from a book, from experiences, from excursions, and from many other places. They should serve as an inter-disciplinary study of the impact of science on the modern world.

Craig indicates that children of any age group can profit from a study of any science problem in which they are interested. The only factors limiting the study are the children's past experiences and the complexity of the principle involved.

You might not even have a science course of study and you need not follow one textbook in a classroom.[11] However, the science program should be planned with the following criteria:

1. It must be a balanced program. Such areas as living things, matter and energy, earth and universe, and how man controls his environment should receive equal treatment.
2. Children should be allowed to ask questions, relate experiences, and try things out.
3. Science learning should be provided through field trips, demonstrations, experiments, use of resource persons, and reading.
4. Books, magazines, pamphlets, pictures, and similar materials should be readily available for children to use.
5. The children should be motivated through meaningful experiences such as observing seasonal changes, making weather reports, preparing temperature records, and caring for plants and animals.
6. Suitable science equipment should be available for children's use.
7. Children should be taught to locate information, distinguish between fact and fancy, and write accurate reports. They should help to select and plan science activities which use the scientific method.
8. Those children capable of high level work in science should be identified and encouraged.
9. Children should be aware of their own progress in science.

In the first grade children might study the following topics: air, changes in weather, how you can change foods, how your body grows, where

[10] Emil T. Hoffman, "Science Education To Meet the Needs of the Modern World," *Science Teacher,* XXXVII, No. 5 (May, 1970), p. 41.

[11] Gerald S. Craig, *Science for the Elementary School Teacher,* Fifth Edition (Waltham, Mass.: Blaisdell Publishing Co., 1966), p. 66.

animals live, how animals move, falling down, floating and sinking, different sounds, water around your earth, being far from earth, care of garden plants, magnets and you, electricity, and use of wheels.[12]

The second grade might consider these topics: our earth, earth moves in space, gravity of earth, air of earth, heat and water, from seeds to plants, seeds are moved about, electricity by rubbing, space around a magnet, our sun in space, water of earth, and science happenings.

Grade three might study the following: finding out what is around you, seasons in many places, paths for electricity, living through many changes, air and you, the moving sun and earth, the changing land of earth, the force of magnetism, plentiful times for living things, living things change the land, and satellites of earth.

The fourth grade might consider these topics: molecules in the universe, the planet earth, the atmosphere, animals and how they are protected, making things move, our solar system, plants and how they are protected, plant and animal communities, magnetic and electrical forces, how animals live together, and exploring the world of sound.

Grade five could explore these topics: plant life on earth, forces and earth changes, moon, earth and sun, inside atoms, theories about electricity and magnetism, being above earth's land and water surfaces, light in the universe, living things and changing climates, chemical changes and atoms, animal life on earth, earth's water resources, and systems in space.

The sixth grade could study the following: ways of thinking and behaving, plants and animals of earth are different, the nature of soil, magnetism everywhere, good health, adaptation of living things, earth's changing atmosphere, explaining electricity, interrelationships in the environment, and moving into space.

Do you see how this program has a spiral organization, and how particular topics are enlarged upon and deepened in each grade?

Here is an example of how the first grade topic "Changes in Weather" might be organized into a unit.[13]

A Sample Science Unit for Grade 1

Title: "The Weather–Causes and Effects and Related Areas"

Introduction: A study of the causes of heat and the differences between heat and cold; the need and method of measuring temperature. The children can be encouraged to discuss their weather experiences; their explanations can be solicited and then contrasted and compared with

[12] These topics are based on the series *Science for You* by Gerald S. Craig and Bernice C. Bryan (Boston: Ginn & Co., 1965).

[13] John Gabriel Navarra and Joseph Zafforoni, *Science Today for the Elementary School Teacher* (New York: Harper and Row, 1960), p. 442.

the explanation offered by science. Illustrations can be shown and discussed on how weather affects clothing and shelter.

The Topics:

a. How is weather indicated?
b. What causes wind motion and storms?
c. What are the different kinds of clouds and winds?
d. How do we predict weather?
e. How is weather valuable to individuals, to farmers, in shipping, and in other situations?
f. What are some detrimental effects of weather?

Activities and Work Projects:

a. Have a child put his finger into pans containing snow, water at room temperature, and heated water. Follow with thermometer readings. Record all readings. Mix snow—in stages—with water, record, and have the child feel mixture. Draw a thermometer on the board.
b. Make a model thermometer with a continuous, movable, control strip (for column, half red and half white).
c. Have as many different types of thermometers for class examination as possible. Illustrate their uses in relation to weather, baking, clinical bath, industry, and home heating.
d. Wave a fan over a radiator; record air temperature; wave a fan over a pan of snow; record air temperature. If this is successful, use to demonstrate origin of cold and warm winds.
e. To demonstrate that air rises when heated, place feather or a fluffy material like dried milkweed seed on table. It remains motionless. When placed over a hot radiator, it sails to the ceiling. Its eventual downward course illustrates the motion of air. If the radiator is hot enough, a pinwheel can be used.
f. Take thermometer readings on floor, eye level, and near ceiling.
g. Have children measure out 20 drops of water into several watch glasses. Set in various places (outside, in sunlit window, shaded window, over radiator, in cool room, etc.). Have children check them periodically to determine the rate of evaporation and record the results each time.
h. Put a toy balloon over the neck of a Pyrex flask. Heat the flask. The balloon will inflate. Submerge the flask in snow or cold water. The balloon will then deflate and depress into the flask. Use this to illustrate air pressure. The flask can be left in a window. Children will be interested in watching the balloon react to heat changes.
i. Have children draw scenery with various weather phases.
j. Utilize songs, poems, stories on weather (to be read, sung, narrated, or recited) and list picturesque words on the chalkboard which have been found in the poems and songs.
k. Keep a weather chart, such as the following.

Date	April 13	April 14
Time	9:15	9:18
Temperature	54	57
Barometer	Falling	Steady
Rainfall	0	0
Wind Direction	West	S.W.
Sky	0	0
Clouds		
Forecast	Fair	Rain

METHOD IN SCIENCE

Science is a thinking subject. The degree to which this potential is realized depends largely upon the teacher's skill in posing problem situations. Units in science should begin and end with problems. When a unit is so structured that answers necessitate application of basic principles learned during the unit, these problems can be a real test of the child's understanding of a topic or area. Carefully planned, they can involve logical and fact-supported thinking.

Such thinking constitutes the scientific method which itself is characterized by five specific elements. The child employs the scientific method by: (a) recognizing problems, (b) formulating hypotheses (guesses), (c) exploring and experimenting, (d) gathering information, (e) drawing conclusions.

You can help children to develop the scientific method with the following procedures:

1. *Show the children how to think clearly.* You can develop clear thinking in every area of the curriculum by furnishing an atmosphere where there is allowance for free expression of feelings and opinions by the children, with an open examination of critical issues. If you guide class discussion by encouraging a full interplay of ideas and permitting no blunt attack or expression of disapproval, you will be teaching children the art of unhurried skillful questioning in the search for truth as well as instilling within them a mutual respect for each individual's worth, ideas, and level of maturity.

Children should become aware that everything they read is not necessarily true, that there are varied points of view on almost any topic. They should come to understand and to recognize the existence of other views although they do not have to agree with them. They might be urged to read articles or books which demonstrate different viewpoints on the same subject.

The children might be encouraged to collect illustrations, stories, anecdotes, and clippings in which scientific thinking was not used, for example, jumping to conclusions or refusal to accept proven data. These items may then be used for class discussion.

You can encourage children to question results and to ask, "Why does this happen?" You can maintain a "Question Box" in which any child can place a question. Once a week, perhaps during a discussion period, the questions in the box could be removed and presented for class discussion and possible solution. The children should talk about finding required answers—by reading, by writing letters to resource people, or by making telephone calls to local experts or to a reference librarian. You should encourage children in their efforts to discover answers through their own experimentation in school or at home. You can give suggestions of simple problems which might be investigated.

2. *Accept children's questions and interests which indicate a readiness for science instruction.* They will ask you, "Why are the leaves falling?" "How can we keep our goldfish healthy?" Here are opportunities to use simple but meaningful experiments. Remember that it is the planning and trying out of theories which is important, rather than the mechanics of the experiment. Allow the children to solve a problem for themselves and suggest their own methods of solution. Provide the children with the problem and the equipment, but let them grope for truth through the challenge of thinking. Provide children *time* for thinking.

The children might ask, "What is wind?" You could set about the classiroom materials such as paper, paper bags, water, glass containers, balloons, and small scales. By using these materials the children might discover that air has weight, exerts pressure, and occupies space. Suppose the experiments the children set up with this equipment fail to solve the problem. Do not consider an activity a failure if the solution is not found. In learning what not to do, the children have moved closer to the truth.

You might have a science center on a designated table or a set of book shelves where children could investigate magnets, examine a collection of rocks on display, or observe fish in a balanced aquarium. In such a science corner books related to the display materials may be featured. If the class is studying birds, bird pictures might be mounted on a nearby bulletin board and books on birds displayed along the chalkboard ledge. A viewmaster and microscope are excellent additions to the science center. A magnifying glass, magnets, batteries, and wire are essential to the science corner if children are to have the science experience of experimenting.

3. *Attempt to identify and encourage the child gifted in science.* You will learn that some children are more able in science than others.[14] This special ability should be provided for within the classroom. You should supply these children with the time, space, and materials which will allow them to pursue their special interests to the fullest. Of course such consideration also should be given to the child gifted in mathematics, language, or the social studies.

[14] Dorothy G. Petersen and Velma D. Hayden, *Teaching and Learning in the Elementary School* (New York: Appleton-Century-Crofts, Inc., 1961), p. 304.

There are many methods of stimulating the gifted child's interest in science. He might teach a science lesson or set up an experiment to demonstrate to the class, explaining the process involved and answering questions. He might prepare a biography of a well-known scientist, collecting clippings about this person, reading books and articles, and preparing a booklet which can be used as reference material in the science center. This booklet might have illustrations, a time line of the scientist's life, and a chart explaining his scientific discoveries.

The gifted child might build a barometer or a rain gauge. He might observe the movements of the sun over a period of time, compiling graphs and charts of the findings. He could study the constellations and their changing positions and keep a record of their course. The science-sophisticated child should be given the opportunity to work with genuine problems and attempt to secure accurate scientific information and insights.

RESEARCH IN SCIENCE

A major objective of science instruction in the elementary school is to "attain understanding of the relationship which connects the answer to the problem." [15] There seems to be much support in the current literature for the view that direct experience with real phenomena is necessary to secure data or information which will help children to formulate concepts. Thus science is "interpretation." There is also a trend to challenge children to understand, preserve, and learn to manage diversity—the ecological diversity of the natural world and the natural diversity of the man-made world.[16] Both children and scientists are involved in the active process of interpreting the physical world.

Studies reveal that children are continuously learning about their environment. This learning is broad in nature since it grows out of experiences with a wide variety of objects and phenomena. It is also fundamental in that it involves the introduction of children to the forces and materials of the universe. In a very real sense a child is developing his own identity with a physical universe.

Interpreting the environment goes on whether there is any science instruction or not. Children seek and make explanations regardless of what goes on in the classroom. This search for an interpretation grows out of the demand of the child for adjustment and equilibrium. The teacher's task is to make certain that children are interpreting the environment and the universe in a scientific manner. This means that children must be taught in an atmosphere of honesty since the procedures of science are

[15] W. Pauli, "Confusion and Problem Solving," *Clearing House*, XXXV, No. 3 (November, 1960), p. 81.

[16] Raymond F. Dasmann, "Ecological Diversity," *The Science Teacher*, XXXVII, No. 4 (April, 1970), p. 21.

honest. Children growing up in a democracy have a right to the most reliable information available and to an understanding of why that information is to be considered reliable.

As a child changes in size and weight, he also changes in his interpretations of the environment. If he suffers from malnutrition, he is handicapped in his physical growth; if he is induced to accept misconceptions, superstitions, and dogmatic beliefs, his outlook on his surrounding world will be stifled. The interpretations that an individual makes of his environment and of the physical world are no small matter to himself or to society. The environment has meaning for every individual and the kind of meaning it possesses for him has much to do with the kind of individual he is. If he thinks his environment is filled with hostile spirits which he fears; if he accepts a set of freakish principles, such as lucky or unlucky numbers; or if he believes that human beings are doomed, he is likely to have stunted mental potentialities in his philosophy of life. If, on the other hand, the individual sees his environment as something that can be studied and intelligently utilized, he will have a more constructive outlook on life. His philosophy of living will have a scientific base.

Science During Elementary Years

By the time a child enters the elementary school, it is quite likely that he has gained certain concepts of roughness, smoothness, lightness, speed, acceleration, pull, push, energy, stability, and many other characteristics found in the environment. He has made beginnings in an understanding of those concepts which in reality are abstractions. That is not to say that he has learned all there is to learn about these abstractions. He has learned—as these concepts are associated with his experiences—what is most fundamental.

In evaluating children's concepts we too frequently place too much emphasis on what is *wrong* with their ideas. It is important for them to know where they have made mistakes, but they must be encouraged to grow from their mistakes, to think through and correct them. They will need guidance and assistance to improve on their conclusions.

Butts studied fourth, fifth, and sixth grade children in a situation where they were confronted with science phenomena and little else, and attempted to evaluate their behavior to see what concept development occurred.[17] He hoped to determine if children would work with perceptions *until they can see them in pattern or a concept.* He asked questions such as: Could the concept be sufficiently defined to enable the children

[17] David P. Butts, "The Degree to Which Children Conceptualize from Science Experience," unpublished doctoral dissertation, The University of Texas, Austin, 1965.

to recognize it in a new experience but in the same pattern? Does the development of one concept aid the development of another unrelated concept? Do factors such as intelligence, chronological age, or science achievement relate to concept development? The four concepts studied were those of (a) displacement, (b) inertia, (c) action–reaction, and (d) depth–pressure relationship.

The children observed an illustration of a science principle while seated around a demonstration table. On the table was the equipment necessary for the experience. The children had pencil and paper and they were asked to predict what would happen when certain things were done and to make a rule explaining why this would happen. During this time, the children observed the demonstration but remained silent. The experiences were designed to afford each child the opportunity to formulate rules for what he thought he would see.

In the question phase which followed the completion of a written response, the children could ask any questions they desired. It was explained, however, that the investigator would only answer those questions which could be answered by "yes or no." If the question did call for an explanation (directed learning), the investigator responded with the question, "How would you find out?" This was an effort to return the child to independent learning. Thus, the children were forced to depend on their individual understanding without having the investigator give information and explanations.

Once the children's inquiries were satisfied, they were permitted to manipulate the apparatus of the demonstration in any way they desired. It was not unusual for children to come to this manipulative session with more ideas about the experience and more questions or suggestions about the verification of their ideas. Information related to the concept that was gained from the question and manipulation phase was a result of what the individual child had searched out and integrated into his thinking.

Butts came to the following conclusions in his study:

1. Children do not develop understanding solely from the manipulation of data in a science experience.
2. There is an orderly improvement in concept understanding between the experiences of the same concept.
3. There is no orderly improvement in conceptual understanding between the experiences of different concepts.
4. There is no relationship between tested intelligence and the change of conceptual understanding which results from individual manipulation of data.
5. There is no relationship between chronological age and the change in conceptual understanding which results from individual manipulation of data.
6. There is no relationship between science achievement and the change in conceptual understanding which results from individual manipulation of data.

This study is one effort to explore how children develop concepts and some of the assumptions of how they learn. The evidence of this study seems to indicate that in order for children to develop a concept, the data and information which are used to build that concept must be related to the child's experience. Other studies may further explore this idea.

CONCLUSION

Mathematics and the sciences are basic tools in discovering, controlling, and utilizing the man-made and natural environment. They are so vital that they should be a part of the curriculum from the very beginning of school. They should be both studied and experienced and are crucial if children are to learn how to apply science to everyday living. Facts are significant in both science and mathematics, and some skills are important. An understanding of relationships is vital in both subjects if children are to learn how to utilize them in varied situations. Innovative programs and methods tend to stress meaning and experience over memorization and drill. New programs and methods have a potentiality for developing in pupils those attitudes and learning tools which will enable individuals to attain the benefits of our scientific age. Research and experimentation are providing clues concerning needed changes in content and methodology to make them relevant and dynamic. In mathematics and the sciences, and indeed in all the content areas, the need for continual teacher growth is very evident.

There is a growing attempt to assess mathematics and science teaching in terms of behaviors and interactions of teachers and children, to classify activities and settings, and to quantify repeating variables.[18]

PROJECTS AND READINGS

1. Paul C. Rosenbloom, Director, Minnesota School Mathematics Center, University of Minnesota, predicts the following five changes to come in elementary school mathematics. See *Educational Leadership,* XVIII, No. 2 (November, 1960), p. 96.

   a. Children will learn skills of reasoning as well as computation. They may discover the proof, for example, that the product of two consecutive whole numbers is always even.
   b. They will be exposed to the laws of the number system. The algorithms will be explained on the basis of the underlying laws of numbers such as,

      "If a and b are numbers; then $a + b = b + a$ and $a \cdot b = b \cdot a$."

[18] For example, J. W. George Tuany and James L. Neujahr, "Inquiring into Science Teaching," *The Science Teacher,* XXXVII, No. 2 (February, 1970), p. 31.

c. A new intrinsic motivation will be introduced into arithmetic by leading children to discover interesting relationships between numbers. The children will attack such problems as,

"Calculate each of the products: 1×3, $3 \times 3 \times 4$, $3 \times 4 \times 5$, $4 \times 5 \times 6$, and so forth."

d. Geometry will probably be taught from kindergarten up and will include an empirical study of the physical space around us with emphasis on observation, experiment, and measurement.

e. Children will be taught to describe nature and society in terms of quantitative data. The children will explore the world around them by counting and measuring. They will learn how a scientist predicts and tests predictions and how we make social decisions on the basis of an analysis of data.

Can you determine why a mathematics program such as Rosenbloom describes is necessary to prepare children for that time in history which we can only vaguely foresee?

2. The publicity that has accompanied many of the recent developments in mathematics education has been received with mixed feelings by teachers, administrators, and school patrons. School people and parents who recall unhappy times in the mathematics classroom may believe that a new era is being prepared for students because the old incomprehensible mathematics is going to be replaced by new and useful mathematics. See Max Beberman, "The Old Mathematics in the New Curriculum," *Educational Leadership,* XIX, No. 6 (March, 1962), p. 373. In what ways are the "old mathematics" (so called) and the "new mathematics" alike and how are they different?

3. Recent interest in science and mathematics has been heightened by the "space race." With its emphasis upon our continuing as the world's scientific leader, the United States government and various private foundations have become interested in aiding mathematicians and mathematics educators in the improvement of school mathematics programs. Many experimental programs have been developed and are now being developed. To what extent do you believe that a national interest in space and armaments should be the criterion for the improvement of the school mathematics program?

4. In the past it was often fashionable to deny method and to deny to it a role in the study of the educational process. Today, it has a major role to play. The complexity of the learning act from a neurological point of view can be seen in the reply of a neurologist to the deceptively simple question, "How does a child learn $3 + 2 = 5$?" This researcher, a member of a medical faculty, replied that some of his colleagues were working on such problems and that if they continued to make the same steady progress, they would have an answer in about 100 years! See Vincent J. Glennon, "Method–Function of a Modern Program as Complement to the Content," *The Arithmetic Teacher,* XII, No. 3 (March, 1963), p. 180. If we know so little of how a child learns, is the method used necessarily so important as long as he secures and can use the language of mathematics?

5. In the broad sense of the word, a program is a plan to be followed. With the many materials available, or becoming available, for use in the elementary classroom, there are many possible plans to be used. We are placed in the position of asking ourselves, "Where does each plan take us? What are we imposing upon the boys and girls in our schools? Why do we believe that the

plan of our choice is the best plan for our children?" See E. Glenadine Gibb, "Do You Have a Mathematics Program?" *The Arithmetic Teacher,* XII, No. 1 (January, 1965), p. 4. What is meant by a *program* in mathematics for the elementary school?

6. In a study of weather and climate, sixth graders have discovered that climatic conditions are affected by latitude, ocean currents, prevailing winds, bodies of water, elevation, and land barriers. The following diagram should challenge the child's ability to apply knowledge acquired during the study. What discoveries and implications should a child make from this diagram?

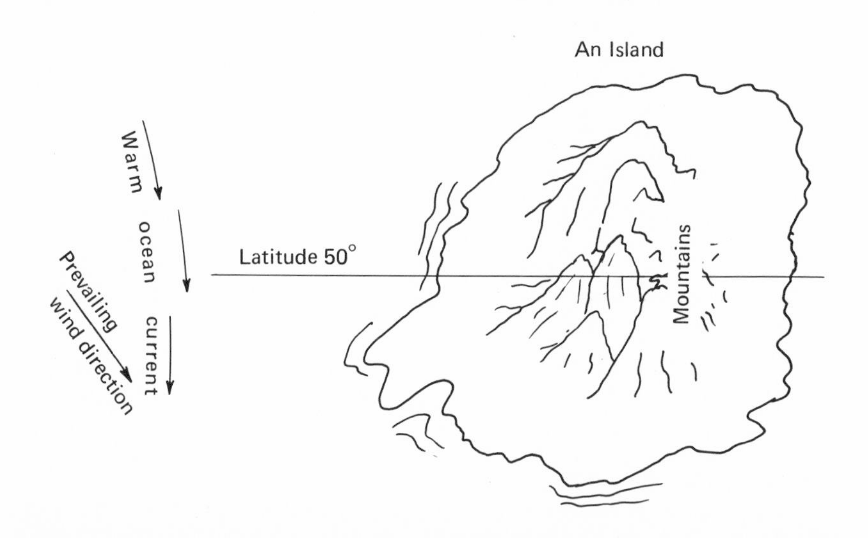

7. Every science teacher should be striving continually to provide his classes with an enriched program of science teaching. Enrichment not only involves the augmentation of course content but also makes use of resources which are readily available. An example: The demonstration has always been a basic component of good science teaching. It presents many opportunities for uses beyond its traditional role, yet sometimes despite proper planning the demonstration does not work as expected. When this occurs, how can the teacher turn the situation into a child's research problem?

8. Teaching science as a process of inquiry depends upon the teacher's ability to develop problem solving skills. Bruner prefers to study problem solving through broad concepts which include hypothetical mode, an organized method of investigation, and intrinsic motivation. Can you construct or set up a broad concept in science which children might study using Bruner's process?

9. These references will give you further insight into the areas of science and mathematics for the elementary school.

a. Paul Kambly and John Suttle, *Teaching Elementary School Science—Methods and Resources* (New York: The Ronald Press Co., 1963), 502 pp. This text helps teachers learn about the value of science in the lives of children and shows how science content and activities may be organized and taught to achieve these values.

b. Ward Bouwsma, Clyde Corle, and Davis Clemson, *Basic Mathematics for Elementary Teachers* (New York: The Ronald Press Co., 1967), 342 pp. The unifying theme of the book is the repeated extension of the universal set of numbers with particular stress laid upon the preservation of the basic laws of arithmetic with each extension.
c. Foster E. Grossnickle, Leo J. Brueckner, and John Reckzeh, *Discovering Meanings in Elementary School Mathematics*, 5th edition (New York: Holt, Rinehart & Winston, Inc., 1968), 458 pp. This book explains how modern mathematics has reached a state of equilibrium and presents a mathematics program that has been tested in a number of elementary schools throughout the country.
d. Oklahoma State Department of Education, State Science Committee, *The Improvement of Science Instruction in Oklahoma Grades K–6* (Oklahoma City: State Department of Education, 1968), 83 pp. This report presents model science lessons for the kindergarten through the sixth grade. Also included is an excellent bibliography pertinent to elementary school science.
e. John W. Renner and William B. Ragan, *Teaching Science in the Elementary School* (New York: Harper & Row, Inc., 1968), 349 pp. The authors emphasize the process approach to science education in the elementary school by drawing upon examples of leading scientists as well as explaining the major objectives of science education in elementary schools.
f. Richard W. Copeland, *How Children Learn Mathematics: Teaching Implications of Piaget's Research* (New York: The Macmillan Co., 1970), 352 pp. This publication places an emphasis on the way in which children learn mathematics and how understanding is developed.
g. Edward Victor, *Science for the Elementary School*, 2nd edition (New York: The Macmillan Co., 1970), 800 pp. This major book describes the changes taking place in elementary science education as a result of the new programs developed by large-scale curriculum projects.

15

Fine and Applied Arts

EXPERIENCING THROUGH THE ARTS

Men through all time have experienced music, pictures, dance, and the theatre. Of course, different people in different times have used them for varying purposes and in varying ways. The arts offer a unique contribution to the social heritage of which children are a part. Any educational program which neglects the study and experiencing of the arts is deficient. The arts are a basic part of a good school curriculum.

The real structure of the arts is to be found in the experiences not apparent to you with which children deal in a highly individualized manner. It is your responsibility to help children derive coherence from a series of experiences in the arts. You cannot tell children to "create something." They should be made aware of experiences upon which they can draw with assurance as they create.

In the elementary grades, the sensitive teacher may discover children's common experiences and general interests which can be used in the arts. The activity should be sufficiently open ended to satisfy all degrees of individual differences.

Thus the common objective of the arts in the elementary school is to help the child to understand his creative self and experience the creative work of others. He should have the opportunity to form aesthetic judgments by learning to appreciate creativity in the arts, through becoming sensitive to aesthetic form, and by sharpening his perceptions of what is seen and heard. This aesthetic judgment will be heightened through a knowledge of the art forms which have enriched and advanced our civilization. You can be the catalyst in attaining this objective. In music, for example, you can secure control, morale, and an inner beat of enthusiasm, as well as creativity. An orchestra, a chorus, or a band is its own argument for creativity; the beauty of a performance is its own lecture on appreciation.

The arts are essential in the total development of the child. They can contribute to the coordination of the entire curriculum. Music, art, the dance, and play acting are as pertinent to the social studies and the language arts as are dates to history. The arts gain strength through integration with the total school curriculum. Their aesthetic principles are pertinent to every program. They contribute to all curriculum areas and yet simultaneously are distinct curriculum areas in their own right. The arts develop the child's humane capacities and help him to attain tranquility and self-actualization.

CONTENT AND METHOD IN MUSIC

Music presents a multiplicity of interesting activities for children in the elementary school. The nature of music is so kaleidoscopic and so filled with varied experiences that every child should find enjoyment through singing, playing, creating, or listening to music or rhythms.

What are the varied functions of music in the elementary school program? Several factors should be considered:

Music should give the child aesthetic appreciation. Music should be taught for its unique aesthetic and spiritual values. The child in the elementary school is capable of responding to beauty and can experience this kind of revelation through an understanding and love of music.

Music should be integrated with other subjects. Music can enrich other parts of the curriculum just as these areas can contribute to the music program. Teaching primary counting songs with finger play can be as important to the arithmetic readiness program as it is to building a musical vocabulary of sound patterns. However, enriching other areas of the curriculum should be a secondary objective. The child should recognize and admit music for its own sake first.

A good music program should develop skills, understandings, attitudes, and appreciations. These will enable the child to realize the ultimate values and abundant richness which music offers. Only through such development can the child secure satisfaction and appreciation of high quality music performed with excellence. Also, through folk music children can learn what people are like.

The music materials selected should be of high quality. Children's musical tastes should be guided carefully, not followed uncritically. Material selected must be of intrinsic, aesthetic worth. Choosing good material is not enough. It must then be presented in that manner which will emphasize its artistic meaning and beauty. The melodic line and the parts, if any, should be taught accurately. The rhythmic structure must be performed according to the intentions of the composer. Attention to the phrase, the dynamics, and the expressive qualities of the work are essential for a truly satisfying musical experience. Material used for listening should also be carefully chosen; for example, records that are of poor quality or that have been played too many times have no fidelity.

The program should stimulate creativity. To be effective, the music program should give ample opportunity for the development of creative capacity. As the child's musical background is broadened—through singing, expressive bodily movement, listening, and music reading—he can gain the necessary facility to crystallize his emotions and feelings into the medium of sound. As this facility grows, his sensitivity to music and its values will increase.

The teacher should be qualified in music. You should be sensitive to music and anxious to bring its rich treasures to children. Unless you have enough facility and understanding to feel confident and competent in the teaching of music, the results of your teaching may be musically sterile. The music lesson should be carefully planned. To have the children select favorite songs merely to fill the class period will not develop an adequate appreciation for music.

Help children secure the popular music of the day. This may be done through television, radio, movies, stage plays, and numerous recording devices. They are surrounded by musical stimuli which present many opportunities for teaching outside the regular music classes directed by a special music teacher. An example is the delightful tunes which children can sing for themselves, for fun and recreation, and for the pure rhythm and physical movement which the music gives. There should be many situations during the day when a song for fun and relaxation would be most appropriate and suitable. Such experiences may contribute much to group cohesiveness.

The child is aware of the new music. Jazz has changed the rhythmic interpretation and dimension of music. The child can sing the TV commercials; he has a collection of the latest popular hits. These should not be excluded from the music program. Perhaps the aesthetic needs of today's child cannot be satisfied unless it has a jazz ingredient because there is a certain excitement from jazz music that has never been known in music before. The child should understand that jazz is the black man's contribution to American music.

He should listen to and sing the black man's folk music as well as that of the colonist and the western pioneer. He should be given the opportunity to hear appropriate symphonies and operas. He will participate in "rock and roll" and those songs which have a natural rhythm and cadence for him. He will sing with relish; he will use those rhythm or musical instruments suited to his maturity and ability with glee if he feels an empathy with a need for that music.

There is no society anywhere that functions without music. There is no child anywhere that cannot participate in some type of music.

Singing in the Classroom

Singing should be the basic activity in any comprehensive music program.[1] It is a kind of expression that is close to the personal interests and experiences of children. Songs should be taught to younger children by rote. A mood for a song can be created through stories, poems, and pictures and then the entire song can be sung. You should go through the song phrase by phrase, singing each phrase alone and then having the children sing it with you. It is possible to use records to introduce songs to children; often the music series have correlated records for each grade level. Using pitch pipes and pianos, where available, can be useful in introducing children to new songs.

When children can read words, they should sing a variety of songs and develop their sense of rhythm. They can be taught to read notes, to sight read songs, to sing, and to understand musical terminology. To help children to reproduce certain intervals which appear frequently in songs, these familiar tunes might be introduced as examples:

"Yankee Doodle"—begins with a fourth.

"Twinkle, Twinkle, Little Star"—begins with a fifth.

"My Bonnie Lies Over the Ocean"—begins with a sixth.

To help children sing with open throats, you can instruct the class to yawn and then sing "ah, oh, ee" on each scale as they slowly move up the scale from middle C to an octave above it. When the children express an interest, you can teach key and time signatures and other musical grammar. Phonograph records can now be purchased which provide model interpretations of the songs to be taught.

Listening to Music

A second objective of the music program is to develop discriminating listeners of music. Listening involves skills which can be developed by carefully guided classroom activities through which children hear and respond to both recorded and live music. To be a good singer, to play in an ensemble, to express rhythm through bodily movement, or to understand the subtle beauties of music, it is necessary to be able to hear

[1] Lilla Belle Pitts *et al.*, *Guide and Teaching Suggestions, Our Singing World Series* (Boston: Ginn & Co., 1952), p. 3.

accurately. You should give careful attention to listening in any instructional program in music.

When using a record, it is important for you to have a discussion preceding and following the listening period. No distracting activity (such as reading or handwork) should be permitted during the listening period. Certain physical factors are conducive to good listening—the record player should be in a proper position, room temperature and lighting should be appropriate, and there should be no competing noises or interest-catching articles on desks.

A necessary listening vocabulary should be gradually acquired by children. New words, both descriptive and musical, should be discussed and explained. You can "set the stage" by relating certain aspects to the general mood or type of music. If Sibelius' "Swan of Tuonela" is presented to a sixth grade class, the lighting could be darkened in keeping with the somber mood of the music. A picture of the dark waters of northern Finland might occupy a central location, and the teacher's voice and facial expression could match the solemn overtones of this legend of the ancient past.[2]

Many classrooms have music corners. A phonograph without an automatic changer can be adapted to provide earphones. Individual children thus can listen to a recorder without disturbing other members of the class.

Playing Instruments

Instrumental activity can provide musical learning and understanding beyond the use of the singing voice. Children can become sensitized to the different sound qualities and mood possibilities of melody and percussion instruments. They can use instruments wherever appropriate to enrich other classroom musical endeavors.

A satisfactory music program in the elementary school should include using classroom percussion, melody, and harmony instruments for song accompaniments; creating melodies with rhythmic interpretations and dramatizations; and exploring tonal and rhythmic relationships. Useful instruments include drums of various kinds, castanets, maracas, triangles, sleigh bells, autoharps, resonator bells, and song flutes.

Simple drums can be made from large coffee cans. After both ends are removed, they can be covered with inner tube rubber or linen coated heavily with shellac. The drumheads can be held in place with twine or cord. Short pieces of doweling can serve as drumsticks. The ends of

[2] Robert E. Nye and Vernice T. Nye, *Music in the Elementary School* (Englewood Cliffs, N.J.: Prentice-Hall, Inc., 1964), p. 248.

the drumsticks can be padded with cloth to secure different effects quite pleasing to primary school children. Other examples are the following:

1. Gourds make good rattles. Boxes or jars in which beans are placed can also be made into attractive rattles.
2. Doweling or broomsticks are an easy type of rhythm instrument to make.
3. Bells can be sewn on wide bands of cloth or elastic.
4. Tubes from paper supplies or combs covered with waxed paper allow the child to produce an interesting effect by humming directly against the paper.
5. Suspended pieces of pipe, metal rods, or large spikes can serve as triangles.

Your responsibility as the classroom teacher is to help the child recognize various musical instruments plus the four major classifications of strings, woodwinds, brasses, and percussions. You may not have the skill to teach children how to play particular instruments, but other members of the school staff or audiovisual aids could supplement your background.

CONTENT AND METHOD IN ART

When we speak of art, we may be thinking of a single object or a creative experience. We may, in fact, be considering the entire process of creation. Art for the child might be both product and process. It might be best to use the term "creative activity" instead of "art" for a program with children. Art is a process of creative activities for children in which a product is the result or record of the experience.[3]

The school should be responsible for developing the child's potential creativity and should provide the conditions which foster such development. Materials and facilities should be available to give the child opportunities to try his ability in a variety of activities and repeat with some regularity those that are of special interest to him. The teacher should also be sufficiently sensitive to guide, suggest, evaluate, and encourage the child. The teacher can create an environment that provides opportunity for creative activity in art. Children are curious by nature, and this curiosity is the food of creativity. It is restrictive for the child to have the art lesson begin with the instructions: "Now, don't make any mistakes. Don't soil your tables. Don't spill the paints. Don't cut your fingers."

[3] Phil H. Rueschhoff and M. Evelyn Swartz, *Teaching Art in the Elementary School—Enhancing Visual Perception* (New York: The Ronald Press Co., 1969).

A Child's View of Art

Even with the finest instruction in procedures, art for the child who has nothing to express becomes a meaningless, mechanical experience. In art the child can organize his thoughts, ideas, feelings, actions, and techniques into a product. If the experience or motivation is shallow, the ideas vague, the feelings diffuse or absent, the product will reflect it. The art product is the record of the complete process. It is through the vehicle of the creative arts that a child can express, freely and openly, his innermost thoughts and feelings.

With the very young child the process is more important than the product. The kindergarten and first grade child may pound out balls or coils of clay day after day before he finally joins them into very simple figure concepts. It is through this repetition that the child gains the sureness of achievement necessary for growth of confidence. The child learns art through experiencing, and hence it is unwise to place undue emphasis on the product as such. The emphasis should be on the process of creating. As the child grows older, the product continually gains in importance.

Childhood is a period when imagination is unfettered. Art activities serve as a wholesome outlet for the many fantasies of children. Children need to have time to wonder, ponder, dream, and experience a positive outlet for their imaginations. To teach art effectively then, you should not only teach procedures but also search for problems calling for personal solutions by children.

Art activities should be creative. Each art project should allow children to think originally and to learn to work independently. To be creative, children should be able to work freely and flexibly, and should be encouraged to attack each problem without the fear of failure. This freedom must be carefully preserved. Both teacher and children should be willing to work toward fresh approaches.

Art should allow the opportunity for growth. Art activities can develop the children's aesthetic abilities. He can have an increasing sensitivity to the organization of ideas and feelings by means of materials, form, color, and texture. Through aesthetic growth, the child will be able to integrate his thinking, feeling, and perceiving into a more harmonious organization.

The art program should allow the opportunities for problem solving. The art project should be given only enough direction by the teacher to assure some measure of success for even the less able child. It must have an "open end" which will provide those conditions by which the child can discover things for himself. He must have the full opportunity to develop his own technique and express himself in an individual manner.

If a craft project is a good one, it quickly "takes over" and demands to be completed in its own way.

The child should be an active participant in a good art program. This does not mean that you should hand out materials and then leave the children to "create" out of a vacuum. You should establish a wholesome climate for creative work, provide good motivation, introduce sufficient orderly procedures to insure good basic foundations on which to work, and then allow the children to use their own ideas for the development of the project. The children should work independently until they reach their own stopping points. Their thinking then should be stimulated to reach a new level of attainment. Children can be helped to value their own ideas by putting them into action. Both teacher and children should learn to value ideas in art which differ from their own. Each piece of art work should be viewed in the context in which it is made: Has this child made a gain? Does this show growth? Is it spontaneous? Is it personal? Is it skillful?

The art program should not be standardized. Each teacher and each school has its own peculiar set of assets and liabilities that affects the arts program. A total art experience starts with a child's idea and develops it into a tangible form. To begin, the teacher needs only the desire for a good program and the barest amount of materials. These materials might be scrap if there is no other source. The child can supply ideas and develop his own techniques.

Art can serve as a link to the past. History can be reconstructed through crafts. In every land and in every period of history, man has worked with clay, fibers, wood, paint, stone, and metal—the same materials with which we work today. Art forms can tell us a great deal about a people. The child should be encouraged to create in the spirit of his times and with the materials of his culture. He can also come to appreciate and secure meaning from great masterpieces out of the past.

An art program has an important function in the school curriculum. An art project should allow the child an opportunity to feel fulfilled. He needs first to conceive an idea and then carry it through to completion. A good arts program allows the child to combine his own ideas with materials, using tools that respond to his will and skill, and creating in tangible form a fresh combination of acts and ideas. This complete involvement with a creative activity helps the child to know himself.

There are three main sources for an art program: nature, function, and material. Nature is not to be copied, but children should have frequent experiences in finding, handling, and sharing their own increasing sensitivity. The interpretation of nature is a primary source of art material. A second source of art is function, which dictates the shape and form an art object is to take. If the art form is a basket, it must be usable for carrying objects; if it is a bowl, it must be suitable for holding water. Finally, there is the material to be worked with. Clay or drawing paper, paints or crayons—each imposes its own limitations on the art activity. The final use of these sources will depend upon the degree of the child's imagination.

It is wise to remember that a relatively small number of children in the classroom will develop into creative and productive *artists,* but all of them should be consumers of art. Everyone is called upon daily to distinguish between good and bad art in clothing, in home furnishings, in cars, in buildings. An effective art program can help to improve the aesthetic taste of art education.

Children should be exposed to tasteful art work—both ancient and modern—which can help them grow in their aesthetic understanding and assist them to redirect their own creative efforts.

Stages of Artistic Growth

Many believe that self-expression in art develops in a general sequential pattern. Lowenfeld has defined the developmental levels of self-expression as: (a) scribbling stages (two to four years), (b) preschematic stage (four to seven years), (c) schematic years (seven to nine years), (d) the stage of dawning realism (nine to eleven years), (e) the pseudo-realistic stage (11 to 13 years), and (f) the period of decision (adolescence).[4] However, D'Amico warns:

> No one would deny the importance of the psychological growth of the individual in the art process, such as the age level characteristics or the particular schema. These general characteristics were originally intended to help us understand the nature of the chilid. Unfortunately, in recent years, they have been misused to classify children according to age level patterns and put them into so many nice pigeonholes—we are confronted with a new and dangerous stereotype: the schematic child! General characteristics should serve only to help us discover the uniqueness in individuals.[5]

You will find children in your classroom in all stages of art development. Thus creative activities should harmonize with each particular child's development. In decorating a classroom for autumn, some children can glue bright leaves on black construction paper. Then cutting a narrow strip around each leaf, black will show around the leaf. These leaves might be scattered on a bulletin board. Another child might arrange brightly colored leaves between two layers of waxed paper which

[4] Viktor Lowenfeld, *Creative and Mental Growth,* Third Edition (New York: The Macmillan Co., 1957), pp. 86–87.

[5] Victor D'Amico, "Coming Events Cast Shadows," *School Arts,* LXXXVIII, No. 4 (September, 1958), p. 11.

are then pressed between newspapers with a warm iron to cause the sheets of waxed paper to adhere to the leaves and to each other. These translucent leaves can be cut out—leaving a wide margin of waxed paper —and hung as mobiles. Some children might compose a collage depicting autumn leaves. Another group might illustrate an autumn scene done in crayon covered by a wash of thin tempera. The creative activities are focused on a central theme, but the method of creativity is adapted to each individual child.

A good art activity is evaluated not by the product but by criteria such as the following:

1. The creative experiences provide an emotional outlet for the child.
2. The child gains some satisfaction from his art work.
3. He grows in ability to evaluate his own work.
4. He can use and accept the criticisms of others.
5. He tries to express things in his own way.
6. He engages in art activities on his own initiative.[6]

CONTENT AND METHOD IN DRAMATIC PLAY

Children in the elementary school can enjoy emotional release through dramatic expression. They often organize their experiences in dramatic play by "living through" the adult life they see going on about them. After an excursion, a child becomes a fireman as he manipulates a homemade fire engine. In the doll corner, children can re-enact family life and conversation. Children can enjoy acting out a familiar story, using spontaneous conversation. Dramatic play can build spontaneity, freedom, and power in creative expression.

Setting the Stage for Drama

You can set the stage for dramatic play. You can read aloud a great deal and you can urge children who read well to read to the group. In addition, you can encourage responses in sketching, painting, singing, and rhythmic activities. You can bring puppets into the classroom, talk about them, and then place them in some secluded spot in the classroom where a few children may experiment with them without an audience. You may find that puppets contain some magic ingredient for releasing the child's inhibitions in dramatics. A child often forgets his own inadequacy as he manipulates a lifelike puppet.

The children may first dramatize with puppets an incident in some beloved and familiar story, using parts that they have written and worked

[6] William B. Ragan, *Teaching America's Children* (New York: Holt, Rinehart & Winston, Inc., 1961), p. 219.

out. You might suggest that it would be easier to manage a hand puppet if the script is made up "as we go along." The children may notice how much greater freedom, zest, and spontaneity the play has. Sometimes a child will secure so much pleasure from making a simple puppet of Batman or of a bandit that he will create quite a different personality for his product when he uses it in a play. It is good to have a few nameless puppets which can be used for many different characters in a dramatic play.

You may find two or three children in your classroom with the initiative, ideas, and enthusiasm to spark creative dramatics. You should give tactful, casual support to these children. Their first attempts at dramatization may be weak in plot and poor in characterization, but they are worth encouraging. It is a single step from puppetry to playing a part in a real dramatic situation.

Procedures in Creative Drama

There are some procedures to follow in developing creative drama with children:

1. Start in a non-methodical fashion at the beginning of a story and plan it through to the end. Time sequence can be arranged later. Begin at a point of exciting action or high enthusiasm. Encourage new ideas for characterization. Avoid negative criticisms.

2. Have the children repeat particular scenes after asking for suggestions on innovations. With such a procedure, scenes leading up to these exciting ones can then be planned. Encourage discussion as to whether the plot is clear and understandable. Now the children in the group can be left on their own to work on the dialogue and the business of the play. Not too much time should be spent polishing the performance. Props should be kept to a bare minimum.

3. Prepare other children in the class to enjoy the production. You could suggest that some children might want to play some of the characters the second time the play is performed. There should be a short class discussion after the play to focus on understanding the personality of a character. The emphasis should be on enjoying the play rather than on talking about it. Through dramatic play you can encourage children's naturalness and inventiveness. Too much discussion may dampen their priceless spontaneity.

4. Encourage children to fashion a play from some appropriate, familiar story or to make one up from their own ideas. They can try it out once or twice within a small group, and then enjoy it with the class as an audience. Several groups may be working on different plays, yet only one might ever reach a completion acceptable in a successful audi-

torium production. It is far better to spend time in creating new plays than in making elaborate preparations for a school assembly or parents'-night performance.

5. Encourage spontaneous dramatic play. Such play gives evidence of children's concepts of social conduct.[7] Their free conversation in dramatization can be more revealing than teacher-made tests. Social understandings and ideas of social behavior manifest themselves more clearly in unsupervised dramatics than under directed teacher effort. If you observe intelligently, you will notice pupil leaders, and you will soon learn children's own social group configurations. Innumerable clues for appraising and guiding social behavior can become apparent in the releasing atmosphere provided by free dramatic play.

6. Allow children to forget themselves and concentrate on the topics at hand. This may be the main value of dramatic play. They should organize their thinking about a given topic, keep others in mind and relate behavior to them and put themselves in the positions of others and think and act accordingly. They should think of reasons for their actions, speech, and manners.

Cross and Cypher state:

> We want students who are able to read between the lines of the printed page. Who can discriminate between the picture sequences of a film or filmstrip. Dramatizations and discussions help in this respect, for they literally project the student into the situation—he is not accepting a message from the page of a book or the projection screen; he is part of an actual experience which has real meaning to him.[8]

Dramatization then must be used with discretion as the need arises.

Children dramatize many things that catch their fancy. In such dramatization they discover needs and meet difficulties and they gain an understanding of the world into which they are growing. As an art, dramatic play has a place in the curriculum. Illustrations of dramatic play are noted below.

1. Primary children can have fun with finger stories. You should first tell the story to the class with the finger actions and then have the children help you to relate it. On another day tell the same story once or twice to enable the children to become acquainted with it gradually. Add other stories as the class displays its readiness.

2. Role playing is another type of dramatic play. Several children could select assigned roles in a given situation. The situation could be described, the roles assigned, the action and script developed as the par-

[7] For a discussion of creative dramatics see Isabel B. Burger, *Creative Play Acting—Learning through Drama,* Second Edition (New York: The Ronald Press Co., 1966).

[8] A. J. Foy Cross and Irene F. Cypher, *Audio-Visual Education* (New York: Thomas Y Crowell Co., 1961), p. 235.

ticipants believe the persons involved in the situation might react. Here is an illustrative situation which might be role played: Mr. and Mrs. Smith have returned from shopping to find they have misplaced the house keys.

3. Scenes from popular television programs might be dramatized. Be sure that all the children know the program which is to be used. Have some children describe the action of the story. Rotate the roles in the program and add parts to permit many children to participate. No scripts should be prepared in written form. The dialogue can simply develop as children explore the story and work with it orally. It is unimportant if a speech varies slightly every time it is given; the significant thing is that the story action moves.

CONTENT AND METHOD IN APPLIED ART

Industrial arts is the common terminology used to refer to applied art. It interprets our industrial world to today's boys and girls but its use is not limited to hobby or vocational craft shops. The objective of applied art is to interest youngsters in learning more about the technological world that surrounds them—its processes, problems, materials, and organization. In many schools children work on individual and group projects with materials and tools of industry in laboratory situations, discover their own abilities and interests, and develop problem-solving skills. As they do so, their core-type learnings cut across many subject matter boundaries, for example, science, social studies, and English. Some classes have even organized corporations, sold stock, and produced inexpensive items to sell to other students. In this way, boys and girls can participate in the various functions of a modern industrial society.

Some leaders in the applied arts field are attempting to minimize the individual type of project activities such as carving leather or making bookends. As the only method of teaching the individual project is too slow and too narrow in its approach. The construction of metal or wood products in themselves does not give children the depth of skill necessary to understand our industrial society. Motor activity in an applied arts program is important; but group projects, unit work, and experimentation in addition to the individual project method enable children to learn more and to learn how to work faster with tools and their hands.

For some children the ability to use materials well and to create acceptable or outstanding results with their hands can give a feeling of satisfaction that may not be possible in other branches of learning. The personal gratification derived from work done to the best of one's ability that has been evaluated carefully often leads to the improvement of general work habits and work standards.

Applied arts should not be considered as an isolated subject, but rather as one that contributes to many areas of experience which in turn are conducive to the growth and development of children. Social studies, play experiences, seasonal interests, a creative urge, or the challenge of environment provide many opportunities for use of manipulative skills and practices.

Knowledge and Skills in Primary Grades

Applied arts for the primary grades might be structured to provide the following capabilities and facts:

What the child should be able to do:

1. Mark pencil line at right angles to straight edge, using try square.
2. Clamp wood to sawhorse with "C" clamp.
3. Saw wood across the grain.
4. Saw wood with the grain.
5. Saw small pieces of wood with backsaw, using mitre box.
6. Saw dowel with backsaw, using mitre box.
7. Bore holes in wood with brace and dowel bit.
8. File curved edges with half-round cabinet file.
9. Drive nails with claw hammer.
10. File edges and ends.
11. Smooth surfaces with sandpaper on a block.
12. Put tools into proper places after work.
13. Apply water paint with brush.
14. Apply shellac over water paint.
15. Clean paint brush after using.
16. Measure in even inches with a rule.
17. Clean file with file card.
18. Drill holes with hand drill.
19. Saw inside openings with key hole saw.
20. Draw nail with claw hammer, using block under claw.

What the child should know:

1. Why it is safe to use the "C" clamp with the lead screw below the work.
2. The importance of keeping hands away from saw teeth.
3. The reason for using a small wooden block when starting a saw cut.
4. The correct position in which to stand out when starting a saw cut.
5. How to use the hammer without injury to self or others.
6. How to clean up after work, using brush, broom, and dustpan.
7. The reason for always keeping the handle on the file for utility and safety.
8. Why it is best to file with the grain.
9. How to select proper size nails for fastening material together.
10. The names of 12 hand tools used.
11. How shellac is thinned with denatured alcohol.
12. How to use a nail in place of a drill for drilling small holes.
13. How to start cuts with keyhole saw by boring holes with brace and dowel bit.
14. How to prevent splitting when the spur of the dowel bit goes through the wood.
15. Why a block is used under the claw hammer head when drawing nails.
16. How to distinguish between brads, finishing nails, and box nails.[9]

[9] Adapted from E. L. Kurth, "Industrial Arts in the Elementary School," *The Industrial Arts Teacher,* XVIII, No. 6 (November–December, 1958), pp. 8–13.

One kindergarten class, through a picture book story, became interested in trains.[10] Few of these children had traveled by train or were ever close to one and so a trip was planned to the nearest railroad station. Returning to the classroom, the children decided to make a train constructed from paper and wood. They built a cab and a coal car of wooden crates for the engineer and fireman, a wooden throttle (fastened so it would move), a cardboard smokestack, and a bell that could be rung by pulling a rope attached to a wooden standard. The children nailed boards together as frames for three railroad cars and they cut windows in the completed cars. They correctly used such words as piston rod, throttle, engine coal car, and passenger cars. Strangely, the children did not play in this train nor take imaginary trips, as they had done on a boat built previously. They did play constantly with the engine and its working parts.

In another school, a group of second grade children studying foods brought so many vegetables to school that they had no place to store or exhibit them and so they decided to build shelves for the vegetables and organize a vegetable market. They brought boards and nails and used a yardstick, try square, saw, and hammer in learning to measure, mark off, saw, and make the shelves the same size. When the vegetables began to spoil, the children decided to cook them and eat them. They borrowed an electric stove, a big kettle, some cups, and spoons, and they made and served vegetable soup. To replenish the vegetable market, they constructed some artificial vegetables from papier-mâché. Some of the children painted a mural that showed foods arriving for their homes by plane, train, boat, wagon, truck, and automobile. Other children made booklets in which they pasted colorful arrangements of pictures of vegetables that were cut from magazines and catalogs. Under each picture the correct spelling for each vegetable was lettered.

The applied arts in the primary grades should be integrated into large learning situations thereby clarifying concepts and contributing to general knowledge and skills.

Enrichment for Older Children

In grades four, five, and six the applied arts can enrich the entire curriculum structure. In the fourth grade the following activities might be appropriate for particular subject areas.

In the language arts, the child might visit a local theater and examine the projector room as well as the stage. He might make scenery and props for plays, design and construct book covers, and make "movie"

[10] "Let's Make It" (Albany: The University of the State of New York, Bureau of Elementary Curriculum Development, 1958), p. 28.

boxes and puppets. In social studies, the child can construct dioramas, models, and maps of those communities he is studying. He can visit a lumberyard to study the various types of lumber. He might lay out and construct model roads, bridges, canals, and airports. Casting bricks of clay, plaster, cement, and building walls of many materials is an excellent experience.

Mathematics and science offer many opportunities for experiences in the applied arts. Advanced abaci can be constructed. The child can concentrate on accuracy in measurement. Graphs on materials production can be drawn, and devices can be made to show a square, circle, rectangle, and triangle. For science, display boxes can be made for rocks, seeds, insects, and minerals. The construction of telegraph sets and model volcanoes in relief are appropriate activities. The child can plant seeds, experiment with the strength of various building materials, and make paper. He might test soils and experiment with the use of fertilizers.

In the fine arts, the fourth grader can weave with textiles and reed and use linoleum blocks for printing. He can make holiday gifts, dye materials, and make candles and wax tablets and scrapbook covers. Presenting puppet shows with homemade puppets and stages and using Indian designs for bracelets, conch belts, medallions, and so forth can be valuable applied arts experiences. Constructing model and life-size totem poles, darning socks, and pressing clothing, as well as using coils and slabs in making pottery, are also valuable. The child can visit a jeweler at work.

To enrich the area of health and safety, the child might repair bicycles or make a first aid kit, stilts, aprons, and smocks. He could record the weights and heights of class members.

The following activities in the applied arts are suitable for the child in the fifth grade. In the language arts the child could make pigeon-hole mailboxes, use the school office duplicating machine, construct scenery and props for dramatics, make book shelves and bookends, use recording machines, and read about industries and industrial processes.

The social studies offers a fertile field for the applied arts. Contour maps of the United States and other countries and models of oil fields, coal mines, or lumber camps are suitable activities. The child could display various types of wood and pictorialize their uses; he could make a relief map of the United States illustrating its products and rivers. Visiting a print shop, collecting and testing building materials, and constructing models to show conservation of land are appropriate. The child can collect and draw pictures of clothing styles, make flags and holders, assemble a diorama of frontier life, and collect and compare textile samples as well as test minerals for chemical makeup.

For industrial arts experiences in mathematics, children might make scale drawings of homes and classroom and construct advanced abaci for decimals. They could visit the office of an architect or engineer and observe how materials are measured with a good deal of accuracy.

In science, the construction of models to show erosion or the cross section of the earth are sound learning experiences. Children can wire bells; build models of dams and reservoirs; fly homemade model gliders; and build a simple apparatus for levers, gears, and inclined planes. They can collect and mount specimens of rocks and soils. They can graft plants and experiment with the strength of textile materials.

The fine arts too, for the fifth grader, can be a rich reservoir of allied activities in the applied arts. Children can make a quilting frame and a patchwork quilt. They can embroider samples, make frames, and work with various other media typical of our country's craft work. Fifth grade children can learn to mend clothing, make camping equipment, and fire and glaze clay work. They might visit a cabinetmaker and learn to make reproductions of boats, planes, and cars.

For the fifth grade child health and safety activities pertinent to applied arts might be building traffic signs for bicycle safety programs, repairing bicycles, and making home plates, bases, and hat stands. Children could experiment with methods of food cooking and preservation. They could make first-aid kits and shoe-shine boxes. In the proper season building a snowball target can be useful as well as preventive!

Children in the sixth grade can compile a school newspaper. They can construct magazine racks and book carts for the school library. They can build scenery and props for class productions as well as design and make scrapbook covers. Sixth grade children can learn to operate a movie projector. They can read about industries and industrial processes.

In social studies, the children can make relief maps showing land formations. They can assemble dioramas of rice fields, jungles, and harbors. It is possible for them to reproduce significant inventions. They might operate a model of canal locks and make hunting, fishing, and trapping devices. Charting industries of states and the making of commerce charts are appropriate activities. The children can learn a great deal from visiting a newspaper plant and governmental offices.

Sixth grade mathematics is easily integrated into the applied arts. Children might design dream houses and learn to read scale drawings and plans. They could construct a decimal divider and a balance scale to weight materials. Making circular and linear fraction boards is good experience.

For science, the child can make a weather vane, anemometer, and rain gauge. Constructing crystal radio sets and developing photographic film are suitable activities. He can visit a telegraph office or a photo studio. Constructing an ant observatory, designing machines to illustrate levers, and experimenting with models of aircraft control surfaces such as rudder, aileron, and elevator are activities directly related to the industrial arts. The child can make electromagnets and electrical quiz boards in studying electricity and rocket ship models in studying the atmosphere.

In the area of the fine arts, sixth grade children might embroider samplers, construct service equipment for lower grades, make tiles and mosaics, experiment with glazers, use linoleum blocks for printing programs for school plays, and print with silk screen and stencils.

The health and safety program lends itself to such applied arts activities as conducting bicycle safety programs, drawing plans of activity areas on the playground, constructing first aid kits, and constructing batting tees.

As the child becomes involved in the above-mentioned activities, safety in the use of tools and materials should be taught constantly to insure a minimum of accidents. Correct and safe use of tools should be taught before a tool is used and at any time when there is a need for review. The handsaw causes more accidents than any other tool; teaching its safe and correct use is a continuous responsibility.

Children today need to understand, as did previous generations, how the things around them are made. They need to learn, appreciate, and value the work of skilled craftsmen. Children should learn how to manipulate materials and tools so they can satisfy their appetite to create.

Planning

Teachers know full well that wholesome learning programs for children do not just happen. While plans for elementary children must always remain flexible, in the applied arts you can nevertheless plan ahead for most of the learning experiences that should occur. You cannot give detailed directions and expect the children to carry them out, but you should think through many possibilities of approach as to how activities in the applied arts might be efficiently integrated into the unit.

Suppose a fourth grade is to make a study of neighborhood facilities. The teacher should first think of possible applied arts activities. A small group of children could construct a child size store for use in the classroom. Another group might construct a large map of the community. Each child might construct a vehicle or implement that is characteristic of some occupation.

Now the teacher must present ideas to the children and have them take an active part in the project. One approach is to lead up to a discussion by centering reading experiences around some community industries and the tools of their trade. Having children make inquiries of their parents is also helpful. Showing appropriate films will also help prepare the class. Finally, the teacher should discuss the overall plan of the study in a general way and then invite suggestions for things to make. It is unwise for the teacher to have detailed plans in mind of the projects he thinks are suitable. Many suggestions should be made by the children. Some children might decide to construct models of public buildings, stores, or factories related to the community map another group is making.

Now the work begins. Since the teacher can foresee that each child will have to use the try square, saw, hammer, file, sandpaper, and paints, he plans to give demonstrations to the entire class a little at a time and progressively as the need arises. (Most children will need advice on methods of attaching wheels on vehicles, for example.)

As the work progresses in a series of work periods, teacher and children periodically evaluate the progress made and attempt to solve some of the problems that arise. Experiences are discussed and subsequent steps planned. It must be remembered that the applied arts experiences are but a small part of this total unit on community facilities. There will be other concomitant learning experiences which have made their contributions to the total study.

A sixth grade might study regions of the world. The teacher must think about the goals he hopes to achieve. One goal might be to have the children recognize the problems of their home region and in turn contrast these with other regions of the world. One of these problems might be the production of food. Teacher and children might decide that a class luncheon, featuring dishes of other lands, would focus on food production. The class could divide into committees. One committee might consider foreign and domestic foods and the problems of their production. Another might organize a shopping trip and budget. The preparation of a menu and musical entertainment are other committee responsibilities as are table conversation and etiquette, table decoration and setting, and food preparation and freezing.

Here again the teacher equips himself with some general ideas and then proceeds to utilize films, textbooks, maps, globes, and other teaching aids in order to prepare and lead the children into discussion and planning sessions for a culminating experience which is the lunchean.

RESEARCH IN THE ARTS

In recent years much research work has been done on creativity and how it is manifested at different educational levels. Many scholars have denied the possibility that young children can do productive thinking (producing something from what is known and remembered). This misconception has led to an overemphasis upon the importance of providing a stimulating environment to the neglect of providing a responsive one, as well as to an emphasis upon recall and reproduction to the neglect of problem solving, creative thinking, and decision-making.

The confusion about the capacity of children for creative thinking has been increased by the tendency for each investigator to limit too seriously the range of his observations of creative manifestations. No single area of observation or test taps all of the child's resources for creative thinking. The same test or kind of observation may not be equally valid or adequate at all age and educational levels. The beginnings of creative thinking may be found in the manipulative, exploratory, and experimental activities of the infant as well as in his use of facial expressions and his efforts to determine meanings from the facial expressions and gestures of others.

Of the many manifestations of creativity during the elementary school years, the greatest attention has been given to creative writing and art. We are now having a renewed recognition of the value of children's writing and their art but are discovering that children can be creative in a variety of other ways which are also important. Generally, educators of the past have considered children in the elementary, and even in the high school, years to be incapable of creative scientific thought.

Assessment of Creativity

During the past 80 years or more, a variety of procedures has been developed for measuring some of the creative thinking abilities. Most of these measures have been utilized exclusively in research, and only now are tests of creative thinking abilities becoming available for use in schools. The weight of evidence seems to indicate that creative thinking is not a unitary ability but that it involves a number of abilities. Thus, attempts to develop a single index of creative thinking or a Creative Quotient should be avoided. According to the most extensive research in this field, the abilities involved are sensitivity to problems, fluency (the ability to produce a large number of ideas), flexibility (the ability to produce a variety of ideas or use a variety of approaches), originality (the ability to produce ideas that are off the beaten track), elaboration (the ability to fill in the details), and rede function (the ability to define or perceive in a way different from the usual, established, or intended way).

The variety of tasks used in assessing the creative thinking abilities at the elementary school level is great. Types of tasks include perceiving ink blots; constructing pictures from dots, circles, squares, parallel lines, incomplete figures, and shapes of colored paper; verbalizing while painting; symbolizing words by lines; designing from standardized materials; developing ideas for product improvement (for example, toys and common objects); developing consequence problems, asking, and guessing;

and guessing sounds or constructing images from sounds. Performances are usually scored for such qualities as fluency, flexibility, originality, and elaboration.

Scores derived from measures of creative thinking have little relationship to performance on intelligence tests. Investigators have consistently urged the use of both types of measures for the identification and study of intellectual talent. Recent studies have shown that if we identify as gifted those scoring in the upper 20 per cent on an intelligence test, we would eliminate about 70 per cent of those who will score in the upper 20 per cent on a measure of creativity. Unquestionably, some minimum level of intelligence is required for outstanding success of a creative nature, but this level cannot now be specified. Many research workers are convinced that cut off points at 135 I.Q. and above, used in most programs for intellectually gifted children, are too high. Several estimates place the minimal level at 120.

From the best research evidence and the observations of many investigators, it has been determined that creative imagination during early childhood seems to reach a peak between four and four and one-half years and is followed by a drop at about age five when the child enters school for the first time. Although this drop has generally been regarded as an inevitable developmental phenomenon of nature, there are now indications that this drop in five-year-olds is a man-made or culture-made phenomenon rather than a natural one.

Findings concerning the stages of creative development during the elementary years have been amazingly consistent, considering the variety of measures, samples of subjects, and periods in history involved. In the United States most of the creative thinking abilities measured by tests show growth from the first through third grades, a sharp drop at about the beginning of the fourth, a rise during the fifth and sixth, and another decline at about the beginning of the seventh grade. The rise in the fifth grade however, is primarily among girls and is in the category of fluency rather than in originality. Some investigators have found that the seventh grade decline extends into the eighth grade. Several studies involving deliberate attempts to keep creative growth alive in the fourth grade and investigations of the development of the creative abilities in cultures outside the United States suggest that the drop which occurs in the fourth grade is a man-made rather than a natural phenomenon.

The weight of research evidence seems to indicate that man fundamentally prefers to learn in creative ways—by exploring, manipulating, questioning, experimenting, risking, testing, and modifying ideas. Recent research suggests that many things can be learned more effiectively and economically in creative ways rather than by imposed ways. It also appears that many individuals who have an especially strong preference for learning creatively learn a great deal when permitted to use their creative thinking abilities but make little educational progress if they are forced to learn. Such research opens exciting possibilities for better ways of individualizing instruction.

Research also indicates that learning by authority brings into play on the part of the learner such abilities as recognition, memory, and logical reasoning—those abilities most frequently assessed by traditional tests of intelligence and scholastic aptitude. In contrast, creative learning involves such abilities as evaluation (especially the ability to sense problems, inconsistencies, and missing elements), divergent production (for example, fluency, flexibility, originality, and elaboration), and redefinition. Studies do indicate that the creative thinking abilities can be important in educational achievement.

Recently researchers have identified 50 or more dimensions of the mind, only a handful of which are included in current I.Q. tests. One attribute which has been identified concerns creativity so that perhaps we may soon be able to measure and test for creativity.

Creativity in the Arts

The arts have long been identified with creativeness, and investigations in the arts will contribute greatly to our understanding of "non-intelligence" or "non-intelligence intellectual activities," as some of these newly discovered or identified attributes of the mind are called. Many studies have indicated that success on the job and success in life are more related to the characteristics of creativity than to traditionally measured intelligence. They suggest a need to re-examine the premises upon which we build many school programs. We are securing a new and more accurate picture of the individual and the various types of giftedness which exist. Any broadening of the concept of giftedness beyond the traditional academic variety must include the arts.

There is a general trend in music education to search for a more efficient and effective method of communicating knowledge. Too, there is a specific interest in the re-examination of music as a school subject to be taught and learned. Current literature reveals a search for a core of musical content that can be accepted as common to the many areas of music education (for example, instrumental, choral, general music, appreciation, and theory classes) and that is appropriate also as a common basis for the musical learning of all segments of the school population. Andrews and Deihl have developed a Battery of Musical Concept Measures, a pioneer effort in the particular area of musical measurement for the identification of children's concepts of pitch, duration, and loudness. The authors indicate, however, that before the measures are acceptable for practical use certain revisions and refinements must be made and the measures must be standardized.

Much of the research conducted with children in the area of music relates to a particular musical aptitude or skill. However, in the area of art education research generally has been concerned with broader, more psychologically oriented aspects of aesthetic expression. Kincaid has made a good summary of such research, including several points reviewed below:

1. The young elementary school child has an innate creative imagination. He is in the process of developing new ideas or insights into known situations. This attitude is characterized by flexibility of approach in being able to redefine objects into new relationships with unique applications.
2. The child is incapable of, and insensitive to, a rational or logical approach to his art. He expresses himself freely and is unconscious as to the structural nature of his environment. His pictorial expressions are generally considered a manifestation of his imagination.
3. Every child is endowed with some degree of potential creativity, but its development into functional creativity is dependent on total environmental influences. Therefore, our schools should play an active part in the unfolding of creative, artistic ability in each individual.[11]

In a similar vein, research in the applied arts indicates that activities in this field in the elementary schools seem to make the abstract more meaningful, learning more effective, and technology better understood. Studies have shown that work-type activities provide opportunities for cooperation, problem solving, planning and evaluation, and worthwhile human relationships within the classroom. These studies also indicate that activities in the applied arts extend the child's interests and develop his talents beyond the limits imposed by mass education in a purely academic setting. They provide opportunities for one kind of creative expression and help to orient the child to his increasingly technical environment. Applied arts activities can help to make school, as well as the whole process of learning, more enjoyable. They can help the teacher to discover individual differences and deal more effectively with them.

The fine and practical arts are an important means of promoting balanced growth; they can enrich perceptions of self, others, and the environment and can provide varied experiences which will enable a child to live effectively, meaningfully, and happily. Furthermore, the arts can contribute meaning, insight, and appreciation to other curriculum areas.

[11] Clarence E. Kincaid, "The Determination and Description of Various Creative Attributes of Children," unpublished doctoral dissertation, The Pennsylvania State University, 1966, pp. 12–13.

The arts significantly add to each individual's capacity to experience the total curriculum.[12]

PROJECTS AND READINGS

1. For several years the University of Chicago Laboratory School has developed an interesting project to expose young children to reproductions of great art. With the use of this project a sense of artistic beauty might be cultivated in children and a respect for the creation of the great artist developed. The reproductions are placed between transparent plastic covers and can be passed around without damage while the teacher leads a discussion of the pictures. Some of the reproductions are large; others are the size of a post card. Some are black and white; some are colored. The collection includes paintings, drawings, prints, sculpture, mobiles, and collages. Illustrations from suitable art magazines and from art books for children and adults also are shown. These reproductions range from representational and storytelling art to the work of the cubist and abstract masters. The art of the West and the art of the Near and Far East are considered. The periods range from prehistoric times, represented by rock carvings, to the present century. What methods would you suggest for exposing the children to these masterpieces? What learnings would you anticipate?

2. If you visit the Lindsey Hopkins Education Center, a large vocational center that serves the Greater Metropolitan Area of Miami, Florida, you could observe children using teaching machines, each in a separate booth or carrel. Each child is reading a small bit of information, selecting his choice of answer, or pushing a button to find out if his choice is correct. Every child may be on a different page or frame and with the large library of programmed materials, every child could be on a different subject. Each goes at his own pace. There seems to be active participation by the child in every phase of learning. Each child is receiving individual attention. His every answer is heard, immediately corrected, and intelligently acted upon. This might be the school of the future. How can a fine arts program be correlated with such a mechanistic approach to learning and with what results?

3. One of the critical problems we are facing in this country is that we are losing respect for people who work with their hands because we have no appreciation of what is involved. Many people have the mistaken idea that laying up a brick wall is a simple thing. "You just take up the mortar and you put it on the brick and you lay it up." But such persons haven't tried putting up a brick wall! What can an applied arts program do to counteract such a trend? Why should it be reversed?

4. Viktor Lowenfeld, one of the great pioneer leaders in studying creativity in children, in his *Creative and Mental Growth* (New York: The Macmillan Co., 1947, p. 7) has stated:

> If the child expresses himself according to his own level, he becomes encouraged in his own independent thinking by expressing his own thoughts and ideas by his own means. The child who imitates

[12] For a comprehensive review of this and other topics, see Kenneth R. Beittel, "Art Education," *Review of Educational Research,* XXXVII, No. 2 (April, 1967), p. 205.

becomes dependent in his thinking, since he relies for his thoughts and expressions upon others. The independent thinking child will not only express whatever comes into his mind but will tackle any problem, emotional or mental, that he encounters in life. Thus his expression serves also as an emotional outlet.

Do you believe that the fine arts are the only form of creative activity for the child? How can creativity be nurtured in other subject areas?

5. Our country is a melting pot of peoples from a wide variety of nations who differ in racial, religious, social, and economic background. Our country is enriched because many different types of people have learned to live together in peace and harmony. It is necessary that children learn to respect and support others' rights as individuals and citizens. The individual child should receive respect and support from his peer group for activities which are sincere and worthwhile. The child also must learn to cooperate in group activities which are worthwhile. What creative activities will help the child receive an understanding of such mutual respect and understanding?

6. The first interest in construction activities concerned with applied arts may be initiated either by a child or by the teacher. It may grow out of basic content related to the grade's program in science, citizenship education, or some other phase of the program. It may be stimulated by taking a trip, viewing a film, looking at a picture book, reading a story, or listening to a radio program. A current event, a community study, or any one of many interests or happenings may stimulate activities. Select an initiating stimulation (for example, a particular story or a TV program) and indicate what construction activities in the applied arts could grow out of it.

7. To increase your understanding in the fine arts as they apply to the elementary school, examine the following sources:

a. Chandler Montgomery, *Art for Teachers of Children* (Columbus, Ohio: Charles E. Merrill Books, Inc., 1968), 200 pp. This book will introduce you to four kinds of aesthetic responses in art education: (1) Individual ventures with suitable materials to externalize one's own aesthetic experience; (2) Searching out and observing this type of aesthetic experience as it occurs in the unorganized environment; (3) Studying its purposeful transformation into works of art; (4) Reading, discussing, thinking about, and projecting extensions and applications of this kind of experience to the needs and interests of children.

b. Charles L. Gary (ed.), *The Study of Music in the Elementary School—A Conceptual Approach* (Washington, D.C.: Music Educators National Conference, 1968). This explains how a child's knowledge of music is secured through intellectual apprehension accompanied by emotional responses and technical proficiency. It is believed the conceptual approach to music brings more from experiences with music to the child's learning, and the benefits will be more appreciated and longer lasting.

c. Gordon O. Wilber and Norman C. Pendered, *Industrial Arts in General Education* (Scranton: International Textbook Co., 1967), 398 pp. This describes the objectives of the industrial arts in the elementary school and particularly how written materials, programmed instruction, overhead transparency projections, 8 mm concept film loops, and closed-circuit television can be used in the classroom to enforce and enrich the applied arts.

d. Frances Webber Aronoff, *Music and Young Children* (New York: Holt, Rinehart & Winston, Inc., 1969), 192 pp. This book presents a working model for the teacher in planning pre-verbal experiences to encourage the young child's cognitive and affective musical growth.
e. Kenneth Lansing, *Art, Artist, and Art Education* (New York: McGraw-Hill Book Co., Inc., 1969), 650 pp. This book presents the nature, purposes, and methodology of curriculum which utilizes the artist, critic, and historian as models of behavior.
f. Robert B. Smith, *Music in the Child's Education* (New York: The Ronald Press Co., 1970), 358 pp. This text offers a structured, sequential approach to presenting a comprehensive and effective music program and includes an impressive collection of songs suitable for children at every level of development.

16

Physical and Mental Health

EDUCATION FOR LEISURE

One theme that has been emphasized in this book is that changes in society are coming so fast that the teacher who is satisfied with the present school program may be left far behind within a few short years. This is an age of routines and conformities by human cogs in an industrial, political complex. It is an age of scientists, dynamic labor leaders, business tycoons, and public relations experts. It is also an epoch of uncomfortable school populations, of overfed and underactive children, of value illness, and of psychological stress contributing to ulcers, coronary heart disease, low back pain, mental disorders, and the tension syndrome. Too, it is a time which urges speed, social status, and the innumerable home and school compulsions and pressures on elementary school children to achieve high marks in the "solid" subjects to prepare for prestigious universities. Yet it is also an era with an increasing amount of free time and abundance of leisure. One of the greatest needs today is for a set of human values which will permit man to live reasonably free from unnecessary illness, stress, and pressure through a balance in work and play. Man needs to discover satisfactions both on the job and during his increasing leisure hours.

Education for leisure may be the key to achieving this balance. Leisure freely chosen and pursued can reap creative, artistic, and spiritual satisfactions which contribute to the individual's inner growth. Work alone is not enough to satisfy, nor is free time if it lacks significance. Wholeness is secured by a proper balance between work and recreation. Recreation is an attitude of mind; in practice, it becomes an outlet to creativity, both physical and spiritual. This becomes particularly true as work for many persons becomes more mechanized and routinized and ceases to be an outlet for original thinking and acting.

John Huston Finley, former editor-in-chief of the *New York Times*, speaks of the child's "rightful heritage of play." He pleads that children be given a real and full chance to play, unregimented and in harmony with their own learnings. If the "heaven of men's dreams" is to have music, poetry, art, and dancing, why not experience such joy now?

CONTENT IN PHYSICAL EDUCATION

Balance Desirable for Children

Physical education has been defined as a system of vigorous activities planned as a developmental experience for children. These activities might include small group games, circle games, simple team games, contests, individual games, and mass play. They involve running–tagging games, throwing–catching games, kicking games, striking games, relays and races, and rhythm games. Sometimes the classification of physical education activities is based on the skills which should be developed at the various levels of the child's school life.

The majority of children are fond of games and physical activities. If given the proper environment and opportunity, they will develop healthy bodies, minds, and characters. A sound mind takes pride in a physically fit body which has alertness, agility, control, balance, poise, and rhythm. No one part of the body should ever be developed at the expense of another or the body itself at the sacrifice of mind and spirit. The balance between physical and mental health is like the Greek ideal—a harmonious rhythm of life, a golden mean without excesses.

The child's joy of living should be preserved through adequate physical and mental health. To secure and maintain such health is one of the most important functions of the school curriculum and the environment it creates. There is an integrated relationship between health and education which is vital to both. For centuries wise people have been saying that a definable relationship exists between the two that makes the contribution of each an absolute necessity to the effective development of the other.

Children need to be educated to develop their physical and mental health, and they need abundant health to make full use of their education.

Health Education

It is no small undertaking to select the appropriate subject matter when planning a health education program. While much progress has been made to increase the health of Americans, new strains and new dangers make health instruction vital. Before deciding what to teach in physical education, you should ask questions pertaining to the children's needs:

1. What are their physical characteristics?
2. How might health and safety practices be integrated into various areas of the curriculum?
3. What health and safety hazards are found within the school and local community?
4. Does the school environment suggest leads for health instruction?
4. What has been learned concerning the children's health from medical examinations and screening tests?
6. What are children's particular interests that relate to health education?
7. What are the experiences and questions of other curriculum areas which pertain to health instruction?
8. What are the basic health needs with which all children must become acquainted?

Vital Topics for Grades K–6. The answers to such questions will move you away from a stereotyped curriculum which is used automatically from year to year. Health knowledge as such can mean very little; for example, many persons continue to use cigarettes in spite of warnings concerning the danger of lung cancer. People continue to overeat and in other ways endanger their health. Mere exposure to knowledge is not enough. However, the following general topics might be integrated in the grades kindergarten through six.

1. Personal cleanliness and appearance.
2. Activity, sleep, rest, and relaxation.
3. Nutrition.
4. Dental health.
5. A knowledge of body structure and operation (including ears and eyes).
6. Prevention and control of disease.
7. Safety and first aid.
8. Mental and emotional health (including alcohol, tobacco, and drugs).
9. Family life education (including sex education).
10. Community health.

An Example of Health Teaching. Such topics should stress those aspects which relate directly to the promotion and maintenance of health; for example, in teaching topic number 5 (a knowledge of body structure and operation) less attention should be paid to the names of particular bones than to the purposes they serve. Factors favorable to their growth and ways that bones facilitate body movement should also be emphasized.

Suppose health education relating to the eye is considered. It might be discussed in grade one, in grade six, and again in high school. In the first grade children could learn about the eye from the experience of having their vision tested to find out "how well they see." The simple Snellen test may be used in combination with teacher observation and children could observe how the test is conducted. They learn that if one does not see well, he should visit an eye doctor and perhaps wear glasses.

Children in the first grade can then develop desirable attitudes and habits toward eye care without knowing the scientific names for any part of the eye. They should learn that vision must be tested regularly, that physicians can help those with defective vision, and that glasses can improve such vision.

Children realize that eyes, like other parts of the body, become tired if used too long. They appreciate good light for reading, coloring, and drawing and should learn to report to parents any difficulty in seeing and any eye fatigue. Thus in the first grade desirable habits and attitudes toward the eye can be formed and reinforced.

In the sixth grade, boys and girls are usually full of questions concerning their bodies and how they function. An example is their interest in their eyes. They should be provided with books, charts, and diagrams which provide information on eyes. They could study the eye and sight by learning about light—its sources and how it travels. The study of light rays, how they are reflected and absorbed by different types of surfaces, and how their direction can be changed by such substances as water and glass could all introduce a study of the eye. The children could be introduced to lenses, convex and concave, and their effect on light rays; and they might learn how a prism affects light and how the eye perceives the color.

The sixth graders then should study the structure of the eye itself, its protective devices, the bony orbit, the eyelashes, eyelids and eyebrows, the layers of tissue over the pupil and the pupil, iris, lens retina, and optic nerves. They should learn also about the muscles of the eye.

They can explore how the eye accommodates to conditions of dim and bright light and how it focuses on objects close by and far away. They could compare the human eye to a camera, but they should learn to appreciate the superiority of the eye. Comparisons may be made between the human eye and the eyes of animals, birds, and fish. An understanding might then be secured of the various adaptations that have resulted to make eyes meet the needs of each type of animal.

Eleven- and twelve-year-olds should learn the causes of farsightedness and nearsightedness and how an oculist or optometrist can correct such defects by prescribing the proper lenses. This background on the structure and function of the eye can reinforce attitudes and habits already practiced and developed. These children should learn why eye infections develop because of unclean habits and why poor light or excessive glare results in eye fatigue.

Health education in the elementary grades should help children to develop desirable health attitudes and habits and the reasons for them. They should think for themselves and make considered judgments. Children are more likely to practice health habits if they understand and approve the reasons for them. The activities suggested for a study of eyes illustrate one of the many ways to make health study meaningful to children.

Drug abuse should be an important ingredient of health education. The elementary grades provide the first opportunity to present formal instruction regarding use and abuse. At this level the subject of drugs should be incorporated as a significant phase of the health education program. Some discussion topics which might be used at the elementary school level are use of medicines for prevention and cure of sickness, dangers of improperly used medicine, hazards posed by abuse of non-medical substances such as glue or gasoline, manner in which boys and girls are introduced to drug abuse, and handling situations in which drugs or other abusable substances are offered. The importance of not "going along with the crowd" or "taking a dare" should be stressed. Effects of drug abuse on general health and social behavior, relationship between drug abuse and juvenile delinquency and crime, import of addiction on one's future, and how students can assist in solving drug abuse problems are important additional topics.[1]

Nutrition

Nutrition is the process by which living bodies take in food and use it. The human body's demand and use of food is a very complicated operation because the body needs certain substances to build new tissues and to repair those that wear out as the result of hard work or play. The child who is well nourished will have strong bones, muscles, and teeth. His skin and blood will be healthy. Children who suffer from malnutrition may have decayed teeth, inflamed eyes, and dry hair. They are likely to be anemic, tired, and listless and may have nervous disorders. The child should early learn what nutrients or food elements are important and necessary to his diet, so that with the proper amount of fresh air, sunshine, exercise, rest, and food he will achieve maximum health.

[1] Smith Kline and French Laboratories in cooperation with the American Association for Health, Physical Education and Recreation, *Drug Abuse: Escape to No Where* (Philadelphia: Smith Kline and French Laboratories, 1967), p. 56.

In the first, second, and third grades the child should learn the ingredients of a balanced meal and a balanced diet. He should understand a daily food plan which consists of the milk group (milk, cheese, and ice cream), the meat group (meat, fish, poultry, eggs, dried beans and peas, and nuts) the bread–cereals group (bread, oatmeal, rice, corn flakes, shredded wheat, spaghetti, macaroni, and crackers), and the vegetable–fruit group (carrots, peas, potatoes, tomatoes, cauliflower, cabbage, lettuce, pineapple, oranges, grapefruit, lemons, apples, bananas, peppers, beans, and strawberries). There are additional foods such as butter, margarine, sugar, and oils which are also important to health.

The young child might cut pictures of these foods out of magazines or draw them and then arrange them for appropriate meals during the day. He might keep a picture record of the foods served in the school cafeteria in the course of a week. This record should be checked to see if there is an overall plan and if the essential foods have been included. You will encounter instances of children whose home diet is scanty or unbalanced. Conferences with the school nurse, the school principal, or the social worker are then advisable. A visit to the child's home, a meeting with the parents, or a program for supplying children with a breakfast and a late afternoon snack in school may help solve such problems.

In the fourth, fifth, and sixth grades the child should realize that proper nutrition supplies the body with energy needs, materials for body growth, and vital chemical regulators. He should understand that hunger is a mechanical and nervous reaction. A stomach ready to receive food is shrunken. Its contracted muscular walls irritate nerve endings which relay impulses that register as hunger in the brain. After eating, the stomach is stretched; its nerves no longer stimulate us. The stomach dictates the need to satisfy hunger.

Appetite on the other hand dictates what one eats to satisfy a hungry stomach. The appetite indicates that certain foods will be more pleasant to eat than others and it stems from a desire to repeat a pleasant experience associated with food. Often we go through life choosing the foods we have tagged as pleasant and avoiding those we consider unpleasant.

The child can be introduced to the social problem of hunger. He should learn how hunger is satisfied by various appetites in different parts of the world. He should know what foods are classified as carbohydrates and that their function is to furnish heat and energy and that their deficiency symptom is a loss of weight. Foods with fat nutrient also furnish heat and energy and supply essential unsaturated fatty acids. A deficiency of fat causes a loss of weight, retarded growth, and abnormal skin. Proteins build, repair, and maintain body tissues. They also build resistance to disease and form regulating substances as well as yield heat and energy. Lack of protein results in poor physical tone, slow mental reactions, lowered resistance to disease, and premature old age.

Calcium is a necessary food nutrient in that it contributes to normal physical development and the maintenance of bones and teeth. It regulates body processes, causes blood to clot, and maintains a normal action of the heart, muscles, and healthy nerves as well as provides for iron utilization. A lack of calcium causes retarded growth, poor tooth formation, rickets, and slow clotting of the blood and porous bones.

Phosphorous also is necessary for the formation of normal bones, teeth, and cell structure and the maintenance of normal blood reaction. Phosphorous develops normal muscle activity; it regulates the output of bodily energy and the metabolism of foods. However, the absence of phosphorous retards growth and causes poor tooth formation, rickets, and porous bones.

Iron is an essential food nutrient in that it is the principal ingredient for the formation of hemoglobin in the red blood corpuscles and in carrying oxygen to body tissues. Its absence as a food nutrient causes anemia and produces weakness and dizziness, loss of weight, and gastric disturbances.

Detailed Study of Nutrition. From these basic fundamentals concerning nutrients, the child can move to a more detailed study of food, its sources, the process of assimilation in the body, vitamins, the energy value of foods, and the variance among people in their calorie needs. The problem of overweight should be discussed and a study made of a height–weight chart. A favorite topic of study with fifth and sixth graders is that of diet fads.

Children in the intermediate grades can construct graphs representing the percentages of daily food requirements in three different kinds of beverages, such as soft drinks, coffee with cream and sugar, and whole milk. Charts will illustrate the essential elements in the human body and what particular foods supply these elements. The sixth grade child could determine the number of calories he needs per pound per hour. Children could also examine the various vitamin supplements on the commercial market and determine their use and value. They can keep an individual daily diary of how many food items and calories are consumed at each meal. The food choices ought to be checked against a foundation food guide.

Children like to plan menus for various occasions, such as parties and camping trips, and for individuals with various physical complaints or for athletes. They could conduct a nutrition experiment with a group of guinea pigs or white rats, in which a comparison is made between a control group and an experimental group to illustrate the effect of the deficiency of the food element in which the children are particularly interested. A study of nutrition is a necessary component in any balanced health program.

Programs in Sex Education

There is a fairly recent interest and development in programmatic sex education for the elementary school.[2] However, knowing how to teach this controversial area as well as knowing what to teach remains a thorny problem. Probably the peer group and the inadvertencies of mass culture will remain the major sources of learning about sex in our society, regardless of the school program.

In many schools sex education is a study of reproductive biology. There is the belief that an understanding of biology tends to lessen the child's tendency to become estranged from his or her own body. Such an approach helps the teacher to control his own anxieties and makes the program less politically vulnerable. It does give the child some understanding of the biological processes pertinent to the sexual components in his life. However, a biological approach to sex education often produces a sense of estrangement in the child between the biological events which he does not experience and the emotional and psychological events which he *does* experience. Sex is represented as something that merely is or something that merely happens. It is seldom presented as something that is experienced, as something that is thought about. It is from television and movies whose representation of the sexual experience is least trustworthy that many children secure a concept of how they might experience the fear, passion, pleasure, and pains of the sexual experience.

With children in the elementary school, sex should be talked about as casually, incidentally, and non-judgmentally as possible. Non-judgmental talk about sex does not mean that widely held negative social attitudes about sexual behavior are ignored or that the legal bans against certain forms of sexual activity are downplayed.

Sex education should not be used as a vehicle for character building or for a predetermined good purpose. An attempt should be made to spell out for the child the options available for him and the risks and joys that are the likely consequences of his choice.

Such an approach to sex education can only be successful with a teacher who feels comfortable with children and whose sexual feelings are sufficiently healthy and normal that he can teach in the service of the children's needs rather than in the service of his own.

The teacher can then talk to the child when, either through developmental maturity or sheer accident, there is a compulsion to ask questions. Sex should be talked about when there is a need to discuss it. It is true that if information is given too soon the content is either meaningless or

[2] See, for example, William Simon and John H. Gagnon, "The Pedagogy of Sex," *Saturday Review*, L, No. 42 (November 18, 1967), p. 74.

anxiety provoking. But if it comes too late it can only be of limited significance.

Nevertheless, sex education in the schools is becoming nationwide. One source indicates that nearly 50 per cent of all schools—including public, private, parochial, and nonsectarian—are already providing it.

In San Diego, California, sex education begins in the sixth grade and consists of 17 lessons, devoted chiefly to the mechanics of reproduction. According to plans, in 1970 all children in the Chicago schools will have been introduced to sex education. One textbook company has made a million dollar investment for the development of a curriculum for kindergarten through twelfth grade in this area.

Psychologists indicate that sexual curiosity begins at about the age of three when children begin to explore their own bodies and discover how other people are made. It is a natural, healthy urge to want to watch each other being undressed and bathed. At the fifth year sexual curiosity normally shifts to other interests. Thus, in kindergarten five-year-olds may be told that having babies is the way fathers and mothers reaffirm their love for each other. In Palo Alto, California, kindergarten teachers often borrow babies from the children's mothers and bathe them in class as an introduction to sex education. In the early primary grades, children might be introduced to the unfolding experience of reproduction, particularly human reproduction. For children of 9 and 10 years, a limited amount of uncomplicated direct teaching in preparation for puberty could be provided. From 10 to 13, the child may and perhaps should be introduced to courses covering the family, interpersonal responsibilities, marriage, and the disparate feelings of boys and girls and how to understand them.

However, there are at present too few school systems with sufficient flexibility to permit an appropriate frankness concerning sex. There is also little understanding as yet of how a commitment to sexuality develops and the role it plays in the child's general personality growth. The teacher must help to establish a climate of mutual trust in which sex education may gain the attention it deserves as new knowledge becomes available.

The American Medical Association indicates that sex education must occur not just in the school—where the current controversy rages—but in the church, the physician's office, and most clearly in the home. Based on past experience, none of these can accomplish the job individually.[3]

Physical Activities

Physical activities do not consist merely of muscular movement or the ability to pass one of the fitness tests that are being used more and more in our schools. Instead, physical fitness is a happy mixture of the best possible bodily health with the physical condition to perform everyday tasks effectively and to meet emergencies as they arise. Hein indicates that this combination in a child or an adult means having the zest and vitality for a full and productive life.[4]

Physical fitness, in a broad sense, may be used to refer to overall well-being, which has moral, intellectual, social, and emotional components as well as physical ones. These aspects of fitness are so closely related that they are virtually inseparable. However, regular and reasonable activity is essential to the improvement and maintenance of this well-being. In addition, a child should eat properly and secure sufficient rest and sleep. He needs to learn how to use his leisure time wisely for recreation and relaxation. He should establish habits of personal cleanliness and learn to be increasingly responsible for securing his own health services. For physical activities to be effective they must be related to the child's entire health program.

For children ages four to six physical activities ought to be based on the following criteria:

1. Exercises and activities should be provided which will develop and maintain posture.
2. Activities should be vigorous and involve all parts of the body.
3. Frequent periods of rest should be provided particularly between vigorous activities.
4. Boys and girls should have the same activities.
5. Activities should develop hand–eye coordination, stationary and moving balance, and general body control.
6. Rhythmic activities should allow for the development of free expression and creativity.
7. Games should be selected which have simple rules, involve small groups, and teach children to take turns.
8. There should be a variety of activities within a unit and within a single lesson.
9. Every game, dance, or self-testing activity should provide an immediate sense of enjoyment and accomplishment.
10. No task should be too difficult for these children and maximum class participation should be stressed.[5]

"Come With Me" is a good game which illustrates these principles for children of this age. A selected child skips around the outer edge of the circle. He tags someone, saying "Come skip with me." The two children hold hands and skip around. The first child then takes a place in the circle while the second one invites the next child to join him, "Come hop with me." The game continues in this way around the circle with each child getting a turn using varied movements.

[3] Editorial, *Today's Health,* XLVIII, No. 2 (February, 1970), p. 31.

[4] Fred V. Hein, "What Is Physical Fitness?" *NEA Journal,* LI, No. 2 (February, 1962), p. 34.

[5] Glenn Kirchner, *Physical Education for Elementary School Children* (Dubuque, Iowa: W. C. Brown Co., 1966), p. 12.

For the child aged seven to nine, the previously stated criteria are applicable. However, additional principles should be emphasized:

1. Activities and exercises should be provided to correct particular posture defects.
2. The growing interest in personal skill development requires the provision of simple evaluative instruments, such as throwing and catching, kicking, and hitting skill tests.
3. At this age there is a growing interest in "team activities." Games should be selected that require a squad leader or captain, group loyalty, and rotation of "important or status positions."
4. Children should be assigned some responsibility for equipment, discipline, and activity selection.
5. Dance activities should be introduced which involve partners and group participation.[6]

Relays are a most popular game for children aged seven to nine. Here are some suggestions for relay games:

Kick a ball around a specified goal and back.
Run while holding ankles.
Duck waddle (squatting).
Crab walk (squatting, then tipped back with hands on ground).
Camel walk (walking on hands and feet with knees straight).
Skip, gallop, hop, walk backward.
Obstacles around which to run, hurdles to jump or scale.
Handball over one player's head and under legs of next.
Elephant walk (one person atop the toes of another).
Caterpillar (hands on floor, feet inching up to meet hands).

For the child aged 9 to 12 the following activities might be appropriate.

1. Team sports, club activities, and intramural competition should be provided. Such activities are most important to the child of this age.
2. For competitive sports and some self-testing activities boys and girls in the fifth and sixth grades should be separated. The separation should be based upon a combination of skill and interest level. This separation may be done by squads within the class, rather than a complete class separation.
3. Opportunities should be provided for folk, square, and social dance.
4. Periods of instruction will be longer with an increased emphasis on skill development.
5. Competitive activities should be provided, with a heavy stress on sportsmanship, leadership, and team loyalty.
6. There should be a variety of self-evaluative devices for all areas of the program.[7]

A variation of volleyball is an excellent indoor sport which permits the whole class to participate. The children can catch the ball, and when

[6] *Ibid.*, p. 14.
[7] *Ibid.*, p. 16.

caught it is immediately put back into play without the use of a special serve.

Many physical fitness tests have been developed to show how well a person performs certain physical tasks. The youth fitness test probably most widely used is the one developed by the American Association for Health, Physical Education, and Recreation (AAHPER). National norms for this test are set for boys and girls from 10 to 17 and for college students. The norms show that if a ten-year-old boy can do one or two pullups on the test, he is doing as well as his peers, but measuring up to the national average on the test does not necessarily indicate that he is as fit as he can be. Boys of this age can generally do better—that they do not have a desirable level of arm and shoulder strength is shown by scores on pullups.

A boy or girl may be extremely well developed in one area of physical fitness and very limited in another. You should watch for these weaknesses and see that children improve their fitness in their limited areas. Physical fitness cannot be measured by a single test item. Fitness tests often vary from a few simple items to a more comprehensive battery of tests. Muscular strength is measured by testing a child's hand grip or his ability to lift a weight. Muscular endurance involving strength and organic functioning is measured by testing his ability to continue to overcome a resistance (that is, weight) through a series of repetitive muscular efforts. Pullups, situps, floor pushups, and parallel bar dips are tests of muscular endurance.

A test of a child's muscular power is his ability to propel his body through space in a vertical jump and a standing or running broad jump. These tests of power are also tests of speed, but not to the same extent as in running where speed must be sustained for a longer time. Periodic testing at regular intervals can enable a youngster to measure his progress by comparing each successive score with the previous one. You should urge the child to keep a personal record of these advances. Then he can see how a regular program of exercise aids his physical development.

There is no simple road to fitness. A child should be taught that he has to expend energy in order to keep fit. If he is willing to make the effort, he can enjoy a physical condition which is first rate.

METHOD IN PHYSICAL EDUCATION

Health Considerations

The *conditions* of your classroom are most pertinent to sound methods in health. Classrooms should be properly heated and ventilated. Shades should be adjusted for proper lighting. The room should be clean. You should watch for children whom you suspect to be ill. During the day you may note children who are unusually listless, irritable, or fatigued. They should be checked by the school nurse, when one is available. If a child is ill, he belongs at home where he can recuperate. Perfect attendance is not a valid goal. A child should know he is not to come to school if he is not well.

You may have to demonstrate the use of health aids such as a handkerchief or toothbrush. Children should be taught to examine themselves for clean skin, clothing, and surroundings. The dangers of putting things in their mouths should be discussed. The classroom should be organized for health and cleanliness. A child might be designated to carry the wastebasket around the room at the close of the day. The children should know where health materials such as tissues and bandaids are kept. When planning the refreshments for a classroom party, remind the children that excessive consumption of candy and soda is generally disapproved by dentists.

Michaelis, Grossman, and Scott describe some interesting teaching strategies for health education:[8]

1. The experimental method allows children to discover key ideas for themselves by engaging in firsthand observation under controlled conditions. Here the children define and state the problem or question, outline the procedures, perform and observe the experiment, and then collect and interpret the data—arriving at and checking the collections. The children could rub a piece of meat over a clean sterilized plate and another piece over a plate which has not been cleaned. The pieces of meat could be placed in two sterile jars, the lids secured tightly, and the differences observed.

2. You might demonstrate a particular health behavior or principle. You could have some children read with eye shades under a strong light and another group read without the shades. After a period of time has elapsed, the groups could compare how much material had been read, how often each had rested the eyes, and other factors.

3. There might be a particular health problem which needs to be discussed and solutions suggested. Many children in the school have colds. Health education might then revolve about the problem of how colds are prevented and how they are cared for.

4. Field trips and surveys constitute a good teaching method. Children can thus observe safety practices and use health service workers as resource persons. Before taking a field trip, the childern should plan the interview, discuss note-taking procedures, and make necessary maps which give directions. The children might visit a food market, a dairy farm, or

[8] John U. Michaelis, Ruth H. Grossman, and Lloyd F. Scott, *New Designs for the Elementary School Curriculum* (New York: McGraw-Hill Book Co., Inc., 1967), p. 291.

a health department. Primary grade children can observe fire safety equipment in different parts of the school.

5. Children might be presented with information, experiences, and activities which can help them reach a generalization concerning physical health. One generalization which they should grasp is that a balanced diet is necessary to good health. The children might read from the textbook a description of the minerals and vitamins of which the body is composed. A chart might then be organized which shows the relationship between the nutrient composition of particular foods and the needs of the body. The children could investigate physical complaints caused by incorrect diets and could compose a play illustrating the body's proper dietary needs.

6. The process of inquiry might be used as a method. The child can *receive* information from a film concerning a proper diet and can *respond* by comparing his daily or weekly diet with the one indicated in the film. Determining how his diet may be improved can cause an *evaluation* of foods and appetites. *Organizing* a suitable diet for himself may be followed by determining how best to discipline oneself to a prescribed diet.

7. Finally, you might use a method that develops particular safety behaviors. It would be primarily concerned with safety education within the school environment, in the community, and in the home. You should help the child become aware of his responsibility for his own personal safety, as well as for the safety and welfare of others. The child should understand safety regulations and their need, and be able to use safety tools suitable to his physical maturity. Specific behaviors necessary for safety should be taught, reviewed, and practiced consistently until they become habitual.

Fire drill and air raid drills should be practiced until they become part of automatic behavior. Using a handkerchief properly, remaining dry in wet weather, and using matches in their correct context are only a few of those essential precautionary behaviors a child should develop.

Probably no other area of the curriculum is so close to the child's personal needs or so important to his total experience as health education. Particular content in health education is related to a particular method.

Physical Education Routines

Much of the success of your program will depend on the smooth routine you establish in preparing children for activities and returning to the regular classroom program upon their completion. There may be individual excuses, changes of costume, showering, and arranging for equipment before the physical education program may proceed.

Children should wear light rubber-soled shoes during physical activities, especially if the gymnasium floor consists of tile. Girls should be permitted to wear shorts or culottes. You should insist that all gym uniforms, including socks and shoes, have the owner's name clearly marked with nonerasable ink. If the children are to wear gym uniforms, they should be kept clean and neat. Friday is a good day for them to be taken home and washed.

To check tardiness, health status, and uniforms quickly and efficiently, children should be taught to take a set position on entering the gymnasium or play area. The children might line up alphabetically or the line formation might be from the tallest to the shortest child or each child might be assigned a number. Squads could be organized, with one child assigned the responsibility of taking roll.

The techniques and standards that you find to be successful in the classroom may not be adaptable to the playground or gymnasium. There may be much vocal enthusiasm and physical movement. However, the children should understand whistle signals. You should use squad leaders and team pressure as much as possible to maintain effective discipline. It is not wise to deny physical activity to the entire class because of the misbehavior of one child. As in every other area of the curriculum, frequent changes of method and activity will stimulate interest and variety.

Teaching children basic formations can increase the efficiency of organization for physical activities. Running and tag games require a specific formation, and many folk dances begin with a circle or line position. Many different formations can be used for conditioning exercises, low organization games, and use of apparatus. You can have each group of children form a circle. A group could form a line with the leader of each group in front, or it might form a fan shape with the leader standing at the opening of the fan.

Essential features of any formation are that each child be able to observe the squad leader and that the activities of one squad do not interfere with those of another.

There are several methods of grouping which one may follow. One way would be on the basis of skills tests or observations of skill ability. Another is to have the children number off in twos, fives, or whatever number of teams you desire. The class may then be arranged in a circle and divided into the desired number of squads. Teams might be selected on the basis of birthdays: for example, children with birthdays in January and February to compose one team, March and April birthdays to compose a second team, etc. You could also use McClay's Index which separates heavier and older children from the lighter and younger children.[9]

[9] Charles H. McClay, *The Measurement of Athletic Power* (New York: A. S. Barnes and Co., 1952), p. 95.

When you introduce a new motor skill, you should give a verbal explanation with a demonstration that every child will have a clear view of. You can divide the skill into its parts or sections and explain each part clearly before moving on to the next. You should check frequently with the children, making certain that each child is following the demonstration and the instructions. If you are unable to demonstrate the skill, ask a child to do it at a speed slower than normally performed. Each child should copy the demonstration of the skill in slow motion. The skill might even be performed by pantomine. Each individual's performance should be checked before the class is organized into smaller practice groups. Now the skill can be practiced in small groups, but you should continue to check for faults and needed corrections. For some children who are less mature physically, it may be necessary to break the skill down into even smaller parts with liberal doses of encouragement and praise.

The length of the physical education period may vary from 10 minutes to an hour, depending on the types of activities performed and the age of the child. Generally, however, it will take about five minutes to prepare for the period and another five minutes to warm up. The explanation and demonstration of the activity may consume about four minutes and the drill about the same amount of time. The activity itself—a game, a dance, self-testing—would take perhaps 10 minutes and the lesson's conclusion two or three minutes. Such a lesson in its entirety would take 30 minutes.

MENTAL HEALTH

Good mental health is often discussed in terms of the absence of pathological symptoms. Mental health is more than the mere absence of emotional disorder or maladaptive behavior. It is not complete control over one's feelings. It is proper and right for a child to become angry, afraid, happy, joyous, or ecstatic. A child who has good mental health may be characterized by a vital, positive, emotional approach to living. Mental health as such has no particular content within the elementary school curriculum. It is primarily concerned with the method, environment, person-to-person relationship, and image of self within the classroom. Promotion of sound mental health for each child is a major school function.

CLASSROOM AND THE INDIVIDUAL

Like a rare musical instrument, each classroom is unique and inimitable and different from the neighboring classroom across the hall. The difference may be caused by the particular socioemotional climate found in that classroom. This atmosphere is often the direct responsibility of the teacher.

A good emotional climate can be built in the classroom when each child knows that he is wanted. The anxiety which children feel concerning their relationship with the teacher is probably greater than most teachers realize. Good mental health can grow in a classroom of good humor, of purpose, of cooperation, and of concern for each individual. The "tyranny of the average"—insistence that each child meet an average academic pace—can cause frustration. Excessive academic pressure is equally frustrating for many children. Reese captures some of sense of futility children may develop:

> "My report card is in my arithmetic book." This was a note written shortly before an 11 year old, Ohio sixth grader put a .45 caliber automatic to his head, pulled the trigger, and killed himself.
>
> What factors have brought such stress to bear on the life of a young person that he or she has seen no alternative but self destruction? The fact that youth do kill themselves is in itself a sizable social and personal tragedy. . . . While the reasons for suicide vary from individual to individual, there is evidence that facets of the educational environment are associated with the act of suicide.[10]

A teacher concerned with sound mental health secures a real understanding of each child's capabilities and potential and he attempts to establish an environment in which they can flourish. A climate of fear is not conducive to sympathetic understanding. The child may fear your authority. He may be afraid of failure. He may fear competition. If you insist on long periods of absolute quiet without physical movement, you may be establishing a negative climate. If you use sarcasm, threats, or continual punishment to keep control you may be causing tensions, hostilities, and fears among the children. If you are continually comparing one child's performance with another, or constantly reminding a child that he is not trying or that he'll never pass, you are creating a very poor environment for mental health. You should not be surprised if such a climate produces outbursts of temper, quarreling, cheating, and stubbornness. The type of classroom setting that you establish will affect the children's mental health.

Person-to-Person Relationships

Probably the most difficult task for any teacher is to secure a person-to-person relationship with particular children. Such children are often the trouble spots during the day. They may be noisy, inattentive, rest-

[10] Frederick D. Reese, "School Age Suicide and the Educational Environment," *Theory into Practice* (Ohio State University College of Education), VII, No. 1 (February, 1968), p. 10.

less, and unable to complete assignments. As a prime measure of securing rapport, you should learn to express your emotions with such children fairly and reasonably and in a manner which demonstrates your humanness and concern.

You must establish routine requirements. Adjusting window shades, distributing supplies, and cleaning the room are not unimportant details in themselves and children should become involved in them. At the beginning of the school year, routine procedures should be established cooperatively between you and the children. It may be a matter of arranging furniture effectively for group work since each child might work in many different groups during the day. Clear directions or illustrations (posted on the bulletin board or mimeographed) concerning the membership and location of each group will lessen confusion in aranging the furniture.

Words often soothe person-to-person relationships. A question or tactful approach leaves you an "out" in case further evidence should prove you to be wrong. Once you have given a challenge or made a demand, you may feel forced to follow through.

If you attempt to cover everything in the curriculum, you may have to minimize human relations. Inevitably the cry is, "The school year is almost over, and I still have so much to do." It is best to plan only a few major goals for yourself and the children. Knowing precisely what you intend to do and checking your achievement will give you a feeling of accomplishment which in turn can affect the children. The sense of well-being that comes with this accomplishment kindles good human relations.

The methods you use in the classroom will strongly affect the child's mental health. Much has been said in this text about suitable methods. However, you should ask yourself the following questions concerning the effects of methods you use in teaching children.

1. Does your method help the child who is continually seeking attention?
2. How are errors and mistakes resolved?
3. How are personal disagreements dissipated?
4. Do the methods allow for humor?
5. Is prejudice absent in the methods used?
6. Does the method instil fear and alienation?
7. Are both sexes challenged by the methods?
8. Do the methods discourage domination by the teacher or other children?
9. Are children involved in group activities?
10. Are assignments interesting and suited to all children?
11. Are the materials used in harmony with the methods?
12. Do the methods have pertinency and conciseness?

Self Image of the Child

Unfortunately many elementary children today have a poor self image. Accepting each child as he is and at the same time believing in him can help the child to improve his self image. Most children want to belong and want to have friends and be liked. Children may have a poor self image as a result of their feelings concerning factors such as poor English, skin color, parents or homes, inferior educational achievements, limited physical abilities, or undesirable physique.

Your attitude toward such children is highly important. It is easy to react favorably to the healthy child with high achievement but you also must accept differences in children and help all of them to feel that they belong in the classroom. When you do not accept a child, it is almost certain that other children will follow your example and reject him. A healthy self image can be secured only if a child is accepted as a person.

Children need to learn how to work and play together in small groups and to gain satisfaction from doing so. Group activities should be organized in the classroom to help children to do this. When a child hesitates to join in, you should work with him individually to discover his interests and help him to overcome certain inadequacies. If you discover that he has an interest or skill that has prestige value among the children, you should gradually bring him into the group. If you voice approval of his efforts, others probably will do likewise.

Feelings of status develop in a child when he knows that the teacher respects him, when he makes good friends, and when his contribution to the group is recognized and appreciated. If most of the children feel good about themselves and others and if they play and work well together, the process of mental health is progressing favorably in your class.

RESEARCH

The Child's Need To Understand

Some studies seem to indicate that children will participate more effectively in programs of physical education if they understand what the particular exercise will do for their growth and development. One study is that conducted by Illinois 4-H clubs. This fitness program emphasizes keeping physically fit,[11] and is a hard conditioning program through which a youth secures a feeling of competence derived from accomplishing a difficult task. This experimental program was not softened with watered-down play activities. Fitness is conceived as consisting of four factors:

[11] D. M. Hall, "A Fitness Program That Works," *The Physical Educator,* XV, No. 3 (October, 1958), p. 123.

1. *A sturdy physique.* This indicates that boys and girls are growing as they should. Their bodies should be well developed for their age and should have the proper proportions of bone, muscle, and fat. If a child's weight is right for his height and body type, this is a good sign that he is growing normally.
2. *Organic fitness.* Everyone's heart and lungs should be strong. Organic fitness requires a good digestive system, normal sensory organs (that is, good eyes, ears, etc.), and freedom from disease and body defects.
3. *Motor fitness.* This means that boys and girls have trained their muscles so they can work and exercise without tiring.
4. *Body protection.* This refers to the ability to protect one's body from dangers. To do this it is necessary to know something about sanitation, disease, safety precautions, and first aid; it is also required to know how to swim.

The chief problem of the Illinois 4-H study was to determine whether a child is growing according to schedule. After repeated weighings and measurements, a growth line was plotted to determine improvement in health. Each child kept a diet scorecard and followed exercise and sleep regimens. A breathing capacity and pulse recovery test was administered; motor fitness was tested through measures of endurance, flexibility, speed, and strength. After a 4-H child received his scores, he was instructed in ways and means for improving them through training and conditioning. Boys and girls will undertake strenuous conditioning activities once they have been told the "whys" of fitness. Activities, seemingly for their own sake, are not enough. Children want to know the reasons why. This experiment indicated that we need not make fitness recreational. It is sufficient in itself as long as boys and girls reap a sense of satisfaction by having accomplished a tough task.

Physical Education for High-Ability Children

There seems to be some evidence that children with high athletic abilities require a physical education program above and beyond that of other children in the same age range.

Clarke and Shelley conducted a study to construct profiles of boys rated as outstanding athletes by their coaches in elementary school and junior high school interschool competition.[12] The profiles were based on measures of maturity, structure strength, motor ability, and intelligence.

[12] H. Harrison Clarke and Morgan E. Shelley, "Maturity Structure Strength Motor Ability and Intelligence Test Profiles of Outstanding Elementary School and Junior High School Athletes," *The Physical Educator,* XVIII, No. 4 (December, 1961), pp. 132–36.

With such profiles a comparison could be made of outstanding athletes with norms for boys of the same chronological age. They also made it possible to observe individual differences among athletes and from these differences to consider ways by which a weakness in one trait was compensated for by strength in another.

A test profile form was specially designed for use in this study. It contained score designations for each of the measures utilized. A profile of the scores made on these tests was drawn for each of the 38 outstanding athletes. Each profile showed a pictorial observation of the athlete's status among boys his own age and each was accompanied by a descriptive sketch of the athlete.

The average outstanding athlete, as compared with samples of boys of his age, was found to be well above the mean in skeletal age. He demonstrated exceptional ability in the motor tests and his measure of strength was high. The average outstanding athlete was slightly above the mean in I.Q., with a score of 107.

In this study athletes were shown to be more mature, have larger bodies, achieve higher scores on the motor ability tests, be much stronger, and have a higher degree of intelligence than their average classmates.

Teacher Factors in Mental Health

Perhaps the first requirement in any mental health program is that the teacher understand his own weaknesses and strengths. A question which might be asked is, "What effect does racial integration have on the classroom teacher and the educational process itself?" An experimental group approach to this problem was initiated at the Beth Israel Hospital in Boston, Massachusetts.[13] The Beth Israel psychiatrists aimed at using group interaction and group material to help the teacher learn more about himself in his function as a teacher. The experiment included teachers from all white schools and teachers from integrated schools—all of the 24 teachers from the all white schools were white; and of the 24 teachers from the integrated schools, only five were white. With the help of psychiatrists the teachers were encouraged and guided to discuss their feelings and attitudes concerning integration.

The experiment seemed successful and worth continuing since the teachers learned from each other about race relations and came to understand their own feelings concerning this issue. This experiment also indicated that the problem faced by the teacher who chooses to participate in social change is more involved than simply presiding over

[13] Norman E. Zinberg, "A Group Approach with the School Teacher in the Integration Crisis," *Mental Hygiene*, V, No. 2 (April, 1967), pp. 289–305.

integrated classes in such a way that no unpleasant incidents occur. He must work with the deeper hurt feelings from past difficulties and with the prejudices that exist by the time children have reached his classroom. Ideas concerning integration problems have a slow rate of change with both children and teachers. This experiment of group meetings may be one way of improving mental health in the classroom.

Interrelationships of Discipline and Aggression

Interesting studies have been made on the relationship between discipline and aggression. These studies seem to indicate that punishment heightens aggression.

In a study of nursery school children observers rated behavior during "free play" periods immediately following a movie designed to induce aggression fantasy.[14] A significant positive correlation was obtained between ratings of anxiety and aggression, indicating that children who exhibited more aggressive behavior were also considered more anxious. Anxiety was inferred from observations of "awkward movements"; incompleted or blocked aggressive acts; tics, thumb sucking, and other "nervous mannerisms"; tense mouth; mask-like expressions; and other symptoms.

In a study by Hollenberg and Sperry it was found that aggressive behavior in a play situation with dolls declined in children who were immediately reproved when they exhibited such behavior. Thus, as he grows older, the child who is severely punished for his aggressive behavior may come to associate punishment with his aggressive acts. Consequently his feelings of aggression may lead to anxiety which then serves as a signal of impending danger. The child's anxiety provides cues that help him to inhibit disapproved behavior in order to avoid anticipated punishment.

Evidence from the foregoing studies suggests that the severely punished child is more hostile than the less severely punished child and that he is more likely to develop anxiety over the expression of aggression which, in turn, causes him to inhibit the expression of overtly hostile acts.

Influence of Words on School Environment

Studies indicate that the words you use in the classroom and the tone with which they are used strongly influence the climate or environment of the classroom in relation to mental health. For example, one teacher admonishes: "I hear noise in the back of this room. Mrs. Cooper doesn't

[14] Opal R. Perdue and Charles D. Spielberger, "Anxiety and the Perception of Punishment," *Mental Hygiene*, L, No. 3 (July, 1966), pp. 390–97.

like noisy children in her room." This is one example of what researchers call an "approval-focused" control technique. Its effect depends upon the relationship between the teacher and the children. A "task-focused" technique dealing with the same problem might sound like this: "I hear noise in the back of the room. We will never finish learning how to do square root if that din continues."

Findings indicated that task-focused control techniques elicit more desirable reactions from children than do approval-focused efforts. When children are convinced that the teacher is an expert in his subject matter, his use of task-focused control techniques demonstrates to them that he has purpose in his lesson and that there is a job to be done. They respect him and will be more inclined to discuss personal matters with him.

Research results seem to suggest several techniques of establishing a positive atmosphere in the classroom:

1. Make use of techniques that are non-threatening, whenever possible.
2. Be sure that control communications are clear, that children know the offender, the offense, and the proper alternative behavior.
3. Increase firmness by changing the tone of voice, moving closer to the offender, or observing him closely until he complies.
4. Focus control techniques on the learning task at hand rather than on teacher approval.
5. Increase subject matter expertness since this contributes to your ability to control classroom misbehavior.

The individual increasingly lives in a world which impairs his physical and mental well-being. You should seek to create an environment, impart knowledge, and organize experiences which contribute to physical and mental health. The major justification should be to help the individual to be his best self which in turn can contribute to effective learning. The school is in a unique position to promote sound health in cooperation with various agencies and organizations as well as with all kinds and ages of people.

CONCLUSION

The development of an urban society has accentuated the necessity for promoting physical and mental health in the schools. Children as well as adults need physical activities, health information, and an environment planned to promote physical and mental health with lifelong benefits. Fortunately, children tend to desire those activities and that kind of environment which contribute to their total health. Not only does good physical and mental health contribute to individual well-being but it also improves the individual's learning capacity. It seems evident that healthy children who have experienced the joys of physical activities are good prospects for other kinds of learning activities. Physical and mental health should be distinct parts of the elementary school curriculum, but they can be correlated with other subjects. In any case, health-related knowledge and skills should be integrated into an overall healthy environment. Understanding and experiencing are as significant in physical and mental health as they are in other curriculum areas. In an urban, technical society, hard labor is done by machines. With increasing leisure there is need for each individual to live joyously and vigorously. Modern man has the time, the means, the techniques, and the knowledge to make this possible—and the possible will become more probable when there is a sound curriculum in physical and mental health.

PROJECTS AND READINGS

1. You will learn through experience that a close relationship exists between physical and mental health. Children will have "off" days when it is difficult for them to concentrate or be cooperative. A child may come to school hungry or hurt. You may notice a child who is particularly tense. Such children are not capable of working at their full potential. Give them a chance to recuperate. Their goal is to regain equilibrium and achieve academically. You might steer them into activities such as painting or quiet reading. You should accept below-par performance without comment. You might even encourage a tired child to rest. You, more than anyone else, will set the emotional tempo of the class. Can you indicate what classroom manner you should assume which indicates your awareness of mental health?

2. The following lesson in physical education may be observed in some schools. Here and there particular children step forward to demonstrate a skill or lead an exercise. Then the class chairman directs team captains to come forward, organize their teams, and walk to the position that each team has been assigned. Teams line up, each team is cheered, captains shake hands, and the relay game begins. Children who are medically disqualified for the relay umpire and keep scores. Five minutes before the end of the period the teacher blows a whistle. The children check scores, cheer for the winning team, change shoes, and line up before the teacher. The entire period took some 30 minutes, 20 of which were given to games. During the period the teacher had moved from team to team, teaching one boy how to tag properly, giving a word of encouragement to a shy umpire, complimenting a child for good sportsmanship, and substituting for a boy called to the office. When they returned to the classroom, the captains recorded the scores on a "Good Sportsmanship Chart." How would you evaluate this lesson?

3. Learning a skill involves appropriate repetition and practice. There are two essential and related parts of this principle. To acquire a skill the child should repeat the movement to the point that it is "overlearned." Once a child has learned to swim, several months may pass without practice, but the child will still be able to swim. The more the skill is overlearned the longer the time

before it is lost. But the repetition must be appropriate. A ten-year-old boy, continually throwing a basketball through a hoop while using improper techniques may experience continual failure. Such repetition is neither appropriate nor effective. What are the implications for physical education from the principle of repetition?

4. You should give the child with high abilities and high achievements more advanced activities. Those with low ability and achievement should receive activities which do not frustrate them. A child with a hearing difficulty should be given a seat near the front of the room to enable him to hear you and the other children. Special attention should be given the child with a visual handicap or any other physical defect. You should observe the child who has a poor attendance record to enable you to discover his interests and help him to like school more. If illness is the cause of poor attendance, you should watch for symptoms and recommend the child for special medical attention. These procedures may lead children to respond favorably to you and thus establish good person-to-person relations. What necessary information should you have concerning each child's past experience to enable you to anticipate how the child may conduct himself in the present situation?

5. Many persons in the school environment are responsible for providing and maintaining conditions for healthy school living. The custodian keeps the school clean; the administrators are responsible for building standards; the nutritionist or cafeteria manager is responsible for balanced meals. You are responsible for adequate ventilation and proper lighting within your classroom. You may be completely or partly responsible for physical education for your class. You should make daily observations of children's health and assist in improving health where possible. You are not only well equipped but well placed as the classroom teacher to provide continual health instruction which will develop in the child positive attitudes and definite behavior towards safe and healthy living. What are some of the ways in which you can capitalize upon incidental opportunities for teaching health and safety? To what extent is it wise to depend upon such occurrences to provide situations which can be related to health and safety instruction? Who are some additional resource persons who can provide assistance? What are some sources of free and inexpensive learning materials?

6. These particular texts will deepen your understanding concerning physical and mental health.

a. Bryant J. Cratty, *Psychology and Physical Activity* (Englewood Cliffs, N.J.: Prentice-Hall, Inc., 1968), 207 pp. The author explains how a program in health and physical education may be evaluated.
b. Brigitta Linner with Richard J. Nitell, *Sin and Society in Sweden* (New York: Pantheon Books, Inc., 1967), 204 pp. The author presents ninety pages of sex education material which should be quite interesting to the teacher.
c. Alexander Frazier (ed.), *The New Elementary School* (Washington: Association for Supervision and Curriculum Development, 1968), 147 pp. The editor presents new knowledge about young children and how they develop and grow.
d. Charles B. Corbin, *Becoming Physically Educated in the Elementary School* (Philadelphia: Lea & Febiger, 1969), 365 pp. This publication presents a basic understanding of what children need to learn in the

elementary school. It should aid the teacher in selecting physical education experiences which will most likely produce desired learning in children.

e. Lester A. Kirkendall and Ruth F. Osborne, *Teacher's Question & Answer Book on Sex Education* (New London, Conn.: Croft Educational Service, Inc., 1969), 112 pp. This exposition provides an overview of the current controversy surrounding sex instruction and public schools and discusses substantive and methodological aspects of sex education programs.

17

Activity Programs

ACTIVITIES IN THE CURRICULUM

An activity is a technique or device which gives focus and direction to the concepts and understandings which are organized for the child's learning. For activities to be of value and pertinency, they must be integrated within the curriculum. An example is a fourth grade unit on Mexico where the activity may be the construction of a life-size goat from cardboard. The essential learning is not the making of the goat but rather the reason why many Mexican farmers own goats rather than cows. Through research and investigation the child learns that many Mexican farmers live on submarginal land, and that goats require much less fodder than cows. They also come to know that in cold weather, when shelter is scarce, the goat can be taken indoors with the family, unlike a cow which would take up too much room. A goat has many uses—it gives milk and meat; its hide can be used for leather; its skin can be used for rugs. Some goats can be trained to pull wagons or plows. Thus the physical activity of constructing a goat involves many learnings which pertain to an understanding of some aspects of Mexican rural life.

Much of the criticism concerning activities or work projects stems from the lack of coordination with so-called "real" learning; they seem to be mere busy work. One newspaper voiced this complaint in an editorial.

Too Many Sandboxes in Schools?

A nation which has been fussing for a decade because Johnny can't read is now fuming because he can't figure either. . . . We must restore learning. It is time we washed our hands of sandbox activities. . . . The first twelve grades of school are for something besides finger painting, self-expression, folk dancing, life guidance, and such other sandbox activity as auto driving, basket weaving, and cheer leading. . . . Sweep the trash out of the curriculum and restore reading, writing, arithmetic, history, geography, science, languages, and the hard core stuff of education.[1]

However, it is well to remember that a definition of curriculum comprises any or all of the following.[2] Curriculum includes:

1. All the experiences the child has regardless of when or how they take place.
2. All the experiences the learner has under the guidance of the school.
3. All the courses which a school offers.
4. The systematic arrangement of certain courses designed for certain curriculum purposes, for example, preparation for high school.
5. Courses offered within a certain subject field, for example, the science curriculum or the language arts curriculum.
6. The program for a special group such as the physically handicapped.
7. Those activities in which an individual child is involved—map making, construction of a mural, a science experiment, a research project, and so forth.

Planned and Incidental Activities

The first definition, that a curriculum embodies life's experiences, indicates that much consideration is given to the child's interests and needs. The second statement implies that the school curriculum is that part of the individual's day for which the school has direct responsibility. However, each of these definitions suggests that out-of-school experiences supplement in-school experiences. Curriculum activities then may include a wide range of projects, some of which are planned for learning potential. Others may not come under the practical interpretation of curriculum responsibility; for example, a child might fall in the classroom and skin his knee badly enough to require medical attention. This unplanned incident may teach the child more about safety and first aid than a whole series of formal lessons. On the other hand a field trip to a drug store or ambulance center will take much planning and organization in the classroom before it can occur. The children should investigate the uses of an ambulance, its equipment, and the various uses of that equipment, before they make the visit. Then the activity can be the vehicle for much learning and it can provide a basic learning experience.

[1] Blanche Adcock, "Editorial," *Coronation Review* (Coronation, Alberta, Canada), (September 15, 1967), p. 2.

[2] Albert J. Oliver, *Curriculum Improvement: A Guide to Problems, Principles, and Procedures* (New York: Dodd, Mead, & Co., Inc., 1965), p. 5.

The problem of air pollution might be identified as an area of study. The children might consider the major causes of air pollution and whose responsibility it is to solve the problem. Children can focus solutions around the following questions. First, what does current research indicate about the causes, dangers, and solutions of air pollution? Second, what local community awareness can be promoted? Third, what kind of community action is necessary?

Learning that is vital is concerned with those aspects of the society in which the child lives, the ways in which these aspects are important to him, and his participation in the activities they represent. Without the use of activities and work projects, it is difficult to study the following: safety in the community; opportunities for play, fun, and recreation; how families in the community earn a living; kinds of homes; how people work together; and how their health is protected. The child's level of maturity, of course, is a significant factor in determining the type and complexity of the activity to be pursued. Children in the primary grades might locate on large floor maps those playgrounds and parks in the immediate area and may construct murals illustrating the regulations concerning the use of such centers. Intermediate grade children might conduct a community survey to ascertain the purposes of these facilities, how they are maintained, and how they could be improved.

Activities and work projects contribute to the children's independence, social effectiveness, and emotional growth. They involve cooperative procedures so that even the very young child develops poise, self-confidence, and personal adjustment, as well as learns mathematics, reading, or science. When children are busy planning and working to complete a project or activity which they value, classroom frustrations and disciplinary problems often take care of themselves. Success in accomplishing these activities in turn builds self-confidence and encourages children to even greater effort. Children welcome responsibilities that are challenging if they are kept within the limits of their abilities. Activities that are cooperative ventures can stress democratic participation in the daily work of the school.

CHILD DEVELOPMENT AND ACTIVITIES

When children join together in an activity or project, they will need help in facing typical problems such as: (a) what work is to be accomplished and how it might be planned and developed, and (b) what is the best way to work together for productivity and efficiency.

With your help, the children themselves should determine their goals and how to achieve them. The plans should be carried out, keeping the goals firmly in mind so that activity will be a cooperative venture. Children should consider one another's ideas carefully, criticize each other constructively, accept and adjust to the personality of each group member, harmonize differences, and do their best to get along.

The assimilation of concepts and skills and the organization of a particular learning activity are closely related. Assuming responsibility for activities is in itself a valuable learning activity for pupils. Learning to select purposes for activities through group cooperation is of additional value. In most activities children should work not only for themselves but also for the total group. In turn, cooperative procedures encourage the use of the individual pupil's insight and initiative, which contribute to his independence in utilizing concepts and skills.

INDEPENDENCE AND CONFIDENCE

You should make a serious attempt to share responsibility with the children for selecting activities, planning them, and evaluating the product.

Recently a speaker addressed some 2,000 elementary children concerning the animals of Australia. The children, with their teachers, were grouped by classes. The children were interested and attentive. To elicit responses from the children at various parts of the presentation, simple questions were asked. Most children of elementary school age could answer the questions but the response was most interesting. In some parts of the auditorium, all the children raised their hands and were eager to be called on. But even though most of the children in the audience probably knew the answers, in several classes no hands were raised at all.

Visiting the classrooms after the presentation, it was noted that in those classes where the children did not respond there were few, if any activities, in progress. In those classes where the children responded enthusiastically, there was involvement in many and varied projects. It would seem that those children who did not raise their hands had not developed the confidence, through projects and activities, to express themselves freely. These children came from classes where they just listened and read a textbook to answer the teacher's questions. In those classes where children raised their hands the children had been given responsibility for developing individual and group activities and had subsequently developed ability, initiative, and confidence in making active contributions to the class.

The discussion on Australian animals in those classes where children had had experience with cooperative activities was easily stimulated. The children asked questions freely and contributed their opinions promptly. In those classrooms where no experience in responsibility for planning and directing work activity had been secured, it was difficult to stimulate a real interest in discussion.

When you encourage children to assume responsibilities for planning and carrying out classroom activities, essentially you are teaching them to be independent of you. When you give them confidence in their own capacity to learn, as well as in their practical ability to plan and execute a project, they are able to work as effectively in your absence as when you are present to guide them. This independence is a significant contribution of work activities and projects.

In developing activities with children, it is important to remember these five points: (a) arouse their curiosity and interest in the project, (b) provide a good work area, (c) guide but don't push, (d) be generous with praise, (e) have a specific goal for each project.

SOCIAL EFFECTIVENESS

Children must learn to adjust to one another's ideas and temperaments. Working together on a mural, a map, or a play, they must deal constantly with human relations problems as important factors in the total classroom situation.

Let us look at some children in a typical fourth grade class. Steve works well with his hands but is a poor planner and is easily lead by others. He has to be told what to do next. Tom is a fast logical thinker. He immediately sees the problem and becomes impatient with those who do not perceive as he does. Vera is clever and charming. She finds it easy to take over and get her own way. However, she is able to reach an understanding with her peer group and is a peacemaker. Virginia is shy, insecure, and introverted. John is a bully who attempts to force his leadership on the group but never pays enough attention to the work going on to lead effectively. Two other children in the class have negative attitudes toward cooperation and are always criticizing the others. Three children cannot be depended upon and never meet their responsibilities. The remaining 20 children in the class cooperate and participate effectively, but their abilities and contributions vary greatly. There are two rather loosely formed but exclusive groups in the class which generate some rivalries and jealousies.

Such a variety in needs and social effectiveness in one class suggests complex problems and multiple demands in guiding activities. You should help the children to recognize and assume their responsibilities in working and living productively with others. You may have to deal with disrupting situations that arise in cooperative work projects. You must be alert to Steve's need to improve on his planning—for Vera is very good at getting others to do her work for her—and to Virginia's need to overcome her lack of confidence. You may be as much concerned with some children's poor emotional adjustment as with John's inability to listen to directions. With your guidance and direction children can learn to be considerate of one another. They must be taught to criticize constructively rather than destructively, to contribute their full share to the activity in progress, and to harmonize the differences that will arise when working with others. This ability to work with others in forming a socially effective group is an essential part of every child's education.

FREEDOM AND RESPONSIBILITY

The following illustration shows how a class can utilize freedom to learn while carrying out group responsibilities. A fifth grade social studies class was beginning a study of Canada and was having exploratory discussions on that nation's size, location, and general physical features. One child asked what Canada's population is. The children searched through their texts and the encyclopedia to secure the answer, and then raised the question why so much land area contained such a relatively small number of people. The children considered this problem carefully. Examining the map in the classroom, they compared Canada's geographic position with that of the United States. They noticed that both nations were between approximately the same lines of longitude, but were quite different in respect to lines of latitude. This comparison led the children to the problem, "Can Canada support a larger population?"

The children then tried to define their problem more explicitly so that they might reach a plausible solution. After a brief investigation they decided that a knowledge of the products, trade, topography, and climate of Canada was essential in order to answer their problem. With some help from the teacher, the children listed on the chalkboard the following questions for investigation:

1. What is Canada's location in relation to the great world trade routes?
2. How much year-round shipping does Canada have from open ports?
3. Where is Canada's present population located?
4. What features in Canada would attract population?
5. Where is Canada's climate most pleasant?

After investigating these questions, they found that Canada has one of the world's highest standards of living. She is also a great manufacturing and trading nation even though her eastern harbors are closed from November to May. They learned that the French Canadians had settled Quebec before the arrival of the Pilgrims in New England. They discovered that Canada's great north land is rich in resources but inhospitable to human habitation.

The children were allowed much freedom in their investigation. They moved from the classroom to the school library as needed. One group of children decided to organize its information into graphs which compared the average temperatures per year with population density. Another group agreed to construct a series of dioramas illustrating Canadian industries and occupations.

When the children had formulated the purposes that were to guide their study, they gained some control over the content to be acquired and also the particular activities which can organize the content. If they understand the kind of work to be done and the appropriate activities to be accomplished, the planning can develop as the work proceeds.

During the process of this activity, the teacher kept constantly in mind that the development of the children's thinking skills was an important educational objective. She continually attempted to help the children learn the processes of active, productive thinking rather than factual outcomes of the thinking of others. She endeavored to raise the level of the children's thinking through the classroom discussions, the children's involvement in those discussions, the type of questions asked, and the degree of student activity.

You should encourage the children to proceed independently of you, to define the kinds of activities they seek to achieve, and to apply the appropriate learning activities. These fifth grade children recognized the need for more information to develop certain activities and turned immediately to the problem of locating sources and collecting desired information. They readily related the facts gathered about topography, population, and climate to a specific activity and thus arrived at a solution. When they checked their first hypothesis against an authoritative source and found that it was not satisfactory, the children turned immediately to the solution of this new problem—to find and correct the mistake they had made. Again they proceeded independently to define the problem, collect the facts needed, and work out a new solution to the activity they had planned. This was done as a group undertaking. The children were able to work together successfully, each participating freely and contributing helpfully in defining the type of work necessary. They could select and apply a suitable activity, graph, mural, or diorama by which they would organize their efforts.

EVALUATION

Evaluation does not occur only at the completion of an activity; it should be carefully made at every point in the process of the activity at which an appraisal will ensure sound progress. Evaluation should take place as the problem is being formulated. It should occur again following the discussion, for example, as to whether a study of Canada's population would give a meaningful understanding of that nation. Then the children have to evaluate the facts collected and determine their relevancy to the solution of the problem. They were concerned as to whether all the important facts involved had been considered. When they were brought face to face with contradictory conclusions of recognized authorities, evaluations were made. A judgment also had to be made as to how the new conclusions affected their previously planned activity.

The children studying Canada secured valuable experience in using their own insight and critical evaluation and in directing their own efforts in carrying out the work. Insight, self-evaluation, and self-direction should be experienced if children are to become independent and competent. Learning comes through self-activity, but the learning should have meaning and direction. Children learn to evaluate by evaluating, and to solve a problem by solving it. They likewise learn to cooperate by cooperating.

A *laissez-faire* attitude towards activity projects which allows children to work haphazardly and often wastefully without learning how to exercise self-direction productively, effectively, and efficiently can be disastrous. Children do not acquire those abilities needed in life by experiences of wasteful self-direction. Starting in kindergarten, children need constant experience in evaluating their learning and activities.

Not all classes are ready to assume immediately the responsibility of evaluation and the freedom associated with it. If the children in your classroom have been accustomed to authoritative direction—and if they have been encouraged to sit, listen, and repeat and have not used what they have learned—you must plan and proceed carefully with the change to self-direction in activity projects. A too sudden shift in methods may be disastrous. You should begin where the children are and proceed from there. Children can evaluate their learning and activities only when they have had experience, understand the processes of planning, and have been involved in planning and processing the activity.

Initially you will be the leader while you gradually increase the children's degree of participation. By building a background of successful experiences, you can develop confidence and competence in the children. Training them in the skills needed to organize activity projects either individually or as groups builds their capacity for self-direction and independent evaluation. New responsibilities in evaluation must be simple, specific, and at the child's level of ability.

PROMOTION OF GROUP WORK

In order to complete a successful activity a group of children must have unity of purpose. There should be control of participation and ideas as the group discusses and plans the execution of the work. The success of a particular project depends upon the understanding of each child in the group of how to proceed in thinking through a problem and reaching a decision.

You probably will meet two general problems in group activity work. First, there will be those situations that disrupt and interfere with the group's work. Then there will be the problem of meeting individual needs which might not affect the work of the group as a whole. There might be a child who does not participate in the activity as well as he should because of lack of confidence, lack of background, inability to express ideas well, or mistreatment by others. A child might be over-aggressive and continually disrupt the functioning of the activity. A child may lack adaptability to other children, to new ideas, and to criticism. There may be personal rivalries and dislikes, intolerance, and lack of respect for others. A particular child may employ delaying tactics to annoy others, or he may simply like to argue.

When such problems arise, you should bring the situation pointedly to the attention of the children for their consideration and possible solution. You should encourage a discussion to determine the causes of the disruption and the children who are responsible for it. Presenting such problems to the class and encouraging the children to suggest a course of action may possibly facilitate problem solutions. However, as the teacher you may have to offer the children a solution in order to make their arrival at a solution less difficult. You may have to assign a segment or part of the problem to a specific child, so that he works alone; but his contribution upon completion can still be integrated into the whole group's activity. You may have to remove him from the group entirely, explaining the reason to him. He may need to work by himself on particular problems which you both solve cooperatively. It may be that three or more such children form a special group to which you need to give special supervision and direction. You should make it quite clear to such children that it is a breach of discipline to disrupt the work of the group or not to abide by the regulations which the group has agreed upon.

There are several guidelines which you might follow in helping children to accept basic responsibilities as individuals participating in a group activity:

The contribution of each child who is doing his best within the group should be considered and respected. Even though his contribution is not as important as that of another participant, he should be accorded the same courteous treatment. Your own reactions, aimed at encouraging and helping individuals to improve, should be an effective demonstration of respect and consideration. It is very easy for a group of children to discourage a timid child by laughing, smiling, raising eyebrows, shrugging shoulders, or showing indifference or contempt in other ways. Children should learn respect for others. It takes time to develop an attitude of respect in the classroom. However, respect is a two-way street; a child should earn as well as deserve considerate treatment.

Each child should try to participate constructively in the group activity. He should be prepared to make constructive contributions to the group discussion. To build a foundation for such participation, you may need to explain assignments carefully to enable each child to understand what is to be done and the responsibilities he is to assume. It is possible to ask children to do too much. The activity may be too complicated and involved, or the group too large for children to succeed.

Each child should understand what the others are contributing. If a child does not understand what others are saying—if he does not listen well and critically—he cannot participate intelligently in an activity. Children should not be allowed to ignore statements which they do not grasp because of poor listening or lack of comprehension. Poor understanding is a primary reason why group activities fail. A child, missing what has been said, loses the thread of the developing discussion and is not able to participate constructively in the activity. A child who is speaking must be listened to, but he also should be challenged to express his ideas clearly and logically. You may have to revise some statements and directions given by a child for full comprehension by all the children. If you sense that there is misunderstanding, you must raise questions yourself, although this responsibility should be gradually shifted to the children as they become more experienced in activity work.

Each child should help with the development of class activity. Children easily become lost but often hesitate to ask for help or direction. You should be patient with a child who indicates, "I don't understand," or "I'm lost." It would help if occasionally you provide a summary to help children to determine how far they have gone and how much further they must go. The more capable child may think a review is a waste of time. You should guard against the temptation of expecting more of a child than he is capable of producing, but at the same time you should challenge him to develop his abilities. The less capable child should be given more time to organize his thinking and produce tangible evidence on his project.

Each child should be free to present his ideas. If the child feels secure as a member of the group, if his ideas have been received in the past, and if he has a wholesome relation with the teacher he is more likely to contribute to the activity. On the other hand if he has no rapport with you, if he is not accepted by other children, and if he does not understand the procedures concerned with the activity his whole attitude toward the activity may be a negative one. A little success is a great stimulant. If you indicate an appreciation of the child's efforts and encourage the other children to make use of their ideas when they are helpful, you can foster the correct attitude in the timid child toward effective participation in the group activity. This backward child greatly needs to have a creditable contribution.

The classroom atmosphere should be open. A child should feel free to defend his ideas and to change them when sufficient evidence is available. Any worthwhile activity can encourage the child to sift evidence and evaluate conclusions. You should encourage a child who believes he has a valid contribution not to give up because of group pressure. He should be open-minded, but he should evaluate opposition carefully. Activities which are worthwhile encourage independent individual thinking and cooperative discussion. Clear thinking does not mean obstinancy or arguing from a weakness or an emotional bias. You may have to interrupt a heated discussion and request that goals and positions be restated.

Each child should earnestly endeavor to improve the activity project. This should be done not for his own selfish reasons but for the benefit of the entire class. It is common for a group organizing a new activity or project to fail to decide on a goal or a procedure. The children can become frustrated if the discussion drags on even though they seem to be working together effectively. Again, you may have to help the children to become organized, reach a compromise, and decide on a goal acceptable to the majority. You should be realistic. There are difficulties and failures in activity work. Children are young, human, and lacking in experience. It is amazing how constructive and creative they can be if their miraculous energy is channeled into constructive and self-directed activities. They should be aided in an understanding of the causes of failures and mistakes and how to prevent them.

COOPERATIVE ACTIVITIES

Activities can assume many forms, depending on the nature of the work, your personal preferences and particular skills, the age and maturity of the children, and the philosophy and climate of the school. The activities in which your children are involved may depend on an abundance of or a lack of supplies. You may have an activity that involves the entire class, an individual child, or a particular group of children. One group of children might prepare a panel discussion, another a dramatization, and another special reports.

In the *kindergarten*, activities should provide experiences which can broaden the children's understandings of themselves, other people, and the world in which they live. Since these children are not yet able to use extensively such tools of learning as reading and interpreting pictures, their activities should depend on firsthand experiences which you may find commonplace but which are new and unexplored to five-year-olds. One activity might involve exploring the school neighborhood for birds, trees, shrubs, weeds, insects, water, woods, and places to cross the street safely and it might include an exploration of the school itself to see what people do. In talking to the custodian, the principal, other teachers, the doctor, and nurse, the children are developing powers of observation and skills in human relationships.

Since children vary in their readiness for learning, your purposes for a particular activity may vary with the children involved. To complete a particular goal, each child in the group may carry out a specific activity.

In the *primary grades,* children should learn to care for and organize such materials as paper, pencils, crayons, clay, wood, tools, plants, books, globes, and maps. They should learn to move about quietly and efficiently in securing necessary materials and to proceed with activities with an increasing degree of independence. You may have to encourage a child with a quiet word or a cheerful smile to act with independence and confidence. You can teach children in these early years to gain a great deal of independence and self-control in activity work which are so necessary for them to build self-initiative and develop responsibility.

In the *intermediate grades,* the physical environment is a profound influence on activity work. Movable chairs and tables are a valuable asset as is a filing cabinet containing a collection of pictures, newspaper clippings, and special pamphlets. Shelves are necessary to hold construction materials. There should be bookcases for reference books, magazines, and particular selections from the school library. There should be varied textbooks available (both single and multiple copies suitable for the grade), as well as a large globe, a large oilcloth outline map, physical maps, political maps, and topographical maps. These should all be appropriate to the children's interest and need. Several large worktables, a broad shelf under the windows, and basic science materials are a few essentials for pre-adolescent activity work.

There is really no end to the type or variety of activities you can use with children in the elementary school. The children might conduct health or diet experiments with mice or guinea pigs. They might attempt to manufacture and cure cheese. They might check safety hazards around the school area. They could construct scrapbooks to send to an African or Vietnamese school. Class representatives could visit a local school board meeting.

For the activity to be worthwhile it should involve planning, initial research and basic investigation, evaluation, and a follow-up. Activities in which children become involved seem to fall into one of the following categories. They collect and evaluate information through visiting, experimenting, observing, taking field trips, and gathering artifacts. They might systematize and present data through the construction of dioramas, murals, posters, or papier-mâché artifacts; the organization and presentation of dramatic plays; the construction of graphs, or maps; and the process of interviewing various kinds of persons.

RECORDS OF ACTIVITIES

In the process of conducting an activity, the children may read books, watch motion pictures and television programs, listen to the radio, and conduct interviews. You and the children should devise some record keeping system. Each child should keep an individual folder or an index card catalogue of activities. A record of his reading might be organized as follows and copies mimeographed for the children:

My name:
The author:
The title:
The date of the book:
Information I collected:
What I think of the book:

The written work of children—stories, poems, and letters—should be kept on file and easily available for children in the group who may wish to use them as a reference. Individual children or a group might find it useful to keep a log or a diary. Essential discussions may be taped for later use by an individual child to clarify goals or direction.

RESEARCH

Taba conducted several studies concerned with the effect of activities on children's learning.[3] The conclusions from her studies of productive learning indicate the following rationale for including activities within the curriculum.

1. The activity, to have learning value, must be related to one or more objectives; otherwise it may be a waste of time. Each different activity represents a different kind of learning behavior and probably requires the use of a differentiated method of learning. It cannot be assumed that

[3] Hilda Taba, *Teachers' Handbook for Elementary Social Studies* (Reading, Mass.: Addison-Wesley Publishing Co., Inc., 1967), pp. 27–86. See also, Hilda Taba and James L. Hills, *Teacher Handbook for Contra Costa Social Studies Grades 1–6* (Hayward, Calif.: Rapid Printers and Lithographers, Inc., 1965).

an activity, in itself, enables the child to interpret the meaning of the activity or make generalizations from it unless both the objective and the method of learning are clearly understood by the child.

2. An activity should involve knowledge, thinking, attitudes, feelings, and sensitivities as well as skills.

3. An activity which produces maximum productive learning experiences can have more than one objective. For example, an activity should help the child to master content as well as to promote a particular skill and thinking process.

4. For the activities which a child experiences during the school year to be effective, they should have some sequence and order. Each new activity should be built on the learnings and skills acquired from the previous one. A child does not secure an attitude or learn the thinking process from a single activity. Attitudes and processes develop gradually; they need to be implemented and repeated in a series of related activities. Initial activities should be concrete and require simple thought processes, but as the school year proceeds they should become increasingly more abstract and require more formal reasoning.

5. As the year progresses, the activities that the child experiences should involve more content and require the performance of more complex skills. There should be an increasing demand to synthesize ideas as the child performs activities. Each activity should demand a bit more than the preceding one, but should not require so much that the child becomes discouraged. Each new activity should be more of a challenge, or a different type of challenge than the previous activity, if maximum learning is to be secured.

6. Learning will be more effective if the child can apply what he has learned in one activity to a new activity. "A continuous effort to apply what is known to explain something new, to predict, and to hypothesize will develop habits and learning sets in school that permit an individual to continue learning beyond school." [4]

7. There are two principal activities which may be used as vehicles of learning. One type of activity simply helps the child to organize, interpret, and express the learning which he has already acquired. The second type of experience challenges the child to accept new content, new ideas, or new skills. It should be an experience which is new and unfamiliar to him. To develop the activity he should either acquire new information or skills or reorganize what he has already learned.

8. The activity should allow the child to organize learning and develop skills as an individual. He should process information independently and should be encouraged to do his own inquiry and his own thinking, as

[4] *Ibid.*, p. 29.

well as work out the activity with his own ideas. The child should come to grips with the activity on his own initiative.

9. Children learn in a multiple of ways—from talking with other children, from listening, from reading, and from watching. Each child has his own method of learning. There should be a wide range of learning activities within the classroom to enable each child to become familiar with that way of learning which is the most efficient and desirable for him. "Although easily overlooked, the expressive and accommodative experiences, which require application or utilization of knowledge, are the very experiences that guarantee internalization of learning and productive use of learning as opposed to stockpiling information." [5]

10. Activities should be open-ended. One group of children might work on a particular activity and develop an entirely different conclusion in content depth and in way of thinking than another group working on the same basic activity. One group might develop its activity with a great deal of abstraction and sophistication while another might develop the same activity on a more concrete and simple level. The activity should be sufficiently open-ended to allow for children's differences in ability, experience, and background.

CONCLUSION

Activities discussed in this chapter are integral rather than peripheral. They should make genuine contributions to the total growth of children since they are not "gimmicks" or "frills" when properly planned and executed. The diverse interests, needs, and skills of individual children can be incorporated into plans for activities. Vital activities enable children to do things by themselves and to share with other children. This helps to create an atmosphere in which each child can help himself to grow while simultaneously stimulating others. If children can plan activities, this will help them to learn how to live together creatively and productively. While the emphasis in this chapter has been on activities closely correlated with the formal curriculum, it is important to note that activities can be valuable before school, after school, on Saturdays, and during summers. Their value is not limited by clock or calendar. The activities which can be cooperatively planned by the teacher and his pupils are an important supplement to traditional kinds of learning activities. Since they are an important part of the school's plan for total growth, the use of the term "extra-curricular" is not applicable—either for activities carried on during the regular school day or for any other time. Activities

[5] *Ibid.*, p. 30.

are an important part of curriculum planning for all subject areas and for all ages.

PROJECTS AND READINGS

1. Douglass indicates that the textbook continues to dominate the work of the teacher. "This is primarily because neither private nor public education can yet provide a sufficient variety of teaching materials to permit the teacher to feel secure about departing from this anchorage. The teacher may find it necessary to rely more heavily on the textbook than he would like. Where the teacher feels that his own subject matter background is weak, he may prefer to rely upon the "authority" which the text provides, rather than on his own judgment, in determining children's activities and projects." [Malcolm P. Douglass, *Social Studies from Theory to Practice in Elementary Education* (Philadelphia: J. B. Lippincott Co., 1967), p. 63. Reprinted by permission.] What activities, which are pedagogically desirable but based on the textbook only, might you find useful?

2. It might be helpful to keep a checklist of the participation of individual children within a group activity with a description of the part each child played. This could give you a record from which you might plan diversified activities. Can you suggest how such a record might be organized and used?

3. In preplanning, it is necessary to formulate objectives, goals, or anticipated outcomes that might be expected from the activity. Of course, the entire class may not be concerned with all the objectives stated, since each group of children may wish to formulate its own goals. However, if you do a good job in activity planning, you can anticipate all or most of the goals. Suppose a more capable group and a less mature group are both working on the same activity. How will their goals be different? How will they be the same?

4. Construction contributes much to those activities which are an integral part of learning. The things to be made are *less significant* than the process and what happens to the children as they plan, execute, and use the things they construct. The materials used should be easy for the children to handle and appropriate for the objects made. Can you think of an activity whose physical product is as important as the process of construction of that product?

5. An activity might be expressed in terms of convergent thinking or of divergent thinking. Guilford suggests that teachers can plan activities with children in two ways in "The Three Faces of Intellect," *The American Psychologist,* XIV, No. 1 (March, 1959), p. 472. Everyone can be directed toward the same or similar type of activities which encourages "convergent thinking." The activity can be planned to develop a rich variety of acceptable learnings which would result in "divergent thinking." He suggests that learning experiences for children should include both kinds. Can you make a discrimination between those activities which are convergent and those which are divergent?

6. The examples of activities cited in this chapter are related to subject areas taught during the school day. There are also "extra-curricular" activities which are scheduled during the school day as well as outside school hours. It would be useful to study the topic of extra-curricular activities to determine which ones are appropriate for the elementary level and what their administrative considerations are: (a) Who will serve as sponsors for activities? (b) How could

they be financed? (c) What safety problems exist if children leave school after safety patrols leave their posts? (d) Should activities be completely school sponsored, or is it appropriate to encourage groups such as the cub scouts to organize activities? (e) What factors should determine whether an activity is more properly scheduled during the day or at the end of the school day? (f) What subject areas should be organized outside school hours, for example, an enrichment program for mathematically gifted children. (g) If an activity is planned by the school, what differentiates it from the basic curriculum?

7. Many elementary pupils participate in activities organized by church and other community groups. What are some of the ways that such activities can be related to the school curriculum? To what extent is it appropriate to use school time to prepare for a non-school sponsored activity, for example, preparing posters for a community contest?

8. Laymen often sponsor activities for elementary children. To what extent does it appear necessary for school personnel to supervise activities to assure that safety and general welfare measures are taken when non-school activities occur on school property?

9. While subject matter may be learned in an activity, the process of learning to work together seems to be the main potential advantage of school activities. What criteria could be used to determine if so much time and energy are spent on activities that other kinds of school learnings will be neglected?

10. Often children who need activities are not inclined to participate in them. At the same time, children participating in activities of their choosing tend to benefit most from them. To what extent do you feel it justifiable to encourage children to participate in activities? How much encouragement can be exerted without its becoming pressure?

11. A pair of gerbils (Asian rodents) is housed in a mathematics laboratory in a Philadelphia elementary school. First and second graders use a stop watch to plot the progress of the animals though a wooden block maze designed and built by the pupils. The teacher, Lore Rasmussen, says, "This is the way children really learn: by doing original research." (Example reported in "What's Right with U.S. Public Schools," a compiled series booklet, *Christian Science Monitor*, June 22, 1965 through August 24, 1965.) What are the advantages of planning for a variety of such activities when developing units? What are some criteria for determining which activities are appropriate for a particular class? How would such experiences contribute to an understanding of the structure of mathematics? What are some other values of such activity?

12. These sources will give you more ideas on activities within the curriculum:

a. Nathaniel Hickerson, *Education for Alienation* (Englewood Cliffs, N.J.: Prentice-Hall, Inc., 1966), 98 pp. This book provides a broad idea of what schools in economically deprived districts are like and gives suggestions for program improvements.

b. Louis E. Raths, Selma Wasserman, Arthur Jonas, and Arnold M. Rothstein, *Teaching for Thinking: Theory and Application* (Columbus, Ohio: Charles C. Merrill Books, Inc., 1967), 374 pp. The authors explain the relationship between theory and learning activities.

c. David Beggs and Edward Buffie, *Nongraded Schools in Action* (Bloomington: Indiana University Press, 1967), 270 pp. The second part of the book describes a collection of individual reports from schools where some degree of non-gradedness has been successfully developed.

d. Ryland W. Crary, *Humanizing the School* (New York: Alfred A. Knopf, 1967), 481 pp. Crary describes the development of a model curriculum which incorporates four dimensions of experience: the humanistic-ethical, the creative-aesthetic, the scientific-quantitative, and the vocational-utilitarian.

e. George Dennison, *The Lives of Children* (New York: Random House, Inc., 1969), 308 pp. Dennison claims that the schools, as institutions, are killing the vital living–learning force natural to every child and shows how learning can become a vibrant, exciting, dynamic force within the lives of children.

18

Facing Today and Tomorrow

CHANGE IN A DEMOCRACY

Seventy per cent of Americans will live on two per cent of the land, contained in a few metropolitan areas, by 1985 if the present trend toward urbanization continues. This is but one of many startling predictions about the changing nature of life in America. The elementary school which seeks to develop a meaningful curriculum must help children to live more effectively today and at the same time must anticipate the kind of world children apparently will live in during their lifetime. It was noted in Chapter 1 that there are tendencies, unless checked by conscious effort, to develop a blind allegiance to the old ways and the old days. In Chapter 11 some of the ways in which changing conditions affect individuals were described. This chapter includes a summary of some anticipated changes and examples of their implications for curriculum. It is appropriate to re-emphasize that change is constant; therefore, curriculum planning and revision will be continuous in a school which takes seriously its responsibilities to individual children and to the total society.

Alcorn, Kinder, and Schunert forcefully point to the crisis of change in education:

> At no time in history has the curriculum maker been confronted with a greater challenge. He is faced with the paradox of attempting to maintain cultural stability and unity in a period of revolutionary change and at the same time attempting to develop a dynamic educational program to keep pace with the needs of a changing world.[1]

[1] Marvin D. Alcorn, James S. Kinder, and Jim R. Schunert, *Better Teaching in Secondary Schools,* Revised Edition (New York: Holt, Rinehart, & Winston, Inc., 1964), p. 369.

Faced with change and challenge as America is today, the country is experiencing some drift toward "nativism," an almost blind tendency to cling to the past as a means of sensing some security in the midst of flux or insecurity. America faces big powers with ideologies which seem to threaten what speakers call, with blurred definitions, "The American Way of Life." There is considerable division and doubt at home at a time when those seeking security through consensus would have the nation making a united attack on external enemies and apparent internal challenges. The teacher who believes that democracy is vital partially as a result of its ability to react *rationally* and *reasonably* in the face of needed change may have difficulties in convincing others that the curriculum of the 1940's, or some other past decade, is not valid today. The American school is dedicated to the democratic ideal devoted to the preservation of individual dignity and worth. The school should seek to develop a curriculum which helps the individual to develop into his maximum potential as an individual seeking his fulfillment in a society which not only gives him freedom *from* fear, exploitation, and domination but also freedom *to become* his unique best self.

One writer claims that education responsive to a changing society should be planned in harmony with the following criteria:

1. The individual should be respected, but he should live cooperatively with the group to be able to respect the individuality of others.
2. While the private aspects of a person's life must be safeguarded, the public component should fulfill social goals and make social systems creative.
3. There should be a free flow of ideas to spread human knowledge and make excellence more prevalent.
4. Decision-making should be based on knowledge, not on ceremony or status of individuals and groups.
5. Democratic institutions should be both humane and efficient to the highest degree possible.
6. Leaders should be elected democratically and should be allowed to function freely during their terms—with reasonable checks and balances operating on them. If removed from office, they should be dismissed through due process of law.[2]

The school which accepts these tenets has some guidelines for evaluating present and needed curricular experiences. These statements suggest the types of behavior needed by the individual in a democratic society. Curricular objectives and means of attaining them can be selected on the basis of their contribution to democratic behavior. Democracy is here presumed to be the basic value taught in American schools.

[2] Harbans Singh Bhola, "The Need for Planned Change . . . In Education," *Theory into Practice* (College of Education, Ohio State University), V, No. 1 (February, 1966), p. 8.

Compatible skills, facts, and values should be stressed to implement the democratic ideal. As conditions change, the *means* of attaining democracy will change—as will curriculum content and the methods designed to strengthen democracy. Democracy in a sense is a constant in the midst of change.

This is an optimistic view in a sense. There is an implication that democracy is a flexible yet stable value, that it has a built-in strength from which its adherents can venture forth on uncharted journeys. Education for democracy is on the frontier of the future. As democracy is widely practiced and individuals in all conditions of life find themselves enriched through it, it can become a stabilizing core for organizing personal and societal ways of meeting change and challenge.

The democratic way of life provides a means of preserving the best of past and present as well as a means of adjusting as needed to help the individual attain his best potentiality. The school thus is both *a preserving agent* for the society since it uses ageless democratic values, and *an agent of change* because it helps children to develop into secure human beings who are capable of critical thinking (about the past as well as the present), creative living, and imaginative approaches to new situations.[3]

EXAMPLES OF CHANGE

The topic of reaction to change is a major one, suitable for volumes rather than paragraphs in one chapter. However, for our purposes here, we will mention a few basic changes and suggest illustrative curricular responses in the hope that this will increase your awareness of change as a significant factor in curriculum planning for the elementary school of today and tomorrow. A more detailed study of societal factors than is possible in this chapter should be conducted as a part of your curriculum analysis.

Mass Society

Americans are being crowded together to a degree beyond that which the frontiersman with his ever present new frontiers could imagine. The city is a place where there are jobs, and hence has been attracting people

[3] In the following sections, the verb form of "will" is used extensively. A statement of changes in several areas of contemporary society is made first; then the "will" verbs are used somewhat dogmatically to imply a degree of optimism that indeed schools *will* make those adjustments and adaptations needed for a meaningful curriculum in a changing world. You may wish to change the verbs to "should" or "may," in case you want to be more "practical" or "objective." Changes are taking place so rapidly that the ideas expressed in this chapter probably are on the conservative side.

by the tens of thousands with amazing rapidity. (There is some tendency to move out of the inner city, but only when access to the inner city can be arranged.) The number of Americans is increasing to such a point that there will be 256 million by 1984, of whom three out of every four will crowd into urban areas concentrated on two per cent of the land space of the nation. These extra millions will probably work in large-scale business or government organizations. They will be governed by big government. Their behavior will be manipulated by advertising, massive in scope, which seeks to convince as many as possible to live in certain manners while utilizing specific products and services. Large pressure groups will struggle for favorable positions of power and rights while individuals may be seen as *units* of power and prestige rather than as individuals.

The curriculum which seeks to maintain the dignity and worth of individuals in a mass society will attempt to foster a sturdy self-reliance and self concept that will enable a person to be someone and something in the midst of millions. It will educate him to think creatively and critically while working cooperatively with others in large-scale bureaucracies that tend to evaluate people in terms of their positions rather than their unique variations. Such a curriculum will condition children to work together efficiently and creatively without sacrificing individual differences. It will assist them to experience some of the enriching diversity of the crowded metropolis, which cannot be done without help. Residents of large cities may have few contacts outside their occupational and neighborhood circles. It will provide relief to individuals trapped by the complexity and impersonality of extensive urbanization and organizations—whether because of race, ability, environment, or limited experiences with learning situations. Special materials, facilities, personnel, and curriculum will be planned when school personnel seek in assisting each individual to avoid being "lost in the shuffle" of mass organizations in crowded urban areas.

Mobility

Large-scale organizations (industrial, military, government, or other) have the tendency to move people and operations. The extent of America's mobility can be seen in two illustrative facts: Three of every ten Americans have moved from their native state; tens of millions Americans may move in a few months' period. An extreme example of intracity mobility is the case of the first grader who had attended seven different schools (her parents moved whenever they could avoid paying rent). Whatever the reason, Americans move often—and frequently very far. Many children have moved to many places around the globe and are likely to continue this fluid mobility into adulthood. Some children have had many experiences in living in other countries, often for periods which exceed residence in America.

The schools will react to mobility in many ways. They will need to accept the fact that children in a particular classroom or school will not have had comparable curricular experiences, and hence each teacher must diagnose the position of each child and ascertain what learning experiences should be planned. Schools will seek to establish loyalties to nation and humanity rather than to a particular community or state. They will strive to help children develop internal security and adaptability, which can provide a reasonable sense of stability in the midst of change. They will help children to establish a sense of worth so that they will not need to strive for status at the sacrifice of self in new communities by means of displays of wealth, power, strength, or other superficial means.

Science and Technology

Some "signs of the times" include: (a) windmill towers used for television antennas; (b) abandoned railroad stations used as residences, restaurants, or repair shops; (c) one room schools used for varied purposes or destroyed; (d) canals grown up with weeds; (e) small grocery stores abandoned. The face of America continues to be changed by science and technology. The National Aeronautics and Space Administration reportedly has estimated that two-thirds of the products that will be available in 1984 have not been developed, and that one half of the children now in grades one through six will work in jobs which do not yet exist. The technological revolution has caused increased demands for persons who are prepared for certain types of positions: professional and technical work, sales work, clerical work, service work, management and ownership, and crafts and supervision. These are jobs which require considerable education and in many cases sophistication in dealing with complexity and abstraction. The jobs which do not require such competencies are on the decline.

Preparation for the type of responsibility needed in modern life in America is tentative in the sense that each individual will have to extend his education or prepare himself for a new type of job to replace the one which has become obsolete. In addition, personal skills needed for successful living will change. Home computers may be developed to set up grocery lists, appointments, and inventories of assets; compute bank balances and write checks; figure income taxes and follow instructions phoned from the office—activated only by the authorized voices of its owners!

Schools confronted with massive scientific and technological change will have to study alternatives and select tentative answers. Education will have to focus upon developing the individual to his maximum *personal* potentiality; with increased roles for automated machinery and computers and decreased work roles for persons, the preparation for work cannot continue as the direct or implied preoccupation of curriculum planning. The constructive use of leisure time and the decline of work as the basis of self concept will become predominant concerns. With knowledge exploding in geometrical frequencies, learning *how to learn* will be more significant than attempting to learn small segments of current knowledge. With computers able to store current specific information and retrieve it with fantastic rapidity when called for, the effort to memorize facts will become archaic since much information is not recalled by slow-functioning minds. Learning to ask questions and to utilize information will be more valuable than rote memorization and meaningless recitation of facts. When there are mechanical means—and teachers who understand how they function—it will become possible for learning to become highly individualized. Children will be aided in learning what they need to know when they need to know it, in order to continue in their progression toward individual goals which they, in cooperation with teachers and parents, have set for themselves.

Economics

An affluent society does not place so much status on the acquisition of goods as does a poor society. The values of the society of scarcity do not motivate human behavior in an affluent society. The economics of a rich, complex society can be learned only through years of experiencing and studying.

The school will need to teach economics (private as well as public and commercial) from the primary grades upward. It will have to use means other than those related to occupations to promote learning since machines and computers will assume major work roles; hence it will turn to intrinsic motivations wherein individual pupils find satisfaction in learning more about their world and the ways in which they relate to it. Individuals will learn the satisfactions of being, rather than the feelings of being units of production. Schools, in cooperation with other institutions of the society, will help children to develop a democratic value system compatible with an economy of affluence. In a hetereogenous society this is difficult, but the schools as reflectors of society will attempt to narrow the lag between what is taught and what is real.

New Groups and Individuals Concerned with Education

As education is increasingly perceived to be the avenue which leads to a better way of life and as pressure groups of all kinds become better organized, there will be irresistible demands that quality education be made available to all. This has been the historic American tradition—schools helping the emerging downtrodden to climb to a brighter future through education.

The schools will attempt to capitalize upon the interest of parents and will help them to realize their aspirations both for children and for themselves. Schools will become focal points for parents and other citizens to seek improvements for individuals of all ages and for the community in general. The gap in communications between school professionals and varied types of laymen will narrow as school people sincerely seek to communicate with and interact with laymen. School people of the future will talk with others instead of talking at them. The concept of the community school (schools extending their influences into the community and in turn bringing the community into the schools to promote learning as well as to learn) will increase the meaningfulness of schools to individual learners in the community. Through contacts with the school staff, those who in the past have felt alienated from the society as a whole, the "disadvantaged," will find the means to what is called "upward mobility"—the attainment of the desired things of life by children in greater quality and quantity than enjoyed by their parents. With hope for progress a reality, frustrations which now lead in many cases to hate will instead be channeled into rational and purposeful choices.

Conformity

Large-scale organizations, mass media, and fluctuating values often may lead individuals to conform to others' views and life patterns. There is a certain security in doing this, particularly for the young and their peer group who may feel that parents are bewildered by and confused about the changing society.

Understanding teachers will establish real communications with children as they competently help them to find meaning in their own lives and accept, but do not necessarily agree with in all cases, their ideas and thoughts. This relationship will to a degree free children from compulsion toward peer conformity and enable each child to find his identity in a changing world. Conformity will be viewed as a symptom of those who do not have the will and the competence to be individuals in a crowded and impersonal world or in organizations which seem to manipulate and to control rather than to care. The school will help parents, whose status is wrapped up in organizational interrelationships, to see that even in a mass society there is need for creative individuality and for a lessening of compulsive efforts to get their children accepted by having them be like everyone else!

Changes in Value

America has been called the melting pot of the world, for it has absorbed diverse nationalities, races, religions, and cultures—as well as diverse socioeconomic classes and differences in education and other factors. There are conflicting value structures for the diverse elements which add both richness and stress to the nation.

The school will not reflect a particular value system. It will select the elements which appear to enhance democratic citizenship and dynamic individual participation in the ongoing society. It will seek to preserve certain values implicit in our heritage, even though this is a difficult task. It will continuously work with its community in assessing ways in which children and teachers can be helped to develop values, which ". . . provide the compass by which the educational process may be steered; they provide a sense of direction basic to any such conscious and direct attempt to influence human behavior as the operation of a formal and institutionalized school system."[4] Decisions about changing circumstances will be evaluated in terms of their impact upon such values as:

Respect for the worth and dignity of every individual.
Equality of opportunity for all children.
Encouragement of variability.
Faith in man's ability to make rational decisions.
Shared responsibility for the common good.
Respect for moral and spiritual values and ethical standards of conduct.[5]

Quality and Quantity

As machines do more and more work and as people live longer and longer, there is a question as to whether the quantity in terms of production and years of living can be matched with the quality of living. Some other societies, for example, the Athenian and to an extent the Roman, at one time had a leisured, affluent society, and eventually lost not only their wealth but also their freedom. Quality and quantity are not automatically paired. As the means to good health are enlarged, good health potentialities may be negated by too much food and too little exercise, to name but one example. Recreation can take forms which are harmful to self and others and leisure time can be boring—or filled with constructive, healthful, and pleasurable activities.

[4] G. Wesley Sowards and Mary Margaret Scobey, *The Changing Curriculum and the Elementary Teacher* (San Francisco: Wadsworth Publishing Co., Inc., 1961), p. 99.

[5] Association for Supervision and Curriculum Development, *Role of Supervisor and Curriculum Director in a Climate of Change,* 1965 Yearbook (Washington: The Association, 1965), p. 39.

Currently leisure time is being used in largely non-educative or non-cultural ways, which are not in themselves "bad." There is a question of *balance,* of what happens as the work week becomes shorter each decade and people spend their time watching television, visiting friends, doing yardwork and gardening, reading magazines, reading books, driving for pleasure, and playing records. Will increasing leisure be spent only on diversion, even when there is little work from which to seek diversion; or will there be an increase in civic, educational, and cultural activities?

The school curriculum will help children to learn a variety of leisurely activities, with balance between physical, recreational, and civic–cultural activities. It will stress not only factual knowledge and attitudes toward constructive leisure but also an environment in which practice is consistent with teaching.

Parental Roles

Families have been increasingly shifted from producing to consuming units, from economic to affectional units. Children have become economic liabilities. Recreational patterns, availability of transportation to take individual family members in different directions, increased tendencies of both parents to work, and other factors have decreased the influence of the family upon children. Dependence upon the peer group for both values and activities has become commonplace. Where there is one or no parent, this dependence may be increased, since an adult model is lacking in many such cases.

The school will seek to develop attitudes and aptitudes suitable for effective family living and also to supplement the family in those areas where it is not functioning. The school will also attempt to become more of a community center where families can profit from educational and recreational programs. Specialized school personnel will find themselves providing guidance for families faced with personal, psychological, economic, and other types of problems, in the conviction that strong school–home ties and mutual aid can increase the likelihood of effective behavioral changes in children.

Expanding Horizons in a Shrinking World

The world has shrunk psychologically. Viewed in the perspective of the immensity of space, almost instantaneous communications, and rapid transportation, the earth seems small. World forces affect each community in America—each has its rolls of dead and injured who responded to America's world role. The American, conscious of past sacrifices for peace and tranquility, may be bothered by cries for peace yet faced with the absence of it and upset by upheavals in other nations. It is difficult to find a strictly local problem; interdependence is recognized either with eagerness by those who see resulting enrichment or with caution by those who fear contamination of the "American Way of Life."

In recognition of a world which seems increasingly interrelated due to modern transportation and communication capabilities the school will redefine "local." It will foster a tolerance of others' views and a rational loyalty to America's heritage, an understanding of different viewpoints and policies, and a set of attitudes which will promote a realistic desire for peace and constructive relationships with diverse peoples. The school will continue to promote factual knowledge of past and present; but the emphasis will be upon present and future and upon functional human relations skills and knowledge such as foreign languages, sociology and anthropology, psychology, economics, political science, geography, and a critical study of history. Literature, music, art, and other expressions of cultures will become more organically related to school efforts to unite mankind into some kind of commonsense cooperation that will increase as nations discover it to be a realistic alternative to unwieldy efforts to maintain power blocs which could destroy most of civilization in a few moments. More teachers and pupils will have communications and contacts with people around the globe—through travel, letters, visual telephone conversations, tape-recorded exchanges, and other means. International and intercultural understanding will extend beyond a subject for study and become a way of living.

Other Challenges

The examples of change noted (and some suggested ways in which the curriculum should be adapted to them) are a very small sample of the total changing scene. Mass, complex, interrelated modern society is faced with change which occurs faster than could have been conceived of even a few years ago. It is the rate and extent of speed which set modern change apart from changes of other time periods when painful adjustments could gradually be completed over a century. Today, there is not a decade in which to adjust. The aspirations of peoples around the world are high, often higher than their apparent resources and there is an insistence that education must guide children into a good today and brighter tomorrow. There is a degree of optimism that through the educated man's way of thinking and living *problems will become challenges,* that through civilized processes difficulties may be solved in a way that is both humane and efficient, and that through democracy changes can occur without destroying the best of the past and without recourse to exploitation of one group for the benefit of others.

In addition to the problems previously discussed, the school will set the stage for a citizenry capable of facing diverse problems brought on by water and air pollution, traffic, junk, and poor management of resources. The curriculum will reflect the explosion of problems caused by change and will help children to develop ways of learning, reacting, and adapting which will be functional in a changing society.

Changing Educational Relationships

The increasing involvement of the state and federal governments, foundations, associations, and business and labor in education was discussed in Chapter 9. We should notice here that the problems and challenges faced by the society are so large that they cannot be met on a strictly local level. New types of educational partnerships will emerge in which efforts will be made to maintain the personal interest of the people in their schools and at the same time utilize the resources, both material and personnel, of the varied agencies concerned with education. The greater involvement of diverse groups and agencies in education is a reflection of the increased recognition that it is the growth industry of the nation, the present frontier which beckons people to extend or rebuild their lives. Education's potentialities make the old West look pale by comparison. Education opens new opportunities in the nation, around the world, and now in space and under the oceans, in ways that can only be perceived dimly in the light of present understandings and skills. The teacher is a part of the exciting and often bewildering days in which we live and into which we are proceeding and often being propelled by circumstances.

It appears obvious that the educators of the future, particularly those in responsible positions, will be among the best educated and most influential people. Many tasks that now consume excessive time and energy will be done by mechanical means or various types of teacher personnel. New organizational patterns will be planned for the diversified responsibilities assumed by the school.

Educators will become not only well educated in content directly related to the organization of curriculum but also in the many disciplines which contribute to an understanding of society and of learners. The teacher who is dedicated to a curriculum that makes sense for today as well as the world of tomorrow will be well educated through formal education and through experiences which will extend his formal education—he will travel; he will attend educative programs; he will read extensively.

The nation's current investment of tens of billions in education each year will increase, and with the increment will come demands that teachers be among the most capable and competent people in the society.

They will be involved in tasks so significant that they will be under scrutiny and pressure to bring about behavioral changes needed to cope with and benefit from societal restructuring of unimaginable magnitude.

EDUCATION FOR PRESENT AND FUTURE

Mayhew assigns a basic significance to contemporary happenings when he states, "Education will eventually be considered an enterprise replacing work as a means by which people will assign meaning to their lives." Education thus is seen as being in the very midst of institutions that are affected by alterations in the economy which are only a part of the basic change in society occurring before our often unperceiving eyes.[6]

Hutchins asks if the schools can prepare children for a future "shrouded" in uncertainty, for a society shifting from an economy of scarcity to one of affluence, for a time when basic strength could be undermined by wealth and leisure.[7] When such questions are raised, they need not be seen as pessimistic but rather viewed as being realistic. Many societies have arisen and fallen. The educator who examines curriculum questions without injecting a realistic appraisal of the present and future is guilty of indifference or blindness.

The staff of the NEA Project on Instruction calls for an urgent examination of the question, What is good education? The urgency, the staff notes, arises from three sources: (a) fundamental and rapid change in contemporary society; (b) the "almost incredible explosion of knowledge," from which selections must be made and which must be organized into instructional form; (c) new knowledge of how different persons learn in a variety of ways, knowledge which should be applied to help children learn so much new knowledge.[8]

The Project writers call for establishment of priorities ". . . premised on a recognition that education is a process of changing behavior and that a changing society requires the capacity for self-teaching and self-adaptation." Priorities suggested for curriculum studies include:

> Learning how to learn, how to attack new problems, how to acquire new knowledge.
> Using rational processes.
> Developing intellectual and vocational competence.
> Exploring values in new experiences.
> Understanding concepts and generalizations.

[6] "The Future that Young People Will Face in America," *U.S. News and World Report*, LVII, No. 7 (August 17, 1964), p. 56.

[7] Robert M. Hutchins, "Are We Educating Our Children for the Wrong Future?" *Saturday Review*, XLVIII, No. 37 (September 11, 1965), p. 66.

[8] National Education Association Project on Instruction, *Schools for the 60's* (Washington: The Association, 1963), pp. v–vi.

"Above all, the school must develop in the pupil the ability to learn under his own initiative and an abiding interest in doing so." [9]

Two of the recommendations of the Project on Instruction are closely related to this chapter; others were made about the content of curriculum in the light of changing conditions. Several other recommendations of the 33 made should also be examined for their relevance to the question at hand.[10] The urgency of these recommendations has been increased as the seventies have begun with rapid and turbulent change.

> Rational discussion of controversial issues should be an important part of the school program. The teacher should help students identify relevant information, learn techniques of critical analysis, make independent judgments, and be prepared to present and support them. The teacher should also help students become sensitive to the continuing need for objective re-examination of issues in the light of new information and changing conditions in society.
>
> . . .
>
> To help the student think critically about current issues, the curriculum should provide opportunities for adequate instruction about social forces and trends. International relations, economic growth, urbanization, population growth, science and technology, and mass media should receive attention commensurate with their significance in modern society.

The same Project staff continues its activities and is now studying the seventies with insights useful to elementary teachers.

We have noted that current changes are extensive. We may safely anticipate that present changes signal even greater ones, for change resembles a pebble thrown into calm water—it produces an ever-widening reaction. But, unlike the pebble's ripples, the effects of change do not diminish and die; rather, they set up their own results which in turn set up corollary effects; the influence of change increases with time and gains in intensity. The days ahead are exciting in potentialities, yet sobering in actuality unless education and other societal institutions make a *concentrated effort* to plan for the present and future. The teacher who understands himself, his pupils, and his society is in position to join in a concerted effort to consummate those long-cherished dreams of mankind that imagined it possible to utilize our material and human resources to build the "good life" for all who respond with vision and vigor. Democracy, dedicated to individual fulfillment, is uniquely flexible in altering its means to attain that end goal. Schools of democracy will reflect this dedication to individual fulfillment both in the present and in the future.

[9] *Ibid.*, p. 9.

[10] National Education Association Project on Instruction, *A Summary Report of the NEA Project on Instruction, Schools for the Sixties* (Washington: The Association, 1963), p. 9.

PROJECTS AND READINGS

1. "By the year 2000, or before, 'teaching' as it is now commonly accepted will be dead, and the job of the educator will be transformed into that of a 'facilitator'—one who creates a rich, responsive environment that will elicit the most learning and change from the student," according to George B. Leonard and John Poppy. Dreamers? Mr. Leonard is managing editor of *Look,* and Mr. Poppy a member of the *Look* staff. They further recommend that children get out into the community and also fly abroad, contending that this kind of experience would cost no more than present "alienation, delinquency, unemployment and war." (*Education U. S. A.*, October 16, 1967.) Are these proposals realistic in terms of conditions reported in this chapter? What proposals would you add to those of Leonard and Poppy, to make the schools relevant in terms of today and tomorrow?

2. "The future can be great only if we can help students learn how to develop a powerful mind—the great goal of all education. . . . Courses of study will increasingly be based on analyses of desirable behavioral outcomes—the information, attitudes, and skills needed for successful performance." [Edgar Dale, "Creating the Future," *The Newsletter* (School of Education, Ohio State University), XXXII, No. 8 (May, 1967).] Looking at the conditions noted in this chapter, what attributes, in addition to powerful minds, appear to be most needed? How can elementary schools help to develop those characteristics and competencies which appear relevant and essential?

3. "Educational environment and activity in the schools are symbolic of what man is today and what he wants to be tomorrow. The design of these symbols is a great art. The study of curriculum should be a preparation for this artistry." [Dwayne Huebner, in Helen F. Robison, ed., *Precedents and Promise in the Curriculum Field* (New York: Teachers College Press, Columbia University, 1966), p. 112.] If you could project elementary school objectives of today into future reality, would the society that would presumably develop be realistic in terms of the emerging future? What would characterize the elementary school of today that prepares children for the future?

4. "In an age of technology, the future leaders of men must increasingly become lifelong students of mankind." This is the essence of a Congressional testimony by Donald N. Michael. Earlier Michael was reported to have claimed that democracy's greatest peacetime challenge is to "provide quickly enough wise men and enough new social institutions through which to use their wisdom." (News release from University of Michigan, September 25, 1967.) The newswriter quoted above was trying to capture the ideas of a scholar concerned with the future. What are the attributes needed by future leaders that you would propose if you could influence governmental actions designed to prepare for the world of the future? What would be included in a proposal which is realistic in terms of future conditions and yet still maintains the democratic heritage of America?

5. "Militancy" is a term commonly applied to certain efforts in the civil rights field and on college campuses. It is activism applied to a challenge of the "Establishment"—depicted by the militants as the collaborating political, economic, and social leaders who seek to maintain their powers and to resist changes which might improve conditions for the poor as well as further justice. Some militants claim that their ends justify varied means, even violence if it

is an effective way to dramatize the need for and means to secure substantial change now. Militancy often has been used with school problems. What in your opinion are the pros and cons of militancy as a strategy for bringing about *social change?* What are the consequences of too slow or too rapid social change? In what ways can militants affect school objectives, policies, and practices—positively and negatively—in contrast to regular school board members and administrators?

6. "Black Power" is a major rallying cry in many communites. Essentially it is a concept which calls for black control—without white collaboration—of power and resources important to blacks (a term preferred to "Negro" by the Black Power advocates). Black Power when applied to education would place schools in predominantly black areas under effective black control of funds, teacher selection, curriculum, and other aspects of school operations. The curriculum would include black history and culture and would emphasize educational relevance to black Americans. How extensively should curriculum stress racial, cultural, and religious uniqueness and separateness, as well as alikeness and commonality? Under what circumstances should neighborhood curriculum objectives and policies replace those of the general school system? What consequences of black power do you anticipate? Are there other minority groups for which the *concept* is valid?

7. Still another pressing topic is the "crisis of the cities." The challenge is accentuated by decay of old cities; the influx of millions of persons, including many who are disadvantaged; the exodus of millions of others to the suburbs; and the acceleration of expectations and needs for expanded services. Can elementary schools meet the pressing needs for future citizens who can live productively and democratically in the cities? Can school staffs, facilities, and other resources be used *now* as centers of community efforts to meet the crises of the cities? How relevant are most elementary schools in relation to the crisis? What steps can be taken to apply the community school concept to the cities? What are the strengths and weaknesses of the Model Cities program, which stresses local, state, and national collaboration?

8. By the year 2018, some behavioral scientists have predicted that man will have technological powers to "control men's feelings, the weather, economic growth and development." (News release, dated June 20, 1968, from Foreign Policy Association.) Living in a controlled society will require a different kind of citizen than is necessary now. What type of elementary education is needed to prepare children for the new kind of world? What aspects of the new world should, and could, be resisted by effective education?

9. Over 2,000 pages of scientific literature are being published every 60 seconds. One billion books are published every year. See R. Freeman Butts, "Charting Our Position on the Way To . . . ," *Reason and Change in Elementary Education,* Second National Conference, The U.S. Office of Education Tri-University Project in Elementary Education, February 1–3, 1968. With knowledge accumulating at such rates, what are the ways for the elementary schools to prepare children for living in a rapidly changing world?

10. A report focused on alternative futures delineates six major future challenges which will confront educators: (a) solving excessive population problems; (b) controlling technological developments; (c) altering values, perceptions, and premises; (d) establishing a sense of national purpose; (e) meeting the educational demands of various groups; (f) educating students

to cope with uncertain futures. [*Alternative Futures and Educational Policy* (Menlo Park: Stanford Research Institute, 1970), 45 pp.] In what ways can the present curricular patterns be adapted to meet such challenges, and to what extent must those patterns be restructured radically? What kinds of attitudes and skills should students be encouraged to learn in preparation for the major challenges that face them?

11. "Cultural shock" is a commonly known reaction to dramatic differences between things in a person's native land and an overseas traveler's experiences. It is possible that many citizens are experiencing "future-shock" when faced with drastic change which challenges their basic orientation to life around them. Unlike the overseas travelers, there is no familiar land to which those suffering from future-shock can return! See June Grant Shane and Harold G. Shane, "Cultural Change and the Curriculum: 1970–2000 A.D.," *Educational Technology*, X, No. 4 (April, 1970), p. 13. Is this danger more real for the teacher than for other adults? What is the significance of the phenomenon to teaching, especially in preparing the young for the inevitability of change?

12. Futurism—the projection of present capabilities and trends into the future—is an important intellectual process. Burdin proposes an examination of 18 such projections (increasingly youthfulness of the population, for example) relative to possible impact on elementary-secondary programs, consequences for school personnel and their preparation programs, and illustrative pre- and in-service activities to prepare for future changes. See Joel L. Burdin, *Futurism: A Needed Process in School Personnel Preparation* (East Lansing: Michigan State University, 1970), 31 pp. How can the curriculum be valid in terms of today's conditions and simultaneously prepare students for future changes? What attitudes and competencies should school personnel develop to enable them to maintain their relevancy in the future?

19

Epilogue and Prologue

TEACHING: KEY ROLE IN SOCIETY

This chapter is an *epilogue*—some concluding words concerning what has been said and unsaid in this book—and a *prologue*—hopefully a challenge for you to begin a lifelong study of curriculum.

When you set out to help children learn to live more effectively, both now and in the future, you have selected a function which is one of the most significant in any society. Education has always been recognized as basic in all societies.

In an increasingly complex world, the day is long past when it is feasible to entrust the education of the young to parents, relatives, and master craftsmen supervising occupational training of apprentices. Change is too pervasive to leave education to chance; education is too varied and comprehensive to proceed without careful planning and implementation. Curriculum, reflecting the nation's educational needs, is an effort to provide those educational experiences which can assure the continued strength and well-being of our democratic society. As a result of helping each individual pupil, individual links are forged which collectively make a strong chain in society.

The task of building a strong educational program is of crucial importance and this is reflected in the increased concern for education at all levels of our society. Congressional polls indicate that education is high on the list of priorities for legislation. We live in a time when the President openly states that education is among his prime concerns. We see the involvement of major political leaders in settling local and national educational crises. We also see parents, who years ago often were thought to be indifferent to education, now actively seeking directly to influence neighborhood schools.

The nation has increased its commitment to education, and it is likely to do more in the future. In 1950 the nation spent, on the average, $209 per pupil; in the 1960's the amount averaged $434 per pupil. This is a part of the trend. In the 1950's the nation saw only 57 per cent of its youth graduating from high school, while in the 1960's the percentage had risen above 72 per cent, with the curve promising to rise sharply in the remainder of the 1970's.

Support for education will increase, for the nation cannot afford to have ill-prepared citizens. Efforts are being made to augment the meaningfulness of school; attendance in school must be more than a percentage figure. Further, the nation is beginning to take seriously the challenge to enable *all* capable students to enroll and succeed in post-secondary education and college.

THE NEW AMERICAN FRONTIER

Great changes are taking place in American education in response to its need. More changes—massive ones—seem inevitable as America awakens to its new frontier: education. Our system of education which has helped in past nation building is now challenged to a massive *re-building*—of aspirations, ideals, competencies, skills, and knowledge. This is what curriculum is about in these changing times and it is a reflection of democracy's crucial capacity to change. A vital and relevant curriculum is a partial fulfillment of our democratic heritage and of our hopes for children and adults.

INNOVATION FOR A CHANGING WORLD

We hope that you have been so challenged to sharpen your intellectual tools and your commitment to one of society's greatest roles—that you will spend a lifetime as an innovator introducing new ideas, methods, and devices as a means of helping learners. Constant change is the only certainty of the future. The school that does not encourage innovators will find itself in the stagnant backwaters rather than in swiftly flowing, powerful rivers. Just as rivers historically have been avenues through which men have communicated ideas, shared commerce, and discovered common purposes, the school that is in the mainstream can best serve man.

There are some chances to be taken even when you seek to innovate in a purposeful and careful way. But innovate you must if you are to meet the rising aspirations of America. You are the recipients of the faith, hope, and will to improve which were the building stones in the nation's past. People do not want blind adherence to the past for its own sake and with your competent leadership they should likewise reject change that is merely for the sake of change. Children are so important that they ought to be protected from either extreme.

The innovator should be an influential guide, in a real sense, a leader, in helping the people to attain their aspirations in harmony with the best of American traditions. Innovators are necessary in order to keep the society vital and responsive to human need. They—you—can serve as a conscience for society at large, which easily can grow accustomed to human need and misery. You should be among those alert, competent, dedicated persons seeking to avoid lethargy and indifference. You can participate in team efforts to provide research, experiments, ideas, insights, and information needed to translate community aspirations into realities. You can be a part of a chain reaction which sweeps the nation. If you learn to work effectively within the increasingly broad educational community, you can translate innovations into general practices. Of course, at this point local, national, and world change will necessitate still further innovation! Today's innovation can become tomorrow's anachronism.

Even constructive change may be resisted for varied reasons. People may feel incapable of effecting change and the apparent security of the status quo is a powerful barrier. There may be honest concerns as to the desirability of proposed changes. If you are to make your maximum contribution, you must develop an attitude that permits you to view possible failures, ridicule, indifference of others, extra work, and other factors attendant to innovation *as part of the job* of a dedicated teacher.

Of course, some innovations are ineffective. They may be more harmful than helpful. One of your major competencies should lie in helping your educational partners—both professional and layman—to differentiate between those innovations which are desirable and those which should be rejected. While many present effective curriculum objectives and practices were bitterly opposed at their birth, many other innovative curriculum proposals were justly rejected. With limited time, resources, and personnel, it is very important to be selective in what you retain and what you choose from innovative proposals that flood the nation.

Prior to attempting innovations in your classroom or school, it is wise to carefully determine objectives, procedures, and means of assessing success and failure. Thoughtful planning can do much to create successful innovations. "Action research"—classroom experimentation—must be carefully carried out. Properly prepared experimentation can be seen for what it is—a continuing effort to secure better education for boys and girls. It can do much to develop a school and community climate in which change is encouraged and even demanded.

Enthusiastic imitators of researchers and experimenters may exaggerate the potentialities of innovation and minimize their problems and limitations. Few practices, whether old or new, can be transported intact from one mind to another, one place to another, and one situation to another. Education is, after all, a complex phenomenon involving people, processes, and products. It is important to listen carefully to the limitations which thoughtful innovators place upon their own works.

Certain questions are appropriate in considering innovative practices: What precisely do research and experimentation show about conditions prevailing where you are teaching? How extensively and carefully was the innovation tested? Were results conclusive or merely suggestive? Have these results been repeated elsewhere? How much retraining of personnel and re-tooling in terms of materials, equipment, and facilities would be necessary if the innovation were adopted in your situation? How many additional resources would have to be secured? How receptive to the innovation are your educational partners, and what is their capability for providing what is needed to make the innovation effective? How much of the effectiveness of the innovation in its original state is a result of the enthusiasm, competence, and experience of the innovator and his colleagues? Could comparable conditions be developed in your school and community?

A similar set of questions should be posed for those who reject change as a matter of course. Neither the old nor the new should be declined indiscriminately or accepted blindly. Advocates of both should accept the challenge to demonstrate the relevance and significance of what they say and do. The basic test of a school curriculum should be its ability to help learners. A test of your skill in human relations will be to help the old—in ideas and inspiration—to accept and *apply* innovations where they are demonstrably desirable. At the same time there is the need to renovate and adapt the old where it will make a valid contribution. You should also help the overly eager innovator to carefully assess the old and the new in terms of what is best for all in the school enterprise.

CURRICULUM STUDY: A COMPLEX, LIFELONG PROCESS

Upon a brief examination of the diverse factors that were noted previously, it becomes obvious that a textbook on curriculum can be only a prologue. This chapter can reiterate the importance of viewing curriculum study as a *beginning*, and for this reason is entitled "Epilogue and Prologue." In earlier chapters we have tried to provide some conceptual tools which will help you to continue your study of curriculum. We have attempted to supply some facts and ideas which will stimulate your persistent efforts to provide a personally significant curriculum for boys and girls. Frankly, we have had some difficulties in separating pure curriculum from methods since what you *do* is a most significant aspect of curriculum.

Effective Curriculum for All

The thrust of American education mainly has been in developing a curriculum that is basically worthwhile, beginning with nursery school and extending through graduate school, and then reaching into the total lifespan. It is now believed that the school must provide for the *unique and total needs of all the people.* It should extend children's total growth to help them attain their maximum potentiality.

Elementary education particularly is seen as the *basic* building block in a sound educational program which begins shortly after birth and extends through the years of retirement. It appears that a child's level of intellectual capability, which will be attained by the age of 17, is half-determined before he begins kindergarten, and that an additional 25 per cent is determined by the age of seven. The child's self concept, learning skills, motivations, and basic concepts are very substantially formed by the time he leaves elementary school. No longer do you find naïve persons saying that *anyone* can teach in the elementary school and claiming that the subject matter is simple and is the major consideration. To build an elementary school curriculum which will be purposeful in the content of contemporary conditions is a challenge of the greatest magnitude and to enable children to experience that curriculum to their fullest potentiality is one of even greater magnitude. Curriculum development and teaching at the elementary level call for human engineering of great sophistication.

Faced with great pressures to serve the total educational needs of the community, educators must develop a curriculum which is relevant and vital to all. Constant change affects curriculum. Historically speaking, facts are facts for fleeting moments of time. Skills become obsolete so rapidly that today's children need those attitudes, abilities, and knowledge which will enable them to re-tool for several jobs in a lifetime. Life is changing drastically since those long centuries when work provided the main meaning and motivation.

The role of the individual varies with those changing conditions. His individuality is severely challenged in a complex society constantly in flux. Society itself, beset by problems with seemingly insurmountable and complicated issues arising at a rapid rate, must become flexible, rational, and capable of diverse responses. Cookbook recipes which provide for a curriculum those factual descriptions of what makes a "good" individual and a "good" society are shallow substitutes for learning that is relevant and vital to both individual and society.

We have suggested that *people* and *processes,* as well as *products,* are key components in a vital curriculum. Knowledge, skills, attitudes, and values which enable people to work constructively together are vital under changed and changing conditions. The processes by which individuals and groups attain constructive goals can be utilized under varied conditions. The very processes of selecting objectives, searching for ways of attaining them, and testing the validity of outcomes are functional responses to a changing and complex world. Curriculum should incorporate an interweaving of people, processes, and outcomes. Such a curriculum is likely to remain important.

Varied Team Members and Means

Whether you are examining the means or ends of curriculum, the tasks appear to be increasingly complex. The job at hand is so varied and so great that there is an increasing need for teams of personnel to do what should be done. We have suggested that the role of the individual teacher has evolved from one in which he primarily dispensed knowledge and maintained discipline. To an extent he continues in this role, but more frequently he serves as a mediator between the child and his environment.

With insights, skills, and information that are not readily available to pupils, you and your educational partners are in a position to help each child to increase his effectiveness in involving himself with his world. You can plan for the interaction of persons, processes of learning, and varied means of learning such as printed materials, broadcast media, and machine-aided learnings. You should be an expert in helping children to attain their maximum growth which involves meeting their personal as well as societal needs. As a helper of individual children, you are also responsible to the society for promoting those kinds of learnings and growth patterns which will maintain and extend a vital and dynamic society.

There is a healthy prospect that many kinds of learning will take place in the community under the direction of individuals who perform various jobs. This suggests that you will serve as a communicator between children and the community and as a coordinator for mutual educational efforts. As children go into the community for many learnings, they (as well as youth and adults of all ages) will also be in school for many kinds of experiences, besides those of learning. The school should be a place where people can learn; the rigid segregation of various ages of learners, in isolation from each other, must be eliminated. In such a setting, your role would be one of specializing in the education of the young and contributing to the education of all ages. Technology should extend your capabilities to enable you to do this.

YOUR HUMAN AND PROFESSIONAL UNIQUENESS

Your specialization, you should carefully note, is in helping individuals to attain their potentiality through learning, broadly conceived. We have suggested that a sound conceptualization of teaching and learning should enable you to adapt to the changing conditions of the moment and of the year. Your competence cannot, under the present challenge, be based primarily upon the quantity of facts which you can recall and verbalize upon demand. You cannot compete with computers, books, programmed learnings of various kinds, broadcast media, and a host of other means for storing, retrieving, and dispensing information and ideas. Yours is a much more dynamic role—that of helping each individual to master his machines and materials, use his time, and convert his resources in a manner which contributes to his dignity and worth. As machines do more, man should be helped to attain his humanness. This is your role, and it is an indispensable one, in our contemporary civilization. Other kinds of roles look pale in comparison.

It will challenge your best efforts to serve as a contributing member of a team while maintaining your own unique contribution to unique individual pupils. It takes a secure, competent, professional person to do what is best for the children and fellow professionals. It requires respect for the worth of each person plus a desire to bring out the best in others while securing personal and professional satisfactions. The complexity of teaching interrelationships in today's and tomorrow's world calls for teachers who are among the best educated persons as well as mature, highly motivated, persevering, and mentally and physically healthy!

The demands of the time are for the best individuals—in terms of personal and professional characteristics and competencies—to nurture America's most important resources: millions of individual boys and girls. They need the best teacher obtainable to do what few others can do so well—to assist them in securing an *education.* This is a magic word when it is translated into a vital curriculum. Transforming magic into reality is the job of anyone who takes the curriculum challenge seriously. No other way is defensible in these days.

You may have noted in this book that many ideas and illustrations, and much information, have not been clarified completely—in effect that loose strands have been left in your conceptualization of curriculum. This is probably inevitable in a subject as broad as curriculum. These strands are potentials which in the hands of a creative weaver can take on completed design and utility.

Competence and Compassion

Our hope is that you will keep an intelligent focus upon your challenge to continually strengthen your ability to utilize the people, processes, and products of curriculum to promote your own growth and that of boys and girls—indeed of all your educational partners. We see nothing in the past, the present, or the future which can substitute for your own competence and compassion extended into the life of children. The needs are there—in the ghetto, in comfortable suburbs, in isolated mountain hamlets, in high rise apartments, in village and metropolis, in town and country. It takes an artist, poet, or writer to depict adequately the hidden and open needs which await your help. The needs of children cry out silently. Their enthusiasm for learning and living, their creativity, their spontaneity—their very childishness in a constructive sense—await a teacher-guide who knows how to translate learning and teaching potentialities into an organized reality—the curriculum.

APPENDIX

Classroom Observation Report

1. *Apathetic* *1 2 3 4 5 6 7 N* *Alert*

Apathetic	Alert
Pupils were inattentive, showed evidence of wandering attention; indifferent to teacher.	Pupils responded eagerly; appeared anxious to recite and participate.
Pupils were listless; spiritless.	Pupils watched teacher attentively when explanation was being made.
Pupils were restless.	Pupils worked concentratedly, appeared immersed in their work.
Pupils participated half-heartedly; assumed a "don't care attitude."	Pupils were prompt and ready to take part in activities.

2. *Obstructive* *1 2 3 4 5 6 7 N* *Responsible*

Obstructive	Responsible
Pupils were rude to teacher and to each other.	Pupils finished work assigned without complaint; demonstrated their accomplishments.
Pupils interrupted one another; were impatient.	Pupils controlled voices.
Pupils were noisy; disturbing.	Pupils were courteous, friendly, and cooperative with teacher and with each other.
Pupils were obstinate; refused to participate in class activities.	Pupils received criticism attentively.
Pupils were quarrelsome, disgruntled; irritable; sullen.	Pupils demonstrated initiative, but sought help freely when necessary.
Pupils demanded attention; appeared selfish; waved hands constantly.	Pupils were orderly without specific directions from teacher.
Pupils engaged in name-calling or "tattling."	Pupils were patient.

[*] John R. Beery, *Professional Preparation and Effectiveness of Beginning Teachers* (Coral Gables, Fla.: Graphic Arts Press, University of Miami, 1960), pp. 71–91, revised from David G. Ryans, *Characteristics of Teachers* (Washington: American Council on Education, 1960). "This instrument was developed and used for research purposes and is not intended for supervisory or administrative purposes," according to Beery in a personal letter dated March 18, 1968. Each characteristic has a range of numbers from 1 through 7 and also includes "N" for not observed. Presumed benefits of studying and using charts such as this were discussed early in the book. While lengthy, this observation system is a valuable approach to conceptualize teacher–learner interaction patterns.

3. *Uncertain*	*1 2 3 4 5 6 7 N* *Confident*
Pupils were afraid to try.	Pupils were willing to try new problems or activities.
Pupils were unsure of themselves; hesitant.	Pupils were undisturbed by mistakes.
Pupils appeared embarrassed.	Pupils entered freely into activities.
Pupils were shy or timid.	Pupils appeared to be relaxed.
Pupils showed tenseness and nervous habits; nail biting; pencil biting.	Pupils spoke with assurance.

4. *Dependent*	*1 2 3 4 5 6 7 N* *Initiating*
Pupils relied on teacher for explicit directions.	Pupils volunteered ideas and made suggestions for further studies.
Pupils showed little ability to work things out for selves; unable to proceed when initiative called for.	Pupils gave evidence of original thinking; were resourceful.
Pupils were reluctant to take lead.	Pupils took the lead willingly.
Pupils were reluctant to accept responsibility.	Pupils assumed responsibility.

5. *Partial*	*1 2 3 4 5 6 7 N* *Fair*
Teacher slighted a pupil.	All pupils were treated equally.
Teacher corrected or criticized certain pupils excessively.	Teacher demonstrated freedom from prejudice toward social, racial, and religious groups.
Teacher gave a pupil special advantages.	In case of controversy, pupil was allowed to explain his side.
Teacher gave most attention to one or a few pupils.	Teacher distributed attention to many pupils.
Teacher showed bias or prejudice (favorable or unfavorable) toward some social, racial, or religious groups.	Teacher rotated leadership impartially.
Teacher showed suspicion of motives of a pupil.	Criticism or praise was based on factual evidence, not hearsay.

6. *Autocratic*	*1 2 3 4 5 6 7 N* *Democratic*
Teacher gave "long distance directions" to pupils; frequently "laid down the law."	Teacher entered into pupils' activities without domination.
Teacher told pupils each step to take.	Teacher exchanged ideas with pupils.
Teacher was intolerant of ideas or suggestions made by pupils.	Teacher encouraged pupils to make own decisions.
Teacher was mandatory in giving directions, gave orders to be obeyed at once.	Teacher guided pupils and made suggestions without being mandatory.
Teacher interrupted pupils.	Teacher asked opinions of pupils.
Teacher insisted on strict order at all times.	Teacher requested criticism of explanations or demonstrations.

7. *Aloof* *1 2 3 4 5 6 7 N* *Responsive*

Aloof	Responsive
Teacher was stiff and formal in relations with a child.	Teacher was approachable to all pupils.
Teacher seemed removed from the group—not a part of the activity.	Teacher was warm in contacts with pupils.
Teacher was condescending to a pupil.	Teacher spoke to a child as to an equal.
Teacher referred to a pupil as "this child" or "that child."	Teacher was tactful in relations with pupils.
Teacher was tactless.	

8. *Restricted* *1 2 3 4 5 6 7 N* *Understanding*

Restricted	Understanding
Teacher recognized only academic accomplishments of pupils; no concern for personal problems.	Teacher showed awareness of a pupil's emotional problems and needs.
Teacher showed little recognition of individual differences in ability and in feelings of pupils.	Teacher was alert to differences in individual ability.
Teacher was not sympathetic with a pupil's failure at a task.	Teacher was tolerant of error on the part of a pupil.
Teacher called attention only to very good or very poor work.	Teacher was patient with a pupil beyond the ordinary limits of patience.
Teacher showed no affection for pupils.	Teacher showed sympathy with a pupil's viewpoint.
Teacher was impatient with a pupil.	Teacher showed affection for a pupil (without) being unduly demonstrative or gushy.

9. *Harsh* *1 2 3 4 5 6 7 N* *Kindly*

Harsh	Kindly
Teacher was hypercritical; faultfinding.	Teacher gave a pupil deserved compliment.
Teacher ridiculed the behavior of a pupil; was sarcastic; depreciated child's efforts.	Teacher was courteous and friendly with pupils at all times.
Teacher used threats.	Teacher found good things to call attention to pupils.
Teacher lost temper; was cross.	Teacher disengaged self from a pupil without bluntness.
Teacher permitted pupils to laugh at mistakes of others.	Teacher was considerate of pupils' feelings.

10. *Dull* *1 2 3 4 5 6 7 N* *Stimulating*

Dull	Stimulating
Teacher seemed blunt; uninteresting; obtuse; was monotonous in presentation materials.	Teacher seemed to challenge and stimulate pupils to do better work; was highly interesting in presentation of materials.
Teacher failed to challenge or stimulate pupils.	Teacher was clever and witty (not smart alecky or wisecracking).
Teacher lacked animation.	Teacher was animated.
Teacher disregarded pupil interests.	Teacher brought lessons successfully to a climax, relating them to major objectives.

11. *Stereotyped*	*1 2 3 4 5 6 7 N*	*Original*
Teacher used routine procedures which were not effective.		Teacher showed initiative in taking a new approach.
Teacher showed no variation in language or procedure under varying conditions.		Teacher showed resourcefulness in making an explanation or demonstration.
Teacher failed to take advantage of a question or a situation to further develop the classes' understanding of a problem.		Teacher used original, interesting, and sometimes relatively unique devices to aid instruction.
Teacher lacked imagination in developing ideas; unoriginal in thought.		Teacher showed evidence of imagination and independence in thought.

12. *Apathetic*	*1 2 3 4 5 6 7 N*	*Alert*
Teacher seemed listless; lacked enthusiasm.		Teacher appeared buoyant; wide-awake; was enthusiastic.
Teacher seemed bored by pupils; was passive in response to pupils.		Teacher was constructively busy.
Teacher was preoccupied; attention seemed to wander.		Teacher was interested in what was going on in class; took lead in thinking.
Teacher was inactive; sat in chair most of time, etc.		Teacher was prompt to "pick up" class when pupils' attention showed signs of lagging.

13. *Unimpressive*	*1 2 3 4 5 6 7 N*	*Attractive*
Teacher was untidy or sloppily dressed.		Teacher was neat and clean.
Teacher was inappropriately dressed; drab, colorless.		Teacher's dress showed good taste.
Teacher's posture and bearing was unattractive.		Teacher's posture and bearing was attractive.
Teacher possessed distracting personal habits.		Teacher possessed personal charm; free from distracting personal habits.
Teacher's voice had disagreeable tone and uninteresting inflection.		Teacher's voice had agreeable tone and interesting inflection.

14. *Evading*	*1 2 3 4 5 6 7 N*	*Responsible*
Teacher shunned responsibility; was reluctant to make a decision; "passed the buck."		Teacher was willing to take responsibility; was conscientious; punctual.
Teacher left learning up to the individual child without giving adequate help.		Teacher suggested aids to learnings; provided "study hints."
Teacher let a difficult situation get out of control.		Teacher controlled difficult situations.
Teacher's assignments were indefinite; did not give adequate direction.		Teacher's assignments were definite; gave adequate direction.
Teacher was not insistent upon standards of quality.		Teacher insisted on standards of quality.

15. *Erratic* *1 2 3 4 5 6 7 N* *Steady*

Erratic	Steady
Teacher was impulsive; uncontrolled; temperamental; unsteady.	Teacher's behavior was decisive, calm, controlled.
Teacher was swayed by circumstances of the moment.	Teacher's behavior with pupils was stable and predictable.
Teacher's behavior was inconsistent.	Teacher's behavior was consistent.

16. *Excitable* *1 2 3 4 5 6 7 N* *Poised*

Excitable	Poised
Teacher was easily disturbed and distracted.	Teacher seemed at ease at all times.
Teacher was flustered by classroom problems, lacked dignity.	Teacher was unruffled by problems developing in the classroom; was dignified without being stiff and formal.
Teacher was hurried in class activities; spoke rapidly using many words and gestures.	Teacher successfully diverted attention from a stress situation in the classroom.
Teacher had nervous habits, was "jumpy."	Teacher was unhurried in class activities; spoke quietly and slowly.

17. *Uncertain* *1 2 3 4 5 6 7 N* *Confident*

Uncertain	Confident
Teacher seemed unsure of self in a situation; faltering, hesitant.	Teacher was sure of self; seemed self-confident in relations with pupils.
Teacher was disturbed and embarrassed by criticism.	Teacher accepted criticism but was undisturbed and unembarrassed by it.
Teacher seemed timid and shy; was artificial.	Teacher had classroom situations under control at all times.

18. *Disorganized* *1 2 3 4 5 6 7 N* *Systematic*

Disorganized	Systematic
Teacher showed no evidence of plan for classwork; poorly prepared.	Teacher gave evidence of careful planning (though procedure was flexible enough to permit adaptations); well-prepared.
Teached seemed undecided what to do next; did not work toward objectives.	Teacher anticipated needs and problems that might arise and was prepared for them.
Teacher wasted time.	Teacher successfully held discussion together; worked toward objectives.
Teacher was careless and shipshod in explanations.	Teacher provided for review and properly spaced learning.

19. *Inflexible* *1 2 3 4 5 6 7 N* *Adaptable*

Inflexible	Adaptable
Teacher was rigid in conforming to routine.	Teacher was flexible in adapting explanations and activities to pupil needs.
Teacher made no attempt to adapt materials to a pupil.	Teacher individualized materials for a pupil

Teacher was incapable of modifying explanations or activities to meet particular situations in the classroom.	Teacher took advantage of pupils' questions to further clarify ideas.
Teacher was impatient with interruptions in or digressions from the usual classroom situation.	Teacher met an unusual classroom situation competently.

20. *Pessimistic* *1 2 3 4 5 6 7 N* *Optimistic*

Teacher was depressed; seemed unhappy.	Teacher was cheerful and good-natured.
Teacher appeared to see and call attention to potential *bad;* was skeptical.	Teacher appeared to see and emphasize potenital *good.*
Teacher was critical of the school, the school system, or the principal.	Teacher joked with pupils on occasion.
Teacher called attention to and emphasized mistakes and errors.	Teacher called attention to and emphasized good work.
Teacher frowned most of the time; had unpleasant facial expression; was irritable.	Teacher spoke of future optimistically.

21. *Immature* *1 2 3 4 5 6 7 N* *Integrated*

Teacher was unrealistic in approach; naïve.	Teacher was realistic in approach; showed good common sense.
Teacher was self-pitying, complaining, demanding; indicated envy or jealousy.	Teacher did not speak of self but of pupil's activities.
Teacher was boastful and conceited.	Teacher was well-controlled emotionally; natural in manner.
Teacher lacked sense of humor.	Teacher possessed good sense of humor.

22. *Narrow* *1 2 3 4 5 6 7 N* *Broad*

Teacher showed evidence of limited background in subject or material; seemed to lack scholarship.	Teacher showed good background in subject; seemed scholarly.
Teacher did not depart from text; failed to enrich discussions with illustrations from related areas.	Teacher drew examples and explanations from various sources and related fields.
Teacher showed little evidence of breadth of cultural background (arts, science, literature, and history).	Teacher showed evidence of broad cultural background (art, science, literature, history).
Teacher's answers to a pupil's questions were incomplete or inaccurate.	Teacher gave complete, accurate and satisfying answers to questions.
Teacher did not approach subject matter critically.	Teacher was constructively critical in approach to subject matter.
Teacher was hesitant or limited in expression.	Teacher was skilled and fluent in expression.

23. The teacher helps the pupils develop understanding, knowledge, and skills.

1 2 3 4 5 6 7 N

Pupils learned nothing.	Pupils learned much.
Information presented in an uninteresting manner.	Information developed with pupils in an interesting manner.
Facts presented without organization.	Facts presented in logical sequence.
Lessons unrelated to previous lessons or learnings.	Lesson built on previous understanding and interests.
No pupil participation.	Wide pupil participation and involvement.

24. The teacher shows sensitivity to individual differences.

1 2 3 4 5 6 7 N

Uniform presentation to entire class.	Evidence of grouping within the class.
Uniform assignments.	Groups or individual assignments.
Instruction based entirely on textbook.	Wide use of reference materials with differential assignments.
No personal interest in the students.	Displays an interest in and has knowledge of students.

25. Teacher maintains good classroom discipline.

1 2 3 4 5 6 7 N

Classroom out of control.	Teacher in control at all times.
Pupils antagonistic to teacher.	Pupil–teacher rapport.
Learning reduced by classroom disorganization.	Classroom organization conducive to learning.
Chaos during recitation and work periods.	Students display good study habits and budget time wisely.
Pupils uncooperative.	Pupils cooperative.

26. Teacher helps the pupil develop efficient study habits.

1 2 3 4 5 6 7 N

Makes no attempt to help pupils develop study skills.	Gives instruction and drill in study skill.
Gives little or no time for study during school day.	Plans for and allows time for pupil to study during class time.
Fails to supervise students during study time.	Gives careful supervision during study time.

27. Teacher provides a healthful and attractive classroom.

1 2 3 4 5 6 7 N

No attention given to heat, light, and ventilation.	Heat, light, and ventilation well adjusted.
Furniture stationary.	Furniture adapted to correlate with activities.
Pupils take no interest in cleanliness of classroom.	Pupils assist in keeping room neat and attractive.
No evidence of pupil or teacher displays.	Teacher exhibits and pupil project work on display.

28. Teacher makes use of a variety of instructional materials.

1 2 3 4 5 6 7 N

No evidence of the use of audio-visual materials.	Evidence found that teacher makes proper use of films, exhibits, bulletin boards, radio, recorder, maps, and field trips.
No evidence of the use of library materials in the instructional program.	Teacher plans for and uses library for individual students, small groups, and entire class.
No evidence of teacher and pupil making learning aids.	Evidence of teacher and pupil ingenuity in the construction of learning aids.

Index